AFRICAN AMERICAN
THEOLOGICAL ETHICS

LIBRARY OF THEOLOGICAL ETHICS

Other books in this series

Basic Christian Ethics, by Paul Ramsey
Christ and the Moral Life, by James M. Gustafson
Christianity and the Social Crisis, by Walter Rauschenbusch
Conscience and Its Problems, by Kenneth E. Kirk
Economic Justice: Selections from Distributive Justice *and* A Living Wage,
    by John A. Ryan
Ethics in a Christian Context, by Paul L. Lehmann
Evangelical Ethics: A Reader, edited by David P. Gushee and Isaac B. Sharp
Feminist Theological Ethics: A Reader, edited by Lois K. Daly
Georgia Harkness: The Remaking of a Liberal Theologian, edited by Rebekah Miles
The Holy Spirit and the Christian Life: The Theological Basis of Ethics, by Karl Barth
Love and Justice: Selections from the Shorter Writings of Reinhold Niebuhr, edited
    by D. B. Robertson
The Meaning of Revelation, by H. Richard Niebuhr
Morality and Beyond, by Paul Tillich
Moral Discernment in the Christian Life: Essays in Theological Ethics, by James M.
    Gustafson and edited and with an introduction by Theo A. Boer and Paul E. Capetz
Moral Man and Immoral Society, by Reinhold Niebuhr
The Nature and Destiny of Man: A Christian Interpretation (2 vols.),
    by Reinhold Niebuhr
Radical Monotheism and Western Culture: With Supplementary Essays,
    by H. Richard Niebuhr
Reconstructing Christian Ethics: Selected Writings, by F. D. Maurice
Religious Liberty: Catholic Struggles with Pluralism, by John Courtney Murray
"The Responsibility of the Church for Society" and Other Essays by H. Richard Niebuhr,
    edited and with an introduction by Kristine A. Culp
The Responsible Self: An Essay in Christian Moral Philosophy, by H. Richard Niebuhr
Selections from Friedrich Schleiermacher's Christian Ethics, edited by James M. Brandt
Situation Ethics: The New Morality, by Joseph Fletcher
The Social Teaching of the Christian Churches (2 vols.), by Ernst Troeltsch
The Structure of Christian Ethics, by Joseph Sittler
The Ten Commandments, edited by William P. Brown
A Theology for the Social Gospel, by Walter Rauschenbusch
Treasure in Earthen Vessels: The Church as Human Community, by James M. Gustafson
War in the Twentieth Century: Sources in Theological Ethics, edited by Richard B. Miller
Womanist Theological Ethics: A Reader, edited by Katie Geneva Cannon, Emilie M.
    Townes, and Angela D. Sims

AFRICAN AMERICAN THEOLOGICAL ETHICS

A Reader

Peter J. Paris, Editor
with Julius Crump

WJK WESTMINSTER
JOHN KNOX PRESS
LOUISVILLE · KENTUCKY

© 2015 Westminster John Knox Press

First edition
Published by Westminster John Knox Press
Louisville, Kentucky

16 17 18 19 20 21 22 23 24 25—10 9 8 7 6 5 4 3 2 1

Book design by Sharon Adams
Cover design by Lisa Buckley
Cover illustration: © David Chmielewski & James Mclaughlin / Getty Images

Library of Congress Cataloging-in-Publication Data
African American theological ethics : a reader / Peter J. Paris, with Julius Crump, editors.
    pages cm. -- (Library of theological ethics)
    Includes index.
    ISBN 978-0-664-23219-1 (alk. paper)
    1. African Americans--Religion. 2. Black theology. 3. Christian ethics. I. Paris, Peter J., 1933- editor.
    BR563.N4A365 2015
    241.089'96073--dc23
                                                                    2015026178

∞ The paper used in this publication meets the minimum requirements
of the American National Standard for Information Sciences—Permanence
of Paper for Printed Library Materials, ANSI Z39.48-1992.

Most Westminster John Knox Press books are available at special quantity discounts
when purchased in bulk by corporations, organizations, and special-interest groups.
For more information, please e-mail SpecialSales@wjkbooks.com.

Contents

Part 3. Opposing Racial Segregation

Part 6. African American Themes and Perspectives

Permissions

Library of Theological Ethics

General Editors' Introduction

The field of theological ethics possesses in its literature an abundant inheritance concerning religious convictions and the moral life, critical issues, methods, and moral problems. The Library of Theological Ethics is designed to present a selection of important texts that would otherwise be unavailable for scholarly purposes and classroom use. The series engages the question of what it means to think theologically and ethically. It is offered in the conviction that sustained dialogue with our predecessors serves the interests of responsible contemporary reflection. Our more immediate aim in offering it, however, is to enable scholars and teachers to make more extensive use of classic texts as they train new generations of theologians, ethicists, and ministers.

The volumes included in the library comprise a variety of types. Some make available English-language texts and translations that have fallen out of print; others present new translations of texts previously unavailable in English. Still others offer anthologies or collections of significant statements about problems and themes of special importance. We hope that each volume will encourage contemporary theological ethicists to remain in conversation with the rich and diverse heritage of their discipline.

ROBIN LOVIN
DOUGLAS F. OTTATI
WILLIAM SCHWEIKER

Preface and Acknowledgments

The idea for this book emerged many years ago when the general editors of the Library of Theological Ethics (LTE) series, namely Robin W. Lovin, Douglas F. Ottati, and William Schweiker, expressed interest in publishing a text on African American theological ethics. After considerable conversation with many colleagues, I decided that a text containing historical and contemporary resources would be helpful to teachers if it presented African Americans as agents in defining, analyzing, and prescribing solutions to the social problems they confronted. It was not a surprise to learn, however, that varying forms of racial oppression constituted the paramount social problem that African Americans have faced throughout their history. Thus, this book contains a selection of significant voices in that struggle, and it is organized in accordance with the various types of opposition they waged in their quests for social justice.

A number of people have been involved in the production of this work. No one believed in its value more than the late Stephanie Egnotovich, the executive editor whose sudden death I continue to mourn. The several meetings I had with her in the last year of her life were always pleasant, perceptive, and encouraging. Subsequent work with the acquisitions editor Jana Reiss was also a very satisfying experience as she supervised the work of securing permissions. In that process, my step-daughter Allison Daniels also provided much help, for which I am grateful. But most of the tedious work in securing permissions and proofing scanned materials was done by Julius Crump, a PhD student at the University of Chicago Divinity School. I am most grateful to him and to his advisor, William Schweiker, who enabled the arrangement. This book would not have been completed without their significant input.

I would also like to thank Cedric Rucker, my research assistant during the year I spent as a visiting professor at Harvard University Divinity School. He undertook the initial task of scanning many of the works in this volume. Further still, I am also grateful to current Executive Editor, Robert A. Ratcliff, and

Director of Production, Julie Tonini, for their excellent work in guiding this book through its final stages of production.

A final word of thanks is reserved for my wife, Adrienne Daniels Paris, whose continuing love and support mean more to me than words can express.

PETER J. PARIS
MIDDLETOWN, DELAWARE
JUNE, 2015

Introduction

The substance of this book evokes the importance of two significant temporal dimensions of the African American experience: namely, memory of the past and hope for the future. Both of those terms capture the historical reality wherein an oppressed people developed their thought and ways of responding to their tragic plight. Accordingly, their theologies and ethics emerged in that cruel and brutal past where their lives were sustained by an undying hope enlivened by their religious imagination.

Brought to these American shores involuntarily four hundred years ago, the suffering of these African people was indescribable. Tens of thousands perished during the so-called middle passage, but many survived as a testimony to the resiliency of the human spirit and its trust in a divine power as the source of abiding hope. Memory of the past coupled with hope for the future constituted the polarities of their temporal experience that came together in every present moment of their lives. As each day's experience was a struggle for survival in the midst of incredible odds, they used all their meager resources, including their religion and morality, in pursuit of that one practical goal. The quality of their endeavors was enhanced by their capacity for creative response. Though badly bruised and broken by their social condition, they were not destroyed.

Contrary to the thought of many observers, their reliance on the help of divine forces did not imply a spirit of passivity. Rather, the practical goal of survival required a partnership between human endeavor and spiritual forces. These Africans had brought that discernment with them through the "middle passage" and eventually integrated its African content with the new substance that they discovered and reshaped in this alien land. The result has been the birth of a hybrid religion and morality known as African American theology and ethics. Both were developed contextually: that is to say, African American theology and African American ethics emerged out of their history of suffering and struggle over a long period of time. The trauma of those experiences helped to strengthen them in their daily endeavors to combat those who denied them their humanity. Alas, the recognition of the value of their religious thought and practice as subjects for academic study and research also involved a struggle.

Toward the end of the turbulent 1960s, a few seminaries and colleges in the United States began offering courses for the first time on a subject that was variously titled: Black Religion in America, The Black Church in America, The Black Religious Experience, to name only a few.[1] In each case the new offerings resulted from the demands of black students in predominantly white colleges, universities, and seminaries for a curriculum that would recognize the historical struggles and accomplishments of black Americans who built churches that have endured for over two centuries. Since there were few academic publications on black religion at that time, and since none of the pioneer teachers had ever had a formal course on the subject, they diligently mined the libraries for source materials only to discover that most of the relevant books[2] were out of print. Yet as soon as their demands became known, new editions of those nearly forgotten materials were quickly published.

Those new courses signaled the beginning of a movement for curricular change in theological and religious studies: a movement that was generated by the demand that two centuries of African American religious history be acknowledged as worthy of academic study, teaching, research, and publications. Those pressures coincided with the nascent discourse about the controversial phenomenon called black theology.[3]

In his first published book, James H. Cone, the progenitor of that new theological genre, leveled a major attack against the classical tradition of theological studies. In brief, he declared that that tradition was guilty of epistemological hegemony as seen by its ignorance, distortion, and devaluation of the religious traditions of oppressed African Americans. Both the challenges and proposed correctives of the black theology advocates received moral support and appreciation from the American Academy of Religion, which approved the formation of a program unit at its annual meetings titled Afro-American Religious History[4] that continues to exist up to the present day. In that same year the Society for

1. Often the term "Afro-American" was used as a synonym for "black."

2. A partial list of those books included the following: W. E. B. DuBois, *The Souls of Black Folk* (Chicago: A. C. McClurg and Co., 1903); Mark Miles Fisher, *Negro Slave Songs in the United States* (New York: The American Historical Society, 1953); E. Franklin Frazier, *The Negro Church in America* (New York: Schocken Books, 1964); Benjamin E. Mays and Joseph W. Nicholson, *The Negro's Church* (New York: Institute of Social and Religious Research, 1933); Benjamin E. Mays, *The Negro's God as Reflected in His Literature,* (n.p.: Chapman and Grimes, Inc., 1938); Howard Thurman, *Jesus and the Disinherited* (Pierce and Smith, 1949); and Carter G. Woodson, *History of the Negro Church* (Washington, DC: The Associated Publishers, 1921). It is important to note that none of the bibliographies in those early years included any texts by women.

3. James H. Cone's first book, *Black Theology and Black Power* (New York: Seabury Press, 1969), appeared in the same year that these courses were being offered for the first time.

4. This program unit was chaired for many years by the late Professor James Melville Washington, one of James Cone's colleagues at Union Theological Seminary in New York.

the Study of Black Religion[5] (SSBR-1970) was organized as a racially separate space aimed at nurturing, supporting, and celebrating the development of black religious scholarship. Most important, the members of the SSBR, inspired by the groundbreaking work of James Cone, focused their energy on developing a new methodological approach to the study of black religion that would do justice to its history and ongoing significance. Clearly, that organization never intended to be an alternative to the American Academy of Religion but rather a locus in which black scholars could strengthen one another for more effective participation within the larger academic academies.

These combined endeavors soon yielded astounding results as evidenced by the gradual increase of African Americans in PhD programs and their consequent appointments to the faculties of seminaries, divinity schools, colleges, and universities. Equally important, by the early 1980s African American women pursuing PhD studies at Union Theological Seminary in New York City began raising their voices in criticism of black male and white feminist theologies for rendering them invisible. Drawing on the novelist Alice Walker's definition of the term "womanist," these women soon gave birth to what they called "womanist studies"[6] in which they determined to study religion from the perspective of African American women's experience.

Increasing numbers of African Americans were soon recognized for their creative productivity in the fields of biblical studies, history, homiletics, theology, ethics, Christian education, pastoral care, and sociology of religion. Suffice it to say that those accomplishments along with the academic works of several other racial and ethnic minorities in the profession eventually resulted in a revolutionary change in the academic study of religion. Numerous diverse voices, long excluded from the mainstream of academic discourse, began the process of making their imprint on religious scholarship by challenging the cultural hegemony within the academy that had excluded them from participation for such a long time.

The aim of this book is to provide a collection of resources that depict a broad range of theological and ethical reasoning that African Americans developed during two centuries of slavery, a subsequent century of racial segregation and

5. One of the principal organizers and the first elected president of The Society for the Study of Black Religion was C. Shelby Rooks, who was at that time the executive director of the Fund for Theological Education, which has continued to provide financial support for African Americans and others in theological education.

6. Two of the earliest writings along these lines were the following: Jacquelyn Grant, "Black Theology and the Black Woman," in *Black Theology: A Documentary History (1966–1979)*, edited by Gayraud S. Wilmore and James H. Cone, (Maryknoll, NY: Orbis, 1982), 418–33 and Delores S. Williams, "The Color of Feminism: Or Speaking the Black Woman's Tongue," in the *Journal of Religious Thought*, 43, no. 1 (Spring–Summer, 1986), 42–58. Three of the earliest books on the subject were published by the following: Katie G. Cannon, *Black Womanist Ethics* (Atlanta, GA: Scholars Press, 1988); Jacquelyn Grant, *White Women's Christ and Black Women's Jesus: Feminist Christology and Womanist Response* (Atlanta, GA: Scholars Press, 1989); and Delores S. Williams, *Sisters in the Wilderness: The Challenge of Womanist God-Talk*, (New York: Maryknoll, 1993).

discrimination, and another half century of continuing inequalities of opportunity and achievement.

Ever since the year 1619 when a small group of Africans were sold into slavery from a Dutch man-of-war in Jamestown, Virginia, America has been a hostile environment for people of African descent. Throughout the colonial period and the first century of this nation's independence, Africans were defined by both popular opinion and the Constitution itself as only partially human. Hence, they were viewed as lacking the natural capacity for equal participation in the nation's political, social, and religious life. The most insidious implication of this definition of Africans as partially human was their tacit removal from the moral realm. Thus, their oppressors felt themselves free from both law and conscience to treat them with impunity. The doctrine of white superiority that reined over all such anthropological discourse has long endured as the first principle of racial reasoning both here and elsewhere. Despite the decreasing numbers of true believers and its legal demise, its spirit has not yet vanished completely from our public domain. Both then and now, its embrace implied the natural inferiority of all African peoples and also, consequently, justified slavery and all subsequent societal practices of racial segregation, discrimination, disrespect, and inequality. Thus Part 1 of this book focuses attention on the signature African American response to that primary anthropological doctrine of white racism.

Although this book does not contain a comprehensive assemblage of African American religious arguments against racial oppression, it does include representative examples of most of them. Since racial oppression assumed many forms over the centuries, African American responses did likewise. Thus, this book is organized in accordance with four organizing practical principles: (1) opposing the doctrine of white supremacy, (2) opposing slavery, (3) opposing racial segregation, and (4) opposing racial discrimination. The book then devotes part 5 to African American religious creativity and part 6 to African American themes and perspectives. An apt conclusion for the book is a poem by James Weldon Johnson on memory and hope, which, since 1919, African Americans have embraced as their national anthem because it expresses in poetic form an overview of the peoples' sufferings and hopes.

Each of the above four organizing principles emerged during a period in black history that was characterized by a dominant form of racial oppression. Parts 5 and 6 comprise respectively overviews of selected African American creative contributions to America's religious culture and selected themes and perspectives with which to guide present-day study and research. Teachers of African American theology and ethics may wish to read these chapters first as contemporary views of the history, methodological issues, and ongoing challenges.

Moreover, it is important to note that African American theological ethics is not an abstract theoretical enterprise. Rather, it is a form of inquiry that is closely related to African American studies in history and sociology both of which either imply or reveal a normative bias for racial justice. Prominent examples of this claim are seen in the works of such scholars as W. E. B. DuBois, Charles S. Johnson, Rayford W. Logan, Benjamin E. Mays, Joseph W. Nicholson, Miles Mark Fisher, and others.

The descriptive and analytical works in this volume were chosen from those of early to mid-twentieth century writers who, along with others, have comprised an unofficial canon for African American religious studies. Yet a growing number of contemporary scholars regularly debate that claim.

Beginning with Richard Allen, the founder of the African Methodist Episcopal Church, many ancestral black religious leaders like Peter Williams, Nathaniel Paul, Martin Delany, Frederick Douglass, Daniel Payne, David Walker, Henry Highland Garnet, Alexander Crummell, and Ida B. Wells-Barnett fully embraced a common historical narrative that highlighted the moral evil of slavery and racial segregation on the one hand and the long struggle of blacks and their allies for freedom on the other hand. Throughout the first half of the twentieth century that narrative was promulgated by The National Association for the Advancement of Colored People, The Southern Christian Leadership Conference, and most of the black churches as an integrationist model aimed at the goal of first class citizenship for all African Americans. Most important, it was viewed as wholly compatible with the principles of the United States Constitution, the Declaration of Independence, and the Christian gospel.

Challenged by the black power movement of the 1960s and the subsequent birth of black studies programs, James H. Cone undertook the valiant endeavor of synthesizing the integrationist and black nationalist traditions in his nascent black theology project. Since black America's most beloved martyrs, Martin Luther King Jr. and Malcolm X, had embodied racial integration and black nationalism respectively, a national public debate ensured concerning the political and cultural value of each.

Inspired by the political independence movements throughout Africa, both the integrationists and nationalists quickly nurtured and created international connections that steadily enabled more expansive spheres of mutual support and enrichment for all concerned.

Since space in this volume does not permit more examples of the nationalist tradition, we recommend that students and teachers augment these readings with selections from the writings of Malxolm X (1925–1965) and Stokeley Carmichael (1941–1998). It is an interesting fact that the two major Pan-Africanists of the twentieth century, Stokely Carmichael and W. E. B. DuBois, emigrated to Guinea and Ghana respectively, where they died and are entombed.

Finally, it is important to note that the responses of African Americans to their oppression have ranged along a continuum from adaptation to wholesale withdrawal from the United States.[7] In between those two extremes we discover

---

7. For a full discussion of these four types of responses, see the introduction to the second edition of my book, *Black Religious Leaders: Conflict in Unity* (Louisville, KY: Westminster/John Knox Press, 1991), 15–28.

differing types of actions aimed at social change via racial self-development, legitimate protest, legislation, insurrection, and emigration. Needless to say, every response required the necessary societal conditions that made it permissible. The common thread that runs through all the various responses, however, is some specific form of resistance to racial oppression and inequality. Clearly, those forms of reasoned resistance were rich in their diversity during every period of African American history.

Some may contend that African Americans did not always resist their oppression but rather accommodated themselves to it. I contend that such a viewpoint is erroneous because accommodation implies adapting to the societal conditions without affirming those conditions. In other words, adaptation means that one does not trespass in the restricted zones but, instead, demonstrates in one's segregated place the contrary implied by the restriction. For example, the view that African Americans were incapable of classical learning was contradicted by their academic achievements in segregated black colleges. Also, the view that African Americans were incapable of founding and managing institutions was contradicted by the achievements of Booker T. Washington at Tuskegee Institute as well as the founding, growth, and endurance of countless black religious institutions. Similarly, a brief glance of black creative achievements in the arts, music, sports, and entertainment under the conditions of their racially segregated world reveals a qualitative deficit that the larger society has suffered by denying a race of people the opportunity to participate. Thus, none should contend that adapting to racism implies affirming it as the deleterious metaphor "Uncle Tom" would imply.

Sadly, at the beginning of this republic, the United States proudly presented itself as the locus for a unique experiment in democracy. Yet the Constitution that the states ratified provided full citizenship rights only to white male property owners. Ironically, it extended the transatlantic slave trade for another twenty years, defined African people as three-fifths human for the sake of voting, and excluded them (along with all women and non-property-owning men) from equal participation in the new democracy. From that time onward, each of the excluded groups has striven to expand the nation's civic laws and practices in order to become included as bona fide citizens with all the rights and privileges pertaining thereto. Thus, their struggles were strikingly similar to those of the colonists who chose to wage a war for their political independence and the right to determine their own destiny in this new world. In contrast to the colonists, however, these subsequent groups were bent on the expansion of democracy rather than its restriction, and that has constituted their indelible contribution to this nation's unfinished legacy.

PART 1
OPPOSING THE DOCTRINE OF WHITE SUPREMACY

Chapter 1

The Origin of Races and Color

Martin R. Delany

Editor's Introduction: One of the greatest threats to the humanity of Africans was the European Christian view that God created Europeans superior in nature to Africans. They based this anthropological understanding on the biblical story of Noah and the curse God placed on his sons. In 1879 the renowned black physician, abolitionist, and advocate for African repatriation, Martin R. Delany (1812–1885), published a small book titled *The Origin of Races and Color* that meticulously provided his reasons for rejecting the doctrine of European supremacy. By integrating the biblical, scientific, and archaeological knowledge of his day, he argued that the diverse races of humankind originated from one common source as told in the Genesis creation story, and after the flood humankind dispersed geographically throughout Africa, Europe, and Asia. While acknowledging the superior status of European cultural progress in the eighteenth century, Delany took great care to demonstrate Africa's high level of civilization in antiquity as evidenced in the abundance of archaeological findings. Most important, he argued that science demonstrates that no amount of racial mixing could ever completely destroy any one of the races. Rather, an infinite regress of racial mixing would result in a reversion to one of the three original races and never the creation of a third race, since the latter would thwart the whole notion of divine creation. Further, Delany sets forth a composite of biblical arguments that people of African descent have embraced as their basic anthropological understanding that the races were created by God: that they originated from a common ancestral source, were intended for community, and that none was either superior or inferior to any of the others. In short, Delany's interpretation of the Biblical sources constituted an alternative anthropology that differed from the anthropology that many Christians of his day were using to support the doctrine of racial supremacy. His argument also repudiated the racial theories that many social Darwinists were advancing in his day. Clearly, Delany's argument set forth the basic structure for all subsequent arguments by African Americans concerning the natural equality and dignity of African peoples. Even a casual reading of the book soon reveals an astounding similarity between many of Delany's arguments and those of modern day African scholars. The latter owe a great debt of gratitude to Martin Delany's genius.

Delany's book contains eighteen chapters in total, dealing with such subjects as the origin of races and color, the progress of races, the progress of the black race, builders of the pyramids, progress in literature, religious polity, a discussion of the gods, wisdom of Ethiopia and Egypt, Garden of Hesperides, serpent of the Garden, modern and ancient Ethiopia, and comparative elements of civilization.

We have selected four chapters for presentation below.

The following excerpts comprise chapters two through five (pp. 11–19) of Martin R. Delany, *The Origin of Races and Color*, (Baltimore, MD: Black Classic Press, 1991)—first published in 1879 as *Principia of Ethnology: The Origin of Races and Color, with an Archeological Compendium of Ethiopian and Egyptian Civilization from Years of Careful Examination and Enquiry* (Philadelphia: Harper and Brother Publishers, 1879).

CHAPTER II
THE CREATION OF MAN

Man, according to Biblical history, commenced his existence in the Creation of Adam. This narration is acceptable to us. The descendants of Adam must have been very numerous, as we read of peoples which we cannot comprehend as having had an existence, as " in the land of Nod, on the east of Eden, whither Cain went from the presence of the Lord and dwelt," where we are told his wife bore Enoch, his first born, though until this circumstance, had we known of the existence of but one woman, Eve the first and mother of Cain, who did not even have a daughter, so far as Moses has informed us in Genesis.

The history of Man from Adam to Noah is very short, as given by Moses in the first chapter in the Bible, and though we learn of the existence of communities and cities, as the first city Enoch built by Cain in the land of Nod, called after his first born; for all we know, there were no legally established general regulations, but each head of a family ruled his own household according to traditional customs, his own desires or notions of propriety, or as circumstances or necessity required.

This view requires a division into periods of the historical events, from the Creation of Man, till after the confusion of tongues, and the dispersion of the people from the Tower of Babel. During the abode of Adam and Eve in the Garden of Paradise, we shall call the period of the "Original Law;" from going out of the Garden till the dispersion from the Tower, the period of the "Law of Necessity;" and after the dispersion on the Plains of Shinar, the period of "Municipal Law."

CHAPTER III
THE ORIGIN OF MAN

Until the Dispersion, Races as such were unknown, but must have become recognized at that time, doubtless at the period of that event, which brings us to the enquiry, What was the Original Man?

There is no doubt that, until the entry into the Ark of the Family of Noah, the people were all of the One Race and Complexion; which leads us to the further enquiry, What was that Complexion?

It is, we believe, generally admitted among linguists, that the Hebrew word Adam (ahdam) signifies red-dark-red as some scholars have it. And it is, we believe, a well-settled admission, that the name of the Original Man was taken from his complexion. On this hypothesis, we accept and believe that the original man was Adam, and his complexion to have been clay color or yellow, more resembling that of the lightest of the pure-blooded North American Indians. And that the peoples from Adam to Noah, including his wife and sons' wives, were all of one and the same color, there is to our mind no doubt.

There are those of the highest intelligence and deepest thoughts, in spite of their orthodox training and Christian predilections, who cannot but doubt the account of the Deluge, touching its universality. On this subject says the Duke of Argyll in his "Primeval Man:" "That the Deluge affected only a small portion of the globe which is *now habitable* is almost certain. But this is quite a different thing from supposing that the Flood affected only a small portion of the world which was *then inhabited.* The wide if not universal prevalence among the heathen nations of a tradition preserving the memory of some such great catastrophe, has always been considered to indicate recollections carried by descent by the surviving few."

Believing as we do in the story of the Deluge, after the subsidence of the waters, there was but one family of eight persons who came forth from the Ark, to re-people the earth—Noah and his wife; their three sons and their wives. And according to Biblical chronology, from the birth of Cain, the first-born of Adam and Eve, to the subsiding of the waters of the Flood, the time was one thousand, six hundred and fifty-five years (1655) the Flood lasting but forty days and forty nights.

"And it came to pass, in the six hundredth and first year, in the first month, the first day of the month, the waters were dried up from off the earth and Noah removing the covering of the Ark and looked, and behold, the face of the ground was dry." *Gen. C. viii, V. 23.* Now, what this six hundredth year means, we do not pretend to know; whether or not it alludes to the age of Noah, is inexplicable. For while chronology curiously enough would seem to make Noah only to have lived about one year after the Flood, the history tells us: "And Noah lived after the flood, three hundred and fifty years." *Gen. C. ix, V. 28.*

From the abatement of the waters to the building of the Tower, chronology makes it but one hundred and two years. This computation of time would seem to agree very well with the number of people who must have accumulated as the offspring of the Four Families who came out of the Ark, the males of which were engaged on the Tower, at the time of the confusion of tongues and dispersion abroad.

CHAPTER IV
THE FAMILY OF NOAH

Noah and family were Adamites, himself and wife being undoubtedly of the same color as that of their progenitors, Adam and Eve. And from the Garden of Eden to the Building of the Tower, there certainly was but one race of people known as such, or no classification of different peoples: "And the Lord said, Behold, the people is one, and they have all one language; and this they began to do and now nothing will be restrained from them which they have imagined to do." *Gen. C. xi, V. 6.*

Here we have inspired testimony of the unity of the people, speaking one language, in consequence of which, they imagined themselves all-powerful, setting all things at defiance. Finally to check this presumption, something had to be done, fully adequate to the end to be accomplished, which was the design of the Divine will. God has a purpose in all that he does, and his purpose in the creation of man, was the promotion of his own glory by the works of man here on earth, as the means of the Creator. And to this end man could best contribute by development and improvement in a higher civilization.

Could this be done by confining himself to a limited space in one quarter of the earth, rearing up a building "whose top may reach unto heaven"? Certainly not, because as the people were all one, and as "like begets like" the acquired manners, habits, customs, and desires of these Tower builders would have been taught and schooled into their descendants, to the neglect of all other employment and industries, confining themselves to comparatively limited spaces, caring nothing for the requirements of community, desiring nothing but to "make brick and burn them thoroughly," and "build a city and a tower whose top may reach unto heaven," and "make for themselves a habitation and a name," lest they be "scattered abroad, upon the face of the whole earth." Here, just what God designed in the Creation of man, these descendants of Noah desired to prevent.

The Progress of Civilization was God's requirement at the hands of man. How could this be brought about, seeing that the people were all one, "speaking one tongue," gathered together and settled in one place? Says his Grace, the Duke of Argyll: "The whole face of nature has been changed, not once, but frequently; not suddenly for the most part, perhaps not suddenly in any case, but slowly and gradually, and yet completely. When once this fact is clearly apprehended whenever we become familiar with the idea that Creation has had a history, we are inevitably led to the conclusion that Creation has also had a method. And then the further question arises—What has this method been? It is perfectly natural that men who have any hopes of solving this question should take that supposition which seems the readiest; and the readiest supposition is, that the agency by which new species are created is the same agency by which new individuals are born."

How applicable is the above extract, to the subject under consideration. Civilization is promoted by three agencies, Revolution, Conquest, and Emigration; the last the most effective, because voluntary, and thereby the more select and choice of the promoters.

The first may come in two ways—morally and peacefully as the Coming of the Messiah; or physically and violently, as a civil war or conquest by military invasion, the worst agencies of civilization; but which do not fail to carry with them much that is useful into the country invaded. A moral revolution is always desirable as an agency in the promotion of civilization.

What then was the "method" of the Creator in effecting this desirable separation and scattering abroad of the people? Why simply the confusion of their tongues, by imparting to, or at least inspiring two divisions of them with a new tongue or dialect comprehended by all of those to whom it was imparted. Though on this subject the Bible is silent, it is reasonable to believe and safe to conclude, that one of the three divisions retained the old original Adamic tongue, so to speak, or that which they spoke when they commenced building; and that one was that which followed after Shem, the progenitor of the Mongolian Race, and eldest of the sons.

By this "method" then, of an All-wise Creator, the people lost interest as communities in each other, and were thereby compelled to separate. And it will certainly be conceded by the intelligent enquirer, that there was a "method" in the manner, if allowed a paradox? But there were other changes said to be necessary to the final separation, in addition to that of the languages: the basis of race distinction, establishing the grand divisions. Is it to be supposed that God wrought a special miracle, by changing for the occasion the external physical characteristics of at least two divisions of the people? He did not. This was not His method; He has a better and even wiser method than a miracle.

Again his lordship the Duke, in combating the Darwinian development theory—and for this we thank his Grace, as a most valuable endorsement of our humble position on the subject of the "Origin of Races and Color"— where his lordship had written his valuable "Primeval Man": "It is not in itself inconsistent with the Theistic argument, or with belief in the ultimate agency and directing power of a Creative Mind. This is clear since we never think of any difficulty in reconciling that belief with our knowledge of the ordinary laws of animal and vegetable production. Those laws may be correctly, and can only be adequately described in the language of religion and theology. 'He who is alone the Author and Creator of all things,' says the present Bishop of Salisbury, 'does not by separate acts of creation give being and life to those creatures which are to be brought forth, but employs His living creatures thus to give effect to His will and pleasure, and as His agents to be the means of communicating life.' "The same language," continues his Grace; "might be applied without the alteration of a word, to the origin of species, if it were indeed true, that new kinds as well as new individuals were created by being born."

CHAPTER V
THE ORIGIN OF RACES

We have shown the "method" of the Creator, in effecting his design for man to "scatter abroad upon the face of the whole earth to "multiply and replenish it." But we have not yet seen how the division was brought about by the confusion of tongues, so as to settle and harmonize the people, instead of distracting and discouraging them. What mark of distinction could there have been given to the multitudes of this "one people" previous to separation, to enable them to recognize any individual of a separate division, without speaking? It must be seen, that such an act of All-wise interposition was essential, to enable each individual of anyone of the now three grand divisions of the new tongues, when seen, to identify the other without speaking; otherwise, there would have been produced a "confusion worse confounded."

"And one of the questions on which testimony bears, is a question of paramount importance in determining the antiquity of the Human Family," says the Duke of Argyll. "That question is not the rise of kingdoms, but the origin of races. The varieties of man are a great mystery. The physical differences which these varieties involve may be indeed, and often are, much exaggerated. Yet these differences are distinct, and we are naturally impelled to ask, When and How did they begin? The question When stands before the question How. The fundamental problem to be solved is this: can such a variety have descended from a single stock? And if they can, then must not a vast indefinite lapse of time have been occupied in the gradual development of divergent types?" This "mystery" we shall hope to solve by the aid of the light of science, and assistance of Divine authority, enabling us to discover the secrets of the laws of nature.

. . . "And the Lord said, Behold the people is one, and they have all one language, let us go down and there confound their language." Behold the people are one; that is they are all of one stock, descended from the same parentage, all still living, consequently they consider themselves all one family. To separate this family, was the paramount object, and to sever their interests in each other, was necessary to this separation.

The sons of Noah were three in number: Shem, Ham and Japheth. That these three sons were the active heads of the people as directors and patriarchal leaders, there is no doubt.

There is to us another fact of as little doubt: that is, that these three sons of Noah all differed in complexion, and proportionate numbers of the people—their dependents in and about the city and around about the Tower—also differed as did the three sons in complexion. And these different complexions in the people, at that early period, when races were unknown, would have no more been noticed as a mark of distinction, than the variation in the color of the hair of those that are white, mark them among themselves as distinct peoples.

That Shem was of the same complexion as Noah his father, and mother—the Adamic complexion—there is no doubt in our mind. And that Ham the second son was swarthy in complexion, we have as little doubt. Indeed, we believe it is generally conceded by scholars, though disputed by some, that the word Ham means "dark," "swarthy," "sable." And it has always been conceded, and never as we know of seriously disputed, that Japheth was white.

Of one thing we are morally certain, that after the confusion of tongues, each one of these three sons of Noah turned and went in different directions with their followers. These followers were just so many and no more than those who spoke one and the same language. And there can be no reasonable doubt in our mind that these people all were of the same complexion with each of the sons of Noah whom they followed. On leaving the Ark, they were one family, relatives, continuing together as "one people," all morally and socially blind and ignorant of any difference of characteristics personal or interests in general, as much so as a family of children with themselves toward the family till years of maturity bring about a change. Hence, when the confusion took place, their eyes became open to their difference in complexion with each other as a division, preferring those of their kind with whom they went, thus permanently uniting their destiny.

Shem settled in Asia, peopling the country around and about the centre from where they scattered. Ham went to the southwest, and Japheth to the northwest. And it will not be disputed, that from then to the present day, the people in those regions where those three sons are said to have located the three grand divisions of the Eastern Hemisphere: Asia, Africa and Europe—are, with the exceptions to be hereafter accounted for, of the distinct complexions of those attributed to Shem, Ham and Japheth; Yellow[1], Black and White. And this confusion of tongues, and scattering abroad in the earth, were the beginning and origin of races.

"But the great question," says the Duke of Argyll, "is not the rise of kingdoms, but the origin of races. When and How did they begin?" This we propose to show, in the next chapter, by an indisputable explanation of the origin of color by transmission of the parents.

---

1. Yellow—called *brown* in South Carolina and the West Indies.

PART 2
OPPOSING SLAVERY

Chapter 2

Opposing the Slave Trade

"An Oration on the Abolition of the Slave Trade in the United States"

Peter Williams Jr.

Editor's Introduction: On March 2, 1807, Congress enacted a law that banned the transatlantic slave trade in the United States intended not to go into effect until January 1, 1808. This was a matter that the framers of the constitution had agreed to delay for twenty years as a compromise in the constitutional debate over slavery. Although the law was habitually abused up to the eve of the Civil War, both black and white abolitionists hailed the event as a major victory in their long, arduous struggle toward their desired goal. A young minister, Reverend Peter Williams Jr. (1780–1840), son of one of the founders of the African Methodist Episcopal Zion Church in New York, delivered the following address in the New York African Church on January 1, 1808, celebrating the act by vividly rehearsing the horrors of the system that had endured for more than two centuries.

Fathers, Brethren, and Fellow Citizens: At this auspicious moment I felicitate you on the abolition of the Slave Trade. This inhuman branch of commerce, which, for some centuries past, has been carried on to a considerable extent, is, by the singular interposition of Divine Providence, this day extinguished. An event so important, so pregnant with happy consequences, must be extremely consonant to every philanthropic heart.

But to us, Africans and descendants of Africans, this period is deeply interesting. We have felt, sensibly felt, the sad effects of this abominable traffic. It has made, if not ourselves, our forefathers and kinsmen its unhappy victims; and pronounced on them, and their posterity, the sentence of perpetual slavery. But benevolent men have voluntarily stepped forward to obviate the consequences of this injustice and barbarity. They have striven assiduously, to restore our natural rights; to guaranty them from fresh innovations; to furnish us with necessary information; and to stop the source from whence our evils have flowed.

The fruits of these laudable endeavors have long been visible; each moment they appear more conspicuous; and this day has produced an event which shall ever be memorable and glorious in the annals of history. We are now assembled to celebrate this momentous era; to recognize the beneficial influences of humane exertions; and by suitable demonstrations of joy, thanksgiving, and gratitude, to return to our heavenly Father, and to our earthly benefactors, our sincere acknowledgments.

Review, for a moment, my brethren, the history of the Slave Trade. Engendered in the foul recesses of the sordid mind, the unnatural monster inflicted gross evils on the human race. Its baneful footsteps are marked with blood; its infectious breath spreads war and desolation; and its train is composed of the complicated miseries of cruel and unceasing bondage.

Before the enterprising spirit of European genius explored the western coast of Africa, the state of our forefathers was a state of simplicity, innocence, and contentment. Unskilled in the arts of dissimulation, their bosoms were the seats of confidence; and their lips were the organs of truth. Strangers to the refinements of civilized society, they followed with implicit obedience the (simple) dictates of nature. Peculiarly observant of hospitality, they offered a place of refreshment to the weary, and an asylum to the unfortunate. Ardent in their affections, their minds were susceptible of the warmest emotions of love, friendship, and gratitude.

Although unacquainted with the diversified luxuries and amusements of civilized nations, they enjoyed some singular advantages from the bountiful hand of nature and from their own innocent and amiable manners, which rendered them a happy people. But alas, this delightful picture has long since vanished; the angel of bliss has deserted their dwelling; and the demon of indescribable misery has rioted, uncontrolled, on the fair fields of our ancestors.

After Columbus unfolded to civilized man the vast treasures of this western world, the desire of gain, which had chiefly induced the first colonists of America to cross the waters of the Atlantic, surpassing the bounds of reasonable acquisition, violated the sacred injunctions of the gospel, frustrated the designs of the pious and humane, and enslaving the harmless aborigines, compelled them to drudge in the mines.

The severities of this employment was so insupportable to men who were unaccustomed to fatigue that, according to Robertson's "History of America," upwards of nine hundred thousand were destroyed in the space of fifteen years on the island of Hispaniola. A consumption so rapid must, in a short period, have deprived them of the instruments of labor, had not the same genius which first produced it found out another method to obtain them. This was no other than the importation of slaves from the coast of Africa.

The Genoese made the first regular importation, in the year 1517, by virtue of a patent granted by Charles of Austria to a Flemish favorite; since which, this commerce has increased to an astonishing and almost incredible degree.

After the manner of ancient piracy, descents were first made on the African coast; the towns bordering on the ocean were surprised, and a number of the inhabitants carried into slavery.

Alarmed at these depredations, the natives fled to the interior, and there united to secure themselves from the common foe. But the subtle invaders were not easily deterred from their purpose. Their experience, corroborated by historical testimony, convinced them that this spirit of unity would baffle every violent attempt; and that the most powerful method to dissolve it would be to diffuse in them the same avaricious disposition which they themselves possessed; and to afford them the means of gratifying it, by ruining each other. Fatal engine: fatal thou hast proved to man in all ages where the greatest violence has proved ineffectual, their undermining principles have wrought destruction. By the deadly power, the strong Grecian arm, which bid the world defiance, fell nerveless; by thy potent attacks, the solid pillars of Roman grandeur shook to their base; and, Oh! Africans! by this parent of the Slave Trade, this grandsire of misery, the mortal blow was struck which crushed the peace and happiness of our country. Affairs now assumed a different aspect; the appearances of war were changed into the most amicable pretensions; presents apparently inestimable were made; and all the bewitching and alluring wiles of the seducer were practiced. The harmless African, taught to believe a friendly countenance, the sure token of a corresponding heart, soon disbanded his fears and evinced a favorable disposition towards his flattering enemies.

Thus the foe, obtaining an intercourse by a dazzling display of European finery, bewildered their simple understandings and corrupted their morals. Mutual agreements were then made; the Europeans were to supply the Africans with those gaudy trifles which so strongly affected them; and the Africans in return were to grant the Europeans their prisoners of war and convicts as slaves. These stipulations, naturally tending to delude the mind, answered the twofold purpose of enlarging their criminal code and of exciting incessant war at the same time that it furnished a specious pretext for the prosecution of this inhuman traffic. Bad as this may appear, had it prescribed the bounds of injustice, millions of unhappy victims might have still been spared. But, extending widely beyond measure and without control, large additions of slaves were made by kidnapping and the most unpalliated seizures.

Trace the past scenes of Africa and you will manifestly perceive these flagrant violations of human rights. The prince who once delighted in the happiness of his people, who felt himself bound by a sacred contract to defend their persons and property, was turned into their tyrant and scourge: he, who once strove to preserve peace and good understanding with the different nations, who never unsheathed his sword but in the cause of justice, at the signal of a slave ship assembled his warriors and rushed furiously upon his unsuspecting friends. What a scene does that town now present, which a few moments past was the abode of tranquility. At the approach of the foe, alarm and confusion pervade every part; horror and dismay are depicted on every countenance; the aged chief, starting from his couch, calls forth his men to repulse the hostile invader: all ages obey the summons; feeble youth and decrepit age join the standard; while the foe, to effect his purpose, fires the town.

Now, with unimaginable terror the battle commences: hear now the shrieks of the women, the cries of the children, the shouts of the warriors, and the groans of the dying. See with what desperation the inhabitants fight in defense of their darling joys. But, alas! overpowered by a superior foe, their force is broken; their ablest warriors fall; and the wretched remnant are taken captives.

Where are now those pleasant dwellings, where peace and harmony reigned incessant, where those beautiful fields, whose smiling crops and enchanting verdure enlivened the heart of every beholder? Alas! those tenements are now enveloped in destructive flames; those fair fields are now bedewed with blood and covered with mangled carcasses. Where are now those sounds of mirth and gladness, which loudly rang throughout the village, where those darling youth, those venerable aged, who mutually animated the festive throng? Alas! those exhilarating peals are now changed into the dismal groans of inconceivable distress; the survivors of those happy people are now carried into cruel captivity. Ah! driven from their native soil, they cast their languishing eyes behind, and with aching hearts bid adieu to every prospect of joy and comfort. A spectacle so truly distressing is sufficient to blow into a blaze the most latent spark of humanity; but, the adamantine heart of avarice, dead to every sensation of pity, regards not the voice of the sufferers, but hastily drives them to market for sale.

Oh Africa, Africa! to what horrid inhumanities have thy shores been witness; thy shores, which were once the garden of the world, the seat of almost paradisiacal joys, have been transformed into regions of woe; thy sons, who were once the happiest of mortals, are reduced to slavery, and bound in weighty shackles, now fill the trader's ship. But, though defeated in the contest for liberty, their magnanimous souls scorn the gross indignity, and choose death in preference to slavery. Painful; Ah! painful, must be that existence which the rational mind can deliberately doom to self-destruction. Thus the poor Africans, robbed of every joy, while they see not the most transient, glimmering, ray of hope to cheer their saddened hearts, sink into the abyss of consummate misery. Their lives, embittered by reflection, anticipation, and present sorrows, they feel burthensome; and death (whose dreary mansions appall the stoutest hearts) they view as their only shelter.

You, my brethren, beloved Africans, who had passed the days of infancy when you left your country, you best can tell the aggravated sufferings of our unfortunate race; your memories can bring to view these scenes of bitter grief. What, my brethren, when dragged from your native land on board the slave ship, what was the anguish which you saw, which you felt, what the pain, what the dreadful forebodings which filled your throbbing bosoms?

But you, my brethren, descendants of African forefathers, I call upon you to view a scene of unfathomable distress. Let your imagination carry you back to former days. Behold a vessel, bearing our forefathers and brethren from the place of their nativity to a distant and inhospitable clime; behold their dejected countenances, their streaming eyes, their fettered limbs; hear them, with piercing cries, and pitiful moans, deploring their wretched fate. After their arrival in port, see them separated without regard to the ties of blood or friendship: husband from wife; parent from child; brother from sister; friend from friend. See the parting tear rolling down their fallen cheeks; hear the parting sigh die on their quivering lips.

But let us no longer pursue a theme of boundless affliction. An enchanting sound now demands your attention. Hail! hail! glorious day, whose resplendent rising disperseth the clouds which have hovered with destruction over the land of Africa, and illumines it by the most brilliant rays of future prosperity. Rejoice, Oh! Africans! No longer shall tyranny, war, and injustice, with irresistible sway, desolate your native country; no longer shall torrents of human blood deluge its delightful plains; no longer shall it witness your countrymen wielding among each other the instruments of death; nor the insidious kidnapper, darting from his midnight haunt, on the feeble and unprotected; no longer shall its shores resound with the awful howlings of infatuated warriors, the deathlike groans of vanquished innocents, nor the clanking fetters of woe doomed captives. Rejoice, Oh, ye descendants of Africans! No longer shall the United States of America, nor the extensive colonies of Great Britain, admit the degrading commerce of the human species; no longer shall they swell the tide of African misery by the importation of slaves. Rejoice, my brethren, that the channels are obstructed through which slavery, and its direful concomitants, have been entailed on the African race. But let incessant strains of gratitude be mingled with your expressions of joy. Through the infinite mercy of the great Jehovah, this day announces the abolition of the Slave Trade. Let, therefore, the heart that is warmed by the smallest drop of African blood glow in grateful transports, and cause the lofty arches of the sky to reverberate eternal praise to his boundless goodness.

Oh, God! we thank Thee, that thou didst condescend to listen to the cries of Africa's wretched sons, and that Thou didst interfere in their behalf. At Thy call humanity sprang forth and espoused the cause of the oppressed; one hand she employed in drawing from their vitals the deadly arrows of injustice; and the other holding a shield, to defend them from fresh assaults; and at that illustrious moment, when the sons of '76 pronounced these United States free and independent; when the spirit of patriotism erected a temple sacred to liberty; when the inspired voice of Americans first uttered those noble sentiments, "We hold these truths to be self-evident, that all men are created equal; that they are endowed by their Creator with certain unalienable rights; among which are life, liberty, and the pursuit of happiness"; and when the bleeding African, lifting his fetters, exclaimed, "Am I not a man and a brother"; then, with redoubled efforts, the angel of humanity strove to restore to the African race the inherent rights of man.

To the instruments of divine goodness, those benevolent men who voluntarily obeyed the dictates of humanity, we owe much. Surrounded with innumerable difficulties, their undaunted spirits dared to oppose a powerful host of interested men. Heedless to the voice of fame, their independent souls dared to oppose the strong gales of popular prejudice. Actuated by principles of genuine philanthropy, they dared to despise the emoluments of ill-gotten wealth, and to sacrifice much of their temporal interests at the shrine of benevolence.

As an American, I glory in informing you that Columbia boasts the first men who distinguished themselves eminently in the vindication of our rights and the improvement of our state.

Conscious that slavery was unfavorable to the benign influences of Christianity, the pious Woolman loudly declaimed against it; and, although destitute of fortune, he resolved to spare neither time nor pains to check its foot and exhorted his brethren, of the denomination of Friends, to abjure the iniquitous custom. These, convinced by the cogency of his arguments, denied the privileges of their society to the slaveholder, and zealously engaged in destroying the aggravated evil. Thus, through the beneficial labors of this pattern of piety and brotherly kindness, commenced a work which has since been promoted by the humane of every denomination. His memory ought therefore to be deeply engraven on the tablets of our hearts; and ought ever to inspire us with the most ardent esteem.

Nor less to be prized are the useful exertions of Anthony Benezet. This inestimable person, sensible of the equality of mankind, rose superior to the illiberal opinions of the age; and, disallowing an inferiority in the African genius, established the first school to cultivate our understandings and to better our condition.

Thus, by enlightening the mind and implanting the seeds of virtue, he banished, in a degree, the mists of prejudice, and laid the foundations of our future happiness. Let, therefore, a due sense of his meritorious actions ever create in us a deep reverence of his beloved name. Justice to the occasion, as well as his merits, forbid me to pass in silence over the name of the honorable William Wilberforce. Possessing talents capable of adorning the greatest subjects, his comprehensive mind found none more worthy his constant attention than the abolition of the slave trade. For this he soared to the zenith of his towering eloquence, and for this he struggled with perpetual ardour. Thus, anxious in defense of our rights, he pledged himself never to desert the cause; and, by his repeated and strenuous exertions, he finally obtained the desirable end. His extensive services have, therefore, entitled him to a large share of our affections, and to a lasting tribute of our unfeigned thanks.

But think not, by brethren, that I pretend to enumerate the persons who have proved our strenuous advocates, or that I have portrayed the merits of those I have mention. No, I have given but a few specimens of a countless number, and no more than the rude outlines of the beneficence of these. Perhaps there never existed a human institution which has displayed more intrinsic merit than the societies for the abolition of slavery.

Reared on the pure basis of philanthropy, they extend to different quarters of the globe, and comprise a considerable number of humane and respectable men. These, greatly impressed with the importance of the work, entered into it with such disinterestedness, engagedness, and prudence, as does honor to their wisdom and virtue. To effect the purposes of these societies no legal means were left untried which afforded the smallest prospects of success. Books were disseminated, and discourses delivered, wherein every argument was employed which the penetrating mind could adduce from religion, justice or reason, to prove the turpitude of slavery, and numerous instances related calculated to awaken sentiments of compassion. To further their charitable intentions, applications were constantly made to different bodies of legislature, and every concession improved to our best possible advantage. Taught by preceding occurrences, that the waves of oppression are ever ready to overwhelm the defenseless, they became the vigilant guardians of all our reinstated joys. Sensible that the inexperienced mind is greatly exposed to the allurements of vice, they cautioned us, by the most salutary precepts and virtuous examples, against its fatal encroachments; and the better to establish us in the path of rectitude they instituted schools to instruct us in the knowledge of letters and the principles of virtue.

By these and similar methods, with divine assistance they assailed the dark dungeon of slavery; shattered its rugged wall, and enlarging thousands of the captives, bestowed on them the blessing of civil society. Yes, my brethren, through their efficiency, numbers of us now enjoy the invaluable gem of liberty; numbers have been secured from a relapse into bondage, and numbers have attained a useful education.

I need not, my brethren, take a further view of our present circumstances, to convince you of the providential benefits which we have derived from our patrons; for if you take a retrospect of the past situation of Africans, and descendants of Africans, in this and other countries, to your observation our advancements must be obvious. From these considerations, added to the happy event which we now celebrate, let ever entertain the profoundest veneration for our munificent benefactors, and return to them from the altars of our hearts the fragrant incense of incessant gratitude. But let not, my brethren, our demonstrations of gratitude be confined to the mere expression of our lips.

The active part which the friends of humanity have taken to ameliorate our sufferings has rendered them, in a measure, the pledges of our integrity. You must be well aware that notwithstanding their endeavors, they have yet remaining, from interest, and prejudice, a number of opposers. These, carefully watching for every opportunity to injure the cause, will not fail to augment the smallest defects in our lives and conversation; and reproach our benefactors with them as the fruits of their actions.

Let us, therefore, by a steady and upright deportment, by a strict obedience and respect to the laws of the land, form an invulnerable bulwark against the shafts of malice. Thus, evincing to the world that our garments are unpolluted by the stains of ingratitude, we shall reap increasing advantages from the favors conferred; the spirits of our departed ancestors shall smile with complacency on the change of our state; and posterity shall exult in the pleasing remembrance. May the time speedily commence when Ethiopia shall stretch forth her hands; when the sun of liberty shall beam resplendent on the whole African race; and its genial influences promote the luxuriant growth of knowledge and virtue.

Chapter 3

Opposing Slavery as the Paramount Moral Evil

"An Address Delivered on the Celebration of the Abolition of Slavery in the State of New York"

Nathaniel Paul

Editor's Introduction: On July 5, 1827, the long gradual process of emancipating slaves in the state of New York had finally come to an end. On that day, the Reverend Nathaniel Paul (1775–1839), pastor of the Hamilton Street Baptist Church in Albany, delivered an address at the celebratory event. In that speech he vividly juxtaposed the joyful beauty of freedom alongside the horrendous brutality of slavery, which he viewed as the greatest moral and religious evil ever perpetrated on humanity. Most important, Paul raised the question of God's omnipotence and mercy in the face of such immense suffering, but he refrains from blaming God. Rather, he said that God has the right to do his will in heaven and earth and that God is able to bring good out of evil while not being the cause of the evil.

Through the long lapse of ages, it has been common for nations to record whatever was peculiar or interesting in the course of their history. Thus when Heaven, provoked by the iniquities of man, has visited the earth with the pestilence which moves in darkness or destruction, that wasteth at noonday, and has swept from existence, by thousands, its numerous inhabitants; or when the milder terms of mercy have been dispensed in rich abundance, and the goodness of God has crowned the efforts of any people with peace and prosperity; they have been placed upon their annals, and handed down to future ages, both for their amusement and profit. And as the nations which have already passed away, have been careful to select the most important events, peculiar to themselves, and have recorded them for the good of the people that should succeed them, so will we place it upon our history; and we will tell the good story to our children and to our children's children, down to the latest posterity, that on the *fourth day of July,* in the year of our Lord 1827, slavery was abolished in the state of New York.

Seldom, if ever, was there an occasion which required a public acknowledgment, or that deserved to be retained with gratitude of heart to the all-wise disposer of events, more than the present on which we have assembled.

It is not the mere gratification of the pride of the heart, or any vain ambitious notion, that has influenced us to make our appearance in the public streets of our city, or to assemble in the sanctuary of the Most High this morning; but we have met to offer our tribute of thanksgiving and praise to almighty God for his goodness; to retrace the acts and express our gratitude to our public benefactors, and to stimulate each other to the performance of every good and virtuous act, which now does, or hereafter may devolve as a duty upon us, as freemen and citizens, in common with the rest of community.

And if ever it were necessary for me to offer an apology to an audience for my absolute inability to perform a task assigned me, I feel that the present is the period. However, relying, for support on the hand of Him who has said, "I will never leave nor forsake"; and confiding in your charity for every necessary allowance, I venture to engage in the arduous undertaking.

In contemplating the subject before us, in connection with the means by which so glorious an event has been accomplished, we find much which requires our deep humiliation and our most exalted praises. We are permitted to behold one of the most pernicious and abominable of all enterprises, in which the depravity of human nature ever led man to engage, entirely eradicated. The power of the tyrant is subdued, the heart of the oppressed is cheered, liberty is proclaimed to the captive, and the opening of the prison to those who were bound, and he who had long been the miserable victim of cruelty and degradation, is elevated to the common rank in which our benevolent Creator first designed, that man should move all of which have been effected by means the most simple, yet perfectly efficient: Not by those fearful judgments of the almighty, which have so often fell upon the different parts of the earth; which have overturned nations and kingdoms; scattered thrones and sceptres; nor is the glory of the achievement, tarnished with the horrors of the field of battle. We hear not the cries of the widow and the fatherless; nor are our hearts affected with the sight of garments rolled in blood; but all has been done by the diffusion and influence of the pure, yet powerful principles of benevolence, before which the pitiful impotency of tyranny and oppression, is scattered and dispersed, like the chaff before the rage of the whirlwind.

I will not, on this occasion, attempt fully to detail the abominations of the traffic to which we have already alluded. Slavery, with its concomitants and consequences, in the best attire in which it can possibly be presented, is but a hateful monster, the very demon of avarice and oppression, from its first introduction to the present time; it has been among all nations the scourge of heaven, and the curse of the earth. It is so contrary to the laws which the God of nature has laid down as the rule of action by which the conduct of man is to be regulated towards his fellow man, which binds him to love his neighbour as himself, that it ever has, and ever will meet the decided disapprobation of heaven.

In whatever form we behold it, its visage is satanic, its origin the very offspring of hell, and in all cases its effects are grievous.

On the shores of Africa, the horror of the scene commences; here, the merciless tyrant, divested of everything human, except the form, begins the action. The laws of God and the tears of the oppressed are alike disregarded; and with more than savage barbarity, husbands and wives, parents and children, are parted to meet no more: and, if not doomed to an untimely death, while on the passage, yet are they for life consigned to a captivity still more terrible; a captivity, at the very thought of which, every heart, not already biased with unhallowed prejudices, or callous to every tender impression, pauses and revolts; exposed to the caprice of those whose tender mercies are cruel; unprotected by the laws of the land, and doomed to drag out miserable existence, without the remotest shadow of a hope of deliverance, until the king of terrors shall have executed his office, and consigned them to the kinder slumbers of death. But its pernicious tendency may be traced still farther: not only are its effects of the most disastrous character, in relation to the slave, but it extends its influence to the slave holder; and in many instances it is hard to say which is most wretched, the slave or the master. . . .

After the fall of man, it would seem that God, foreseeing that pride and arrogance would be the necessary consequences of the apostasy, and that man would seek to usurp undue authority over his fellow, wisely ordained that he should obtain his bread by the sweat of his brow; but contrary to this sacred mandate of heaven, slavery has been introduced, supporting the one in all the absurd luxuries of life, at the expense of the liberty and independence of the other. Point me to any section of the earth where slavery, to any considerable extent exists, and I will point you to a people whose morals are corrupted; and when pride, vanity and profusion are permitted to range unrestrained in all their desolating effects, and thereby idleness and luxury are promoted, under the influence of which, man, becoming insensible of his duty to his God and his fellow creature; and indulging in all the pride and vanity of his own heart, says to his soul, thou hast much goods laid up for many years. But while thus sporting, can it be done with impunity? Has conscience ceased to be active?

Are there no forebodings of a future day of punishment, and of meeting the merited avenger? Can he retire after the business of the day and repose in safety? Let the guards around his mansion, the barred doors of his sleeping room, and the loaded instruments of death beneath his pillow, answer the question. And if this were all, it would become us, perhaps, to cease to murmur, and bow in silent submission to that providence which had ordained this present state of existence, to be but a life of degradation and suffering.

Since affliction is but the common lot of men, this life, at best, is but a vapor that ariseth and soon passeth away. Man, said the inspired sage, that is born of a woman, is of few days and full of trouble; and in a certain sense, it is not material what our present situation may be, for short is the period that humbles all to the dust, and places the monarch and the beggar, the slave and the master, upon equal thrones. But although this life is short, and attended with one entire scene of anxious perplexity, and few and evil are the days of our pilgrimage; yet man is advancing to another state of existence, bounded only by the vast duration of eternity in which happiness or misery await us all. The great author of our existence has marked out the way that leads to the glories of the upper world, and through the redemption which is in Christ Jesus, salvation is offered to all. But slavery forbids even the approach of mercy; it stands as a barrier in the way to ward off the influence of divine grace; it shuts up the avenues of the soul, and prevents its receiving divine instruction; and scarce does it permit its miserable captives to know that there is a God, a Heaven or a Hell!

Its more than detestable picture has been attempted to be portrayed by the learned, and the wise, but all have fallen short, and acknowledged their inadequacy to the task, and have been compelled to submit, by merely giving an imperfect shadow of its reality. Even the immortal Wilberforce, a name that can never die while Africa lives, after exerting his ingenuity, and exhausting the strength of his masterly mind, resigns the effort, and calmly submits by saying, "never was there, indeed, a system so replete with wickedness and cruelty to whatever part of it we turn our eyes; we could find no comfort, no satisfaction, no relief." It was the gracious ordinance of providence, both in the natural and moral world, that good should often arise out of evil. Hurricanes clear the air; and the propagation of truth was promoted by persecution, pride, vanity, and profusion contributed often, in their remoter consequences, to the happiness of mankind. In common, what was in itself evil and vicious, was permitted to carry along with it some circumstances of palliation. The Arab was hospitable, the robber brave; we did not necessarily find cruelty associated with fraud or meanness with injustice. But here the case was far otherwise. It was the prerogative of this detestable traffic, to separate from evil its concomitant good, and to reconcile discordant mischief. It robbed war of its generosity, it deprived peace of its security. We saw in it the vices of polished society, without its knowledge or its comforts, and the evils of barbarism without its simplicity; no age, no sex, no rank, no condition, was exempt from the fatal influence of this wide wasting calamity. Thus it attained to the fullest measure of its pure, unmixed, unsophisticated wickedness; and scorning all competition or comparison, it stood without a rival in the secure and undisputed possession of its detestable pre-eminence.

Such were the views which this truly great and good man, together with his fellow philanthropists, took of this subject, and such are the strong terms in which he has seen fit to express his utter abhorrence of its origin and effects. Thus have we hinted at some of the miseries connected with slavery. And while I turn my thoughts back and survey what is past, I see our forefathers seized by the hand of the rude ruffian, and torn from their native homes and all that they held dear or sacred. I follow them down the lonesome way, until I see each safely placed on board the gloomy slave ship; I hear the passive groan, and the clanking of the chains which bind them. I see the tears which follow each other in quick succession down the dusky cheek.

I view them casting the last and longing look towards the land which gave them birth, until at length the ponderous anchor is weighed, and the canvass spread to catch the favored breeze; I view them wafted onward until they arrive at the destined port; I behold those who have been so unfortunate as to survive the passage, emerging from their loathsome prison, and landing amidst the noisy rattling of the massy fetters which confine them; I see the crowd of traffickers in human flesh gathering, each anxious to seize the favored opportunity of enriching himself with their toils, their tears and their blood. I view them doomed to the most abject state of degraded misery, and exposed to suffer all that unrestrained tyranny can inflict, or that human nature is capable of sustaining.

Chapter 4

Opposing the Hypocrisy of Slave-Owning Christians

Appendix to his 1845 *Narrative of the Life of Frederick Douglass, an American Slave, Written by Himself*

Frederick Douglass

Editor's Introduction: No one has described more adequately the experience of slavery than Frederick Douglass (1817–1895), premier escaped slave, abolitionist, orator, autobiographer, editor, statesman, and the most renowned African American of the nineteenth century. For a half century, Douglass was the indisputable authoritative black voice on all matters pertaining to slavery and the struggle for freedom and justice. Fully aware of the contradictory role that Christianity played in sustaining the institution, Douglass leveled some of his most severe condemnations of the hypocrisy of slave-owning and slave-supporting Christianity. His analysis of the contradiction between authentic biblical Christianity and the American practice of Christianity was published as an appendix to his 1845 *Narrative of the Life of Frederick Douglass, An American Slave, Written by Himself.* Its prophetic argument fully expressed then and now the African American perspective on slavery and all who support such an evil system.

APPENDIX

I find since reading over the foregoing Narrative, that I have, in several instances, spoken in such a tone and manner, respecting religion, as may possibly lead those unacquainted with my religious views to suppose me an opponent of all religion. To remove the liability of such misapprehension, I deem it proper to append the following brief explanation. What I have said respecting and against religion, I mean strictly to apply to the *slaveholding religion* of this land, and with no possible reference to Christianity proper; for, between the Christianity of this land, and the Christianity of Christ, I recognize the widest possible difference—so wide, that to receive the one as good, pure, and holy, is of necessity to reject the other as bad, corrupt, and wicked. To be the friend of the one, is of necessity to be the enemy of the other. I love the pure, peaceable, and impartial Christianity of Christ: I therefore hate the corrupt, slaveholding, women-whipping, cradle-plundering, partial and hypocritical Christianity of this land. Indeed, I can see no reason, but the most deceitful one, for calling the religion of this land Christianity. I look upon it as the climax of all misnomers, the boldest of all frauds, and the grossest of all libels. Never was there a clearer case of "stealing the livery of the court of heaven to serve the devil in." I am filled with unutterable loathing when I contemplate the religious pomp and show, together with the horrible inconsistencies, which everywhere surround me. We have men-stealers for ministers, women-whippers for missionaries, and cradle-plunderers for church members. The man who wields the blood-clotted cowskin during the week fills the pulpit on Sunday, and claims to be a minister of the meek and lowly Jesus. The man who robs me of my earnings at the end of each week meets me as a class-leader on Sunday morning, to show me the way of life, and the path of salvation. He who sells my sister, for purposes of prostitution, stands forth as the pious advocate of purity. He who proclaims it a religious duty to read the Bible denies me the right of learning to read the name of the God who made me. He who is the religious advocate of marriage robs whole millions of its sacred influence, and leaves them to the ravages of wholesale pollution. The warm defender of the sacredness of the family relation is the same that scatters whole families—sundering husbands and wives, parents and children, sisters and brothers—leaving the hut vacant, and the hearth desolate. We see the thief preaching against theft, and the adulterer against adultery. We have men sold to build churches, women sold to support the gospel, and babes sold to purchase Bibles for the *poor heathen all for the glory of God and the good of souls!* The slave auctioneer's bell and the church-going bell chime in with each other, and the bitter cries of the heart-broken slave are drowned in the religious shouts of his pious master. Revivals of religion and revivals in the slave-trade go hand in hand together. The slave prison and the church stand near each other. The clanking of fetters and the rattling of chains in the prison, and the pious psalm and solemn prayer in the church, may be heard at the same time. The dealers in the bodies and souls of men erect their stand in the presence of the pulpit, and they mutually help each other. The dealer gives his blood-stained gold to support the pulpit, and the pulpit, in return, covers his infernal business with the garb of Christianity. Here we have religion and robbery the allies of each other-devils dressed in angels' robes, and hell presenting the semblance of paradise.

> "Just God! and these are they,
> Who minister at thine altar, God of right!
> Men who their hands, with prayer and blessing lay
> On Israel's ark of light.

> "What! preach, and kidnap men?
> Give thanks, and rob thy own afflicted poor?
> Talk of thy glorious liberty, and then
> Bolt hard the captive's door?

> "What! servants of thy own
> Merciful Son, who came to seek and save
> The homeless and the outcast, fettering down
> The tasked and plundered slave!

> "Pilate and Herod friends!
> Chief priests and rulers, as of old, combine!
> Just God and holy! is that church which lends
> Strength to the spoiler theme.

The Christianity of American is a Christianity, of whose votaries it may be as truly said, as it was of the ancient scribes and Pharisees, "They bind heavy burdens, and grievous to be borne, and lay them on men's shoulders, but they themselves will not move them with one of their fingers. All their works they do for to be seen of men. They love the uppermost rooms at feasts, and the chief seats in the synagogues, . . . and to be called of men, Rabbi, Rabbi.—But woe unto you, scribes and Pharisees, hypocrites! For ye shut up the kingdom of heaven against men; for ye neither go in yourselves, neither suffer ye them that are entering to go in. Ye compass sea and land to make one proselyte, and when he is made, ye make him twofold more the child of hell than yourselves.—Woe unto you, scribes and Pharisees, hypocrites! For ye pay tithe of mint, and anise, and cumin, and have omitted the weightier matters of the law, judgment, mercy, and faith; these ought ye to have done, and not to leave the other undone. Ye blind guides! Which strain at a gnat, and swallow a camel. Woe unto you, scribes and Pharisees, hypocrites! For ye make clean the outside of the cup and of the platter; but within, they are full of extortion and excess.—Woe unto you, scribes and Pharisees, hypocrites! For ye are like unto whited sepulchers, which indeed appear beautiful outward, but are within full of dead men's bones, and of all uncleanness. Even so ye also outwardly appear righteous unto men, but within ye are full of hypocrisy and iniquity."[See Matthew 23:4–28.]

Dark and terrible as is this picture, I hold it to be strictly true of the overwhelming mass of professed Christians in America. They strain at a gnat, and swallow a camel. Could anything be more true of our churches? They would be shocked at the proposition of fellowshipping a *sheep-stealer*, and at the same time they hug to their communion a *man-stealer*, and brand me with being an infidel, if I find fault with them for it. They attend with Pharisaical strictness to the outward forms of religion, and at the same time neglect the weightier matters of the law, judgment, mercy, and faith. They are always ready to sacrifice, but seldom to show mercy. They are they who are represented as professing to love God whom they have not seen, whilst they hate their brother whom they have seen. They love the heathen on the other side of the globe. They can pray for him, pay money to have the Bible put into his hand, and missionaries to instruct him; while they despise and totally neglect the heathen at their own doors. Such is, very briefly, my view of the religion of this land; and to avoid any misunderstanding, growing out of the use of general terms, I mean, by the religion of this land, that which is revealed in the words, deeds, and actions, of those bodies, north and south, calling themselves Christian churches, and yet in union with slaveholders. It is against religion, as presented by these bodies, that I have felt it my duty to testify.

I conclude these remarks by copying the following portrait of the religion of the south, (which is, by communion and fellowship, the religion of the north) which I soberly affirm is "true to the life," and without caricature or the slightest exaggeration. It is said to have been drawn, several years before the present anti-slavery agitation began, by a northern Methodist preacher, who, while residing at the south, had an opportunity to see slaveholding morals, manners, and piety, with his own eyes. "Shall I not visit for these things? saith the Lord. Shall not my soul be avenged on such a nation as this?" [Jeremiah 5:9.]

"Come, saints and sinners, hear me tell
How pious priests whip Jack and Nell,
And women buy and children sell,
And preach all sinners down to hell,
And sing of heavenly union.

"They'll bleat and baa, [go on] like goats,
Gorge down black sheep, and strain at motes,
Array their backs in fine black coats,
seize their negroes by their throats,
And choke, for heavenly union.

"They'll church you if you sip a dram,
And damn you if you steal a lamb;
Yet rob old Tony, Doll, and Sam,
Of human rights, and bread and ham;
Kidnapper's heavenly union.

"They'll loudly talk of Christ's reward,
And bind his image with a cord,
And scold, and swing the lash abhorred,
And sell their brother in the Lord
To handcuffed heavenly union.

"They'll read and sing a sacred song,
And make a prayer both loud and long,
And teach the right and do the wrong,
Hailing the brother, sister throng,
With words of heavenly union.

"We wonder how such saints can sing,
Or praise the Lord upon the wing,
Who roar, and scold, and whip, and sting,
And to their slaves and mammon cling,
In guilty conscience union.

"They'll raise tobacco, corn, and rye,
And drive, and thieve, and cheat, and lie,
And lay up treasures in the sky,
By making switch and cowskin fly,
In hope of heavenly union.

"They'll crack old Tony on the skull,
And preach and roar like Bashan bull,
Or braying ass, of mischief full,
Then seize old Jacob by the wool,
And pull for heavenly union.

"A roaring, ranting, sleek man-thief,
Who lived on mutton, veal, and beef,
Yet never would afford relief
To needy, sable sons of grief,
Was big with heavenly union.

"'Love not the world,' the preacher said,
And winked his eye, and shook his head;
He seized on Tom, and Dick, and Ned,
Cut short their meat, and clothes, and bread,
Yet still loved heavenly union.

"Another preacher whining spoke
Of One whose heart for sinners broke:
He tied old Nanny to an oak,
And drew the blood at every stroke,
And prayed for heavenly union.

"Two others oped their iron jaws,
And waved their children-stealing paws;
There sat their children in gewgaws;
By stinting negroes' backs and maws,
They kept up heavenly union.

"All good from Jack another takes,
And entertains their flirts and rakes,
Who dress as sleek as glossy snakes,
And cram their mouths with sweetened cakes;
And this goes down for union."

Sincerely and earnestly hoping that this little book may do something toward throwing light on the American slave system, and hastening the glad day of deliverance to the millions of my brethren in bonds—faithfully relying upon the power of truth, love, and justice, for success in my humble efforts—and solemnly pledging myself anew to the sacred cause, I subscribe myself,

FREDERICK DOUGLASS
LYNN, MASS., APRIL 28, 1845.

Chapter 5

Opposing Slavery by Escaping

Harriet Tubman
and the Underground Railroad

Editor's Introduction: Though slaves frequently escaped from slavery long before the nineteenth century, they began doing so in ever increasing numbers around the turn of the century. In fact, abolitionists organized the so-called Underground Railroad that comprised a network of sympathizers bent on helping slaves to escape from their bondage and enjoy freedom either in the northern states or Canada. Those who participated in the enterprise had no moral qualms about doing so because they viewed slavery as an illicit system wholly outside the moral realm. Hence, they viewed escape as the only means of moral redemption for both the nation and those whom it enslaved. From the middle of the nineteenth century onwards the most prominent leader in the Underground Railroad had been an amazing woman named Harriet Tubman (1820–1913). In our time she is viewed as a veritable national icon deeply embedded in myth, folklore, and history. Since she was illiterate, she has left no written narrative of her work. Rather, virtually everything known about her has come to us as stories told by others. This statement would not be complete apart from the following biographical summary preserved by the Library of Congress.

Born: c. 1820, Dorchester County, Maryland
Died: March 10, 1913, Auburn, New York
Harriet Tubman was a runaway slave from Maryland who became known as the "Moses of her people." Over the course of 10 years, and at great personal risk, she led hundreds of slaves to freedom along the Underground Railroad, a secret network of safe houses where runaway slaves could stay on their journey north to freedom. She later became a leader in the abolitionist movement, and during the Civil War she was a spy for the federal forces in South Carolina as well as a nurse.

After Harriet Tubman escaped from slavery, she returned to slave-holding states many times to help other slaves escape. She led them safely to the northern free states and to Canada. It was very dangerous to be a runaway slave. There were rewards for their capture, and ads like you see here described slaves in detail. Whenever Tubman led a group of slaves to freedom, she placed herself in great danger. There was a bounty offered for her capture because she was a fugitive slave herself, and she was breaking the law in slave states by helping other slaves escape. What do you think Tubman did when someone she was helping became frightened and wanted to turn back?

If anyone ever wanted to change his or her mind during the journey to freedom and return, Tubman pulled out a gun and said, "You'll be free or die a slave!" Tubman knew that if anyone turned back, it would put her and the other escaping slaves in danger of discovery, capture or even death. She became so well known for leading slaves to freedom that Tubman became known as the "Moses of Her People." Many slaves dreaming of freedom sang the spiritual "Go Down Moses." Slaves hoped a savior would deliver them from slavery just as Moses had delivered the Israelites from slavery.

Chapter 6

Opposing Slavery through Abolitionism
"Slavery Brutalizes Man"

Daniel A. Payne

Editor's Introduction: The Anti-Slavery Society in the United States was organized in 1833. Its most prominent leaders were William Lloyd Garrison, Frederick Douglass, Harriet Beecher Stowe, Theodore Weld, and Robert Purvis, to mention only a few. Most important, abolitionism had strong religious roots that included Quakers, Evangelicals of the Second Great Awakening, and growing numbers of Methodists, Presbyterians, and Baptists in the free states of the north.

One of the best arguments in support of abolitionism was delivered in a speech by Daniel A. Payne (1811–1893) at Fordsboro, New York, on the occasion of his ordination to the Lutheran ministry in 1839. His argument that slavery brutalized man was grounded in the notion that God created humans a little lower than the angels and, hence, humans are creatures of immense dignity and value. Thus, when humans demean others by making them slaves, they demean themselves. Consequently, slavery is not a racial matter. Rather, it pertains to human beings as such because the practice not only subverts the capacity of moral agency but it also subverts the moral governance of the divine creator. This powerful argument helped persuade the Lutherans to accept their synod's recommendation to end slavery.

Two years later Payne left the Lutheran church and joined the African Methodist Episcopal Church, which elected him a bishop in 1846. In 1863 he became president of Wilberforce University, thus becoming the first African American ever elected to a university presidency anywhere.

Mr. President: I move the adoption of the Report, because it is based upon the following propositions: American Slavery brutalizes man—destroys his moral agency, and subverts the moral government of God. Sir, I am opposed to slavery, not because it enslaves the black man, but because it enslaves man. And were all the slaveholders in this land men of color, and the slaves white men, I would be as thorough and uncompromising an abolitionist as I now am; for whatever and whenever I may see a being in the form of a man, enslaved by his fellow man, without respect to his complexion, I shall lift up my voice to plead his cause, against all the claims of his proud oppressor; and I shall do it not merely from the sympathy which man feels towards suffering man, but because God, the living God, whom I dare not disobey, has commanded me to open my mouth for the dumb, and to plead the cause of the oppressed.

Slavery brutalizes man. We know that the word man, in its primitive sense, signifies. But the intellectual and moral structure of man, and the august relations which he sustains to the Deity, have thrown around the name, and being designated by it, a halo of glory, brightened by all the ideas, that are ennobling on earth, and blessed in eternity. This being God created but a little lower than the angels, and crowned him with glory and honor; but slavery hurls him down from his elevated position, to the level of brutes, strikes this crown of glory from his head and fastens upon his neck the galling yoke, and compels him to labor like an ox, through summer's sun and winter's snow, without remuneration. Does a man take the calf from the cow and sell it to the butcher? So slavery tears the child from the arms of the reluctant mother, and barters it to the soul trader for a young colt, or some other commodity! Does the bird catcher tear away the dove from his mate? So slavery separates the groaning husband from the embraces of his distracted and weeping wife! And are the beasts of the forest hunted, tortured and slain at the pleasure of the cruel hunter? So are the slaves hunted, tortured and slain by the cruel monster slavery! To treat a man like a brute is to brutalize him. We have seen that slavery treats man like a brute, therefore slavery brutalizes man! But does slavery stop here? Is it content with merely treating the external man like a brute? No, sir, it goes further, and with a heart as brazen as that of Belshazzar and hands still more sacrilegious, it lays hold of the immortal mind, seizes the will, and binds that which Jehovah did not bind—fetters that which the Eternal made as free to move and act as the breath of Heaven. "It destroys moral agency!" To destroy moral agency is to fetter or obstruct the will of man. Now let us see if slavery is innocent of this. The very moment that a man conceives the diabolic design of enslaving his brother's body, that very moment does he also conceive the still more heinous design of fettering his will, for well does he know that in order to make his dominion supreme over the body, he must fetter the living spring of all its motions. Hence, the first lesson the slave is taught is to yield his will unreservedly and exclusively to the dictates of his master. And if a slave desire to educate himself or his children, in obedience to the dictates of reason or the laws of God, he does not, he cannot do it without the consent of his master. Does reason and circumstances and the Bible command a slave to preach the gospel of his brethren? Slavery arises, and with a frown, an oath and a whip, fetters or obstructs the holy volition of his soul! I knew a pious slave in Charleston who was a licensed exhorter in the Methodist Episcopal Church; this good man was in the habit of spending his Saturday nights on the surrounding plantations, preaching to the slaves. One night, as usual, he got into a canoe, sailed upon James Island. While in the very act of preaching the unsearchable riches of Christ to dying men, the patrols seized him and whipped him in the most cruel manner, and compelled him to promise that he would never return to preach again to those slaves. In the year 1834, several colored brethren, who were also exhorters in the Methodist Episcopal Church commenced preaching to several destitute white families, who gained a subsistence by cultivating some poor lands about three or four miles from Charleston. The first Sunday I was present; the house was nearly filled with these poor white farmers. The master of the house was awakened to a sense of his lost condition. During the following week he was converted. On the third Sunday from the day he was convinced of sin he died in the triumphs of faith, and went to heaven. On the fourth Sunday from the time the dear brethren began to preach, the patrols scented their tract, and put them to chase. Thus, an end was put to their labors. Their willing souls were fettered, and the poor whites constrained to go without the preaching of the gospel. In a word, it is in view of man's moral agency that God commands him to shun vice, and practice virtue. But what female slave can do this? I lived twenty-four years in the midst of slavery and never knew but six female slaves who were reputedly virtuous! What profit is to the female slave that she is disposed to be virtuous? Her will, like her body, is not her own; they are both at the pleasure of her master; and he brands them at his will. So it subverts the moral government of God.

In view of the moral agency of man, God hath most wisely and graciously given him a code of laws, and certain positive precepts, to control and regulate moral actions. This code of laws, and these positive precepts, with the divine influence which they are naturally calculated to exert on the mind of man, constitutes his moral government.

Now, to nullify these laws—to weaken or destroy their legitimate influence on the human mind, or to hinder man from yielding universal and entire obedience to them is to subvert the moral government of God.

Now, slavery nullifies these laws and precepts—weakens and destroys their influence over the human mind, and hinders men from yielding universal and entire obedience to them; therefore slavery subverts the moral government of God. This is the climax of the sin of slavery! This is the blackest, foulest, and most horrid feature of the heaven-daring Monster! He stretcheth out his hand against God, and strengtheneth himself against the Almighty—he runneth on him, even on his neck, upon the thick bosses of his buckler. Thus saith the Lord, "Thou shalt not commit adultery." But does the man who owns a hundred females obey the law? Does he not nullify it and compel the helpless woman to disobey God? Concerning the religious instruction of children, thus saith the Lord, "Bring them up in the nurture and admonition of the Lord." But what saith slavery? "They are my property, and shall be brought up to serve me." They shall not even learn to read his word, in order that they may be brought up in his nurture and admonition. If any man doubts this, let him read the slave code of Louisiana and see if it is not death to teach slaves. Thus saith the Lord, "Remember the Sabbath day, to keep it holy." Does not slavery nullify this law, and compel the slave to work on the Sabbath? Thus saith the Lord, "Obey thy father and thy mother." Can the slave children obey this command of God? Does not slavery command the children to obey the master and let him alone? Thus saith the Son of God, "What God hath joined together let no man put asunder." Does not slavery nullify this law, by breaking the sacred bands of wedlock, and separating the husband and wife forever? Thus saith the Son of God, "Search the Scriptures." Does not slavery seal up the word of God and make it criminal for the slave to read it? In 1834, the legislature of South Carolina enacted a law prohibiting the instruction of any slave; and Mr. Lawrence in a pamphlet which he published in 1835, to defend this law, declared that if the slaves were permitted to read the Bible, ninety of them would become infidels, like Voltaire, where ten would become Christians. "Go ye into all the world, and preach the Gospel unto every creature," saith the Son of God. Does slavery permit it? In 1835, a minister of the Episcopal Church, in the city of Charleston, appealed to the civil authority for permission to preach to the free population of an evening, but they would not permit him.

The objector may reply, that at the present moment there are four Methodist missionaries, and one Lutheran, laboring among the slave population of South Carolina. We answer, that this is true, and we are glad of it; but this fact does not overthrow our proposition, nor falsify what we have stated, for although a few planters have permitted the Gospel to be preached to their slaves, the majority of them prohibit it, and this permission is extraneous to slavery and is no part of its creed or code. Slavery never legislates for the religious instruction of slaves, but, on the contrary, legislates to perpetuate their ignorance; and there are laws this very moment in the statute books of South Carolina and other states, prohibiting the religious instruction of slaves. But this is not all that slavery does to subvert the moral government of God. The slaves are sensible of the oppression exercised by their masters; and they see these masters on the Lord's day worshiping in his holy Sanctuary. They hear their masters professing Christianity; they see their masters preaching the Gospel; they hear these masters praying in their families, and they know that oppression and slavery are inconsistent with the Christian religion; therefore they scoff at religion itself, mock their masters, and distrust both the goodness and justice of God. Yes, I have known them even to question His existence. I speak not of what others have told me, but of what I have both seen and heard from the slaves themselves. I have heard the mistress ring the bell for family prayer, and I have seen the servants immediately begin to sneer and laugh; and have heard them declare they would not go in to prayers, adding, if I go in she will only just read, "Servants obey your masters"; but she will not read, "Break every yoke, and let the oppressed go free." I have seen colored men at the church door, scoffing at the ministers, while they were preaching, and saying, you had better go home, and set your slaves free. A few nights ago between ten and eleven o'clock a runaway slave came to the house where I live for safety and succor. I asked him if he was a Christian. "No sir," said he, "white men treat us so bad in Mississippi that we can't be Christians."

Sir, I taught school in Charleston five years. In 1834 the legislature of our state enacted a law to prohibit colored teachers. My school was filled with children and youth of the most promising talents; and when I looked upon them and remembered that in a few more weeks this school shall be closed and I be permitted no more to teach them, notwithstanding I had been a professor seven years, I began to question the existence of the Almighty and to say, if indeed there is a God, does he deal justly? Is he a just God? Is he a holy Being? If so, why does he permit a handful of dying men thus to oppress us? Why does he permit them to hinder me from teaching these children, when nature, reason and Revelation command me to teach them? Thus I began to question the divine government and to murmur at the administration of His providence. And could I do otherwise, while slavery's cruelties were pressing and grinding my soul in the dust, and robbing me and my people of those privileges which it was hugging to its breast, and giving thousands to perpetuate the blessing which it was tearing away from us? Sir, the very man who made the law alluded to, did that very year, increase the property of South Carolina College.

Chapter 7

Opposing Slavery by Repudiating the American Colonization Society

"Slavery and Colonization"

Reverend Peter Williams Jr.

Editor's Introduction: Like his father, who was one of the organizers of the African Methodist Episcopal Zion Church in New York City in 1796, the Reverend Peter Williams Jr. founded the first black Episcopal church in New York in 1814: namely, St. Philips African Episcopal Church, which exists to this day. In fact, he was also the first black in America to be ordained as an Episcopal priest. In a July 4 oration in 1830 he strongly condemned the American Colonization Society, which he believed was motivated wholly by the desire to rid America of all colored people, whether slave or free. His speech enumerated the many inconsistencies that permeated the rhetoric of the colonists, the most prominent of which being their presumed interest in improving the lives of the Africans in America by sending them to a continent that the colonists had long condemned as uncivilized and woefully lacking in all the resources necessary for an improved quality of life. Since he was not against colonization as such, he discussed the opportunity presently made available for blacks to purchase land on Lake Huron in Canada at a reasonable price. Most important, he approved such a venture because it was introduced by blacks and not by racist whites whose sole interest was that of removing blacks from American soil.

On this day the fathers of this nation declared, "We hold these truths to be self-evident, that all men are created equal, that they are endowed by their Creator with certain unalienable rights, among which are life, liberty, and the pursuit of happiness." These truly noble sentiments have secured to their author a deathless fame. The sages and patriots of the Revolution subscribed them with enthusiasm and "pledged their lives, their fortunes, and their sacred honour" in their support.

The result has been the freedom and happiness of millions, by whom the annual returns of this day are celebrated with the loudest and most lively expressions of joy.

But although this anniversary affords occasion of rejoicing to the mass of the people of the United States, there is a class, a numerous class, consisting of nearly three millions, who participate but little in its joys, and are deprived of their unalienable rights by the very men who so loudly rejoice in the declaration that "all men are born free and equal."

The festivities of this day serve but to impress upon the minds of reflecting men of colour a deeper sense of the cruelty, the injustice, and oppression, of which they have been the victims. While others rejoice in their deliverance from a foreign yoke, they mourn that a yoke a thousandfold more grievous is fastened upon them. Alas, they are slaves in the midst of freedom; they are slaves to those who boast that freedom is the unalienable right of all; and the clanking of their fetters, and the voice of their wrongs, make a horrid discord in the songs of freedom which resound through the land.

No people in the world profess so high a respect for liberty and equality as the people of the United States, and yet no people hold so many slaves, or make such great distinctions between man and man.

From various causes (among which we cheerfully admit a sense of justice to have held no inconsiderable rank) the work of emancipation has within a few years been rapidly advancing in a number of States. The State we live in, since the 4th of July, 1827, has been able to boast that she has no slaves, and other States where there still are slaves appear disposed to follow her example.

These things furnish us with cause of gratitude to God, and encourage us to hope that the time will speedily arrive when slavery will be universally abolished. Brethren, what a bright prospect would there be before us in this land had we no prejudices to contend against after being made free.

But, alas! the freedom to which we have attained is defective. Freedom and equality have been "put asunder." The rights of men are decided by the colour of their skin; and there is as much difference made between the rights of a free white man and a free coloured man as there is between a free coloured man and a slave.

Though delivered from the fetters of slavery, we are oppressed by an unreasonable, unrighteous, and cruel prejudice, which aims at nothing less than the forcing away of all the free coloured people of the United States to the distant shores of Africa. Far be it from me to impeach the motives of every member of the African Colonization Society. The civilizing and Christianizing of that vast continent, and the extirpation of the abominable traffic in slaves (which notwithstanding all the laws passed for its suppression is still carried on in all its horrors), are no doubt the principal motives which induce many to give it their support.

But there are those, and those who are most active and most influential in its cause, who hesitate not to say that they wish to rid the country of the free coloured population, and there is sufficient reason to believe, that with many, this is the principal motive for supporting that society; and that whether Africa is civilized or not, and whether the Slave Trade be suppressed or not, they would wish to see the free coloured people removed from this country to Africa.

Africa could certainly be brought into a state of civil and religious improvement without sending all the free people of colour in the United States there.

A few well-qualified missionaries, properly fitted out and supported, would do more for the instruction and improvement of the natives of that country than a host of colonists, the greater part of whom would need to be instructed themselves, and all of whom for a long period would find enough to do to provide for themselves instead of instructing the natives.

How inconsistent are those who say that Africa will be benefited by the removal of the free people of colour of the United States there, while they say they are the most vile and degraded people in the world. If we are as vile and degraded as they represent us, and they wish the Africans to be rendered a virtuous, enlightened and happy people, they should not think of sending us among them, lest we should make them worse instead of better.

The colonies planted by white men on the shores of America, so far from benefiting the aborigines, corrupted their morals, and caused their ruin; and yet those who say we are the most vile people in the world would send us to Africa to improve the character and condition of the natives. Such arguments would not be listened to for a moment were not the minds of the community strangely warped by prejudice.

Those who wish that that vast continent should be compensated for the injuries done it, by sending thither the light of the gospel and the arts of civilized life, should aid in sending and supporting well-qualified missionaries, who should be wholly devoted to the work of instruction, instead of sending colonists who would be apt to turn the ignorance of the natives to their own advantage, and do them more harm than good.

Much has also been said by Colonizationists about improving the character and condition of the people of colour of this country by sending them to Africa. This is more inconsistent still. We are to be improved by being sent far from civilized society. This is a novel mode of improvement. What is there in the burning sun, the arid plains, and barbarous customs of Africa, that is so peculiarly favourable to our improvement? What hinders our improving here, where schools and colleges abound, where the gospel is preached at every corner, and where all the arts and sciences are verging fast to perfection? Nothing, nothing but prejudice. It requires no large expenditures, no hazardous enterprises to raise the people of colour in the United States to as highly improved a state as any class of the community. All that is necessary is that those who profess to be anxious for it should lay aside their prejudices and act towards them as they do by others. We are NATIVES of this country, we ask only to be treated as well as FOREIGNERS. Not a few of our fathers suffered and bled to purchase its independence; we ask only to be treated as well as those who fought against it. We have toiled to cultivate it, and to raise it to its present prosperous condition; we ask only to share equal privileges with those who come from distant lands, to enjoy the fruits of our labour. Let these moderate requests be granted, and we need not go to Africa nor anywhere else to be improved and happy. We cannot but doubt the purity of the motives of those persons who deny us these requests, and would send us to Africa to gain what they might give us at home.

But they say the prejudices of the country against us are invincible; and as they cannot be conquered, it is better that we should be removed beyond their influence. This plea should never proceed from the lips of any man who professes to believe that a just God rules in the heavens.

The African Colonization Society is a numerous and influential body. Would they lay aside their own prejudices, much of the burden would be at once removed; and their example (especially if they were as anxious to have justice done us here as to send us to Africa) would have such an influence upon the community at large as would soon cause prejudice to hide its deformed head.

But, alas! the course which they have pursued has an opposite tendency.

By the scandalous misrepresentations which they are continually giving of our character and conduct we have sustained much injury, and have reason to apprehend much more.

Without any charge of crime we have been denied all access to places to which we formerly had the most free intercourse; the coloured citizens of other places, on leaving their homes, have been denied the privilege of returning; and others have been absolutely driven out.

Has the Colonization Society had no effect in producing these barbarous measures?

They profess to have no other object in view than the colonizing of the free people of colour on the coast of Africa, with their own consent; but if our homes are made so uncomfortable that we cannot continue in them, or, if like our brethren of Ohio and New Orleans, we are driven from them, and no other door is open to receive us but Africa, our removal there will be anything but voluntary.

It is very certain that very few free people of colour wish to go to that land. The Colonization Society know this, and yet they do certainly calculate that in time they will have us all removed there.

How can this be effected but by making our situation worse here, and closing every other door against us?

God in His good providence has opened for such of us as may choose to leave these States an asylum in the neighbouring British Providence of Canada.

There is a large tract of land on the borders of Lake Huron, containing a million of acres, which is offered to our people at $1.50 per acre. It lies between the 42nd and 44th degrees of north latitude. The climate is represented as differing but little from this; the soil as good as any in the world; well-timbered and watered. The laws are good, and the same for the coloured man as the white man. A powerful sympathy prevails there in our behalf, instead of the prejudice which here oppresses us; and everything encourages the hope, that by prudence and industry we may rise to as prosperous and happy a condition as any people under the sun.

To secure this land as a settlement for our people it is necessary that a payment of $6,000 be made on or before the 10th of November next.

This sum it is proposed to lay out in the purchase of 4,000 acres, and when paid will secure the keeping of the remainder in reserve for coloured emigrants ten years. The land so purchased is to be sold out by agents, or trustees to emigrants, and the moneys received in return to be appropriated to a second purchase, which is to be sold as at first, and the returns again laid out in land, until the whole tract is in their possession; and then the capital so employed is to be expended on objects of general utility.

The persons who have bargained for the land have found it necessary to apply to the citizens of the United States to aid them by their donations in raising the amount necessary to make their first purchase, and also to aid a number of emigrants who were driven away in a cruel manner, and in a destitute condition from Cincinnati, to seek a home where they might, and who have selected the Huron tract as their future abode.

Each of these particulars present powerful claims to your liberality. "Cast thy bread upon the waters," says the wise man in the text, "and thou shalt find it after many days. Give a portion to seven and also to eight, for thou knowest not what evil shall be upon the earth." Oh! truly we "know not what evil shall be upon the earth."

When we look at the course of events, relative to our people in this country, we find reason to conclude that it is proper we should provide a convenient asylum to which we and our children may flee in case we should be so oppressed as to find it necessary to leave our present homes. The opinion is daily gaining ground, and has been often openly expressed, that it would be a great blessing to the country if all its free coloured population could be removed to Africa. As this opinion advances, recourse will naturally be had to such measures as will make us feel it necessary to go. Its operation has been already much felt in various States.

The coloured population of Cincinnati were an orderly, industrious and thriving people, but the white citizens, having determined to force them out, first entered into a combination that they would give none of them employment; and finally resorted to violent measures to compel them to go. Should the anxiety to get rid of us increase, have we not reason to fear that some such courses may be pursued in other places.

Satan is an inventive genius. He often appears under the garb of an angel of light, and makes religion and patriotism his plea for the execution of his designs. Our Lord foretold His disciples that "the time cometh, when whosoever killeth you, will think that he doeth God service." Brethren, the time is already come when many think that whosoever causeth us to remove from our native home does service to his country and to God.

Ah! to many in other places beside Cincinnati and New Orleans the sight of free men of colour is so unwelcome that we know not what they may think themselves justifiable in doing to get rid of them. Will it not then be wise for us to provide ourselves with a convenient asylum in time. We have now a fair opportunity of doing so; but if we neglect it, it may be occupied by others, and I know of none likely to be offered which promises so many advantages. Indeed, I feel warranted in saying, that if they are not speedily secured, attempts will be made to prevent our securing them hereafter, and that propositions have actually been made, by influential men, to purchase them, in order that the coloured people may not get them in their possession.

It is true that Africa and Haiti, and perhaps some other countries, will still afford us a place of refuge, yet it will not certainly be amiss to have Canada also at our choice. Some may prefer going there to any other place. But suppose we should never stand in need of such an asylum (and some think that our having provided it will make it less necessary, an effect we should all rejoice in, as we have no wish to go if we can stay in comfort); suppose we should never stand in need of such an asylum, still the amount required to secure it is so small that we can never regret parting with it for such an object. What is $6,000 to be raised by the coloured people throughout the United States? How few are so poor that they cannot give a few shillings without missing it? Let it have the amount which is usually spent by our people in this city on the Fourth of July in celebrating the national independence, and it will make up a very considerable part of it. I have been informed that at the suggestion of one of our coloured clergymen the members of one of the societies who intended to dine together tomorrow have agreed to give the money which would have been paid for dinner tickets to this object. This is truly patriotic. I would say to each of you, brethren "go and do likewise." Give what you would probably expend in celebrating the Fourth of July to the colony of your brethren in Canada; and on the birthday of American freedom secure the establishment of a colony in which you and your children may rise to respectability and happiness. Give it, and you will be no poorer than if you gave it not; and you will secure a place of refuge to yourselves in case of need. "Give a portion to seven and also to eight, for thou knowest not what evil shall be upon the earth."

You are strongly urged to liberality on this occasion by a regard to your future welfare. No scheme for our colonization that has ever yet been attempted has so few objections, or promises so many advantages; but if you withhold your aid until every imaginable objection is removed, you will never effect any object beneficial to yourselves or to your brethren.

Brethren, it is no time to cavil, but to help. If you mean to help the colony, help now. The amount of the first purchase must be paid by the 10th of November, or not at all. Brethren, this scheme of colonization opens to us a brighter door of hope than was ever opened to us before, and has a peculiar claim upon our patronage, because it has originated among our own people. It is not of the devising of the white men, nor of foreigners, but of our own kindred and household. If it succeeds, ours will be the credit. If it succeeds not, ours will be the fault. I am happy, however, to find that it meets the approbation of most, if not of all, of those wise and good men who have for many years been our most zealous and faithful friends, and it evidently appears to be specially favoured by Providence. But the occasion has not only an appeal to your interest, but to your charity.

Your brethren exiled from Cincinnati for no crime but because God was pleased to clothe them with a darker skin than their neighbours cry to you from the wilderness for help. They ask you for bread, for clothing, and other necessaries to sustain them, their wives and their little ones, until by their industry they can provide themselves the means of support. It is true, there are some among them that are able to help themselves; but for these we do not plead. Those who can help themselves, will; but as the ablest have been sufferers in the sacrifice of their property, and the expenses and dangers of their forced and hurried removal, they are not able to assist their destitute brethren.

Indeed, most of the wealthy men of colour in Cincinnati arranged so as to remain until they could have a chance of disposing of their property to advantage; but the poor were compelled to fly without delay, and consequently need assistance. Brethren, can you deny it to them? I know you too well to harbour such a thought. It is only necessary to state to you their case to draw forth your liberality. Think then what these poor people must have suffered in being driven with their wives and their little ones from their comfortable homes late in autumn to take up their residence in a wide and desolate wilderness. Oh, last winter must have been to them a terrible one indeed! We hope that they, by their own efforts, will be better prepared for the next; but they must yet stand in need of help. They have the rude forest to subdue, houses to build, food to provide. They are the pioneers for the establishment of a colony, which may be a happy home for thousands and tens of thousands of our oppressed race. Oh, think of the situation of these, your brethren, whom the hand of oppression has driven into exile, and whom the providence of God has perhaps doomed, like Joseph, to suffering, that at some future day much people may be saved alive. Think of them, and give to their relief as your hearts may dictate. "Cast thy bread upon the waters," etc.

Chapter 8

Opposing Slavery by Force

Appeal, in Four Articles; Together
with a Preamble, to the Coloured
Citizens of the World, but
in Particular, and Very Expressly,
to Those of the United States of America

David Walker

Editor's Introduction: In 1829 David Walker (1785–1830)
published an incendiary pamphlet titled *David Walker's Appeal,*
in Four Articles; Together with a Preamble, to the Coloured Citizens
of the World, but in Particular, and Very Expressly, to Those of the
United States of America. The treatise was condemned everywhere
in the South as well as among many abolitionists in the North.
Many viewed the pamphlet as incitement to rebellion because
of its passionate repudiation of the arbitrary doctrine of white
superiority, the hypocrisy of Christians and their clergy, the
unspeakable brutality of chattel slavery, and the racist proposals to
repatriate blacks to Africa. Arguably, this pamphlet represented the
first attempt by a black man to provide the slaves themselves with
a strong literary attack on the system of bondage. Having traveled
widely in the country, Walker was a popular speaker and writer in
abolitionist circles. As a tailor who repaired uniforms of sailors for
resale, he smuggled his pamphlet into the South by sewing copies
of it into the pockets of the uniforms. One of his most persistent
arguments was that slavery degraded the body, mind, and soul

of the slave to such an extent that one's humanity demanded the preference of death over life. Most important, the last part of Article 4 draws a parallel relationship between the opponents of slavery and those who wrote the Declaration of Independence. Walker's sudden premature death in Boston soon after the third edition of his pamphlet led many to suspect foul play.

ARTICLE III

Religion, my brethren, is a substance of deep consideration among all nations of the earth. The Pagans have a kind, as well as the Mahometans, the Jews and the Christians. But pure and undefiled religion, such as was preached by Jesus Christ and his apostles, is hard to be found in all the earth. God, through his instrument, Moses, handed a dispensation of his Divine will, to the children of Israel after they had left Egypt for the land of Canaan or of Promise, who through hypocrisy, oppression and unbelief, departed from the faith.—He then, by his apostles, handed a dispensation of his, together with the will of Jesus Christ, to the Europeans in Europe, who, in open violation of which, have made *merchandise* of us, and it does appear as though they take this very dispensation to aid them in their *infernal* depredations upon us. Indeed, the way in which religion was and is conducted by the Europeans and their descendants, one might believe it was a plan fabricated by themselves and the *devils* to oppress us. But hark! My master has taught me better than to believe it—he has taught me that his gospel as it was preached by himself and his apostles remains the same, notwithstanding Europe has tried to mingle blood and oppression with it.

It is well known to the Christian world, that Bartholomew Las Casas, that very notoriously avaricious Catholic priest or preacher, and adventurer with Columbus in his second voyage, proposed to his countrymen, the Spaniards in Hispaniola to import the Africans from the Portuguese settlement in Africa, to dig up gold and silver, and work their plantations for them, to effect which, he made a voyage thence to Spain, and opened the subject to his master, Ferdinand then in declining health, who listened to the plan: but who died soon after, and left it in the hand of his successor, Charles V. This wretch, ("Las Casas, the Preacher,") succeeded so well in his plans of oppression, that in 1503, the first blacks had been imported into the new world. Elated with this success, and stimulated by sordid avarice only, he importuned Charles V. in 1511, to grant permission to a Flemish merchant, to import 4000 blacks at one time. Thus we see, through the instrumentality of a pretended preacher of the gospel of Jesus Christ our common master, our wretchedness first commenced in America—where it has been continued from 1503, to this day, 1829. A period of three hundred and twenty-six years. But two hundred and nine, from 1620 [1619]—when twenty of our fathers were brought into Jamestown, Virginia, by a Dutch man of war, and sold off like brutes to the highest bidders; and there is not a doubt in my mind, but that tyrants are in hope to perpetuate our miseries under them and their children until the final consumation of all things.—But if they do not get dreadfully deceived, it will be because God has forgotten them.

The Pagans, Jews and Mahometans try to make proselytes to their religions, and whatever human beings adopt their religions but they extended to them their protection. But Christian Americans, not only hinder their fellow creatures, the Africans, but thousands of them *will absolutely beat a coloured person nearly to death, if they catch him on his knees, supplicating the throne of grace.* This barbarous cruelty was by all the heathen nations of antiquity, and is by the Pagans, Jews and Mahometans of the present day, left entirely to Christian Americans to inflict on the Africans and their descendants, that their cup which is nearly full may be completed. I have known tyrants or usurpers of human liberty in different parts of this country to take their fellow creatures, the coloured people, and beat them until they would scarcely leave life in them; what for? Why they say "The black devils had the audacity to be found *making prayers and supplications to the God who made them!!!!*"

Yes, I have known small collections of coloured people to have convened together, for no other purpose than to worship God Almighty, in spirit and in truth, to the best of their knowledge; when tyrants, calling themselves *patrols,* would also convene and wait almost in breathless silence for the poor coloured people to commence singing and praying to the Lord our God, as soon as they had commenced, the wretches would burst in upon them and drag them out and commence beating them as they would rattle-snakes—many of whom, they would beat so unmercifully, that they would hardly be able to crawl for weeks and sometimes for months. Yet the American ministers send out missionaries to convert the heathen, while they keep us and our children sunk at their feet in the most abject ignorance and wretchedness that ever a people was afflicted with since the world began. Will the Lord suffer this people to proceed much longer? Will he not stop them in their career? Does he regard the heathens abroad, more than the heathens among the Americans? Surely the Americans must believe that God is partial, notwithstanding his Apostle Peter, declared before Cornelius and others that he has no respect to persons, but in every nation he that feareth God and worketh righteousness is accepted with him.—"The word," said he, "which God sent unto the children of Israel, preaching peace, by Jesus Christ, (he is Lord of all."[1]) Have not the Americans the Bible in their hands? Do they believe it? Surely they do not. See how they treat us in open violation of the Bible!! They no doubt will be greatly offended with me, but if God does not awaken them, it will be, because they are superior to other men, as they have represented themselves to be. Our divine Lord and Master said, "all things whatsoever ye would that men should do unto you, do ye even so unto them." But an American minister, with the Bible in his hand, holds us and our children in the most abject slavery and wretchedness. Now I ask them, would they like for us to hold them and their children in abject slavery and wretchedness? No, says one, that never can be done—you are too abject and ignorant to do it—you

---

1. See Acts of the Apostles, chap. x. v.—25–27. [The citation should be to Acts 10:36. Ed.]

are not men—you were made to be slaves to us, to dig up gold and silver for us and our children. Know this, my dear sirs, that although you treat us and our children now, as you do your domestic beast—yet the final result of all future events are known but to God Almighty alone, who rules in the armies of heaven and among the inhabitants of the earth, and who dethrones one earthly king and sits up another, as it seemeth good in his holy sight. We may attribute these vicissitudes to what we please, but the God of armies and of justice rules in heaven and in earth, and the whole American people shall see and know it yet, to their satisfaction. I have known pretended preachers of the gospel of my Master, who not only held us as their natural inheritance, but treated us with as much rigor as any Infidel or Deist in the world—just as though they were intent only on taking our blood and groans to glorify the Lord Jesus Christ. The wicked and ungodly, seeing their preachers treat us with so much cruelty, they say: our preachers, who must be right, if any body are, treat them like brutes, and why cannot we?—They think it is no harm to keep them in slavery and put the whip to them, and why cannot we do the same!—They being preachers of the gospel of Jesus Christ, if it were any harm, they would surely preach against their oppression and do their utmost to erase it from the country; not only in one or two cities, but one continual cry would be raised in all parts of this confederacy, and would cease only with the complete overthrow of the system of slavery, in every part of the country.

But how far the American preachers are from preaching against slavery and oppression, which have carried their country to the brink of a precipice; to save them from plunging down the side of which, will hardly be affected, will appear in the sequel of this paragraph, which I shall narrate just as it transpired. I remember a Camp Meeting in South Carolina, for which I embarked in a Steam Boat at Charleston, and having been five or six hours on the water, we at last arrived at the place of hearing, where was a very great concourse of people, who were no doubt, collected together to hear the word of God, (that some had collected barely as spectators to the scene, I will not here pretend to doubt, however, that is left to themselves and their God.)

Myself and boat companions, having been there a little while, we were all called up to hear; I among the rest went up and took my seat—being seated, I fixed myself in a complete position to hear the word of my Saviour and to receive such as I thought was authenticated by the Holy Scriptures; but to my no ordinary astonishment, our Reverend gentleman got up and told us (coloured people) that slaves must be obedient to their masters—must do their duty to their masters or be whipped—the whip was made for the backs of fools, &c. Here I pause for a moment, to give the world time to consider what was my surprise, to hear such preaching from a minister of my Master, whose very gospel is that of peace and not of blood and whips, as this pretended preacher tried to make us believe. What the American preachers can think of us, I aver this day before my God, I have never been able to define. They have newspapers and monthly periodicals, which they receive in continual succession, but on the pages of which, you will scarcely ever find a paragraph respecting slavery, which is ten thousand times more injurious to this country than all the other evils put together; and which will be the final overthrow of its government, unless something is very speedily done; for their cup is nearly full.—Perhaps they will laugh at or make light of this; but I tell you Americans! that unless you speedily alter your course, *you* and your *Country are gone*!!!!!! For God Almighty will tear up the very face of the earth!!! Will not that very remarkable passage of Scripture be fulfilled on Christian Americans? Hear it Americans!! "He that is unjust, let him be unjust still:—and he which is filthy, let him be filthy still: and he that is righteous, let him be righteous still: and he that is holy, let him be holy still."[2] I hope that the Americans may hear, but I am afraid that they have done us so much injury, and are so firm in the belief that our Creator made us to be an inheritance to them for ever, that their hearts will be hardened, so that their destruction may be sure. This language, perhaps is too harsh for the American's delicate ears. But Oh Americans! Americans!! I warn you in the name of the Lord, (whether you will hear, or forbear,) to repent and reform, or you are ruined!!! Do you think that our blood is hidden from the Lord, because you can hide it from the rest of the world, by sending out missionaries, and by your charitable deeds to the Greeks, Irish, &c.? Will he not publish your secret crimes on the house top? Even here in Boston, pride and prejudice have got to such a pitch, that in the very houses erected to the Lord, they have built little places for the reception of coloured people, where they must sit during meeting, or keep away from the house of God, and the preachers say nothing about it—much less go into the hedges and highways seeking the lost sheep of the house of Israel, and try to bring them in to their Lord and Master. There are not a more wretched, ignorant, miserable, and abject set of beings in all the world, than the blacks in the Southern and Western sections of this country, under tyrants and devils. The preachers of America cannot see them, but they can send out missionaries to convert the heathens, notwithstanding. Americans! unless you speedily alter your course of proceeding, if God Almighty does not stop you, I say it in his name, that you may go on and do as you please for ever, both in time and eternity—never fear any evil at all!!!!!!!!

⇒ ADDITION.—The preachers and people of the United States form societies against Free Masonry and Intemperance, and write against Sabbath breaking, Sabbath mails, Infidelity, &c. &c. But the fountain head[3], compared with which, all those other evils are comparatively nothing, and from the bloody and murderous head of which, they receive no trifling support, is hardly noticed by the Americans. This is a fair illustration of the state of society in this country— it shows what a bearing *avarice* has upon a people, when they are nearly given up by the Lord to a hard heart and a reprobate mind, in consequence of afflicting their fellow creatures. God suffers some to go on until they are ruined for ever!!!!! Will it be the case with the whites of the United States of America?—We hope

---

2. See Revelation, chap. xxii. 11.

3. Slavery and oppression. [The allusion to Free Masonry refers to the furor following the threatened revelation of Masonic secrets by Williams Morgan in 1826 and Morgan's subsequent murder. Ed.]

not—We would not wish to see them destroyed notwithstanding, they have and do now treat us more cruel than any people have treated another, on this earth since it came from the hands of its Creator (with the exceptions of the French and the Dutch, they treat us nearly as bad as the Americans of the United States.) The will of God must however, in spite of us, *be done.*

The English are the best friends the coloured people have upon earth. Though they have oppressed us a little and have colonies now in the West Indies, which oppress us *sorely.—Yet* notwithstanding they (the English) have done one hundred times more for the melioration of our condition, than all the other nations of the earth put together. The blacks cannot but respect the English as a nation, notwithstanding they have treated us a little cruel.

There is no intelligent *black man* who knows any thing, but esteems a real Englishman, let him see him in what part of the world he will—for they are the greatest benefactors we have upon earth. We have here and there, in other nations, good friends. But as a nation, the English are our friends.

How can the preachers and people of America believe the Bible? Does it teach them any distinction on account of a man's colour? Hearken, Americans! to the injunctions of our Lord and Master, to his humble followers . . . [The rest of this quotation is from Article IV that is titled, Our Wretchedness in Consequence of the Colonizing Plan.]

But remember, Americans, that as miserable, wretched, degraded and abject as you have made us in preceding, and in this generation, to support you and your families, that some of you, (whites) on the continent of America, will yet curse the day that you ever were born. You want slaves, and want us for your slaves!!! My colour will yet, root some of you out of the very face of the earth!!!!!! You may doubt it if you please. I know that thousands will doubt they think they have us so well secured in wretchedness, to them and their children, that it is impossible for such things to occur.[4] So did the antideluvians doubt Noah, until the day in which the flood came and swept them away. So did the Sodomites doubt, until Lot had got out of the city, and God rained down fire

4. Why do the Slave-holders or Tyrants of America and their advocates fight so hard to keep my brethren from receiving and reading my Book of Appeal to them?—Is it because they treat us so well?—Is it because we are satisfied to rest in Slavery to them and their children?—Is it because they are treating us like men, by compensating us all over this free country!! for our labours?—But why are the Americans so very fearfully terrified respecting my Book?—Why do they search vessels, &c. when entering the harbours of tyrannical States, to see if any of my Books can be found, for fear that my brethren will get them to read. Why, I thought the Americans proclaimed to the world that they are a happy, enlightened, humane and Christian people, all the inhabitants of the country enjoy equal Rights!! America is the Asylum for the oppressed of all nations!!!

Now I ask the Americans to see the fearful terror they labor under for fear that my brethren will get my Book and read it—and tell me if their declaration is true—viz, if the United States of America is a Republican Government?—Is this not the most tyrannical, unmerciful, and cruel government under Heaven—not excepting the Algerines, Turks and Arabs?—I believe if any candid person would take the trouble to go through the Southern and Western sections of this country, and could have the heart to see the cruelties inflicted by these Christians on us, he would say, that the Algerines, Turks and Arabs treat their dogs a thousand times better than we are treated by the Christians.—But perhaps the Americans do their very best to keep my Brethren from receiving and

and brimstone from Heaven upon them, and burnt them up. So did the king of Egypt doubt the very existence of a God; he said, "who is the Lord, that I should let Israel go?" Did he not find to his sorrow, who the Lord was, when he and all his mighty men of war, were smothered to death in the Red Sea? So did the Romans doubt, many of them were really so ignorant, that they thought the whole of mankind were made to be slaves to them; just as many of the Americans think now, of my colour. But they got dreadfully deceived. When men got their eyes opened, they made the murderers scamper. The way in which they cut their tyrannical throats, was not much inferior to the way the Romans or murderers, served them, when they held them in wretchedness and degradation under their feet. So would Christian Americans doubt, if God should send an Angel from Heaven to preach their funeral sermon. The fact is, the Christians having a name to live, while they are dead, think that God will screen them on that ground.

See the hundreds and thousands of us that are thrown into the seas by Christians, and murdered by them in other ways. They cram us into their vessel holds in chains and in hand-cuffs—men, women and children, all together!! O! save us, we pray thee, thou God of Heaven and of earth, from the devouring hands of the white Christians!!!

> Oh! thou Alpha and Omega!
> The beginning and the end,
> Enthron'd thou art, in Heaven above,
> Surrounded by Angels there.
>
> From whence thou seest the miseries
> To which we are subject;
> The whites have murder'd us, O God!
> And kept us ignorant of thee.
>
> Not satisfied with this, my Lord!
> They throw us in the seas:

---

reading my "Appeal" for fear they will find in it an extract which I made from their Declaration of Independence, which says, "we hold these truths to be self-evident, that all men are created equal," &c. &c. &c. If the above are not the causes of the alarm among the Americans, respecting my Book, I do not know what to impute it to, unless they are possessed of the same spirit with which Demetrius the Silversmith was possessed—however, that they may judge whether they are of the same avaricious and ungodly spirit with that man, I will give here an extract from the Acts of the Apostles, chapter xix,—verses 23, 24, 25, 26, 27.

"And the same time there arose no small stir about that way. For a certain man named Demetrius, a silversmith, which made silver shrines for Diana, brought no small gain unto the craftsmen; whom he called together with the workmen of like occupation, and said, Sirs, ye know that by this craft we have our wealth: moreover, ye see and hear, that not alone at Ephesus, but almost throughout all Asia, this Paul hath persuaded and turned away much people, saying, that they be no gods which are made with hands: so that not only this our craft is in danger to be set at nought; but also that the temple of the great goddess Diana should be despised, and her magnificence should be destroyed, whom all Asia and the world worshippeth."

I pray you Americans of North and South America, together with the whole European inhabitants of the world, (I mean Slave-holders and their advocates) to read and ponder over the above verses in your minds, and judge whether or not you are of the infernal spirit with that Heathen Demetrius, the Silversmith: In fine I beg you to read the whole chapter through carefully.

Be pleas'd, we pray, for Jesus' sake,
To save us from their grasp.

We believe that, for thy glory's sake,
Thou wilt deliver us;
But that thou may'st effect these things,
Thy glory must be sought.

In conclusion, I ask the candid and unprejudiced of the whole world, to search the pages of historians diligently, and see if the Antideluvians—the Sodomites—the Egyptians—the Babylonians—the Ninevites—the Carthagenians—the Persians—the Macedonians—the Greeks—the Romans—the Mahometans—the Jews—or devils, ever treated a set of human beings, as the white Christians of America do us, the blacks, or Africans. I also ask the attention of the world of mankind to the declaration of these very American people, of the United States.

A DECLARATION MADE JULY 4, 1776.

It says,[5] "When in the course of human events, it becomes necessary for one people to dissolve the political bands which have connected them with another, and to assume among the Powers of the earth, the separate and equal station to which the laws of nature and of nature's God entitle them. A decent respect for the opinions of mankind requires, that they should declare the causes which impel them to the separation.—We hold these truths to be self evident—that all men are created equal, that they are endowed by their Creator with certain unalienable rights: that among these, are life, liberty, and the pursuit of happiness that, to secure these rights, governments are instituted among men, deriving their just powers from the consent of the governed; that when ever any form of government becomes destructive of these ends, it is the right of the people to alter or to abolish it, and to institute a new government laying its foundation on such principles, and organizing its powers in such form, as to them shall seem most likely to effect their safety and happiness. Prudence, indeed, will dictate, that governments long established should not be changed for light and transient causes; and accordingly all experience hath shewn, that mankind are more disposed to suffer, while evils are sufferable, than to right themselves by abolishing the forms to which they are accustomed. But when a long train of abuses and usurpations, pursuing invariably the same object, evinces a design to reduce them under absolute despotism, it is their right it is their duty to throw off such government, and to provide new guards for their future security." See your Declaration Americans!!! Do you understand your own language? Hear your language, proclaimed to the world, July 4th, 1776— ⇒ "We hold these truths to be self evident—that ALL MEN ARE CREATED EQUAL!! that they

5. See the Declaration of Independence of the United States.

are endowed by their Creator with certain unalienable rights; that among these are life, *liberty,* and the pursuit of happiness!!" Compare your own language above, extracted from your Declaration of Independence, with your cruelties and murders inflicted by your cruel and unmerciful fathers and yourselves on our fathers and on us—men who have never given your fathers or you the least provocation!!!!!!

Hear your language further! ⇒ " "But when a long train of abuses and usurpation, pursuing invariably the same object, evinces a design to reduce them under absolute despotism, it is their *right,* it is their *duty,* to throw off such government, and to provide new guards for their future security."

Now, Americans! I ask you candidly, was your sufferings under Great Britain, one hundredth part as cruel and tyranical as you have rendered ours under you? Some of you, no doubt, believe that we will never throw off your murderous government and "provide new guards for our future security." If Satan has made you believe it, will he not deceive you?[6] Do the whites say, I being a black man, ought to be humble, which I readily admit? I ask them, ought they not to be as humble as I? or do they think that they can measure arms with Jehovah? Will not the Lord yet humble them? or will not these very coloured people whom they now treat worse than brutes, yet under God, humble them low down enough? Some of the whites are ignorant enough to tell us, that we ought to be submissive to them, that they may keep their feet on our throats. And if we do not submit to be beaten to death by them, we are bad creatures and of course must be damned, &c. If any man wishes to hear this doctrine openly preached to us by the American preachers, let him go into the Southern and Western sections of this country—I do not speak from hear say—what I have written, is what I have seen and heard myself. No man may think that my book is made up of conjecture—I have travelled and observed nearly the whole of those things myself, and what little I did not get by my own observation, I received from those among the whites and blacks, in whom the greatest confidence may be placed.

The Americans may be as vigilant as they please, but they cannot be vigilant enough for the Lord, neither can they hide themselves, where he will not find and bring them out . . .

⇒

---

6. The Lord has not taught the Americans that we will not some day or other throw off their chains and hand-cuffs, from our hands and feet, and their devilish lashes (which some of them shall have enough of yet) from off our backs.

Chapter 9

Opposing Slavery by Rebelling
"Call to Rebellion"

Henry Highland Garnet

Editor's Introduction: In August 1843, Henry Highland Garnet (1815–1882), a Black Presbyterian minister, presented a memorable argument to the National Negro Convention in Buffalo in which he praised the theological and moral virtues of those courageous people who would be willing to fight to the death for their freedom. He later admitted that his reasoning was similar to that advocated by David Walker in his Appeal. In any case he was bent on leading blacks away from the method of moral suasion to that of political activism in pursuit of racial justice. Even though his fiery address failed to receive the endorsement of the convention by only one vote, it did serve to give theological and ethical credibility to the earlier endeavors of insurrectionists like Denmark Vesey, Gabriel Prosser, and Nat Turner. In any case, that speech confirmed Garnet's mission in life as an abolitionist as well as a believer in the Bible because both traditions treated Africans fairly as human beings. His longtime friend Alexander Crummell had embodied that vision by spending twenty years in Liberia as had his friend Edward Blyden. He was also friends with Henry McNeal Turner

55

and Frederick Douglass in spite of the latter's objection to his call for rebellion. As a prominent Presbyterian minister, he served both the Shiloh Presbyterian Church in Troy, New York, and the Fifteenth Street Presbyterian Church in Washington, DC. He longed to go to Africa and to be buried there, desires that were realized just a few months before his death and shortly afterward.

Brethren and Fellow Citizens:—Your brethren of the North, East, and West have been accustomed to meet together in National Conventions, to sympathize with each other, and to weep over your unhappy condition. In these meetings we have addressed all classes of the free, but we have never, until this time, sent a word of consolation and advice to you. We have been contented in sitting still and mourning over your sorrows, earnestly hoping that before this day your sacred liberty would have been restored. But, we have hoped in vain. Years have rolled on, and tens of thousands have been borne on streams of blood and tears, to the shores of eternity. While you have been oppressed, we have also been partakers with you; nor can we be free while you are enslaved. We, therefore, write to you as being bound with you. Many of you are bound to us, not only by the ties of a common humanity, but we are connected by the more tender relations of parents, wives, husbands, children, brothers, and sisters, and friends. As such we most affectionately address you.

Slavery has fixed a deep gulf between you and us, and while it shuts out from you the relief and consolation which your friends would willingly render, it affects and persecutes you with a fierceness which we might not expect to see in the fiends of hell. But still the Almighty Father of mercies has left to us a glimmering ray of hope, which shines out like a lone star in a cloudy sky. Mankind are becoming wiser, and better—the oppressor's power is fading, and you, every day, are becoming better informed, and more numerous. Your grievances, brethren, are many. We shall not attempt, in this short address, to present to the world all the dark catalogue of this nation's sins, which have been committed upon an innocent people. Nor is it indeed necessary, for you feel them from day to day, and all the civilized world look upon them with amazement.

Two hundred and twenty seven years ago, the first of our injured race were brought to the shores of America. They came not with glad spirits to select their homes in the New World. They came not with their own consent, to find an unmolested enjoyment of the blessings of this fruitful soil. The first dealings they had with men calling themselves Christians, exhibited to them the worst features of corrupt and sordid hearts; and convinced them that no cruelty is too great, no villainy and no robbery too abhorrent for even enlightened men to perform, when influenced by avarice and lust. Neither did they come flying upon the wings of Liberty, to a land of freedom. But they came with broken hearts, from their beloved native land, and were doomed to unrequited toil and deep degradation. Nor did the evil of their bondage end at their emancipation by death. Succeeding generations inherited their chains, and millions have come from eternity into time, and have returned again to the world of spirits, cursed and ruined by American slavery.

The propagators of the system, or their immediate ancestors, very soon discovered its growing evil, and its tremendous wickedness, and secret promises were made to destroy it. The gross inconsistency of a people holding slaves, who had themselves "ferried o'er the wave" for freedom's sake, was too apparent to be entirely overlooked. The voice of Freedom cried, "Emancipate yourselves." Humanity supplicated with tears for the deliverance of the children of Africa. Wisdom urged her solemn plea. The bleeding captive plead his innocence, and pointed to Christianity who stood weeping at the cross. Jehovah frowned upon the nefarious institution, and thunderbolts, red with vengeance, struggled to leap forth to blast the guilty wretches who maintained it. But all was in vain. Slavery had stretched its dark wings of death over the land, the Church stood silently by the priests prophesied falsely, and the people loved to have it so. Its throne is established, and now it reigns triumphant.

Nearly three millions of your fellow citizens are prohibited by law and public opinion, (which in this country is stronger than law,) from reading the Book of Life. Your intellect has been destroyed as much as possible, and every ray of light they have attempted to shut out from your minds. The oppressors themselves have become involved in the ruin. They have become weak, sensual, and rapacious—they have cursed you—they have cursed themselves—they have cursed the earth which they have trod.

The colonists threw the blame upon England. They said that the mother country entailed the evil upon them, and that they would rid themselves of it if they could. The world thought they were sincere, and the philanthropic pitied them. But time soon tested their sincerity.

In a few years the colonists grew strong, and severed themselves from the British Government. Their independence was declared, and they took their station among the sovereign powers of the earth. The declaration was a glorious document. Sages admired it, and the patriotic of every nation reverenced the God like sentiments which it contained. When the power of Government returned to their hands, did they emancipate the slaves? No; they rather added new links to our chains. Were they ignorant of the principles of Liberty? Certainly they were not. The sentiments of their revolutionary orators fell in burning eloquence upon their hearts, and with one voice they cried, Liberty or Death. Oh what a sentence was that! It ran from soul to soul like electric fire, and nerved the arm of thousands to fight in the holy cause of Freedom. Among the diversity of opinions that are entertained in regard to physical resistance, there are but a few found to gainsay that stern declaration. We are among those who do not. Slavery! How much misery is comprehended in that single word. What mind is there that does not shrink from its direful effects? Unless the image of God be obliterated from the soul, all men cherish the love of Liberty. The nice discerning political economist does not regard the sacred right more than the untutored African who roams in the wilds of Congo. Nor has the one more right to the full enjoyment of his freedom than the other. In every man's mind the good seeds of liberty are planted, and he who brings his fellow down so low, as to make him contented with a condition of slavery, commits the highest crime against God and man. Brethren, your oppressors aim to do this. They endeavor to make you as much like brutes as possible. When they have blinded the eyes of your mind when they have embittered the sweet waters of life then, and not till then, has American slavery done its perfect work.

TO SUCH DEGRADATION IT IS SINFUL IN THE EXTREME FOR YOU TO MAKE VOLUNTARY SUBMISSION. The divine commandments you are in duty bound to reverence and obey. If you do not obey them, you will surely meet with the displeasure of the Almighty. He requires you to love him supremely, and your neighbor as yourself—to keep the Sabbath day holy—to search the Scriptures—and bring up your children with respect for his laws, and to worship no other God but him. But slavery sets all these at nought, and hurls defiance in the face of Jehovah. The forlorn condition in which you are placed, does not destroy your moral obligation to God. You are not certain of heaven, because you suffer yourselves to remain in a state of slavery, where you cannot obey the commandments of the Sovereign of the universe. If the ignorance of slavery is a passport to heaven, then it is a blessing, and no curse, and you should rather desire its perpetuity than its abolition. God will not receive slavery, nor ignorance, nor any other state of mind, for love and obedience to him. Your condition does not absolve you from your moral obligation. The diabolical injustice by which your liberties are cloven down, NEITHER GOD, NOR ANGELS, OR JUST MEN, COMMAND YOU TO SUFFER FOR A SINGLE MOMENT. THEREFORE IT IS YOUR SOLEMN AND IMPERATIVE DUTY TO USE EVERY MEANS, BOTH MORAL, INTELLECTUAL, AND PHYSICAL THAT PROMISES SUCCESS. If a band of heathen men should attempt to enslave a race of Christians, and to place their children under the influence of some false religion, surely Heaven would frown upon the men who would not resist such aggression, even to death. If, on the other hand, a band of Christians should attempt to enslave a race of heathen men, and to entail slavery upon them, and to keep them in heathenism in the midst of Christianity, the God of heaven would smile upon every effort which the injured might make to disenthral themselves.

Brethren, it is as wrong for your lordly oppressors to keep you in slavery, as it was for the man thief to steal our ancestors from the coast of Africa. You should therefore now use the same manner of resistance, as would have been just in our ancestors when the bloody foot prints of the first remorseless soul thief was placed upon the shores of our fatherland. The humblest peasant is as free in the sight of God as the proudest monarch that ever swayed a sceptre. Liberty is a spirit sent out from God, and like its great Author, is no respecter of persons.

Brethren, the time has come when you must act for yourselves. It is an old and true saying that, "if hereditary bondmen would be free, they must themselves strike the blow." You can plead your own cause, and do the work of emancipation better than any others. The nations of the world are moving in the great cause of universal freedom, and some of them at least will, ere long, do you justice. The combined powers of Europe have placed their broad seal of disapprobation upon the African slave trade. But in the slave-holding parts of the United States, the trade is as brisk as ever. They buy and sell you as though you were brute beasts. The North has done much—her opinion of slavery in the abstract is known. But in regard to the South, we adopt the opinion of the New York Evangelist—We have advanced so far, that the cause apparently waits for a more effectual door to be thrown open than has been yet. We are about to point out that more effectual door. Look around you, and behold the bosoms of your loving wives heaving with untold agonies! Hear the cries of your poor children! Remember the stripes your fathers bore. Think of the torture and disgrace of your noble mothers. Think of your wretched sisters, loving virtue and purity, as they are driven into concubinage and are exposed to the unbridled lusts of incarnate devils. Think of the undying glory that hangs around the ancient name of Africa—and forget not that you are native born American citizens, and as such, you are justly entitled to all the rights that are granted to the freest. Think how many tears you have poured out upon the soil which you have cultivated with unrequited toil and enriched with your blood; and then go to your lordly enslavers and tell them plainly, that you are determined to be free. Appeal to their sense of justice, and tell them that they have no more right to oppress you, than you have to enslave them. Entreat them to remove the grievous burdens which they have imposed upon you, and to remunerate you for your labor. Promise them renewed diligence in the cultivation of the soil, if they will render to you an equivalent for your services. Point them to the increase of happiness and prosperity in the British West Indies since the Act of Emancipation. Tell them in language which they cannot misunderstand, of the exceeding sinfulness of slavery, and of a future judgment, and of the righteous retributions of an indignant God. Inform them that all you desire is FREEDOM, and that nothing else will suffice. Do this, and for ever after cease to toil for the heartless tyrants, who give you no other reward but stripes and abuse. If they then commence the work of death, they, and not you, will be responsible for the consequences. You had better all die immediately, than live slaves and entail your wretchedness upon your posterity. If you would be free in this generation, here is your only hope. However much you and all of us may desire it, there is not much hope of redemption without the shedding of blood. If you must bleed, let it all come at once—rather die freemen, than live to be slaves. It is impossible like the children of Israel, to make a grand exodus from the land of bondage. The Pharaohs are on both sides of the blood red waters! You cannot move en masse, to the dominions of the British Queen—nor can you pass through Florida and overrun Texas, and at last find peace in Mexico. The propagators of American slavery are spending their blood and treasure, that they may plant the black flag in the heart of Mexico and riot in the halls of the Montezumas. In the language of the Rev.

Robert Hall, when addressing the volunteers of Bristol, who were rushing forth to repel the invasion of Napoleon, who threatened to lay waste the fair homes of England, "Religion is too much interested in your behalf, not to shed over you her most gracious influences."

You will not be compelled to spend much time in order to become inured to hardships. From the first moment that you breathed the air of heaven, you have been accustomed to nothing else but hardships. The heroes of the American Revolution were never put upon harder fare than a peck of corn and a few herrings per week. You have not become enervated by the luxuries of life. Your sternest energies have been beaten out upon the anvil of severe trial. Slavery has done this, to make you subservient, to its own purposes; but it has done more than this, it has prepared you for any emergency. If you receive good treatment, it is what you could hardly expect; if you meet with pain, sorrow, and even death, these are the common lot of slaves.

Fellow men! Patient sufferers! behold your dearest rights crushed to the earth! See your sons murdered, and your wives, mothers and sisters doomed to prostitution. In the name of the merciful God, and by all that life is worth, let it no longer be a debatable question whether it is better to choose Liberty or death.

In 1822, Denmark Veazie [Vesey], of South Carolina, formed a plan for the liberation of his fellow men. In the whole history of human efforts to overthrow slavery, a more complicated and tremendous plan was never formed. He was betrayed by the treachery of his own people, and died a martyr to freedom. Many a brave hero fell, but history, faithful to her high trust, will transcribe his name on the same monument with Moses, Hampden, Tell, Bruce and Wallace, Toussaint L'Ouverture, Lafayette and Washington. That tremendous movement shook the whole empire of slavery. The guilty soul thieves were overwhelmed with fear. It is a matter of fact, that at that time, and in consequence of the threatened revolution, the slave States talked strongly of emancipation. But they blew but one blast of the trumpet of freedom and then laid it aside. As these men became quiet, the slaveholders ceased to talk about emancipation; and now behold your condition today! Angels sigh over it, and humanity has long since exhausted her tears in weeping on your account!

The patriotic Nathaniel Turner followed Denmark Veazey [Vesey]. He was goaded to desperation by wrong and injustice. By despotism, his name has been recorded on the list of infamy, and future generations will remember him among the noble and brave.

Next arose the immortal Joseph Cinqué, the hero of the Amistad. He was a native African, and by the help of God he emancipated a whole ship load of his fellow men on the high seas. And he now sings of liberty on the sunny hills of Africa and beneath his native palm trees, where he hears the lion roar and feels himself as free as that king of the forest.

Next arose Madison Washington that bright star of freedom, and took his station in the constellation of true heroism. He was a slave on board the brig Creole, of Richmond, bound to New Orleans, that great slave mart, with a hundred and four others. Nineteen struck for liberty or death. But one life was taken, and the whole were emancipated, and the vessel was carried into Nassau, New Providence.

Noble men! Those who have fallen in freedom's conflict, their memories will be cherished by the true hearted and the God fearing in all future generations; those who are living, their names are surrounded by a halo of glory.

Brethren, arise, arise! Strike for your lives and liberties. Now is the day and the hour. Let every slave throughout the land do this, and the days of slavery are numbered. You cannot be more oppressed than you have been—you cannot suffer greater cruelties than you have already. Rather die freemen than live to be slaves. Remember that you are FOUR MILLIONS!

It is in your power so to torment the God cursed slaveholders that they will be glad to let you go free. If the scale was turned, and black men were the masters and white men the slaves, every destructive agent and element would be employed to lay the oppressor low. Danger and death would hang over their heads day and night. Yes, the tyrants would meet with plagues more terrible than those of Pharaoh. But you are a patient people. You act as though, you were made for the special use of these devils. You act as though your daughters were born to pamper the lusts of your masters and overseers. And worse than all, you tamely submit while your lords tear your wives from your embraces and defile them before your eyes. In the name of God, we ask, are you men? Where is the blood of your fathers? Has it all run out of your veins? Awake, awake; millions of voices are calling you! Your dead fathers speak to you from their graves. Heaven, as with a voice of thunder, calls on you to arise from the dust.

Let your motto be resistance! resistance! RESISTANCE! No oppressed people have ever secured their liberty without resistance. What kind of resistance you had better make, you must decide by the circumstances that surround you, and according to the suggestion of expediency. Brethren, adieu! Trust in the living God. Labor for the peace of the human race, and remember that you are FOUR MILLIONS.

Chapter 10

Opposing Slavery by Emigrating to Africa
"The Regeneration of Africa"

Alexander Crummell

Editor's Introduction: Alexander Crummell (1819–1898), born free in New York City, graduated from the Oneida Institute, and despite his rejection by General Theological Seminary he was consecrated an Episcopal priest in Boston in 1844. He immigrated to England, where he graduated from Cambridge and spent two decades in Liberia bent on providing moral support to the African émigrés to that American colony. Like most of his contemporaries, he viewed Africans as uncivilized heathens in need of the benefits of Western colonization, civilization, and Christianity. Most important, he considered repatriated African slaves from America and the Caribbean as the effective agents of Africa's redemption because of their ancestral solidarity with Africa. Further, he argued that since these black émigrés from the Americas would be permanent settlers among the native Africans, they were ideally suited to model all the virtues of Western civilization and Christianity for them. This, he believed, would be a much more effective means for the transformation of Africa than anything that European missionaries could accomplish. His views of Africa and the paternalistic role of ex-slaves in its redemption informed the perspectives of Africans in the diaspora for many generations thereafter. The following was delivered in 1865 at the Pennsylvania Colonization Society.

The great principle which lies at the basis of all successful propagation of the Gospel is this, namely, the employment of all indigenous agency. Christianity never secures *thorough* entrance and complete authority in any land, save by the use of men and minds somewhat native to the soil. And from the very start of the Christian faith this idea has always been illustrated in the general facts of its conquest.

In the work of Jewish evangelization our Lord himself employed the agency of Jews. For the evangelization of Greeks, he employed, indeed, Jews, but Jews who had become *hellenized.* At an early period the Romans were to be brought under the influence of Christianity; and although the faith was introduced among them by an agency which was exotic, yet Romans themselves stamped the impress of the faith upon the Empire, and strangled nigh to death, in less than three centuries, its fierce and vulpine paganism. So, in like manner, it became rooted in the soil of Britain. So, likewise, at a later period, in Russia and Scandinavia. Hardly a generation passed away, in either of these cases, ere the zealous and adventurous pioneers of the new system resigned their work, and handed over their prerogatives to the hardy and convicted sons of the soil.

It seems clear, then, that for the evangelization of *any* country, the main instrumentality to be set to work is that of men of like sentiments, feelings, blood and ancestry, with the people whose evangelization is desired. The faith, so to speak, must needs become incorporated with a people's mental, moral, and even physical constitution, vitalize their being, and run along the channels of their blood.

Now this principle applies, in common with all other lands, to Africa. It is, under God, the condition of the success of the Cross throughout that vast continent.

All this, however, is but theory. The facts which more especially prove it, are the successful missions of the English in West Africa, both Episcopal and Wesleyan. Nothing can be more glorious than the heroic, almost god-like self-sacrifice of their missionaries, for nigh forty years, to introduce Christianity among the natives; nothing, on the other hand, more discouraging than the small results which at first followed their efforts. But by-and-by, one native and then another, and another was raised up, fitted and prepared to be preachers of the Gospel. The Christian faith had become engrafted upon the native stock. It swelled with the inspirations of their breath; it coursed along the channels of their veins. Then the truth began to spread; it had lodged itself in a new race and began to assert its authority in a new land. The new soil was genial; and the Divine principle, although transplanted, put forth all its original vitality. As when a new plant or seed is brought from some distant country to a new land, akin in soil and climate to its parent bed, it shoots up and spreads abroad with all its former vigor and luxuriance; so Christianity, so soon as it became indigenous to Africa, commenced a successful career; and now mission stations are to be found two thousand miles along the coast; catechists, by scores are employed; ministers are preaching the Gospel on the coast and in the interior. Missions conducted by native clergymen, are being carried into the strongholds of ancient, sanguinary kingdoms; and are advancing, with authority and power, up the great Niger, towards the very heart of the continent.

And in all this we see illustrated the great principle that, for the propagation of the faith, the main lever and agency must needs be indigenous. The faith, at first, is an exotic, in all new lands; but, in order to make its roots strike deep into the new soil, men, native in blood, lineage, feelings, and sentiments, must needs be raised up and put to active effort.

Now, the Almighty, in a most marvelous manner, has been providing just this agency, with almost every indigenous quality, for the propagation of the faith on the continent of Africa. Millions of the Negro race have been stolen from the land of their fathers. They have been the serfs, for centuries, on the plantations and in households, in the West Indies and the United States, of civilized and Christian people. By contact with Anglo-Saxon culture and religion, they have, themselves, been somewhat permeated and vitalized by the civilization and the Christian principles of their superiors. Numbers of them have become emigrants, settlers, denizens of a free Republic, and of thriving colonies of the British on the West Coast of Africa; and numbers more of them ever and anon emigrate from the lands of their past thraldom back, not unfrequently, to the very spots whence their parents were first stolen. And these emigrants almost invariably profess the faith of Jesus. They are *Christian* emigrants, journeying across the wide ocean, with Bibles, and Prayer Books, and Tracts, and Sermons, and family altars, seeking a new home amid the heathen population of Africa.

Now, I say, that when you send out such companies of people, you send Christianity to Africa; and I would fain emphasize this remark, and invite attention to it.

If you send a missionary to Africa, you send, indeed, a good, holy, faithful minister; but he is but an individual; he may, or he may not, plant Christianity in the field. The probability is that he will not; for the greatest of saints can only represent a partial Christianity. Hence the likelihood, the almost certainty is, that his work will have to be followed up by others. When, therefore, you send a single individual, as a missionary, you do not necessarily send Christianity to Africa; albeit you send a devoted Christian.

On the other hand, when you send out a *company of Christian emigrants,* you send a *church.* Planted on the coast of Africa, its rootlets burst forth on one side and another like the "little daughters" of the plantain in a tropical soil.

But facts are more powerful, more convincing than mere theories. I will, therefore, attempt briefly to illustrate this principle by facts:

1. The Presbyterians have a school in Pennsylvania called the "Ashmun Institute"; for the training of colored men for missionary duty in Africa. A few

years ago, three of these students left the United States with their families, as emigrants to Liberia. Now, when the Presbyterians sent forth this little company of Christians, they sent out organized Christianity to heathen Africa. In each of those little bands, there was "the church in the house;" with the Bible and the preacher, and baptized children; the germs of a new outgrowth of Christianity in the future. Civilization, moreover, was allied to all their life, work and habits, in their new homes.

And these men, settled at Liberia, take root there; increase is given to their families there as well as here. Native heathen also come into their families, work for them in their gardens, in their work-shops, and on their farms; are touched by their civilized habits, and moved by their family prayers and Sunday teachings. As their children grow up, they, in their turn, become the centres, to other heathen, of new and wider influences, both civilizing and Christian. Native converts become incorporated with them in the household of faith. By-and-by these native converts raise up Christian children; who, in some cases, are married to persons of the emigrant stock; and thus the native and the emigrant blood, at times, *both* Christianized, flow, mingled together, through the veins of a new race, thoroughly indigenous and native.

Now, just *such* power, strength, and permanent influence cannot go forth from your foreign missionary; because he is an exotic. Beneath the burning sun of Africa he withers and pines away, and alas, too often dies, a glorious martyr for Christianity! And when he departs to paradise, his wife and children return to Europe or America, weak, enfeebled, bereaved; but they rarely have permanent influence in Africa!

The black Christian emigrant, on the other hand, is indigenous, in blood, constitution, and adaptability. Two centuries of absence from the continent of Africa, has not destroyed his physical adaptation to the land of his ancestors. There is a tropical fitness, which inheres in our constitution, whereby we are enabled, when we leave this country, to sit down under an African sun; and soon, and with comparative ease, feel ourselves at home, and move about in the land as though we had always lived there. Children, too, are born to us in our adopted country, who have as much strength and vitality as native children; and soon we find ourselves establishing families right beside those of our heathen kinsfolk.

Now you can easily see what a powerful influence that denomination of Christians—the Presbyterians—can wield by such an agency as I have described, to bless and save Africa. They send thither living, concrete, organic, indigenous Christianity in the young men and their families, trained at their Institute; send it there to abide; to be reproduced in their children; to be spread out in their families; and not to be an evanescent and fugitive thing, without root in the soil, and void of bud, and fruit, and flower; nor yet a tender exotic, needing a hot-house carefulness and nurture; but a thing of life and robustness, mindless of sun and dews, and storms and tempests, fitted to every circumstance of life and nature!

Such is the great power which the Almighty has given our Presbyterian brethren for planting Christianity in Africa.

2. But here is another illustration of the same power, which, just at this time, is given the Baptists of this country, for the same blessed work for Christianity and Africa. Only two months ago, one hundred and fifty colored Baptists in Virginia applied for passage to Liberia for themselves and children. No inducements were held out to them; no persuasions used among them. It was a spontaneous movement of their own. I may add, here, that I am told by a student in the Episcopal "Divinity School:" in this city, that he had seen in Virginia colored Baptist ministers, men moved, we may believe, by the Spirit of God, who were seeking opportunities to get to Africa to preach the Gospel. These ministers, these emigrants, wish to go to Africa to *remain* there. They are seeking a home for themselves and their children in that, the land of their sires. They desire to go back to their fatherland, and to root themselves and their offspring in the ancestral soil, and to send down their blood and lineage, amid the scenes and the rights which were familiar to their unfortunate ancestors.

3. And now tell me what nobler plan could the great Baptist denomination fall upon, than just this providential movement, to effect that which is dear to their hearts, and to the hearts of all Christians—the redemption of Africa! And what a living thing would not their work be, if perchance, they could plant some half dozen compact, intelligent, enterprising villages of such Christian people, amid the heathen populations of West Africa!

4. But now, even at the risk of wearying you, I will advert briefly to one more distinct and providential illustration of this principle. There is the island of Barbadoes, a British colony; it contains a black population of 130,000 people. For years these people have had organizations among themselves, intending emigration to West Africa. Two years ago the President of Liberia extended an official invitation to the sons of Africa in the West Indies to come over to Liberia, and aid us in the great work of Christianity and civilization which God has imposed upon us. And the response from these our brethren was immediate. Just a week before I sailed from Liberia, the brig "Corn," from Barbadoes, arrived in the "Roads of Monrovia" with 346 emigrants. The most of these persons were Episcopalians; well-trained handicraftsmen, skillful sugar-makers, intelligent, spirited, well-educated persons. Not merely hundreds, but *thousands* more of their kinsfolk and fellow-islanders, in Barbadoes, stand ready, nay, anxious, to colonize themselves in the Republic of Africa.

Whose work is this? Who has prompted this movement of Christian black men from Barbadoes, back to the land of their ancestors; laden with gifts, and talents; sanctified, as numbers of them are, by the spirit of grace? Who, but the Spirit of God is moving these Christian "remnants" of black society—this seed of civilization—from the West Indies and America, to the coast of Africa. Who but God himself has called and elected this germ of Christianity to a great work of duty in the land of their fathers? And what more facile and effectual means could the Episcopalians of this country use than this, that is to seize upon this movement to plant their own phase of Christianity in villages and towns along the coast, and in the interior of Africa?

Does any man doubt this assertion of distinctive providence? Come, then, with me for a moment to the West Coast of Africa—take your position, say at Sierra Leone; run your eye along the whole line of the coast, from Gambia to the Cameroons, and watch that steady, quiet, uninterrupted emigration of cultivated colored men, who are coming over from Jamaica, Antigua, Barbadoes, St. Kitts, St. Thomas and Demarara; many of them men who have "ate their terms" at the Inns of London; some graduates of Edinburg, St. Augustine's, Canterbury, Codrington College, and other great schools—coming over to the West Coast of Africa, and becoming merchants, planters, postmasters, government officials, lawyers, doctors, judges, and blessed be God, catechists and clergymen, at British settlements in Western Africa! Then go down two hundred miles to the Republic of Liberia, and see there 14,000 black emigrants from more than half of the States of America; and see there, too, how that God, after carrying on His work of preparation in the black race in America in dark, mysterious and distressful ways, has at length brought out a "remnant" of them and placed them in a free Republic, to achieve high nationality, to advance civilization and to subserve the highest interests of the Cross and the Church! have rested this matter, this evening, almost, if not quite, entirely, upon the one single point, that is, THE EVANGELIZATION OF AFRICA. I can present and urge it upon no lower, no inferior consideration. I recognize the need of Trade, Agriculture, Commerce, Art, Letters and Government, as the collateral and indispensable aids to the complete restoration of my fatherland. That man must be blind who does not see *that*. But they are but *collateral* and auxiliary; not the end, and aim, and object of that divine will and providence which the Almighty has been working out by the means of institutions and governments, by afflictions and sufferings, and even oppressions, during the course of centuries.

PART 3
OPPOSING RACIAL
SEGREGATION

Chapter 11

Opposing Racial Segregation by Withdrawing from Racist Churches

The Life Experiences and Gospel Labors of the Rt. Rev. Richard Allen

Richard Allen

Editor's Introduction: While the constitution of the new republic was being ratified, so-called freemen and women in northern cities began separating themselves voluntarily from the racist practices of the white churches—a process that soon resulted in the founding of autonomous black congregations and denominations. The most prominent leader in that endeavor was a black preacher, Richard Allen (1760–1831) who, in 1789 emptied St. George's Methodist Church in Philadelphia of its black members and organized the Bethel African Methodist Episcopal Church, which eventually became the mother church of the first black denomination. He described that event in his diary that was discovered in a trunk after his death. He discussed the primary reason for their departure from the church accordingly: ". . . we were so scandalously treated in the presence of all the congregation present." Yet the spirit of their separation did not entail any absolute disassociation from the white Methodists, as evidenced in the financial support the African Methodists received from them as well as their retention of the doctrines and polity of the white Methodists. Further, Bishop

71

Francis Asbury dedicated The Bethel African Methodist Episcopal Church in 1794 and ordained Allen as a Methodist bishop in 1799. Most important, Allen believed that God was with him and his people, blessing them every step of the way. Suffice it to say that he has been revered throughout African American church history as the father of the independent black church movement, which eventually expressed itself in many denominational forms in which the vast majority of black Christians continue to hold membership.

A number of us usually attended St. George's church in Fourth street; and when the colored people began to get numerous in attending the church, they moved us from the seats we usually sat on, and placed us around the wall, and on Sabbath morning we went to church and the sexton stood at the door, and told us to go in the gallery. He told us to go, and we would see where to sit. We expected to take the seats over the ones we formerly occupied below, not knowing any better. We took those seats. Meeting had begun, and they were nearly done singing, and just as we got to the seats, the elder said, "Let us pray." We had not been long upon our knees before I heard considerable scuffling and low talking. I raised my head up and saw one of the trustees, H-___M___, having hold of the Rev. Absalom Jones, pulling him up off of his knees, and saying, "You must get up—you must not kneel here." Mr. Jones replied, "Wait until prayer is over." Mr. H___ M___ said "No, you must get up now, or I will call for aid and force you away." Mr. Jones said, "Wait until prayer is over, and I will get up and trouble you no more." With that he beckoned to one of the other trustees, Mr. L___ S___ to come to his assistance. He came, and went to William White to pull him up. By this time prayer was over, and we all went out of the church in a body, and they were no more plagued with us in the church. This raised a great excitement and inquiry among the citizens, in so much that I believe they were ashamed of their conduct. But my dear Lord was with us, and we were filled with fresh vigor to get a house erected to worship God in. Seeing our forlorn and distressed situation, many of the hearts of our citizens were moved to urge us forward; notwithstanding we had subscribed largely towards finishing St. George's church, in building the gallery and laying new floors, and just as the house was made comfortable, we were turned out from enjoying the comforts of worshipping therein. We then hired a store-room, and held worship by ourselves. Here we were pursued with threats of being disowned, and read publicly out of meeting if we did continue worship in the place we had hired; but we believed the Lord would be our friend. We got subscription papers out to raise money to build the house of the Lord. By this time we had waited on Dr. Rush and Mr. Robert Ralston, and told them of our distressing situation. We considered it a blessing that the Lord had put it into our hearts to wait upon those gentlemen. They pitied our situation, and subscribed largely towards the church, and were very friendly towards us, and advised us how to go on. We appointed Mr. Ralston our treasurer. Dr. Rush did much for us in public by his influence. I hope the name of Dr. Benjamin Rush and Robert Ralston will never be forgotten among us. They were the first two gentlemen who espoused the cause of the oppressed, and aided us in building the house of the Lord for the poor Africans to worship in. Here was the beginning and rise of the first African church in America. But the elder of the Methodist Church still pursued us. Mr. John McClaskey called upon us and told us if we did not erase our names from the subscription paper, and give up the paper, we would be publicly turned out of meeting. We asked him if we had violated any rules of discipline by so doing. He replied, "I have the charge given to me by the Conference, and unless you submit I will read you publicly out of meeting." We told him we were willing to abide by the discipline of the Methodist Church, "And if you will show us where we have violated any law of discipline of the Methodist Church, we will submit; and if there is no rule violated in the discipline we will proceed on." He replied, "We will read you all out." We told him if he turned us out contrary to rule of discipline, we should seek further redress. We told him we were dragged off of our knees in St. George's church, and treated worse than heathens; and we were determined to seek out for ourselves, the Lord being our helper. He told us we were not Methodists, and left us. Finding we would go on in raising money to build the church, he called upon us again, and wished to see us all together. We met him. He told us that he wished us well, that he was a friend to us, and used many arguments to convince us that we were wrong in building a church. We told him we had no place of worship; and we did not mean to go to St. George's church any more, as we were so scandalously treated in the presence of all the congregation present; "and if you deny us your name, you cannot seal up the scriptures from us, and deny us a name in heaven. We believe heaven is free for all who worship in spirit and truth." And he said, "So you are determined to go on." We told him "Yes, God being our helper." He then replied, "We will disown you all from the Methodist connection." We believed if we put our trust in the Lord, he would stand by us. This was a trial that I never had to pass through before. I was confident that the great head of the church would support us. My dear Lord was with us. We went out with our subscription paper, and met with great success. We had no reason to complain of the liberality of the citizens. The first day the Rev. Absalom Jones and myself went out we collected three hundred and sixty dollars. This was the greatest day's collection that we met with. We appointed a committee to look out for a lot— the Rev. Absalom Jones, William Gray, William Wilcher and myself. We pitched upon a lot at the corner of Lombard and Sixth streets. They authorized me to go and agree for it. I did accordingly. The lot belonged to Mr. Mark Wilcox. We entered into articles of agreement for the lot. Afterwards the committee found a lot in Fifth Street, in a more commodious part of the city, which we bought; and the first lot they threw upon my hands, and wished me to give it up. I told them they had authorized me to agree for the lot, and they were all well satisfied with the agreement I had made, and I thought it was hard that they would throw it upon my hands. I told them I would sooner keep it myself than to forfeit the agreement I had made. And so I did.

We bore much persecution from many of the Methodist connection; but we have reason to be thankful to Almighty God, who was our deliverer. The day was appointed to go and dig the cellar. I arose early in the morning and addressed the throne of grace, praying that the Lord would bless our endeavors. Having by this time two or three teams of my own—as I was the first proposer of the African church, I put the first spade in the ground to dig a cellar for the same. This was the first African Church or meetinghouse that was erected in the United States of America. We intended it for the African preaching-house or church; but finding that the elder stationed in this city was such an opposer to our proceedings of erecting a place of worship, though the principal part of the directors of this church belonged to the Methodist connection, the elder stationed here would neither preach for us, nor have anything to do with us. We then held an election, to know what religious denomination we should unite with. At the election it was determined there were two in favor of the Methodist, the Rev. Absalom Jones and myself, and a large majority in favor of the Church of England. The majority carried. Notwithstanding we had been so violently persecuted by the elder, we were in favor of being attached to the Methodist connection; for I was confident that there was no religious sect or denomination would suit the capacity of the colored people as well as the Methodist; for the plain and simple gospel suits best for any people; for the unlearned can understand, and the learned are sure to understand; and the reason that the Methodist is so successful in the awakening and conversion of the colored people, the plain doctrine and having a good discipline. But in many cases the preachers would act to please their own fancy, without discipline, till some of them became such tyrants, and more especially to the colored people. They would turn them out of society, giving them no trial, for the smallest offense, perhaps only hearsay. They would frequently, in meeting the class, impeach some of the members of whom they had heard an ill report, and turn them out, saying, "I have heard thus and thus of you, and you are no more a member of society"—without witnesses on either side. This has been frequently done, notwithstanding in the first rise and progress in Delaware state, and elsewhere, the colored people were their greatest support; for there were but few of us free; but the slaves would toil in their little patches many a night until midnight to raise their little truck and sell to get something to support them more than what their masters gave them, but we used often to divide our little support among the white preachers of the Gospel. This was once a quarter. It was in the time of the old Revolutionary War between Great Britain and the United States. The Methodists were the first people that brought glad tidings to the colored people. I feel thankful that ever I heard a Methodist preach. We are beholden to the Methodists, under God, for the light of the Gospel we enjoy; for all other denominations preached so high-flown that we were not able to comprehend their doctrine. Sure am I that reading sermons will never prove so beneficial to the colored people as spiritual or extempore preaching. I am well convinced that the Methodist has proved beneficial to thousands and ten times thousands. It is to be awfully feared that the simplicity of the Gospel that was among them fifty years ago, and that they conform more to the world and the fashions thereof, they would fare very little better than the people of the world. The discipline is altered considerably from what it was. We would ask for the good old way, and desire to walk therein.

In 1793 a committee was appointed from the African Church to solicit me to be their minister, for there was no colored preacher in Philadelphia but myself. I told them I could not accept of their offer, as I was a Methodist. I was indebted to the Methodists, under God, for what little religion I had; being convinced that they were the people of God, I informed them that I could not be anything else but a Methodist, as I was born and awakened under them, and I could go no further with them, for I was a Methodist, and would leave you in peace and love. I would do nothing to retard them in building a church as it was an extensive building, neither would I go out with a subscription paper until they were done going out with their subscription. I bought an old frame that had been formerly occupied as a blacksmith shop, from Mr. Sims, and hauled it on the lot in Sixth near Lombard Street, that had formerly been taken for the Church of England. I employed carpenters to repair the old frame, and fit it for a place of worship. In July 1794, Bishop Asbury being in town I solicited him to open the church for us which he accepted. The Rev. John Dickins sung and prayed, and Bishop Asbury preached. The house was called bethel, agreeable to the prayer that was made. Mr. Dickins prayed that it might be a bethel to the gathering in of thousands of souls. My dear Lord was with us, so that there were many hearty "amen's" echoed through the house. This house of worship has been favored with the awakening of many souls, and I trust they are in the Kingdom, both white and colored. Our warfare and troubles now began afresh. Mr. C. proposed that we should make over the church to the Conference. This we objected to, he asserted that we could not be Methodists unless we did; we told him he might deny us their name, but they could not deny us a seat in Heaven. Finding that he could not prevail with us so to do, he observed that we had better be incorporated, then we could get any legacies that were left for us, if not, we could not. We agreed to be incorporated. He offered to draw the incorporation himself, that it would save us the trouble of paying for to get it drawn. We cheerfully submitted to his proposed plan. He drew the incorporation, but incorporated our church under the Conference, our property was then all consigned to the Conference for the present bishops, elders, ministers, etc., that belonged to the white Conference, and our property was gone. Being ignorant of incorporations we cheerfully agreed thereto. We labored about ten years under this incorporation, until James Smith was appointed to take the charge in Philadelphia; he soon waked us up by demanding the keys and books of the church, and forbid us holding any meetings except by orders from him; these propositions we told him we could not agree to. He observed he was elder, appointed to the charge, and unless we submitted to him, he would read us all out of meeting. We told him the house was ours, we had bought it, and paid for it. He said he would let us know it was not ours, it belonged to the Conference; we took counsel on it; counsel informed us we had been taken in; according to the incorporation it belonged to the white connection. We asked him if it couldn't be altered; he told us if two-thirds of the society agreed to have it altered, it could be altered. He gave me a transcript to lay before them; I called the society together and laid it before them. My dear Lord was with us. It was unanimously agreed to, by both male and female. We had another incorporation drawn that took the church from Conference, and got it passed, before the elder knew anything about it. This raised a considerable rumpus, for the elder contended that it would not be good unless he had signed it. The elder, with the trustees of St. George's, called us together, and said we must pay six hundred dollars a year for their services, or they could not serve us. We told them we were not able so to do. The trustees of St. George's insisted that we should or should not be supplied by their preachers. At last they made a move that they would take four hundred; we told them that our house was considerably in debt, and we were poor people, and we could not agree to pay four hundred, but we agreed to give them two hundred. It was moved by one of the trustees of St. George's that the money should be paid into their treasury; we refused paying it into their treasury, but we would pay it to the preacher that served; they made a move that the preacher should not receive the money from us. The Bethel trustees made a move that their funds should be shut and they would pay none; this caused a considerable contention. At length they withdrew their motion. The elder supplied us preaching five times in a year for two hundred dollars. Finding that they supplied us so seldom, the trustees of Bethel church passed a resolution that they would pay but one hundred dollars a year, as the elder only preached five times in a year for us; they called for the money, we paid him twenty-five dollars a quarter, but he being dissatisfied, returned the money back again, and would not have it unless we paid him fifty dollars. The trustees concluded it was enough for five sermons, and said they would pay no more; the elder of St. George's was determined to preach for us no more, unless we gave him two hundred dollars, and we were left alone for upwards of one year.

Mr. Samuel Royal being appointed to the charge of Philadelphia, declared unless we should repeal the Supplement, neither he nor any white preacher, travelling or local, should preach any more for us; so we were left to ourselves. At length the preachers and stewards belonging to the Academy, proposed serving us on the same terms that we had offered to the St. George's preachers, and they preached for us better than twelve months, and then demanded $150 per year; this not being complied with, they declined preaching for us, and were once more left to ourselves, as an edict was passed by the elder, that if any local preacher should serve us, he should be expelled from the connection. John Emory, then elder of the Academy, published a circular letter, in which we were disowned by the Methodists. A house was also hired and fitted up for worship, not far from Bethel, and an invitation given to all who desired to be Methodists to resort thither. But being disappointed in this plan, Robert R. Roberts, the resident elder, came to Bethel, insisted on preaching to us and taking the spiritual charge of the congregation, for we were Methodists he was told he should come on some terms with the trustees; his answer was, that "He did not come to consult with Richard Allen or other trustees, but to inform the congregation, that on next Sunday afternoon, he would come and take the spiritual charge." We told him he could not preach for us under existing circumstances. However, at the appointed time he came, but having taken previous advice we had our preacher in the pulpit when he came, and the house was so fixed that he could not get but more than half way to the pulpit. Finding himself disappointed he appealed to those who came with him as witnesses, that "That man (meaning the preacher), had taken his appointment." Several respectable white citizens who knew the colored people had been ill-used, were present, and told us not to fear, for they would see us righted, and not suffer Roberts to preach in a forcible manner, after which Roberts went away.

The next elder stationed in Philadelphia was Robert Birch, who, following the example of his predecessor, came and published a meeting for himself. But the method just mentioned was adopted and he had to go away disappointed. In consequence of this, he applied to the Supreme Court for a writ of mandamus, to know why the pulpit was denied him. Being elder, this brought on a lawsuit, which ended in our favor. Thus by the Providence of God we were delivered from a long, distressing and expensive suit, which could not be resumed, being determined by the Supreme Court. For this mercy we desire to be unfeignedly thankful.

About this time, our colored friends in Baltimore were treated in a similar manner by the white preachers and trustees, and many of them driven away who were disposed to seek a place of worship, rather than go to law.

Many of the colored people in other places were in a situation nearly like those of Philadelphia and Baltimore, which induced us, in April 1816, to call a general meeting, by way of Conference. Delegates from Baltimore and other places which met those of Philadelphia, and taking into consideration their grievances, and in order to secure the privileges, promote union and harmony among themselves, it was resolved: "That the people of Philadelphia, Baltimore, etc., etc., should become one body, under the name of the African Methodist Episcopal Church." We deemed it expedient to have a form of discipline, whereby we may guide our people in the fear of God, in the unity of the Spirit, and in the bonds of peace, and preserve us from that spiritual despotism which we have so recently experienced—remembering that we are not to lord it over God's heritage, as greedy dogs that can never have enough. But with long suffering and bowels of compassion, to bear each other's burdens, and so fulfill the Law of Christ, praying that our mutual striving together for the promulgation of the Gospel may be crowned with abundant success.

> The God of Bethel heard her cries,
> He let his power be seen;
> He stopp'd the proud oppressor's frown,

And proved himself a King.
Thou sav'd them in the trying hour,
Ministers and councils joined,
And all stood ready to retain
That helpless church of Thine.
Bethel surrounded by her foes,
But not yet in despair,
Christ heard her supplicating cries;
The God of Bethel heard.

Chapter 12

Opposing Racial Segregation through Self-Help Programs
"The Atlanta Exposition Address"

Booker T. Washington

Editor's introduction: Even though accommodating to the conditions of oppression was widespread throughout the period of slavery, Booker T. Washington, 1856–1915, articulated his philosophy more clearly and persuasively than any black leader had ever done previously. The occasion was the opening of the Atlanta Cotton States and International Exposition in Atlanta, Georgia, on September 18, 1895. His speech was a tour de force in rhetorical excellence, and soon thereafter he became the most powerful black leader in the nation. Clearly, it was not the first time he had addressed a mix audience of northern and southern white social and economic elites. Rather, at the beginning of his public career, he was asked to address the 1885 meeting of the National Educational Association in Madison, Wisconsin, which was attended by over four thousand people, including a large representation from Alabama. Similarly, he was asked to give a five minute address at an international meeting of Christian workers in Atlanta in 1893. The audience comprised about two thousand men and women from both north and south. The newspapers in both regions reported on those speeches quite favorably, which was unique for the time. But his public address of paramount importance was the 1895 speech, often referred to as "The Atlanta Compromise." In that speech, Washington set forth the basic principles for racial cooperation between the North and the South and between blacks and whites for the next half century by repudiating both the political interests of blacks along with all claims for racial social equality. Thus, he emphasized the wisdom of cultivating friendly relations between blacks and whites; the embrace of skilled labor as the primary means for economic self-development; the assurance that blacks would remain a patient, law-abiding, unresentful, and faithful people as they have always been; belief that the mutuality of the races centered around industrial, commercial, civil, and religious interests and that God would bless racial cooperation in the South as the means for ushering in a new heaven and a new earth. While many have condemned this address as a conservative embrace of second-class citizenship, I contend that it was a mild form of opposition to the prevailing societal ethos of racial oppression by its embrace of a cooperative venture for separate yet mutual development under the conditions of racial oppression. At that time, Washington's approach seemed to be the only viable choice. All others invariably led to violent rejection.

MR. PRESIDENT AND GENTLEMEN OF THE BOARD OF DIRECTORS AND CITIZENS:

One-third of the population of the South is of the Negro race. No enterprise seeking the material, civil, or moral welfare of this section can disregard this element of our population and reach the highest success. I but convey to you, Mr. President and Directors, the sentiment of the masses of my race when I say that in no way have the value and manhood of the American Negro been more fittingly and generously recognized than by the managers of this magnificent Exposition at every stage of its progress. It is a recognition that will do more to cement the friendship of the two races than any occurrence since the dawn of our freedom.

Not only this, but the opportunity here afforded will awaken among us a new era of industrial progress. Ignorant and inexperienced, it is not strange that in the first years of our new life we began at the top instead of at the bottom; that a seat in Congress or the state legislature was more sought than real estate or industrial skill; that the political convention or stump speaking had more attractions than starting a dairy farm or truck garden.

A ship lost at sea for many days suddenly sighted a friendly vessel. From the mast of the unfortunate vessel was seen a signal, "Water, water; we die of thirst" The answer from the friendly vessel at once came back, "Cast down your bucket where you are." A second time the signal, "Water, water; send us water!" ran up from the distressed vessel, and was answered, "Cast down your bucket where you are." And a third and fourth signal for water was answered, "Cast down your bucket where you are." The captain of the distressed vessel, at last heeding the injunction, cast down his bucket, and it came up full of fresh, sparkling water from the mouth of the Amazon River. To those of my race who depend on bettering their condition in a foreign land or who underestimate the importance of cultivating friendly relations with the Southern white man, who is their next-door neighbour, I would say: "Cast down your bucket where you are"—cast it down in making friends in every manly way of the people of all races by whom we are surrounded.

Cast it down in agriculture, mechanics, in commerce, in domestic service, and in the professions. And in this connection it is well to bear in mind that whatever other sins the South may be called to bear, when it comes to business, pure and simple, it is in the South that the Negro is given a man's chance in the commercial world, and in nothing is this Exposition more eloquent than in emphasizing this chance. Our greatest danger is that in the great leap from slavery to freedom we may overlook the fact that the masses of us are to live by the productions of our hands, and fail to keep in mind that we shall prosper in proportion as we learn to dignify and glorify common labour and put brains and skill into the common occupations of life; shall prosper in proportion as we learn to draw the line between the superficial and the substantial, the ornamental gewgaws of life and the useful. No race can prosper till it learns that there is as much dignity in tilling a field as in writing a poem. It is at the bottom of life we must begin, and not at the top. Nor should we permit our grievances to overshadow our opportunities.

To those of the white race who look to the incoming of those of foreign birth and strange tongue and habits for the prosperity of the South, were I permitted I would repeat what I say to my own race, "Cast down your bucket where you are." Cast it down among the eight millions of Negroes whose habits you know, whose fidelity and love you have tested in days when to have proved treacherous meant the ruin of your firesides. Cast down your bucket among these people who have, without strikes and labour wars, tilled your fields, cleared your forests, builded your railroads and cities, and brought forth treasures from the bowels of the earth, and helped make possible this magnificent representation of the progress of the South. Casting down your bucket among my people, helping and encouraging them as you are doing on these grounds, and to education of head, hand, and heart, you will find that they will buy your surplus land, make blossom the waste places in your fields, and run your factories. While doing this, you can be sure in the future, as in the past, that you and your families will be surrounded by the most patient, faithful, law-abiding, and unresentful people that the world has seen. As we have proved our loyalty to you in the past, in nursing your children, watching by the sick-bed of your mothers and fathers, and often following them with tear-dimmed eyes to their graves, so in the future, in our humble way, we shall stand by you with a devotion that no foreigner can approach, ready to lay down our lives, if need be, in defense of yours, interlacing our industrial, commercial, civil, and religious life with yours in a way that shall make the interests of both races one. In all things that are purely social we can be as separate as the fingers, yet one as the hand in all things essential to mutual progress.

There is no defense or security for any of us except in the highest intelligence and development of all. If anywhere there are efforts tending to curtail the fullest growth of the Negro, let these efforts be turned into stimulating, encouraging, and making him the most useful and intelligent citizen. Effort or means so invested will pay a thousand per cent interest. These efforts will be twice blessed—blessing him that gives and him that takes. There is no escape through law of man or God from the inevitable:

> *The laws of changeless justice*
> *Bind oppressor with oppressed;*
> *And close as sin and suffering joined*
> *We march to fate abreast.*

Nearly sixteen millions of hands will aid you in pulling the load upward, or they will pull against you the load downward. We shall constitute one-third and more of the ignorance and crime of the South, or one-third its intelligence and progress; we shall contribute one-third to the business and industrial prosperity of the South, or we shall prove a veritable body of death, stagnating, depressing, retarding every effort to advance the body politic.

Gentlemen of the Exposition, as we present to you our humble effort at an exhibition of our progress, you must not expect overmuch. Starting thirty years ago with ownership here and there in a few quilts and pumpkins and chickens (gathered from miscellaneous sources), remember the path that has led from these to the inventions and production of agricultural implements, buggies, steam-engines, newspapers, books, statuary, carving, paintings, the management of drugstores and banks, has not been trodden without contact with thorns and thistles. While we take pride in what we exhibit as a result of our independent efforts, we do not for a moment forget that our part in this exhibition would fall far short of your expectations but for the constant help that has come to our educational life, not only from the Southern states, but especially from Northern philanthropists, who have made their gifts a constant stream of blessing and encouragement.

The wisest among my race understand that the agitation of questions of social equality is the extremest folly, and that progress in the enjoyment of all the privileges that will come to us must be the result of severe and constant struggle rather than of artificial forcing. No race that has anything to contribute to the markets of the world is long in any degree ostracized. It is important and right that all privileges of the law be ours, but it is vastly more important that we be prepared for the exercises of these privileges. The opportunity to earn a dollar in a factory just now is worth infinitely more than the opportunity to spend a dollar in an opera-house.

In conclusion, may I repeat that nothing in thirty years has given us more hope and encouragement, and drawn us so near to you of the white race, as this opportunity offered by the Exposition; and here bending, as it were, over the altar that represents the results of the struggles of your race and mine, both starting practically empty handed three decades ago, I pledge that in your effort to work out the great and intricate problem which God has laid at the doors of the South, you shall have at all times the patient, sympathetic help of my race; only let this be constantly in mind, that, while from representations in these buildings of the product of field, of forest, of mine, of factory, letters, and art, much good will come, yet far above and beyond material benefits will be that higher good, that, let us pray God, will come, in a blotting out of sectional differences and racial animosities and suspicions, in a determination to administer absolute justice, in a willing obedience among all classes to the mandates of law. This, coupled with our material prosperity, will bring into our beloved South a new heaven and a new earth.

Chapter 13

Opposing Racial Segregation by Condemning Lynching
"This Awful Slaughter"

Ida B. Wells-Barnett

Editor's Introduction: Ida B. Wells-Barnett (1862–1931) was
forced to leave Memphis, Tennessee, at the risk of losing her life
because she dared to write in her newspaper that the success of three
African American men as business men prompted the envy of the
whites who lynched them. Thus, she urged blacks in Memphis to
emigrate to the West. Her newspaper office was destroyed while she
was away on a business trip, and she was advised not to return. She
then launched her lifelong career as a crusader against lynching by
carefully gathering and analyzing factual information to demonstrate
that the reasons for lynching lay in the economics and politics of
racial oppression rather than the alleged propensity of black men as
rapists of white women. Her writings also gave public visibility to
the taboo subject of white men raping black women which, under
the conditions of chattel slavery, resulted in the development of
a mixed race as permanent evidence of such a horrific practice.
Wells-Barnett traveled to England in 1893/94, where she lectured
widely on the subject, which inspired the British to form an Anti-
Lynching Society. Upon her return she laid the groundwork for the

continuation of her campaign in two organizations in which she was a founding member: namely, the National Association of Colored Women and the National Association for the Advancement of Colored People. In fact, the following speech was delivered on May 18, 1909, at the first annual meeting of the NAACP in Atlanta, Georgia. Thereafter, she would have the support of a strong ally in her long anti-lynching crusade. By any measure she was among the most courageous and militant leaders of her day. Most important, she saw women's suffrage and their role in social protest as necessary instruments for the emancipation of black people.

The lynching record for a quarter of a century merits the thoughtful study of the American people. It presents three salient facts: First, lynching is color-line murder. Second, crimes against women is the excuse, not the cause. Third, it is a national crime and requires a national remedy. Proof that lynching follows the color line is to be found in the statistics which have been kept for the past twenty-five years. During the few years preceding this period and while frontier law existed, the executions showed a majority of white victims. Later, however, as law courts and authorized judiciary extended into the far West, lynch law rapidly abated, and its white victims became few and far between. Just as the lynch-law regime came to a close in the West, a new mob movement started in the South.

This was wholly political, its purpose being to suppress the colored vote by intimidation and murder. Thousands of assassins banded together under the name of Ku Klux Klans, "Midnight Raiders," "Knights of the Golden Circle," et cetera, et cetera, spread a reign of terror, by beating, shooting and killing colored in a few years, the purpose was accomplished, and the black vote was suppressed. But mob murder continued. From 1882, in which year fifty-two were lynched, down to the present, lynching has been along the color line. Mob murder increased yearly until in 1892 more than two hundred victims were lynched and statistics show that 3,284 men, women and children have been put to death in this quarter of a century. During the last ten years from 1899 to 1908 inclusive the number lynched was 959. Of this number 102 were white, while the colored victims numbered 857. No other nation, civilized or savage, burns its criminals; only under that Stars and Stripes is the human holocaust possible. Twenty-eight human beings burned at the stake, one of them a woman and two of them children, is the awful indictment against American civilization—the gruesome tribute which the nation pays to the color line.

Why is mob murder permitted by a Christian nation? What is the cause of this awful slaughter? This question is answered almost daily—always the same shameless falsehood that "Negroes are lynched to protect womanhood." Standing before a Chautauqua assemblage, John Temple Graves, at once champion of lynching and apologist for lynchers, said: "The mob stands today as the most potential bulwark between the women of the South and such a carnival of crime as would infuriate the world and precipitate the annihilation of the Negro race." This is the never-varying answer of lynchers and their apologists. All know that it is untrue. The cowardly lyncher revels in murder, then seeks to shield himself from public execration by claiming devotion to woman. But truth is mighty and the lynching record discloses the hypocrisy of the lyncher as well as his crime.

The Springfield, Illinois, mob rioted for two days, the militia of the entire state was called out, two men were lynched, hundreds of people driven from their homes, all because a white woman said a Negro assaulted her. A mad mob went to the jail, tried to lynch the victim of her charge and, not being able to find him, proceeded to pillage and burn the town and to lynch two innocent men. Later, after the police had found that the woman's charge was false, she published a retraction, the indictment was dismissed and the intended victim discharged. But the lynched victims were dead. Hundreds were homeless and Illinois was disgraced.

As a final and complete refutation of the charge that lynching is occasioned by crimes against women, a partial record of lynchings is cited; 285 persons were lynched for causes as follows: Unknown cause, 92; no cause, 10; race prejudice, 49; miscegenation, 7; informing, 12; making threats, 11; keeping saloon, 3; practicing fraud, 5; practicing voodooism, 1; refusing evidence, 2; political causes, 5; disputing, 1; disobeying quarantine regulations, 2; slapping a child, 1; turning state's evidence, 3; protecting a Negro, 1; to prevent giving evidence, 1; knowledge of larceny, 1; writing letter to white woman, 1; asking white woman to marry; 1; jilting girl, 1; having smallpox, 1; concealing criminal, 2; threatening political exposure, 1; self-defense, 6; cruelty, 1; insulting language to woman, 5; quarreling with white man, 2; colonizing Negroes, 1; throwing stones, 1; quarreling, 1; gambling, 1.

Is there a remedy, or will the nation confess that it cannot protect its protectors at home as well as abroad? Various remedies have been suggested to abolish the lynching infamy, but year after year, the butchery of men, women and children continues in spite of plea and protest. Education is suggested as a preventive, but it is as grave a crime to murder an ignorant man as it is a scholar. True, few educated men have been lynched, but the hue and cry once started stops at no bounds, as was clearly shown by the lynchings in Atlanta, and in Springfield, Illinois.

Agitation, though helpful, will not alone stop the crime. Year after year statistics are published, meetings are held, resolutions are adopted and yet lynchings go on. Public sentiment does measurably decrease the sway of mob law, but the irresponsible bloodthirsty criminals who swept through the streets of Springfield, beating an inoffensive law-abiding citizen to death in one part of the town, and in another torturing and shooting to death a man who for threescore years had made a reputation for honesty; integrity and sobriety, had raised a family and had accumulated property; were not deterred from their heinous crimes by either education or agitation.

The only certain remedy is an appeal to law. Lawbreakers must be made to know that human life is sacred and that every citizen of this country is first a citizen of the United States and secondly a citizen of the state in which he belongs. This nation must assert itself and protect its federal citizenship at home as well as abroad. The strong arm of the government must reach across state lines whenever unbridled lawlessness defies state laws and must give to the individual under the Stars and Stripes the same measure of protection it gives to him when he travels in foreign lands.

Federal protection of American citizenship is the remedy for lynching. Foreigners are rarely lynched in America. If, by mistake, one is lynched, the national government quickly pays the damages. The recent agitation in California against the Japanese compelled this nation to recognize that federal power must yet assert itself to protect the nation from the treason of sovereign states. Thousands of American citizens have been put to death and no President has yet raised his hand in effective protest, but a simple insult to a native of Japan was quite sufficient to stir the government at Washington to prevent the threatened wrong. If the government has power to protect a foreigner from insult, certainly it has power to save a citizen's life.

The practical remedy has been more than once suggested in Congress. Senator Gallinger, of New Hampshire, in a resolution introduced in Congress called for an investigation "with the view of ascertaining whether there is a remedy for lynching which Congress may apply." The Senate Committee has under consideration a bill drawn by A. E. Pillsbury, formerly Attorney General of Massachusetts, providing for federal prosecution of lynchers in cases where the state fails to protect citizens or foreigners. Both of these resolutions indicate that the attention of the nation has been called to this phase of the lynching question.

As a final word, it would be a beginning in the right direction if this conference can see its way clear to establish a bureau for the investigation and publication of the details of every lynching, so that the public could know that an influential body of citizens has made it a duty to give the widest publicity to the facts in each case; that it will make an effort to secure expressions of opinion all over the country against lynching for the sake of the country's fair name; and lastly, but by no means least, to try to influence the daily papers of the country to refuse to become accessory to mobs either before or after the fact.

Several of the greatest riots and most brutal burnt offerings of the mobs have been suggested and incited by the daily papers of the offending community. If the newspaper which suggests lynching in its accounts of an alleged crime, could be held legally as well as morally responsible for reporting that "threats of lynching were heard"; or, "it is feared that if the guilty one is caught, he will be lynched"; or, "there were cries of 'lynch him,' and the only reason the threat was not carried out was because no leader appeared," a long step toward a remedy will have been taken.

In a multitude of counsel there is wisdom. Upon the grave question presented by the slaughter of innocent men, women and children there should be an honest, courageous conference of patriotic, law-abiding citizens anxious to punish crime promptly, impartially and by due process of law, also to make life, liberty and property secure against mob rule.

Time was when lynching appeared to be sectional, but now it is national—a blight upon our nation, mocking our laws and disgracing our Christianity. "With malice toward none but with charity for all" let us undertake the work of making the "law of the land" effective and supreme upon every foot of American soil—a shield to the innocent; and to the guilty, punishment swift and sure.

Chapter 14

Opposing Racial Segregation by Moral Suasion

"To the Nations of the World"

W. E. B. DuBois

Editor's Introduction: William Edward Burghardt DuBois (1868–
1963) was renowned as Black America's greatest intellectual; lifelong
writer and activist in the struggle for racial justice; a founder of the
National Association for the Advancement of Colored People and
editor of that body's Crisis Magazine for three decades; organizer of
the first five Pan-African Congresses; inspired by the philosophies
of Karl Marx, William James, and Max Weber; welcomed in the
newly independent Ghana as an honorary citizen; honored with a
state funeral in Ghana; and memorialized by the establishment of
a museum and a crypt in Accra, where he and his wife lived from
1958 until his death in 1963. In the following speech given on
July 25, 1900, at the Pan-African Congress at Westminster Hall,
London, DuBois uttered his most quoted words: "The problem of
the twentieth century is the problem of the color line . . ." The
speech clearly reveals that at that early period in his long career,
DuBois was deeply committed to the art of moral suasion as the
preferred method for effecting racial justice for African peoples
around the world.

In the metropolis of the modern world, in this the closing year of the nineteenth century, there has been assembled a congress of men and women of African blood, to deliberate solemnly upon the present situation and outlook of the darker races of mankind. The problem of the twentieth century is the problem of the color line, the question as to how far differences of race—which show themselves chiefly in the color of the skin and the texture of the hair—will hereafter be made the basis of denying to over half the world the right of sharing to utmost ability the opportunities and privileges of modern civilization.

To be sure, the darker races are today the least advanced in culture according to European standards. This has not, however, always been the case in the past. And certainly the world's history, both ancient and modern, has given many instances of no despicable ability and capacity among the blackest races of men. In any case, the modern world must remember that in this age when the ends of the world are being brought so near together the millions of black men in Africa, America and the Islands of the Sea, not to speak of the brown and yellow myriads elsewhere, are bound to have a great influence upon the world in the future, by reason of sheer numbers and physical contact.

If now the world of culture bends itself towards giving Negroes and other dark men the largest and broadest opportunity for education and self-development, then this contact and influence is bound to have a beneficial effect upon the world and hasten human progress. But if, by reason of carelessness, prejudice, greed and injustice, the black world is to be exploited and ravished and degraded, the results must be deplorable, if not fatal—not simply to them, but to the high ideals of justice, freedom and culture which a thousand years of Christian civilization have held before Europe.

And now, therefore, to these ideals of civilization, to the broader humanity of the followers of the Prince of Peace, we, the men and women of Africa in world congress assembled, do now solemnly appeal: Let the world take no backward step in that slow but sure progress which has successively refused to let the spirit of class, of caste, of privilege, or of birth, debar from life, liberty and the pursuit of happiness a striving human soul. Let no color or race be a feature of distinction between white and black men, regardless of worth or ability.

Let not the natives of Africa be sacrificed to the greed of gold, their liberties taken away, their family life debauched, their just aspirations repressed, and avenues of advancement and culture taken from them. Let not the cloak of Christian missionary enterprise be allowed in the future, as so often in the past, to hide the ruthless economic exploitation and political downfall of less developed nations, whose chief fault has been reliance on the plighted faith of the Christian church.

Let the British nation, the first modern champion of Negro freedom, hasten to crown the work of Wilberforce, and Clarkson, and Buxton, and Sharpe, Bishop Colenso, and Livingston, and give as soon as practicable, the rights of responsible government to the black colonies of Africa and the West Indies. Let not the spirit of Garrison, Phillips, and Douglass wholly die out in America; may the conscience of a great nation rise and rebuke all dishonesty and unrighteous oppression toward the American Negro, and grant to him the right of franchise, security of person and property, and generous recognition of the great work he has accomplished in a generation toward raising nine millions of human beings from slavery to manhood.

Let the German Empire, and the French Republic, true to their great past, remember that the true worth of colonies lies in their prosperity and progress, and that justice, impartial alike to black and white, is the first element of prosperity. Let the Congo Free State become a great central Negro state of the world, and let its prosperity be counted not simply in cash and commerce, but in the happiness and true advancement to its black people.

Let the nations of the world respect the integrity and independence of the free Negro states of Abyssinia, Liberia, Haiti, and the rest, and let the inhabitants of these states, the independent tribes of Africa, the Negroes of the West Indies and America, and the black subjects of all nations take courage, strive ceaselessly, and fight bravely, that they may prove to the world their incontestable right to be counted among the great brotherhood of mankind. Thus we appeal with boldness and confidence to the Great Powers of the civilized world, trusting in the wide spirit of humanity, and the deep sense of justice and of our age, for a generous recognition of the righteousness of our cause.

Chapter 15

Opposing Racial Segregation by Rebuilding Africa
"Declaration of the Rights of the Negro Peoples of the World"

Marcus Garvey

Editor's Introduction: Marcus Mosiah Garvey Jr. (1887–1940) was born in Jamaica. He arrived in the United States in 1916 bent on visiting Booker T. Washington, whom he believed had developed a significant venture in racial self-development: namely, a program that he thought symbolized his own black nationalist perspective. He did not know that Washington had died the previous year. His arrival coincided with the emigration of tens of thousands of blacks from the rural south to northern cities, where they experienced considerable frustration and anxiety. Soon thereafter many black veterans returned from the war to face racial discrimination, segregation, disrespect, and violence. Experienced in community organizing, journalism, and public speaking, he addressed their condition by organizing the Universal Negro Improvement Association (UNIA) with the mission to organize all people of African descent around a program to reclaim African sovereignty for their ancestral homeland. Most important, he believed that the solution to the racial problem in America and elsewhere lay in this enterprise. Undoubtedly, his movement revived the hopes of working class black folk for a better life and spawned the largest social movement ever witnessed in the United States. Though he was later tried, convicted, and deported for unintentional mismanagement of funds, the spirit of his movement lived on to inspire the nascent Nation of Islam, the Rastafarians, and numerous African independence movements. His development of a Pan-African nationalist philosophy constitutes his legacy, which has been publicly memorialized in Jamaica, the United States, Canada, and Great Britain. The following principles—found in Garvey's "Declaration of the Rights of the Negro Peoples of the World": The Principles of the Universal Negro Improvement Association—underlay his extensive writings and speeches.

PREAMBLE

Be It Resolved, That the Negro people of the world, through their chosen representatives in convention assembled in Liberty Hall, in the City of New York and United States of America, from August 1 to August 31, in the year of Our Lord one thousand nine hundred and twenty, protest against the wrongs and injustices they are suffering at the hands of their white brethren, and state what they deem their fair and just rights, as well as the treatment they propose to demand of all men in the future.

We complain:

1. That nowhere in the world, with few exceptions, are black men accorded equal treatment with white men, although in the same situation and circumstances, but, on the contrary, are discriminated against and denied the common rights due to human beings for no other reason than their race and color.

We are not willingly accepted as guests in the public hotels and inns of the world for no other reason than our race and color.

2. In certain parts of the United States of America our race is denied the right of public trial accorded to other races when accused of crime, but are lynched and burned by mobs, and such brutal and inhuman treatment is even practiced upon our women.

3. That European nations have parceled out among them and taken possession of nearly all of the continent of Africa, and the natives are compelled to surrender their lands to aliens and are treated in most instances like slaves.

4. In the southern portion of the United States of America, although citizens under the Federal Constitution, and in some States almost equal to the whites in population and are qualified land owners and taxpayers, we are, nevertheless, denied all voice in the making and administration of the laws and are taxed without representation by the State governments, and at the same time compelled to do military service in defense of the country.

5. On the public conveyances and common carriers in the southern portion of the United States we are jim-crowed and compelled to accept separate and inferior accommodations and made to pay the same fare charged for first-class accommodations, and our families are often humiliated and insulted by drunken white men who habitually pass through the jim-crow cars going to the smoking car.

6. The physicians of our race are denied the right to attend their patients while in the public hospitals of the cities and States where they reside in certain parts of the United States.

Our children are forced to attend inferior separate schools for shorter terms than white children, and the public school funds are unequally divided between the white and colored schools.

7. We are discriminated against and denied an equal chance to earn wages for the support of our families, and in many instances are refused admission into labor unions and nearly everywhere are paid smaller wages than white men.

8. In the Civil Service and departmental offices we are everywhere discriminated against and made to feel that to be a black man in Europe, America and the West Indies is equivalent to being an outcast and a leper among the races of men, no matter what the character attainments of the black men may be.

9. In the British and other West Indian islands and colonies Negroes are secretly and cunningly discriminated against and denied those fuller rights of government to which white citizens are appointed, nominated and elected.

10. That our people in those parts are forced to work for lower wages than the average standard of white men and are kept in conditions repugnant to good civilized tastes and customs.

11. That the many acts of injustices against members of our race before the courts of law in the respective islands and colonies are of such nature as to create disgust and disrespect for the white man's sense of justice.

12. Against all such inhuman, unchristian and uncivilized treatment we here and now emphatically protest, and invoke the condemnation of all mankind.

In order to encourage our race all over the world and to stimulate it to overcome the handicaps and difficulties surrounding it, and to push forward to a higher and grander destiny, we demand and insist on the following Declaration of Rights:

1. Be it known to all men that whereas all men are created equal and entitled to the rights of life, liberty and the pursuit of happiness, and because of this we, the duly elected representatives of the Negro peoples of the world, invoking the aid of the just and Almighty God, do declare all men, women and children of our blood throughout the world free citizens and do claim them as free citizens of Africa, the Motherland of all Negroes.

2. That we believe in the supreme authority of our race in all things racial; that all things are created and given to man as a common possession; that there should be an equitable distribution and apportionment of all such things, and in consideration of the fact that as a race we are now deprived of those things that

are morally and legally ours, we believed it right that all such things should be acquired and held by whatsoever means possible.

3. That we believe the Negro, like any other race, should be governed by the ethics of civilization, and therefore should not be deprived of any of those rights or privileges common to other human beings.

4. We declare that Negroes, wheresoever they form a community among themselves should be given the right to elect their own representatives to represent them in Legislatures, courts of law, or such institutions as may exercise control over that particular community.

5. We assert that the Negro is entitled to even-handed justice before all courts of law and equity in whatever country he may be found, and when this is denied him on account of his race or color such denial is an insult to the race as a whole and should be resented by the entire body of Negroes.

6. We declare it unfair and prejudicial to the rights of Negroes in communities where they exist in considerable numbers to be tried by a judge and jury composed entirely of an alien race, but in all such cases members of our race are entitled to representation on the jury.

7. We believe that any law or practice that tends to deprive any African of his land or the privileges of free citizenship within his country is unjust and immoral, and no native should respect any such law or practice.

8. We declare taxation without representation unjust and tyran[n]ous, and there should be no obligation on the part of the Negro to obey the levy of a tax by any law-making body from which he is excluded and denied representation on account of his race and color.

9. We believe that any law especially directed against the Negro to his detriment and singling him out because of his race or color is unfair and immoral, and should not be respected.

10. We believe all men are entitled to common human respect and that our race should in no way tolerate any insults that may be interpreted to mean disrespect to our race or color.

11. We deprecate the use of the term "nigger" as applied to Negroes, and demand that the word "Negro" be written with a capital "N."

12. We believe that the Negro should adopt every means to protect himself against barbarous practices inflicted upon him because of color.

13. We believe in the freedom of Africa for the Negro people of the world, and by the principle of Europe for the Europeans and Asia for the Asiatics, we also demand Africa for the Africans at home and abroad.

14. We believe in the inherent right of the Negro to possess himself of Africa and that his possession of same shall not be regarded as an infringement of any claim or purchase made by any race or nation.

15. We strongly condemn the cupidity of those nations of the world who, by open aggression or secret schemes, have seized the territories and inexhaustible natural wealth of Africa, and we place on record our most solemn determination to reclaim the treasures and possession of the vast continent of our forefathers.

16. We believe all men should live in peace one with the other, but when races and nations provoke the ire of other races and nations by attempting to infringe upon their rights[,] war becomes inevitable, and the attempt in any way to free one's self or protect one's rights or heritage becomes justifiable.

17. Whereas the lynching, by burning, hanging or any other means, of human beings is a barbarous practice and a shame and disgrace to civilization, we therefore declare any country guilty of such atrocities outside the pale of civilization.

18. We protest against the atrocious crime of whipping, flogging and overworking of the native tribes of Africa and Negroes everywhere. These are methods that should be abolished and all means should be taken to prevent a continuance of such brutal practices.

19. We protest against the atrocious practice of shaving the heads of Africans, especially of African women or individuals of Negro blood, when placed in prison as a punishment for crime by an alien race.

20. We protest against segregated districts, separate public conveyances, industrial discrimination, lynchings and limitations of political privileges of any Negro citizen in any part of the world on account of race, color or creed, and will exert our full influence and power against all such.

21. We protest against any punishment inflicted upon a Negro with severity, as against lighter punishment inflicted upon another of an alien race for like offense, as an act of prejudice and injustice, and should be resented by the entire race.

22. We protest against the system of education in any country where Negroes are denied the same privileges and advantages as other races.

23. We declare it inhuman and unfair to boycott Negroes from industries and labor in any part of the world.

24. We believe in the doctrine of the freedom of the press, and we therefore emphatically protest against the suppression of Negro newspapers and periodicals in various parts of the world, and call upon Negroes everywhere to employ all available means to prevent such suppression.

25. We further demand free speech universally for all men.

26. We hereby protest against the publication of scandalous and inflammatory articles by an alien press tending to create racial strife and the exhibition of picture films showing the Negro as a cannibal.

27. We believe in the self-determination of all peoples.

28. We declare for the freedom of religious worship.

29. With the help of Almighty God we declare ourselves the sworn protectors of the honor and virtue of our women and children, and pledge our lives for their protection and defense everywhere and under all circumstances from wrongs and outrages.

30. We demand the right of an unlimited and unprejudiced education for ourselves and our posterity forever[.]

31. We declare that the teaching in any school by alien teachers to our boys and girls, that the alien race is superior to the Negro race, is an insult to the Negro people of the world.

32. Where Negroes form a part of the citizenry of any country, and pass the civil service examination of such country, we declare them entitled to the same consideration as other citizens as to appointments in such civil service.

33. We vigorously protest against the increasingly unfair and unjust treatment accorded Negro travelers on land and sea by the agents and employee of railroad and steamship companies, and insist that for equal fare we receive equal privileges with travelers of other races.

34. We declare it unjust for any country, State or nation to enact laws tending to hinder and obstruct the free immigration of Negroes on account of their race and color.

35. That the right of the Negro to travel unmolested throughout the world be not abridged by any person or persons, and all Negroes are called upon to give aid to a fellow Negro when thus molested.

36. We declare that all Negroes are entitled to the same right to travel over the world as other men.

37. We hereby demand that the governments of the world recognize our leader and his representatives chosen by the race to look after the welfare of our people under such governments.

38. We demand complete control of our social institutions without interference by any alien race or races.

39. That the colors, Red, Black and Green, be the colors of the Negro race.

40. Resolved, That the anthem "Ethiopia, Thou Land of Our Fathers etc.," shall be the anthem of the Negro race. . . .

41. We believe that any limited liberty which deprives one of the complete rights and prerogatives of full citizenship is but a modified form of slavery.

42. We declare it an injustice to our people and a serious impediment to the health of the race to deny to competent licensed Negro physicians the right to practice in the public hospitals of the communities in which they reside, for no other reason than their race and color.

43. We call upon the various governments of the world to accept and acknowledge Negro representatives who shall be sent to the said governments to represent the general welfare of the Negro peoples of the world.

44. We deplore and protest against the practice of confining juvenile prisoners in prisons with adults, and we recommend that such youthful prisoners be taught gainful trades under humane supervision.

45. Be it further resolved, That we as a race of people declare the League of Nations null and void as far as the Negro is concerned, in that it seeks to deprive Negroes of their liberty.

46. We demand of all men to do unto us as we would do unto them, in the name of justice; and we cheerfully accord to all men all the rights we claim herein for ourselves.

47. We declare that no Negro shall engage himself in battle for an alien race without first obtaining the consent of the leader of the Negro people of the world, except in a matter of national self-defense.

48. We protest against the practice of drafting Negroes and sending them to war with alien forces without proper training, and demand in all cases that Negro soldiers be given the same training as the aliens.

49. We demand that instructions given Negro children in schools include the subject of "Negro History," to their benefit.

50. We demand a free and unfettered commercial intercourse with all the Negro people of the world.

51. We declare for the absolute freedom of the seas for all peoples.

52. We demand that our duly accredited representatives be given proper recognition in all leagues, conferences, conventions or courts of international arbitration wherever human rights are discussed.

53. We proclaim the 31st day of August of each year to be an international holiday to be observed by all Negroes.

54. We want all men to know that we shall maintain and contend for the freedom and equality of every man, woman and child of our race, with our lives, our fortunes and our sacred honor.

These rights we believe to be justly ours and proper for the protection of the Negro race at large, and because of this belief we, on behalf of the four hundred million Negroes of the world, do pledge herein the sacred blood of the race in defense, and we hereby subscribe our names as a guarantee of the truthfulness and faithfulness hereof, in the presence of Almighty God, on this 13th day of August, in the year of our Lord one thousand nine hundred and twenty.

Chapter 16

Opposing Racial Segregation and Discrimination by Demanding Civil Rights

"Behold the Land"

W. E. B. DuBois

Editor's Introduction: On October 20, 1946, W. E .B. DuBois delivered one of his last major public addresses at the closing session of the Southern Youth Legislature in Columbia, South Carolina, titled "Behold the Land." He used the occasion to inspire the youth to continue the struggle for freedom and justice to which he had devoted his life for more than a half century. His speech contains elements of a socialist critique of capitalism and a strong belief that the solution to the race problem lay in the recognition that blacks and the white working class have common interests and should be persuaded to work cooperatively for a better life for all. Most important, his speech makes an urgent plea for the value of reason over force in their common pursuit. In retrospect, this speech can be viewed as a rationale for the nonviolent civil rights movement that would begin less than a decade later with the Montgomery Bus Boycott under the leadership of Martin Luther King Jr.

The future of American Negroes is in the South. Here three hundred and twenty-seven years ago, they began to enter what is now the United States of

America; here they have made their greatest contribution to American culture; and here they have suffered the damnation of slavery, the frustration of recon-struction and the lynching of emancipation. I trust then that an organization like yours is going to regard the South as the battle-ground of a great crusade. Here is the magnificent climate; here is the fruitful earth under the beauty of the southern sun; and here, if anywhere on earth, is the need of the thinker, the worker and the dreamer. This is the firing line not simply for the emancipation of the American Negro but for the emancipation of the African Negro and the Negroes of the West Indies; for the emancipation of the colored races; and for the emancipation of the white slaves of modern capitalistic monopoly.

Remember here, too, that you do not stand alone. It may seem like a failing fight when the newspapers ignore you; when every effort is made by white people in the South to count you out of citizenship to act as though you did not exist as human beings while all the time they are profiting by your labor; gleaning wealth from your sacrifices and trying to build a nation and a civilization upon your gradation. You must remember that despite all this, you have allies and allies even in the white South. First and greatest of these possible allies are the white working classes about you. The poor whites whom you have been taught to despise and who in turn have learned to fear and hate you. This must not deter you from efforts to make them understand, because in the past in their ignorance and suffering they have been led foolishly to look upon you as the cause of most of their distress. You must remember that this attitude is hereditary from slavery and that it has been deliberately cultivated ever since emancipation.

Slowly but surely the working people of the South, white and black, must come to remember that their emancipation depends upon their mutual cooperation; upon their acquaintanceship with each other; upon their friendship; upon their social intermingling. Unless this happens each is going to be made the football to break the heads and hearts of the other.

WHITE YOUTH IS FRUSTRATED

White youth in the South is peculiarly frustrated. There is not a single great ideal which they can express or aspire to, that does not bring them into flat contradic-tion with the Negro problem. The more they try to escape it, the more they land into hypocrisy, lying and double-dealing; the more they become, what they least wish to become, the oppressors and despisers of human beings. Some of them, in larger and larger numbers, are bound to turn toward the truth and recognize you as brothers and sisters, as fellow travelers toward the dawn.

There has always been in the South that intellectual elite who saw Negro problem clearly. They have always lacked and some still lack the courage to stand up for what they know is right. Nevertheless they can be depended on in the long run to follow their own clear thinking and their own decent choice. Finally even the politicians must eventually recognize the trend in the world, in this country, and the South. James Byrnes, that favorite son of this commonwealth, and Secretary of State of the United States, is today occupying an indefensible and impossible position; and if he survives in the memory of men, he must begin to help establish in his own South Carolina something of that democracy which he has been recently so loudly preaching to Russia. He is the end of a long series of men whose eternal damnation is the fact that they looked truth in the face and did not see it; John C. Calhoun, Wade Hampton, Ben Tillman are men whose names must ever be besmirched by the fact that they fought against freedom and democracy in a land which was founded upon democracy and freedom.

Eventually this class of men must yield to the writing in the stars. That great hypocrite, Jan Smuts, who today is talking of humanity and standing beside Byrnes for a United Nations, is at the same time oppressing the black people of South Africa to an extent which makes their two countries, South Africa and the American South, the most reactionary peoples on earth. Peoples whose exploitation of the poor and helpless reaches the last degree of shame. They must in the long run yield to the forward march of civilization or die.

WHAT DOES THE FIGHT MEAN?

If now you young people, instead of running away from the battle here in Carolina, Georgia, Alabama, Louisiana and Mississippi, instead of seeking freedom and opportunity in Chicago and New York—which do spell opportunity—nevertheless grit your teeth and make up your minds to fight it out right here if it takes every day of your lives and the lives of your children's children; if you do this, you must in meetings like this ask yourselves what does the fight mean? How can be carried on? What are the best tools, arms, and methods? And where does it lead?

I should be the last to insist that the uplift of mankind never calls for force and death. There are times, as both you and I know, when

> "Tho' love repine and reason chafe,
> There came a voice without reply,
> 'Tis man's perdition to be safe
> When for truth he ought to die."

At the same time and even more clearly in a day like this, after the millions of mass murders that have been done in the world since 1914, we ought to be the last to believe that force is ever the final word. We cannot escape the clear fact that what is going to win in this world is reason if this ever becomes a reasonable world. The careful reasoning of the human mind backed by the facts of science is the one salvation of man. The world, if it resumes its march toward civilization, cannot ignore reason. This has been the tragedy of the South in the past; it is still its awful and unforgivable sin that it has set its face against reason and against the fact. It tried to build slavery upon freedom; it tried to build tyranny upon democracy; it tried to build mob violence on law and law on lynching and in all that despicable endeavor, the state of South Carolina has led the South for a century. It began not the Civil War—not the War between the States—but the War to Preserve Slavery; it began mob violence and lynching and today it stands in the front rank of those defying the Supreme Court on disfranchisement.

Nevertheless reason can and will prevail; but of course it can only prevail with publicity—pitiless blatant publicity. You have got to make the people of the United States and of the world know what is going on in the South. You have got to use every field of publicity to force the truth into their ears, and before their eyes. You have got to make it impossible for any human being to live in the South and not realize the barbarities that prevail here. You may be condemned for flamboyant methods; for calling a congress like this; for waving your grievances under the noses and in the faces of men. That makes no difference; it is your duty to do it. It is your duty to do more of this sort of thing than you have done in the past. As a result of this you are going to be called upon for sacrifice. It is no easy thing for a young black man or a young black woman to live in the South today and to plan to continue to live here; to marry and raise children; to establish a home. They are in the midst of legal caste and customary insults; they are in continuous danger of mob violence; they are mistreated by the officers of the law and they have no hearing before the courts and the churches and public opinion commensurate with the attention which they ought to receive. But that sacrifice is only the beginning of battle, you must re-build this South.

There are enormous opportunities here for a new nation, a new economy, a new culture in a South really new and not a mere renewal of an old South of slavery, monopoly and race hate. There is a chance for a new cooperative agriculture on renewed land owned by the state with capital furnished by the state, mechanized and coordinated with city life. There is chance for strong, virile trade unions without race discrimination, with high wage, closed shop and decent conditions of work, to beat back and hold in check the swarm of land-lords, monopolists and profiteers who are today sucking the blood out of this land. There is chance for cooperative industry, built the cheap power of T.V.A. and its future extensions. There is chance opportunity to organize and mechanize domestic service with decent and high wage and dignified training.

"BEHOLD THE LAND"

There is a vast field for consumers cooperation, building business on public service and not on private profit as the main-spring of Industry. There is chance for a broad, sunny, healthy home life, shorn the fear of mobs and liquor, and rescued from lying, stealing politicians, who build their deviltry on race prejudice.

Here in this South is the gateway to the colored millions of the West Indies, Central and South America. Here is the straight path to Africa, the Indies, China and the South Seas. Here is the path to the greater, freer, truer world. It would be shame and cowardice to surrender this glorious land and its opportunities for civilization and humanity to the thugs and lynchers, the mobs and profiteers, the monopolists and gamblers who today choke its soul and steal its resources. The oil and sulphur; the coal and iron; the cotton and corn; lumber and cattle belong to you the workers, black and white, not to the thieves who hold them and use them to enslave you. They can be rescued and restored to the people if you have the guts to strive for the real right to vote, the right to real education, the right to happiness and health and the total abolition of the father of these scourges of mankind, poverty.

"Behold the beautiful land which the Lord thy God hath given thee." Behold the land, the rich and resourceful land, from which for a hundred years its best elements have been running away, its youth and hope, black and white, scurrying North because they are of each other, and dare not face a future of equal, independent, upstanding human beings, in a real and not a sham democracy.

To rescue this land, in this way, calls for the Great Sacrifice; this is the thing that you are called upon to do because it is the right thing to do. Because you are embarked upon a great and holy crusade, the emancipation of mankind, black and white; the upbuilding of democracy; the breaking down, particularly here in the South, of forces of evil represented by race prejudice in South Carolina; by lynching in Georgia; by disfranchisement in Mississippi; by ignorance in Louisiana and by all these and monopoly of wealth in the whole South.

There could be no more splendid vocation beckoning to the youth of the twentieth century, after the flat failures of white civilization, after the flamboyant establishment of an industrial system which creates poverty and the children of poverty which are ignorance and disease and crime; after the crazy boasting of a white culture that finally ended in wars which ruined civilization in the whole world; in the midst of allied peoples who have yelled about democracy and I never practiced it either in the British Empire or in the American Commonwealth or in South Carolina.

Here is the chance for young women and young men of devotion to lift again the banner of humanity and to walk toward a civilization which will be free and intelligent; which will be healthy and unafraid; and build in the world a culture led by black folk and joined by peoples of all colors and all races—without poverty, ignorance and disease! . . .

Chapter 17

Opposing Racial Segregation and Discrimination by Legal Redress

"Remarks on the Bicentennial of the Constitution"

Thurgood Marshall

Editor's Introduction: Thurgood Marshall (1908–1993), great grandson of a slave, was the first African American on the Supreme Court of the United States. Prior to his nomination to the court in 1967 by President Lyndon Johnson he was renowned as the lawyer who argued for the Brown v. Board of Education decision and persuaded the court to overthrow the separate but equal doctrine that had been established in 1896 by the Plessy v. Ferguson ruling. More than anything else, that action laid the legal groundwork for the subsequent civil rights movement that began the following year with the Montgomery Bus Boycott. Marshall delivered the following speech at the annual seminar of the San Francisco Patent and Trademark Law Association, Maui, Hawaii, May 1987. Contrary to the expectations of his audience, he focused attention on the imperfection of the original constitution as written by its founders and the subsequent need for numerous amendments as well as a civil war to resolve. Most important, he demonstrated the importance of the law in both denying and granting civil rights.

1987 marks the 200th anniversary of the United States Constitution. A Commission has been established to coordinate the celebration. The official meetings, essay contests, and festivities have begun.

The planned commemoration will span three years, and I am told that 1987 is "dedicated to the memory of the Founders and the document they drafted in Philadelphia." We are to "recall the achievements of our Founders and the knowledge and experience that inspired them, the nature of the government they established, its origins, its character, and its ends, and the rights and privileges of citizenship, as well as its attendant responsibilities."

Like many anniversary celebrations, the plan for 1987 takes particular events and holds them up as the source of all the very best that has followed. Patriotic feelings will surely swell, prompting proud proclamations of the wisdom, foresight and sense of justice shared by the Framers and reflected in a written document now yellowed with age. This is unfortunate not in the patriotism itself, but the tendency for the celebration to oversimplify, and overlook the many other events that have been instrumental to our achievements as a nation. The focus of this celebration invites a complacent belief that the vision of those who debated and compromised in Philadelphia yielded the "more perfect Union" it is said we now enjoy.

I cannot accept this invitation, for I do not believe that the meaning of the Constitution was forever "fixed" at the Philadelphia Convention. Nor do I find the wisdom, foresight, and sense of justice exhibited by the Framers particularly profound. To the contrary, the government they devised was defective from the start, requiring several amendments, a civil war, and momentous social transformation to attain the system of constitutional government, and its respect for the individual freedoms and human rights, we hold as fundamental today. When contemporary Americans cite "The Constitution," they invoke a concept that is vastly different from what the Framers barely began to construct two centuries ago.

For a sense of the evolving nature of the Constitution we need look no further than the first three words of the document's preamble: "We the People." When the Founding Fathers used this phrase in 1787, they did not have in mind the majority of America's citizens. "We the People" included, in the words of the Framers, "the whole number of free Persons." On a matter so basic as the right to vote, for example, Negro slaves were excluded, although they were counted for representational purposes at three fifths each. Women did not gain the right to vote for over a hundred and thirty years.

These omissions were intentional. The record of the Framers' debates on the slave question is especially clear: the Southern States acceded to the demands of the New England States for giving Congress broad power to regulate commerce, in exchange for the right to continue the slave trade. The economic interests of the regions coalesced: New Englanders engaged in the "carrying trade" would profit from transporting slaves from Africa as well as goods produced in America by slave labor. The perpetuation of slavery ensured the primary source of wealth in the Southern States.

Despite this clear understanding of the role slavery would play in the new republic, use of the words "slaves" and "slavery" was carefully avoided in the original document. Political representation in the lower House of Congress was to be based on the population of "free Persons" in each State, plus three-fifths of all "other Persons." Moral principles against slavery, for those who had them, were compromised, with no explanation of the conflicting principles for which the American Revolutionary War had ostensibly been fought: the self-evident truths "that all men are created equal, that they are endowed by their Creator with certain unalienable Rights, that among these are Life, Liberty and the pursuit of Happiness."

It was not the first such compromise. Even these ringing phrases from the Declaration of Independence are filled with irony, for an early draft of what later became that Declaration assailed the King of England for suppressing legislative attempts to end the slave trade and for encouraging slave rebellions. The final draft adopted in 1776 did not contain this criticism. And so again at the Constitutional Convention's eloquent objections to the institution of slavery went unheeded, and its opponents eventually consented to a document which laid a foundation for the tragic events that were to follow.

Pennsylvania's Governor Morris provides an example. He opposed slavery and the counting of slaves in determining the bases for representation in Congress. At the Convention he objected that

> the inhabitant of Georgia or South Carolina who goes to the coast of Africa, and in defiance of the most sacred laws of humanity tears away his fellow creatures from their dearest connections and damns them to the most cruel bondage, shall have more votes in a Government instituted for protection of the rights of mankind, than the Citizen of Pennsylvania or New Jersey who views with a laudable horror, so nefarious a practice.

And yet Governor Morris eventually accepted the three-fifths accommodation. In fact, he wrote the final draft of the Constitution, the very document the bicentennial will commemorate.

As a result of compromise, the right of the southern States to continue importing slaves was extended, officially, at least until 1808. We know that it actually lasted a good deal longer, as the Framers possessed no monopoly on the ability to trade moral principles for self-interest. But they nevertheless set an unfortunate example. Slaves could be imported, if the commercial interests of the North were protected. To make the compromise even more palatable, customs duties would be imposed at up to ten dollars per slave as a means of raising public revenues.

No doubt it will be said, when the unpleasant truth of the history of slavery in America is mentioned during this bicentennial year, that the Constitution was a product of its times, and embodied a compromise which, under other circumstances, would not have been made. But the effects of the Framers' compromise have remained for generations. They arose from the contradiction between guaranteeing liberty and justice to all, and denying both to Negroes.

The original intent of the phrase, "We the People," was far too clear for any ameliorating construction. Writing for the Supreme Court in 1857, Chief Justice Taney penned the following passage in the Dred Scott case, on the issue whether, in the eyes of the Framers, slaves were "constituent members of the sovereignty," and were to be included among "We the People":

> We think they are not, and that they are not included, and were not intended to be included. They had for more than a century before been regarded as beings of an inferior order, and altogether unfit to associate with the white race; and so far inferior, that they had no rights which the white man was bound to respect; and that the Negro might justly and lawfully be reduced to slavery for his benefit. Accordingly, a Negro of the Africa race was regarded as an article of property, and held, and brought and sold as such. No one seems to have doubted the correctness of the prevailing opinion of the time.

And so, nearly seven decades after the Constitutional Convention, the Supreme Court reaffirmed the prevailing opinion of the Framers regarding the rights of Negroes in America. It took a bloody civil war before the 13th Amendment could be adopted to abolish slavery, though not the consequences slavery would have for future Americans.

While the Union survived the civil war, the Constitution did not. In its place arose a new, more promising basis for justice and equality, the 14th Amendment, ensuring protection of the life, liberty, and property of all persons against deprivations without due process, and guaranteeing equal protection of the laws. And yet almost another century would pass before any significant recognition was obtained of the rights of black Americans to share equally even in such basic opportunities as education, housing, and employment, and to have their votes counted, and counted equally. In the meantime, blacks joined America's military to fight its wars and invested untold hours working in its factories and on its farms, contributing to the development of this country's magnificent wealth and waiting to share in its prosperity.

What is striking is the role legal principles have played throughout America's history in determining the condition of Negroes. They were enslaved by law, emancipated by law, disenfranchised and segregated by law; and, finally, they have begun to win equality by law. Along the way, new constitutional principles have emerged to meet the challenges of a changing society. The progress has been dramatic, and it will continue.

The men who gathered in Philadelphia in 1787 could not have envisioned these changes. They could not have imagined, nor would they have accepted, that the document they were drafting would one day be construed by a Supreme Court to which had been appointed a woman and the descendent of an African slave. "We the People" no longer enslaved, but the credit does not belong to the Framers. It belongs to those who refused to acquiesce in outdated notions of "liberty," "justice," and "equality," and who strived to better them.

And so we must be careful, when focusing on the events which took place in Philadelphia two centuries ago, that we not overlook the momentous events which followed, and thereby lose our proper sense of perspective. Otherwise, the odds are that for many Americans the bicentennial celebration will be little more than a blind pilgrimage to the shrine of the original document now stored in a vault in the National Archives. If we seek, instead, a sensitive understanding of the Constitution's inherent defects, and its promising evolution through 200 years of history, the celebration of the "Miracle at Philadelphia" will, in my view, be a far more meaningful and humbling experience. We will see that the true miracle was not the birth of the Constitution, but its life, a life nurtured through two turbulent centuries of our own making, and a life embodying much good fortune that was not.

Thus, in this bicentennial year, we may not all participate in the festivities with flag waving fervor. Some may more quietly commemorate the suffering, struggle, and sacrifice that has triumphed over much of what was wrong with the original document, and observe the anniversary with hopes not realized and promises not fulfilled. I plan to celebrate the bicentennial of the Constitution as a living document, including the Bill of Rights and the other amendments protecting individual freedoms and human rights.

Chapter 18

Opposing Racial Segregation by Direct Nonviolent Protest

"A Realistic Look at the Question of Progress in the Area of Race Relations"

Martin Luther King Jr.

Editor's Introduction: Martin Luther King Jr. (1929–1968), a well-educated Baptist minister, assumed the pastorate of Dexter Avenue Baptist Church in Montgomery, Alabama, in 1955 directly out of his PhD studies at Boston University School of Theology. Soon thereafter he was propelled into national visibility by the Montgomery Bus Boycott, which was set in motion by the arrest of Rosa Parks, who refused to give up her seat to a white man who had boarded the bus after all seats in the section for whites were filled. Organized initially by the Women's Political Council and the indefatigable work of JoAnn Robinson as a one-day boycott, it lasted for 382 days, when it was brought to an end by the Supreme Court's declaration that racial segregation on the buses was unconstitutional. For the next twelve years King worked tirelessly as the undisputed leader of the Civil Rights Movement. During that time he received countless threats, his house was bombed, and he was arrested numerous times. In 1964 he became the youngest person ever to win the Nobel Peace Prize. By the time of his death he had turned his attention to the tasks of ending poverty and the war in Vietnam. Suffice it to say that his thought and action inspired many other oppressed groups to adopt similar tactics in protesting their respective conditions. All of his thought and work were grounded in a theological perspective. He received many honors posthumously including the Presidential Medal of Freedom in 1977 and the Congressional Gold Medal to him and Coretta Scott King in 2014. In 1986 Martin Luther King Jr. Day was established as a national holiday to celebrate his birth.

In April of 1957 King delivered the following address to a Freedom Rally sponsored by the Citizens Committee of Greater Saint Louis, a collection of ministerial groups. The transcript below includes responses from the audience.

Mr. Chairman [*W. E. W. Brown*], distinguished platform associates, citizens of this great city, ladies and gentlemen, I need not pause to say how delighted I am to be here this evening and to be a part of this very rich fellowship. I want to express my appreciation to you for your kindness and loyalty. And I am indeed honored to share the platform with so many distinguished clergymen and civic leaders, some of whom I knew before coming here and others that I had not met before. But we all have a deep unity, a spiritual unity. I think of some of our very good friends like Dr. [*John E.*] Nance, Dr. Brown, Dr. Huntley, who lived in Montgomery at one time and pastored one of our very fine churches there. Certainly we will remain indebted to him for his leadership and for his scholarship. His most provocative and inspiring book that has influenced minds in this nation and over the world, *As I Saw It.* I look back and see my former schoolmate from Morehouse College, Earl Nance. And so that I am not at all a stranger around here in St. Louis. And all of the other persons, I want to thank you for your personal courtesies and all the things that you have done to make our struggle in Montgomery less difficult. Certainly I owe a deep debt of gratitude to brother [*Lafayette*] Thompson, whom I met some months ago. Then later in Hot Springs, Arkansas, just about two or three months ago, we had the privilege of having dinner together and talking over some very vital matters. And I am indebted to him for contacts made and for making so many vital things possible. Then I am indebted to Dr. Nance for this very gracious introduction.

It's good to be in St. Louis, for I'm happy to see the progress that has been made and that is being made in the area of human relations. In a quiet and dignified manner, integration has moved on amazingly well and this city is to be commended. Certainly the deeper cities in the Deep South have a great deal to learn from a city like St. Louis. It proves that integration can be brought into being without a lot of trouble, that it can be done smoothly and peacefully. This city is to be commended for that.

I bring you greetings from Montgomery, Alabama, a city that has been known over the years as the Cradle of the Confederacy. But I bring you special greetings from the fifty-thousand Negroes of that city who came to see a little more than a year ago that it is ultimately more honorable to walk in dignity than ride in humiliation. [*applause*] I bring you greetings from fifty-thousand people who decided one day to substitute tired feet for tired souls and walk the streets of Montgomery until the sagging walls of segregation were finally crushed by the battering rams of surging justice. [*applause*] I bring you greetings from a humble people who heard the words of Jesus and decided to follow him, even if it meant going to Calvary. A people who decided that love is a basic principle of the universe. [*applause; word inaudible*]

But I didn't come here this evening to talk only about Montgomery. I want to try to grapple with a question that continually comes to me. And it is a question on the lips of men and women all over this nation. People all over are wondering about the question of progress in race relations. And they are asking, "Are we really making any progress?" I want to try to answer that question. And if I would use a subject for what I plan to say this evening, I would use a rather lengthy subject: A Realistic Look at the Question of Progress in the Area of Race Relations.

There are three basic attitudes that one can take toward the question of progress in the area of race relations. And the first attitude that can be taken is that of extreme optimism. Now the extreme optimist would argue that we have come a long, long way in the area of race relations. He would point proudly to the marvelous strides that have been made in the area of civil rights over the last few decades. From this he would conclude that the problem is just about solved, and that we can sit comfortably by the wayside and wait on the coming of the inevitable.

The second attitude that one can take toward the question of progress in the area of race relations is that of extreme pessimism. The extreme pessimist would argue that we have made only minor strides in the area of race relations. He would argue that the rhythmic beat of the deep rumblings of discontent that we hear from the Southland today is indicative of the fact that we have created more problems than we have solved. He would say that we are retrogressing instead of progressing. He might even turn to the realms of an orthodox theology and argue that hovering over every man is the tragic taint of original sin and that at bottom human nature cannot be changed. He might even turn to the realms of modern psychology and seek to show the determinative effects of habit structures and the inflexibility of certain attitudes that once become molded in one's being. (*Yes*) From all of this he would conclude that there can be no progress in the area of race relations. (*Alright, Alright*)

Now you will notice that the extreme optimist and the extreme pessimist have at least one thing in common: they both agree that we must sit down and do nothing in the area of race relations. (*Yes*) The extreme optimist says do nothing because integration is inevitable. The extreme pessimist says do nothing because integration is impossible. But there is a third position that is another attitude that can be taken, and it is what I would like to call the realistic position. The realist in the area of race relations seeks to reconcile the truths of two opposites while avoiding the extremes of both. (*Yeah*) So the realist would agree with the optimist that we have come a long, long way. But, he would go on to balance that by agreeing with the pessimist that we have a long, long way to go. (*Amen*) [*applause*] And it is this basic theme that I would like to set forth this evening. We have come a long, long way (*Yes*) but we have a long, long way to go. (*Amen*) [*applause*]

Now let us notice first that we've come a long, long way. You will remember that it was in the year of 1619 that the Negro slaves first landed on the shores of this nation. They were brought here from the shores of Africa. Unlike the Pilgrim fathers who landed at Plymouth a year later, they were brought here against their wills. Throughout slavery the Negro was treated in a very inhuman fashion. He was a thing to be used, not a person to be respected. (*Yeah, That's Right*) He was merely, [*applause*] he was merely a depersonalized cog in a vast plantation machine. (*Yeah*) The famous Dred Scott decision of 1857 well illustrates the status of the Negro during slavery. For it was in this decision that the Supreme Court of the nation said, in substance, that the Negro is not a citizen of this nation. He is merely property subject to the dictates of his owner. Living under these conditions many Negroes lost faith in themselves. Many came to feel that perhaps they were less than human. So long as the Negro accepted this place assigned to him, so long as the Negro patiently accepted injustice and exploitation, a sort of racial peace was maintained.

But it was an uneasy peace. (*Yeah*) It was a negative peace in which the Negro was forced patiently to accept injustice and exploitation. For you see, true peace is not merely the absence of some negative force, but it is a presence of some positive force. (*Amen*) I think that is what Jesus meant when one day his disciples stood before him with their glittering eyes, wanting to hear something good, and Jesus looked at them and said, in no uncertain terms, "Brethren, I come not to bring peace, but a sword." He didn't mean, "I come to bring a physical sword." He didn't mean, "I come not to bring positive peace." What Jesus is saying, "I come not to bring this old negative peace which makes for deadening passivity and stagnant complacently. And whenever I come a conflict is precipitated between the old and the new. (*Yes*) Whenever I come, (*Yes*) there is a lashing out between justice and injustice. (*Yes*) Whenever I come, (*Yes*) there is a division between the forces of light and the forces of darkness." (*Yes*) Peace is not merely the absence of tension, but it is the presence of justice. (*Yes*) [*applause*] And the peace which existed at that time was a negative, obnoxious peace devoid of any positive meaning.

But then something happened to the Negro. Moving on up in the nineteen-hundreds it became necessary for him to travel more. Circumstances made it necessary. His rural, plantation background gradually gave way to urban, industrial life. And his cultural life was gradually rising through the steady decline of crippling illiteracy, (*Yes, sir*) and even the economic life of the Negro was gradually rising. And all of these forces conjoined (*Yes, sir*) to cause the

Negro to take a new look at himself. Negro masses all over began to reevaluate themselves. The Negro came to feel that he was somebody. (*Yes, sir*) His religion revealed to him, [*applause*] he had read his Bible enough, his religion revealed to him that God loves all of his children (*Amen*) and that all men are made in his image. And somehow the Negro came to see that every man from a bass black to a treble white he is significant on God's keyboard. [*applause*] And so he could now cry out in his own soul with the eloquent poet:

Fleecy locks and black complexion
cannot forfeit nature's claims
Skin may differ, but affection
Dwells in black and white the same. (Yes, sir)
Were I so tall as to reach the pole
Or to grasp the ocean at a span,
I must be measured by my soul
The mind is the standard of the man. [applause] (Go ahead)

And with this new sense of dignity and this new self-respect, a brand new Negro emerged and the tension which we witness in the Southland today can be explained in part by the revolutionary change in the Negro's evaluation of his nature and destiny and his determination to struggle, suffer, sacrifice, and even die if necessary until the walls of segregation crumble. [*applause*]

You see, all I'm trying to say to you is that we've come a long, long way since 1619. (*Yes*) But not only has the Negro come a long, long way in reevaluating his own intrinsic worth, but he's come a long, long way in achieving civil rights. We must admit that. Fifty years ago or twenty-five years ago, a year hardly passed that numerous Negroes were not brutally lynched by some vicious mob. But now the day of lynching has just about passed. We've come a long, long way. Twenty-five or fifty years ago, most of the Southern states had the poll tax, which was designed to keep the Negro from becoming a registered voter. And now the poll tax has been eliminated in all but five states. We've come a long, long way. (*Amen*) We have even come a long, long way in achieving the ballot— far from what it ought to be and particularly in the Deep South. We've come a long, long way there. As late as 1948, there were just seven-hundred and fifty thousand Negro registered voters in the South, and by 1952 that number had leaped to one million three-hundred thousand. We've come a long, long way. [*applause*] Not only that, we've come a long, long way in economic growth. The Negro wage earner today makes four times more than the Negro wage earner in 1940. Whether you know it or not the national income of the Negro is now more than fifteen billion dollars a year. That's more than all of the exports of the United States and more than the national income of Canada. We've come a long, long way. [*applause*]

Not only that, in our generation we have been able to see the walls of segregation gradually crumble. For awhile it looked like we would never get away from it. You will remember back in 1896, the Supreme Court of this nation established the doctrine of "separate but equal" as the law of the land. And as a result of this doctrine we were thrown and left in the Egypt of segregation. At every moment there was always some pharaoh with a hardened heart who, amid the cry of every Moses, would not allow us to get out of Egypt. There was always a Red Sea before us with its glaring dimensions. (*Yes*) Then one day through the providence of God and the decision of the Supreme Court, May 17, 1954, the Red Sea opened. (*Yes*) Supreme Court said the old *Plessy* doctrine must go. (*Yes*) [*recording interrupted*] To segregate an individual on the basis of his race is to deny that individual of equal protection of the law. (*Yes*) And so in our generation, if I may speak figuratively, we have been able to see old man segregation on his death bed. And I'm sure, [*applause*] and I'm sure that most of us would be very happy to see the old brother pass on because he's been a disturbing factor to the whole community. [*applause*]

And so we've come a long, long way since 1896. And my friends I've been talking now for about fifteen or twenty minutes and I wish I could stop here. It would be beautiful to stop here. But I've tried to tell you about how far we've come, and it would be fine if every speaker in America could stop right there. (*Yeah, That's right*) But if we stopped here we would be the victims of a dangerous optimism. (*Yeah*) [*applause*] If we stopped here we would be the victims of an illusion wrapped in superficiality. (*Yeah*) If we stopped here we would be the victims of an optimism which makes for deadening complacency and stagnant passivity. In order to tell the truth we must move on. [*applause*] See, not only have we come a long, long way, but truth impels us to admit that we have a long, long way to go. (*Yes*)

It's quite true that lynchings have about ceased in the South, but other things are happening that are quite tragic. Many states have risen up in open defiance, and the legislative halls of the Deep South ring loud with such words as "interposition" and "nullification." Ku Klux Klan is marching again. And a modern version of the Ku Klux Klan has arisen in the form of so-called "respectable" White Citizens Councils. (*Yes*) Not only that, the voice of a little boy fourteen years old is crying out from the waters of Mississippi. (*Yes*) Men and women are being shot because they merely have a desire to stand up and vote as first class citizens. The homes of ministers and civic leaders are being bombed. More tragic than all of that, the house of God is being bombed. (*Yes*) We got a long, long way to go, (*Yes*) a long, long way. (*Yes*)

Oh, I like to think about the fact that we've come a long, long way in economic development, but we have a long, long way to go. The poverty of the Negro is still appalling, (*Yeah*) in spite of all of our growth. We must face the fact that forty-three percent of the Negro families of America still make less than two thousand dollars a year. Compare that with the fact that just seventeen percent of the white families make less than two thousand dollars a year. Twenty-one percent of the Negro families still make less than a thousand dollars a year. Compare that with the fact that just seven percent of the white families make less than a thousand dollars a year. Eighty-eight percent of the Negro families of America make less than five thousand dollars a year. Compare that with the fact that sixty percent of the white families make less than five thousand dollars a year. To put it another way, just twelve percent of the Negro families of America make five thousand dollars or more a year, while forty percent of the white families of America make five thousand dollars or more a year. We've come a long, long way, but we have a long, long way to go in economic equality. [*applause*]

Then my friends, we must face the fact that segregation is still a reality in America. We still confront it in the South in its glaring and conspicuous forms. We still confront it in the North, in the border states in its hidden and subtle forms. (*Yeah, Amen*) Now it's true as I just said, speaking figuratively, that old man segregation is on his deathbed. But history has proven that social systems have a great last-minute breathing power and the guardians of the *status quo* are always on hand with their oxygen tents to keep the old order alive. [*applause*] So my friends, segregation is still a fact. But we know this evening as we assemble here that if democracy is to live segregation must die. [*applause*] Segregation is a tragic cancer which must be removed before our democratic health can be realized. Segregation is something of a, a tragic sore that debilitates the white as well as the Negro community. Segregation is nothing but slavery covered up with certain niceties of complexity. [*applause*] The underlying philosophy of segregation is diametrically opposed to the underlying philosophy of democracy and Christianity, and all the dialectics of the logicians cannot make them lie down together. Segregation is utterly un-Christian. So we have, [*applause*] and so we have the Christian and moral responsibility to work courageously until segregation and discrimination have been removed from every aspect and every area of our nation's life.

Yes, we must continue to gain the ballot. One of the great needs of the hour is for the Negro to gain political power through the ballot. And I have come to see in the last few months that one of the most decisive steps that [*recording interrupted*] that short walk to the voting booth. My friends, those of you here in St. Louis and those who live in states that are moving on in integration and states in the North that have already moved on have the moral responsibility to use the ballot and use it well because you don't have the problems gaining the ballot that we have in Alabama. You have no excuse. And it is your challenge to go down and get it in your hand and use it wisely. This is one of the great things that you can do for power. [*applause*] People in the North ask me from time to time, "What can we do to help in the South?" And I [outline?] a lot of things, but I always come back to this saying, "Get the ballot and through gaining the ballot you gain political power." And you can call the politicians and tell them that certain things will have to be done because you helped put them in office. (*Yeah*) This is an important thing. [*applause*]

I would like to say to you my friends, in this period we must continue to go down in our pockets and give big money for the cause of freedom. (*Yeah*) We have a long, long way to go and we are going to have to spend some money to get there. (*That's right*) Integration is not some lavish dish that the white man will pass out on a silver platter while the Negro merely furnishes their appetite. [*laughter*] If we are going to get it, we are going to have to work for it, and we are going to have to give our money for it. [*applause*] It seems to be the strategy in the Deep South now, on the part of the White Citizens Councils and other reactionary organizations, to stall this thing as long as possible. They know as well as we know that segregation is on its deathbed, but they have decided that they are going to delay it as long as possible by keeping the Negro bogged down in court cases and litigation. And in order to destroy this stalling process, we are going to have to give big money for the cause of freedom. [*applause*]

And I admonish you to continue to support the NAACP. For no matter if they do outlaw it in Alabama, in Texas, and Louisiana, the fact still remains that this organization has done more to achieve the civil rights of Negroes over any other organization that I can point to. [*applause*] We cannot afford to desert the NAACP at this hour. (*Amen*) Let us give. Let us not waste our money on frivolities. This is time now to give big money for the cause of freedom. And we can't say that we don't have it any longer. We have it for so many other things that we want. (*Yes, sir*) We have the biggest cars that have ever been let loose into history. [*applause*] I am always appalled when I see how much whiskey and beer Negroes are drinking. [*applause*] And I think it would be an indictment on the integrity and practical wisdom of the Negro if historians look back and have to record that at the height of the twentieth century the Negro spent more on frivolities than he did on the eternal values of freedom and the cause of justice. (*Yeah*) [*applause*]

My friends, we've got to continue to persuade the federal government to use all of its powers to enforce the law of the land. [*recording interrupted*] And while I am on this point, I would like to say to you that on the seventeenth of May, just a few weeks from now, we are calling upon every freedom-loving Negro, from all over the nation, who can get off of work that day to come to Washington. We are having a Pilgrimage of Prayer for Freedom to Washington. We are not going there to make any threats. We are not going there to say what you have to do. We are simply going there to thank God for what has already been done, and to ask him for his guidance through the other period of transition, and to appeal to the conscience of the nation to do something about the violence in the South and to carry through the civil rights bill that is now being argued in Congress. We are asking every minister of this nation to be there. Every congregation should send its pastor to Washington on the seventeenth of May. We have the backing of the most powerful organizations in the nation. [*applause*] We met in Washington just last week. The most powerful Negro leaders of this nation assembled there and all endorse this plan with hearty enthusiasm. Bishop Greene, and Bishop Walls of the AME Zion church, Bishop Greene of the AME church, Bishop Spottswood of the AME Zion church, Bishop D. Ward Nichols of the AME church, Dr. Jackson and Dr. Jemison of the National Baptist Convention, Dr. Borders, and ministers from all over the South, Mr. Roy Wilkins, Mr. A.

Philip Randolph, A. Clayton Powell, Charlie Diggs. All of the leading citizens and fighters for civil rights assembled there and endorsed this plan with hearty enthusiasm, and we intend to assemble there in Washington, [*applause*] on the seventeenth of May and we want to see you there. This is the time that we must register our protest in a humble, Christian, nonviolent spirit and say to the nation, say to the officials in Washington, Come over and help us. (*Yes*) This is a time that we need you. And we need you to take a stand and to enforce the laws of the land. We've got to get it over to the nation. (*Yes, sir*) And there is a bit of urgency about this thing.

I'm aware of the fact that there are some people telling us to slow up. They are saying all over. There are some writing letters from the South to the North saying, Slow up, you are going too fast. Well, I've never quite understood that. They talk about gradualism and I always felt that at least gradualism meant starting and moving, and how in the world can you slow up when you haven't even started? (*Laughter*) [*applause*] The gradualism that we hear so much talk about in the South now is an escape, is an excuse rather for do-nothingism and escapism which ends up in stand-stillism. [*recording interrupted*]

We are not fighting for ourselves alone but we are fighting for this nation. (*Amen*) Go back and tell those people who are telling us to slow up that there are approximately two billion four hundred million people in this world. Go back and tell them that two-thirds of these people are colored. (*Yes, sir*) Go back and tell them that one billion six hundred million of the people of the world are colored. (*Yes*) Most of them live on two continents. Six hundred million in China. Four hundred million in India and Pakistan. A hundred million in Indonesia. Two hundred million in Africa. Eighty-six million in Japan. These people for years have lived under the bondage of colonialism and imperialism. (*Yes, sir*) One day they got tired. One day these people got tired of being trampled over by the iron feet of oppression. (*Yes*) One day they got tired of being pushed out of the glittering sunlight of life's July, left standing in the piercing chill of an alpine November. So as a result of their tiredness they decided to rise up and protest against colonialism and imperialism. As a result of their rising up, more than one billion three hundred million of the colored peoples of the world have broken aloose from colonialism and imperialism. (*Yes, sir*) They have broken aloose from the Egypt of colonialism. [*applause*] They have broken aloose from the Egypt of colonialism, and now they are moving through the wilderness of adjustment toward the Promised Land of cultural integration. And as they look back you know what they are saying? Racism and colonialism must go in this world. (*Yes*) They assembled in Bandung some months ago and that was the word that echoed from Bandung: "Racism and colonialism must go." [*applause*]

Just two weeks ago, in Africa and Europe, I talked with some of the major leaders of Asia and Africa. And this was the one point they stressed over and over again. Prime Minister Nkrumah and his finance minister N. K. Gbedema said to me, "Our sympathies are with the free world." There is something about America that we like but we are making it clear in the U.N. and in the other diplomatic circles around the world that beautiful words and extensive handouts cannot be substitutes for the basic simple responsibility of giving freedom and justice to our colored brothers all over the United States. [*applause*] That is what they are saying around the world. And I say to you my friends, because of our love for America we cannot slow up. (*Yes*)

Oh, the hour is getting late. (*Yes*) The clock of destiny is ticking out. (*Go ahead*) We've got to say this to the nation that we are not fighting for ourselves alone, we are fighting for this nation. (*Yes*) For if America doesn't wake up, she will one day arise and discover that the uncommitted peoples of the world will have given their allegiance to a false communistic ideology. I just wish this evening that somebody would take a fast plane over to Washington, (*Go ahead*) and just plead with Senator Eastland and his colleagues, (*Alright*) and say to him that the civil rights issue is not some ephemeral, evanescent domestic issue that can be kicked around by reactionary and hypocritical politicians. (*Yes*) But it is an eternal moral issue which may well determine the destiny of our nation in its ideological struggle with communism. (*Oh, yeah*) [*applause*] The destiny of our nation is involved. We can't afford to slow up. (*Yes, sir*) The motor is now cranked up. We are moving up the highway of freedom toward the city of equality and we can't afford to slow up because our nation has a date with destiny. We've got to keep moving. We've got to keep moving. [*applause*]

I'm about through now, but that is a warning signal, a signal that must forever stand before us. (*Yes*) I've tried to say that we've come a long, long way and we have a long, long way to go. I've tried to suggest some of the things that we must do in order to go the additional miles ahead. My friends, I cannot leave you without saying that as we move on let us be sure that our methods are thoroughly moral and Christian. (*Yes*) [*applause*] This is one of the basic things confronting our nation. No matter what we suffer. I know it's really hard when we think of the tragic midnight of injustice and oppression that we've had to live under so many years, but let us not become bitter. Let us never indulge in hate campaigns, for we can't solve the problem like that. (*No*) Somebody must have sense in this world. (*Amen*) And to hate for hate does nothing but intensify the existence of hate in the universe. (*Amen*) We must not use violence. Maybe sometimes we will have to be the victims of violence but never let us be the perpetrators of violence (*Amen*). For if we succumb to the temptation of using violence in our struggle, unborn generations would be the recipients of a long and desolate night of bitterness (*Yes*) and our chief legacy to the future would be an endless rain of meaningless chaos. We must not use violence. Oh, sometimes as we struggle it will be necessary to boycott. But let us remember as we boycott that a boycott is never an end. A boycott is merely means to awaken within the oppressor the sense of shame and to let him know that we don't like how we are being treated; but the end my friends is reconciliation, the end is redemption. (*Yeah*) And our aim must never be to defeat the white man or to humiliate him. Our aim must be to win his friendship and his understanding. [*applause*]

Oh, no matter how much we are mistreated there is still a voice crying through the vistas of time saying, "Love your enemy." (*Yeah*) "Bless them that curse you, pray for them that despitefully use you." [*applause*] And then, and only then, can you matriculate into the university of eternal life. (*Yes*) We must get a hold of this simple principle of love and let it be our guiding principle throughout our struggle.

This means that through this period we will need leaders on every hand and at every scene who will stress this. This is a time for sound and sane leadership. (*Yes, sir*) This no period for rabble-rousers, whether the rabble-rouser be white or Negro. (*That's right*) We are grappling and dealing with the most complex, one of the most weighty and complex social issues of the centuries. (*Go ahead, Go ahead, sir*) This problem is deeply rooted in the emotions, deeply rooted in the customs and traditions of the South. And we can't solve the problem with misguided emotionalism. (*No*) This is a period for sane, sound, rational leadership. (*Yes*) We must be calm and yet positive at the same time. We must avoid the extremes of hard-headedness and uncle-Tomism. (*Yes*) Oh, this is a period for leaders. Leaders not in love with publicity, but in love with humanity. (*Yes, sir*) Leaders not in love with money, but in love with justice. (*Yes*) Leaders who can subject their particular egos to the greatness of the cause. (*Yes*)

Oh, God give us leaders. (*Yes*)
A time like this demands great leaders. (*Yes, sir*)
Leaders whom the lust of office cannot kill;
Leaders whom the spoils of life cannot buy; (*Yes*)
Leaders who possess opinions and will; (*Yes*)
Leaders who will not lie;
Leaders who can stand before a demagogue and damn his
treacherous flatteries without winking. (*Yes*)
Tall leaders, (*Yes*) sun-crowned, who live above the fog
in public duty and in private thinking.

And this is the need my friends of the hour. This is the need all over the nation. In every community there is a dire need for leaders (*Yes*) who will lead the people, who stand today amid the wilderness toward the promise land of freedom and justice. God grant that ministers, and lay leaders, and civic leaders, and businessmen, and professional people all over the nation will rise up and use the talent and the finances that God has given them, and lead the people on toward the Promised Land of freedom with rational, calm, nonviolent means. This is the great challenge of the hour. (*Yes*)

And if we will do this my friends we will be able to speed up the coming of this new order, (*Yes*) which is destined to come. (*Yes*) This new world in which men will be able to live together as brothers. (*Yes*) This new world in which all men will respect the dignity and worth of all human personality. This new world in which men will beat their swords into plowshares and their spears into pruning hooks. (*Yes*) Yes, this new world in which men will no longer take necessities from the masses to give luxuries to the classes. (*Yes, sir*) This new world in which men will learn the old principle of the fatherhood of God and the brotherhood of man. They will hear once more the voice of Jesus crying out through the generations saying, "Love everybody." (*Yes*) This is that world. (*Yes*) Then right here in America we will be able to sing with new meaning:

> My country 'tis of thee, (Amen)
> Sweet land of liberty, (Amen)
> Of thee I sing.
> Land where my fathers died,
> Land of the Pilgrims pride,
> From every mountain side,
> Let freedom ring.

As I heard a powerful orator say not long ago that must become literally true. (*Yes*) Freedom must ring from every mountain side. Let us go out this evening with that determination. Yes, let it ring from the snow-capped Rockies of Colorado. (*Yes*) Let it ring from the prodigious hill tops of New Hampshire. Let it ring from the mighty Alleghenies of Pennsylvania. Let it ring from the curvaceous slopes of California. But not only that. From every mountain side let freedom ring. (*Yes*) Yes, let us go out and be determined that freedom will ring from every mole hill in Mississippi. (*Yes*) Let it ring from Stone Mountain of Georgia. (*Yes*) Let it ring from Lookout Mountain of Tennessee. (*Yes*) Let it ring from every mountain and hill of Alabama. (*Yes*) From every mountain side (*Yes*) let freedom ring. (*Yes*) And when that happens we will be able to go out and sing a new song (*Yeah, Yes*): "Free at last, free at last, great God almighty I'm free at last." [*applause*]

Chapter 19

Opposing Racial Segregation through Congressional Legislation

"Speech on Civil Rights"

Adam Clayton Powell Jr.

Editor's Introduction: Adam Clayton Powell Jr. (1908–1972) succeeded his father in 1937 as pastor of Harlem's most prestigious black congregation, Abyssinian Baptist Church. Deeply committed to social justice, he regularly campaigned for better housing and jobs for the poor people of Harlem. In 1941 he became the first black to be elected to the city council of New York, and in 1945 he was elected to the United States Congress. His popularity in his district enabled him to be reelected over and over again. His outspokenness and flamboyant style did not endear him to his congressional colleagues, especially those from the south whose racism he regularly challenged with what became known as the Powell amendment, which he attached to most bills. The Powell amendment stated that federal monies could not be used by enterprises that practiced racial segregation and discrimination. In 1961, after fifteen years in Congress, he became Chair of the influential Committee on Education and Labor. During the ensuing years he was successful in helping to pass a record number of bills through the house, all of which expanded social justice in ways

121

that helped racial minorities and the poor. Much of that legislation pertained to President Kennedy's New Frontier programs and those of President Johnson's Great Society. Alas Powell was stripped of his chairmanship in 1967 because of his refusal to pay a libel suit that he had lost, and the Congress refused to seat him, pending the report of a judicial investigation. In 1968 he was reelected to the House, though without seniority. In 1969 the Supreme Court ruled that Congress had acted wrongly in refusing to seat him. He lost his first reelection bid in 1970 to Congressman Charles Rangel. The following speech was delivered in Congress on February 2, 1955.

Mr. Speaker, the United States Congress is a 19th century body in a 20th century world. In the field of civil rights we are still conducting ourselves along the pattern of yesterday's world. Tremendous changes are taking place in our country eradicating the concept of second-class citizenship. Yet the United States Congress has done absolutely nothing in this sphere. We are behind the times. We are a legislative anachronism. In an age of atomic energy, our dynamic is no more powerful than a watermill.

The executive and the judicial branches of our Government have passed us by so completely and are so far ahead that the peoples of our Nation do not even look to the United States Congress any longer for any dynamic leadership in the field of making democracy real. So many changes, tremendous changes, have taken place under our Supreme Court and under the leadership of President Eisenhower that many of the civil rights bills which I used to introduce are no longer of any value. This year, for instance, I did not introduce the bill to abolish segregation in the Armed Forces—it was not needed. Nor did I introduce the bill to guarantee civil rights in the District of Columbia—it was not needed.

I think it highly significant to point out that the appointment of my distinguished colleagues, Representatives Diggs, of Detroit, Mich., and Dawson, of Chicago, Ill., to the Veterans' Affairs Committee and the District of Columbia Committee, respectively, was due entirely to the changing climate.

Two years ago the leadership of this House, Republican or Democrat, would not have dared to place a Negro on either of these two committees because both were committees which dealt with segregation.

Our Veterans' Administration rigidly maintained the bars of segregation, especially in our veterans' hospitals. Two years ago, this Capital was a cesspool of democracy where not only I, as a Negro congressman, was banned from a public places but also visiting chiefs of state and their representatives, if their skin happened to be dark. But under the vigorous leadership of H.V. Higley, Administrator of Veterans' Affairs, there is no longer any segregation in any veterans hospital. And under the leadership of District Commissioner Samuel Spencer, from Mississippi, if you please, this Capital has become a glorious place, truly representative of the finest of our American way of life. And, again I repeat, all of this was done without the help of the Congress and ofttimes done in spite of the opposition of the Congress.

For 10 years, my colleagues and I have introduced civil rights amendment after amendment, civil rights bill after bill, pleading, praying that you good ladies and gentlemen would give to this body the glory of dynamic leadership that it should have. But you have failed and history has recorded it.

I am proud to be a Member of the Congress of the United States. I am proud to be a Member of the legislative branch of the United States Government and I know you are too. But I beseech you to transform this emotion of pride into the deed of leadership. This is an hour for boldness. This is an hour when a world waits breathlessly, expectantly, almost hungrily, for this Congress, the 84th Congress, through legislation to give some semblance of democracy in action. Our President and our Supreme Court cannot do all this by themselves and, furthermore, we should not expect it. We are derelict in our duty if we continue to plow looking backward. No man is fit for this new world, for this new kingdom of God on earth, who plows looking backward. And it is coming with or without us. Time is running out, ladies and gentlemen; Asia has almost slipped from our grasp and Africa will be next. There is no guaranty of our position in Europe. Only a resolute three-pronged drive can make democracy live, breathe, and move now. Only legislative, judicial and executive action can completely guarantee the victory of the free world.

The legislative branch—this Congress—must immediately change its childish, immature, compromising, 19th century attitude and not just become a part of the 20th century world but a leader.

Therefore I ask all of you, on both sides of the aisle, to support this year the bill to eradicate segregation in interstate transportation; to support the omnibus civil rights bill offered by Representative Emanuel Celler, chairman of the Judiciary Committee. Prompt hearings on these bills should be held immediately and swift passage with a minimum of friction should be brought about. We should have a bipartisan approach to domestic democracy or our bipartisan foreign policy approach will be utterly meaningless.

The fair employment opportunities bill did languish in the Committee on Education and Labor, of which I am a member, under the chairmanship of both the Republican and the Democratic leaders, and that should immediately be considered.

The opponents of a fair employment opportunities bill state that they do not believe that the Federal Government should intrude in States rights. I do not agree with them, but until such time as we do pass a national FEPC, I am introducing today an FEPC bill for the District of Columbia. There can be no argument of violation of States rights now. An FEPC bill for the District of Columbia would automatically allow this Congress to become a part of the glorious, victorious, forward march of our executive and judicial branches in the District of Columbia.

We who believe in civil rights urge first: Unity of thought and action for the passage of an interstate antisegregation bill to ban segregation on all interstate carriers. This bill has been introduced by the gentleman from Massachusetts, Representative Heselton. Also I have introduced a companion bill.

Last year when the House Committee on Interstate and Foreign Commerce was considering legislation to end segregation in interstate travel, a 29 year old witness appeared. He was Lt. Thomas Williams, formerly of the United States Air Force. Lieutenant Williams had volunteered for duty when he was 19 years old. He served in the Air Force with merit until 1953 when he was dropped following his arrest in the State of Florida because he refused to move from a so-called white section of an interstate bus. That young man, in the uniform of his country, was jailed and fined even though the United States Supreme Court had told carriers to end racial segregation. That case is still before the courts on appeal. After he was dropped by the United States Air Force, Lieutenant Williams was so eager to serve his country that he enlisted in the New Jersey National Guard. He served for nearly a year. About 2 weeks ago, while flying a jet plane, he was killed serving his country before he had a chance to see democracy come to pass.

We believe in the second place in unity of thought and action towards the passage of an omnibus civil-rights bill.

We believe in the third place in unity of thought and action for the passage of a fair employment opportunities act.

I would like to serve notice that some of us intend after a reasonable time of waiting for our committees and our committee chairmen to act to use every parliamentary device we can to bring before this Congress civil-rights bills of worth and value. We intend to use, after a reasonable period of time, Calendar Wednesdays and discharge petitions. I trust that the leadership will give us cooperation and that we will not be stymied by the use of counter parliamentary methods to prevent us from bringing Calendar Wednesday forward.

On this day, when we bow our heads and hearts in the memory of one of the greatest human beings that ever lived, Franklin Delano Roosevelt, may we not use some of the breadth of his greatness in our hearts and minds, realizing those great words of his that "We have nothing to fear but fear."

> So let us be strong.
> We are not here to play, to dream, to drift.
> We have hard work to do, loads to lift
> Shun not the struggle that is God's gift.
> Be strong. It matters not how deep entrenched the wrong.
> Nor how hard the battle goes, nor the night how long.
> Faint not, fight on.
> Tomorrow will come the dawn.

PART 4
OPPOSING RACIAL DISCRIMINATION

Chapter 20

Advancing in Politics

"From Protest to Politics"

Bayard Rustin

Editor's Introduction: The civil rights struggle for first class citizenship for African Americans achieved its legislative goals with the presidential signing of the Civil Rights Act of 1964 and the Voting Rights Act of 1965. Some viewed the significance of those achievements as the final end of the Civil War. The remaining task was to seize that formal opportunity and to effect the substance of equal citizenship politically, socially, and economically. From the time of the Montgomery Bus Boycott onward, Bayard Rustin (1910–1987) functioned behind the scenes as one of Dr. King's major advisors. In fact, he had been one of the founders of the Congress of Racial Equality (CORE) and a peace activist deeply committed to the philosophy of nonviolent resistance. In 1965 he published an essay in Commentary titled "From Protest to Politics," which has endured over the years as a major guide in the political struggle for racial equality and (though often debated) a basic text in the study of African American political leadership. In 1965 only five blacks were members of Congress. By 1971, when the Congressional Black Caucus was formed, that number had increased to thirteen and many more in succeeding years.

. . . What is the value of winning access to public accommodations for those who lack money to use them? The minute the movement faced this question, it was compelled to expand its vision beyond race relations to economic relations, including the role of education in modern society. And what also became clear is that all these interrelated problems, by their very nature, are not soluble by private, voluntary efforts but require government action or politics. Already Southern demonstrators had recognized that the most effective way to strike at the police brutality they suffered from was by getting rid of the local sheriff and that meant political action, which in turn meant, and still means, political action within the Democratic party where the only meaningful primary contests in the South are fought.

And so, in Mississippi, thanks largely to the leadership of Bob Moses, a turn toward political action has been taken. More than voter registration is involved here. A conscious bid for *political power* is being made, and in the course of that effort a tactical shift is being effected: direct action techniques are being subordinated to a strategy calling for the building of community institutions or power bases. Clearly, the implications of this shift reach far beyond Mississippi. What began as a protest movement is being challenged to translate itself into a political movement. Is this the right course? And if it is, can the transformation be accomplished?

The very decade which has witnessed the decline of legal Jim Crow has also seen the rise of *de facto* segregation in our most fundamental socio economic institutions. More Negroes are unemployed today than in 1954, and the unemployment gap between the races is wider. The median income of Negroes has dropped from 57 per cent to 54 per cent of that of whites. A higher percentage of Negro workers is now concentrated in jobs vulnerable to automation than was the case ten years ago. More Negroes attend *de facto* segregated schools today than when the Supreme Court handed down its famous decision; while school integration proceeds at a snail's pace in the South, the number of Northern schools with an excessive proportion of minority youth proliferates. And behind this is the continuing growth of racial slums, spreading over our central cities and trapping Negro youth in a milieu which, whatever its legal definition, sows an unimaginable demoralization. Again, legal niceties aside, a resident of a racial ghetto lives in segregated housing, and more Negroes fall into this category than ever before.

These are the facts of life which generate frustration in the Negro community and challenge the civil rights movement. At issue, after all, is not *civil rights*, strictly speaking, but social and economic conditions. Last summer's riots were not race riots; they were outbursts of class aggression in a society where class and color definitions are converging disastrously. How can the (perhaps misnamed) civil rights movement deal with this problem? . . .

This matter of economic role brings us to the greater problem—the fact that we are moving into an era in which the natural functioning of the market does not by itself ensure every man with will and ambition a place in the productive process. The immigrant who came to this country during the late 19th and early 20th centuries entered a society which was expanding territorially and/ or economically. It was then possible to start at the bottom, as an unskilled or semi-skilled worker, and move up the ladder, acquiring new skills along the way. Especially was this true when industrial unionism was burgeoning, giving new dignity and higher wages to organized workers. Today the situation has changed. We are not expanding territorially, the western frontier is settled, labor organizing has leveled off, and our rate of economic growth has been stagnant for a decade. And we are in the midst of a technological revolution which is altering the fundamental, structure of the labor force, destroying unskilled and semi-skilled jobs in which Negroes are disproportionately concentrated.

Whatever the pace of this technological revolution may be the *direction* is clear: the lower rungs of the economic ladder are being lopped off. This means that an individual will no longer be able to start at the bottom and work his way up; he will have to start in the middle or on top, and hold on tight. It will not even be enough to have certain specific skills, for many skilled jobs are also vulnerable to automation. A broad educational background, permitting vocational adaptability and flexibility, seems more imperative than ever. We live in a society where, as Secretary of Labor Willard Wirtz puts it, machines have the equivalent of a high school diploma. Yet the average educational attainment of American Negroes is 8.2 years . . .

Let me sum up what I have thus far been trying to say: the civil rights movement is evolving from a protest movement into a full-fledged *social movement*—an evolution calling its very name into question. It is now concerned not merely with removing the barriers to full *opportunity* but with achieving the fact of *equality*. From sit-ins and freedom rides we have gone into rent strikes, boycotts, community organization, and political action. As a consequence of this natural evolution, the Negro today finds himself stymied by obstacles of far greater magnitude than the legal barriers he was attacking before: automation, urban decay, *de facto* school segregation. These are problems which, while conditioned by Jim Crow, do not vanish upon its demise. They are more deeply rooted in our socio economic order; they are the result of the total society's failure to meet not only the Negro's needs, but human needs generally. . . .

The revolutionary character of the Negro's struggle is manifest in the fact that this struggle has done more to democratize life for whites than for Negroes. Clearly, it was the sit-in movement of young Southern Negroes which, as it galvanized white students, banished the ugliest features of McCarthyism from the American campus and resurrected political debate. It was not until Negroes assaulted *de facto* school segregation in centers that the issue of quality education for *all* children stirred into motion. Finally, it seems reasonably clear that the civil rights movement, directly and through the resurgence of social conscience it kindled, did more to initiate the war on poverty than any other single force . . .

Neither that movement nor the country's twenty million black people can win political power alone. We need allies. The future of the Negro struggle depends on whether the contradictions of this society can be resolved by a coalition of progressive forces which becomes the *effective* political majority in the United States. I speak of the coalition which staged the March on Washington, passed the Civil Rights Act, and laid the basis for the Johnson landslide—Negroes, trade unionists, liberals, and religious groups. . . .

The role of the civil rights movement in the reorganization of American political life is programmatic as well as strategic. We are challenged now to broaden our social vision, to develop functional programs with concrete objectives. We need to propose alternatives to technological unemployment, urban decay, and the rest. We need to be calling for public works and training, for national economic planning, for federal aid to education, for attractive public housing—all this on a sufficiently massive scale to make a difference. We need to protest the notion that our integration into American life, so long delayed, must now proceed in an atmosphere of competitive scarcity instead of in the security of abundance which technology makes possible. We cannot claim to have answers to all the complex problems of modern society. That is too much to ask of a movement still battling barbarism in Mississippi. But we can agitate the right questions by probing at the contradictions which still stand in the way of the "Great Society." The questions having been asked, motion must begin in the larger society, for there is a limit to what Negroes can do alone.

Chapter 21

Supporting the Equal Rights Amendment

"I Am for the Equal Rights Amendment"

Shirley Chisholm

Editor's Introduction: In 1968 Shirley Chisholm (1924–2005) became the first African American woman ever elected to Congress. She was a strong leader for the rights of women, children, blacks, and the poor. She was a founder of the National Organization of Women (NOW) and of the Congressional Black Caucus. In 1972 she shocked many by her announcement to run for the democratic nomination for the presidency of the United States. She once said that her gender had been a greater handicap than her race. Thus, her argument for women's equality was built on similar arguments for racial equality. In fact, she viewed the unequal treatment of either women or blacks as irrational, antiquated, and unjust. Her proabortion stance and opposition to the war in Vietnam made her a popular speaker on the university circuit. The following speech was given on the floor of the House on August 10, 1970.

Mr. Speaker, House Joint Resolution 264, before us today, which provides for equality under the law for both men and women, represents one of the most clear-cut opportunities we are likely to have to declare our faith in the principles that shaped our Constitution. It provides a legal basis for attack on the most subtle, most pervasive, and most institutionalized form of prejudice that exists. Discrimination against women, solely on the basis of their sex, is so widespread that is seems to many persons normal, natural and right.

Legal expression of prejudice on the grounds of religious or political belief has become a minor problem in our society. Prejudice on the basis of race is, at least, under systematic attack. There is reason for optimism that it will start to die with the present, older generation. It is time we act to assure full equality of opportunity to those citizens who, although in a majority, suffer the restrictions that are commonly imposed on minorities, to women.

The argument that this amendment will not solve the problem of sex discrimination is not relevant. If the argument were used against a civil rights bill, as it has been used in the past, the prejudice that lies behind it would be embarrassing. Of course laws will not eliminate prejudice from the hearts of human beings. But that is no reason to allow prejudice to continue to be enshrined in our laws—to perpetuate injustice through inaction.

The amendment is necessary to clarify countless ambiguities and inconsistencies in our legal system. For instance, the Constitution guarantees due process of law, in the 5th and 14th amendments. But the applicability of due process of sex distinctions is not clear. Women are excluded from some State colleges and universities. In some States, restrictions are placed on a married woman who engages in an independent business. Women may not be chosen for some juries. Women even receive heavier criminal penalties than men who commit the same crime. What would the legal effects of the equal rights amendment really be? The equal rights amendment would govern only the relationship between the State and its citizens—not relationships between private citizens. The amendment would be largely self-executing, that is, and Federal or State laws in conflict would be ineffective one year after date of ratification without further action by the Congress or State legislatures.

Opponents of the amendment claim its ratification would throw the law into a state of confusion and would result in much litigation to establish its meaning. This objection overlooks the influence of legislative history in determining intent and the recent activities of many groups preparing for legislative changes in this direction.

State labor laws applying only to women, such as those limiting hours of work and weights to be lifted would become inoperative unless the legislature amended them to apply to men. As of early 1970 most States would have some laws that would be affected. However, changes are being made so rapidly as a result of title VII of the Civil Rights Act of 1964, it is likely that by the time the equal rights amendment would become effective; no confliction of State laws would remain.

In any event, there has for years been great controversy as to the usefulness to women of these State labor laws. There has never been any doubt that they worked a hardship on women who need or want to work overtime and on women who need or want better paying jobs, and there has been no persuasive evidence as to how many women benefit from the archaic policy of the laws. After the Delaware hours law was repealed in 1966, there were no complaints from women to any of the State agencies that might have been approached.

Jury service laws not making women equally liable for jury service would have been revised. The selective service law would have to include women, but women would not be required to serve in the Armed Forces where they are not fitted any more than men are required to serve. Military service, while a great responsibility, is not without benefits, particularly for young men with limited education or training.

Since October 1966, 246,000 young men who did not meet the normal mental or physical requirements have been given opportunities for training and correcting physical problems. This opportunity is not open to their sisters. Only girls who have completed high school and meet high standards on the educational test can volunteer. Ratification of the amendment would not permit application of higher standards to women.

Survivorship benefits would be available to husbands of female workers on the same basis as to wives of male workers. The Social Security Act and the civil service and military service retirement acts are in conflict. Public schools and universities could not be limited to one sex and could not apply different admission standards to men and women. Laws requiring longer prison sentences for women than men would be invalid, and equal opportunities for rehabilitation and vocational training would have to be provided in public correctional institutions. Different ages of majority based on sex would have to be harmonized. Federal, State, and other governmental bodies would be obligated to follow nondiscriminatory practices in all aspects of employment, including public school teachers and State university and college faculties.

What would be the economic effects of the equal rights amendment? Direct economic effects would be minor. If any labor laws applying only to women still remained, their amendment or repeal would provide opportunity for women in better-paying jobs in manufacturing. More opportunities in public vocational and graduate schools for women would also tend to open up opportunities in better jobs for women.

Indirect effects could be much greater. The focusing of public attention on the gross legal, economic, and social discrimination against women by hearings and debates in the Federal and State legislatures would result in changes in attitude of parents, educators, and employers that would bring about substantial economic changes in the long run.

Sex prejudice cuts both ways. Men are oppressed by the requirements of the Selective Service Act, by enforced legal guardianship of minors, and by alimony laws. Each sex, I believe, should be liable when necessary to serve and defend this country. Each has a responsibility for the support of children.

There are objections raised to wiping out laws protecting women workers. No one would condone exploitation. But what does sex have to do with it. Working conditions and hours that are harmful to women are harmful to men; wages that are unfair for women are unfair for men. Laws setting employment limitations on the basis of sex are irrational, and the proof of this is their inconsistency from State to State. The physical characteristics of men and women are not fixed, but cover two wide spans that have a great deal of overlap. It is obvious, I think, that a robust woman could be more fit for physical labor than a weak man. The choice of occupation would be determined by individual capabilities, and the rewards for equal works should be equal.

This is what it comes down to: artificial distinctions between persons must be wiped out of the law. Legal discrimination between the sexes is, in almost every instance, founded on outmoded views of society and the pre-scientific beliefs about psychology and physiology. It is time to sweep away these relics of the past and set further generations free of them.

Federal agencies and institutions responsible for the enforcement of equal opportunity laws need the authority of a Constitutional amendment. The 1964 Civil Rights Act and the 1963 Equal Pay Act are not enough; they are limited in their coverage—for instance, one excludes teachers, and the other leaves out administrative and professional women. The Equal Employment Opportunity Commission has not proven to be an adequate device, with its power limited to investigation, conciliation, and recommendation to the Justice Department. In its cases involving sexual discrimination, it has failed in more than one-half. The Justice Department has been even less effective. It has intervened in only one case involving discrimination on the basis of sex, and this was on a procedural point. In a second case, in which both sexual and racial discrimination were alleged, the racial bias charge was given far greater weight.

Evidence of discrimination on the basis of sex should hardly have to be cited here. It is in the Labor Department's employment and salary figures for anyone who is still in doubt. Its elimination will involve so many changes in our State and Federal laws that, without the authority and impetus of this proposed amendment, it will perhaps take another 194 years. We cannot be parties to continuing a delay. The time is clearly now to put this House on record for the fullest expression of that equality of opportunity which our founding fathers professed. They professed it, but they did not assure it to their daughters, as they tried to do for their sons.

The Constitution they wrote was designed to protect the rights of white, male citizens. As there were no black Founding Fathers, there were no founding mothers—a great pity, on both counts. It is not too late to complete the work they left undone. Today, here, we should start to do so.

Chapter 22

Speaking for the Common Good

"Who Then Will Speak
for the Common Good?"

Barbara Jordan

Editor's Introduction: In 1966 Barbara Jordan (1936–1996)
was the first African American woman to be elected to the Texas
State Senate and later to chair a major committee. In 1972 she and
Andrew Young were the first African Americans from the South
to be elected to the United States Congress since Reconstruction.
Her persuasive oratory contributed to her selection by the House
Judiciary Committee to present the committee's opening statement
on July 25, 1974, as it began its proceedings to impeach President
Richard Nixon. Heard and seen by millions, that speech catapulted
her into worldwide visibility. Its captivating opening deserves
duplication here:

> Earlier today we heard the beginning of the Preamble to the Con-
> stitution of the United States, 'We, the people.' It is a very eloquent
> beginning. But when that document was completed, on the seven-
> teenth of September in 1787, I was not included in that "We, the
> people." I felt somehow for many years that George Washington
> and Alexander Hamilton just left me out by mistake. But through
> the process of amendment, interpretation, and court decision I have

135

finally been included in 'We, the people.' Today I am an inquisitor. I believe hyperbole would not be fictional and would not overstate the solemnness that I feel right now. My faith in the Constitution is whole, it is complete, it is total.

On July 12, 1976, Jordan was the first African American ever to give the keynote address at the Democratic National Convention. Moreover, she was invited to do so again at the convention in 1992 fifteen years after she retired from Congress.

Thank you ladies and gentlemen for a very warm reception.

It was one hundred and forty-four years ago that members of the Democratic Party first met in convention to select a Presidential candidate. Since that time, Democrats have continued to convene once every four years and draft a party platform and nominate a Presidential candidate. And our meeting this week is a continuation of that tradition. But there is something different about tonight. There is something special about tonight. What is different? What is special?

I, Barbara Jordan, am a keynote speaker.

When—A lot of years passed since 1832, and during that time it would have been most unusual for any national political party to ask a Barbara Jordan to deliver a keynote address. But tonight, here I am. And I feel—I feel that notwithstanding the past that my presence here is one additional bit of evidence that the American Dream need not forever be deferred.

Now—Now that I have this grand distinction, what in the world am I supposed to say? I could easily spend this time praising the accomplishments of this party and attacking the Republicans—but I don't choose to do that. I could list the many problems which Americans have. I could list the problems which cause people to feel cynical, angry, frustrated: problems which include lack of integrity in government; the feeling that the individual no longer counts; the reality of material and spiritual poverty; the feeling that the grand American experiment is failing or has failed. I could recite these problems, and then I could sit down and offer no solutions. But I don't choose to do that either. The citizens of America expect more. They deserve and they want more than a recital of problems.

We are a people in a quandary about the present. We are a people in search of our future. We are a people in search of a national community. We are a people trying not only to solve the problems of the present, unemployment, inflation, but we are attempting on a larger scale to fulfill the promise of America. We are attempting to fulfill our national purpose, to create and sustain a society in which all of us are equal.

Throughout—Throughout our history, when people have looked for new ways to solve their problems and to uphold the principles of this nation, many times they have turned to political parties. They have often turned to the Democratic Party. What is it? What is it about the Democratic Party that makes it the instrument the people use when they search for ways to shape their future? Well I believe the answer to that question lies in our concept of governing. Our concept of governing is derived from our view of people. It is a concept deeply rooted in a set of beliefs firmly etched in the national conscience of all of us.

Now what are these beliefs? First, we believe in equality for all and privileges for none. This is a belief—This is a belief that each American, regardless of background, has equal standing in the public forum—all of us. Because—Because we believe this idea so firmly, we are an inclusive rather than an exclusive party. Let everybody come.

I think it no accident that most of those immigrating to America in the 19th century identified with the Democratic Party. We are a heterogeneous party made up of Americans of diverse backgrounds. We believe that the people are the source of all governmental power; that the authority of the people is to be extended, not restricted.

This—This can be accomplished only by providing each citizen with every opportunity to participate in the management of the government. They must have that, we believe. We believe that the government which represents the authority of all the people, not just one interest group, but all the people, has an obligation to actively—underscore _actively_—seek to remove those obstacles which would block individual achievement—obstacles emanating from race, sex, economic condition. The government must remove them, seek to remove them. We.

We are a party—We are a party of innovation. We do not reject our traditions, but we are willing to adapt to changing circumstances, when change we must. We are willing to suffer the discomfort of change in order to achieve a better future. We have a positive vision of the future founded on the belief that the gap between the promise and reality of America can one day be finally closed. We believe that.

This, my friends is the bedrock of our concept of governing. This is a part of the reason why Americans have turned to the Democratic Party. These are the foundations upon which a national community can be built. Let all understand that these guiding principles cannot be discarded for short-term political gains. They represent what this country is all about. They are indigenous to the American idea. And these are principles which are not negotiable.

In other times—In other times, I could stand here and give this kind of exposition on the beliefs of the Democratic Party and that would be enough. But today that is not enough. People want more. That is not sufficient reason for the majority of the people of this country to decide to vote Democratic. We have made mistakes. We realize that. We admit our mistakes. In our haste to do all things for all people, we did not foresee the full consequences of our actions. And when the people raised their voices, we didn't hear. But our deafness was only a temporary condition, and not an irreversible condition.

Even as I stand here and admit that we have made mistakes, I still believe that as the people of America sit in judgment on each party, they will recognize that our mistakes were mistakes of the heart. They'll recognize that.

And now—now we must look to the future. Let us heed the voice of the people and recognize their common sense. If we do not, we not only blaspheme our political heritage, we ignore the common ties that bind all Americans. Many fear the future. Many are distrustful of their leaders, and believe that their voices are never heard. Many seek only to satisfy their private work—wants; to satisfy their private interests. But this is the great danger America faces—that we will cease to be one nation and become instead a collection of interest groups: city against suburb, region against region, individual against individual; each seeking to satisfy private wants. If that happens, who then will speak for America? Who then will speak for the common good?

This is the question which must be answered in 1976: Are we to be one people bound together by common spirit, sharing in a common endeavor; or will we become a divided nation? For all of its uncertainty, we cannot flee the future. We must not become the "New Puritans" and reject our society. We must address and master the future together. It can be done if we restore the belief that we share a sense of national community, that we share a common national endeavor. It can be done.

There is no executive order; there is no law that can require the American people to form a national community. This we must do as individuals, and if we do it as individuals, there is no President of the United States who can veto that decision.

As a first step—As a first step, we must restore our belief in ourselves. We are a generous people, so why can't we be generous with each other? We need to take to heart the words spoken by Thomas Jefferson:

Let us restore the social intercourse—"Let us restore to social intercourse that harmony and that affection without which liberty and even life are but dreary things."

A nation is formed by the willingness of each of us to share in the responsibility for upholding the common good. A government is invigorated when each one of us is willing to participate in shaping the future of this nation. In this election year, we must define the "common good" and begin again to shape a common future. Let each person do his or her part. If one citizen is unwilling to participate, all of us are going to suffer. For the American idea, though it is shared by all of us, is realized in each one of us.

And now, what are those of us who are elected public officials supposed to do? We call ourselves "public servants" but I'll tell you this: We as public servants must set an example for the rest of the nation. It is hypocritical for the public official to admonish and exhort the people to uphold the common good if we are derelict in upholding the common good. More is required—More is required of public officials than slogans and handshakes and press releases. More is required. We must hold ourselves strictly accountable. We must provide the people with a vision of the future. If we promise as public officials, we must deliver. If—If we as public officials propose, we must produce. If we say to the American people,

"It is time for you to be sacrificial"—sacrifice. If the public official says that, we [public officials] must be the first to give.

We must be. And again, if we make mistakes, we must be willing to admit them. We have to do that. What we have to do is strike a balance between the idea that government should do everything and the idea, the belief, that government ought to do nothing. Strike a balance.

Let there be no illusions about the difficulty of forming this kind of a national community. It's tough, difficult, not easy. But a spirit of harmony will survive in America only if each of us remembers that we share a common destiny; if each of us remembers, when self-interest and bitterness seem to prevail, that we share a common destiny.

I have confidence that we can form this kind of national community.

I have confidence that the Democratic Party can lead the way.

I have that confidence.

We cannot improve on the system of government handed down to us by the founders of the Republic. There is no way to improve upon that. But what we can do is to find new ways to implement that system and realize our destiny.

Now I began this speech by commenting to you on the uniqueness of a Barbara Jordan making a keynote address. Well I am going to close my speech by quoting a Republican President and I ask you that as you listen to these words of Abraham Lincoln, relate them to the concept of a national community in which every last one of us participates:

"As I would not be a slave, so I would not be a master." This—This—"This expresses my idea of Democracy. Whatever differs from this, to the extent of the difference, is no Democracy."

Thank you.

Chapter 23

Common Ground

"Keep Hope Alive"

Jesse Louis Jackson Sr.

Editor's Introduction: Jesse Louis Jackson Sr. (1941–) civil rights
activist, religious and political leader, negotiator and ambassador of
good will, founder and President of the Rainbow PUSH Coalition,
has traveled around the world seeking justice and peace. His career
began when he was a student at North Carolina Agricultural and
Technical State University and became involved in the sit-in
movement. Soon thereafter, Martin Luther King Jr. appointed
him director of the Operation Breadbasket program in Chicago,
which was the economic arm of the Southern Christian Leadership
Conference. In 1972 he formed his own independent organization
and gradually built a national and international sphere of influence
for himself and his organization. His principal goal has always been
economic empowerment and justice for the poor in general and for
blacks in particular. He ran for President of the United States in
1984 and in 1988 and developed a political base that enabled him to
effect significant changes in the Democratic Party, both at the local
and national levels. He has received countless honors including the
Presidential Medal of Freedom and was appointed Special Envoy

to Africa by President Bill Clinton. His son Jesse Louis Jackson Jr. was a congressman from 1995 to 2012. The following speech was delivered July 19, 1988, at the Democratic National Convention in the Omni Coliseum, Atlanta, Georgia.

Tonight, we pause and give praise and honor to God for being good enough to allow us to be at this place at this time. When I look out at this convention, I see the face of America: Red, Yellow, Brown, Black and White. We are all precious in God's sight—the real rainbow coalition.

All of us—all of us who are here think that we are seated. But we're really standing on someone's shoulders. Ladies and gentlemen, Mrs. Rosa Parks—the mother of the civil rights movement.

[Mrs. Rosa Parks is brought to the podium.]

I want to express my deep love and appreciation for the support my family has given me over these past months. They have endured pain, anxiety, threat, and fear. But they have been strengthened and made secure by our faith in God, in America, and in you. Your love has protected us and made us strong. To my wife Jackie, the foundation of our family; to our five children whom you met tonight; to my mother, Mrs. Helen Jackson, who is present tonight; and to our grandmother, Mrs. Matilda Burns; to my brother Chuck and his family; to my mother-in-law, Mrs. Gertrude Brown, who just last month at age 61 graduated from Hampton Institute—a marvelous achievement.

I offer my appreciation to Mayor Andrew Young who has provided such gracious hospitality to all of us this week.

And a special salute to President Jimmy Carter. President Carter restored honor to the White House after Watergate. He gave many of us a special opportunity to grow. For his kind words, for his unwavering commitment to peace in the world, and for the voters that came from his family, every member of his family, led by Billy and Amy, I offer my special thanks to the Carter family.

My right and my privilege to stand here before you has been won, won in my lifetime, by the blood and the sweat of the innocent.

Twenty-four years ago, the late Fannie Lou Hamer and Aaron Henry—who sits here tonight from Mississippi—were locked out onto the streets in Atlantic City; the head of the Mississippi Freedom Democratic Party.

But tonight, a Black and White delegation from Mississippi is headed by Ed Cole, a Black man from Mississippi; twenty-four years later.

Many were lost in the struggle for the right to vote: Jimmy Lee Jackson, a young student, gave his life; Viola Liuzzo, a White mother from Detroit, called "nigger lover," and brains blown out at point blank range; [Michael] Schwerner, [Andrew] Goodman and [James] Chaney—two Jews and a Black—found in a common grave, bodies riddled with bullets in Mississippi; the four darling little girls in a church in Birmingham, Alabama. They died that we might have a right to live.

Dr. Martin Luther King Jr. lies only a few miles from us tonight. Tonight he must feel good as he looks down upon us. We sit here together, a rainbow, a coalition—the sons and daughters of slavemasters and the sons and daughters of slaves, sitting together around a common table, to decide the direction of our party and our country. His heart would be full tonight.

As a testament to the struggles of those who have gone before; as a legacy for those who will come after; as a tribute to the endurance, the patience, the courage of our forefathers and mothers; as an assurance that their prayers are being answered, that their work has not been in vain, and, that hope is eternal, tomorrow night my name will go into nomination for the Presidency of the United States of America.

We meet tonight at the crossroads, a point of decision. Shall we expand, be inclusive, find unity and power; or suffer division and impotence?

We've come to Atlanta, the cradle of the Old South, the crucible of the New South. Tonight, there is a sense of celebration, because we are moved, fundamentally moved from racial battlegrounds by law, to economic common ground. Tomorrow we'll challenge to move to higher ground.

Common ground. Think of Jerusalem, the intersection where many trails met. A small village that became the birthplace for three great religions—Judaism, Christianity, and Islam. Why was this village so blessed? Because it provided a crossroads where different people met, different cultures, different civilizations could meet and find common ground. When people come together, flowers always flourish—the air is rich with the aroma of a new spring.

Take New York, the dynamic metropolis. What makes New York so special? It's the invitation at the Statue of Liberty, "Give me your tired, your poor, your huddled masses who yearn to breathe free." Not restricted to English only. Many people, many cultures, many languages with one thing in common: They yearn to breathe free. Common ground.

Tonight in Atlanta, for the first time in this century, we convene in the South; a state where Governors once stood in school house doors; where Julian Bond was denied a seat in the State Legislature because of his conscientious objection to the Vietnam War; a city that, through its five Black Universities, has graduated more black students than any city in the world. Atlanta, now a modern intersection of the New South.

Common ground. That's the challenge of our party tonight—left wing, right wing. Progress will not come through boundless liberalism nor static conservatism, but at the critical mass of mutual survival—not at boundless liberalism nor static conservatism, but at the critical mass of mutual survival. It takes two wings to fly. Whether you're a hawk or a dove, you're just a bird living in the same environment, in the same world.

The Bible teaches that when lions and lambs lie down together, none will be afraid, and there will be peace in the valley. It sounds impossible. Lions eat lambs. Lambs sensibly flee from lions. Yet even lions and lambs find common ground. Why? Because neither lions nor lambs want the forest to catch on fire.

Neither lions nor lambs want acid rain to fall. Neither lions nor lambs can survive nuclear war. If lions and lambs can find common ground, surely we can as well—as civilized people.

The only time that we win is when we come together. In 1960, John Kennedy, the late John Kennedy, beat Richard Nixon by only 112,000 votes—less than one vote per precinct. He won by the margin of our hope. He brought us together. He reached out. He had the courage to defy his advisors and inquire about Dr. King's jailing in Albany, Georgia. We won by the margin of our hope, inspired by courageous leadership. In 1964, Lyndon Johnson brought both wings together—the thesis, the antithesis, and the creative synthesis—and together we won. In 1976, Jimmy Carter unified us again, and we won. When do we not come together, we never win. In 1968, the division and despair in July led to our defeat in November. In 1980, rancor in the spring and the summer led to Reagan in the fall. When we divide, we cannot win. We must find common ground as the basis for survival and development and change and growth.

Today when we debated, differed, deliberated, agreed to agree, agreed to disagree, when we had the good judgment to argue a case and then not self-destruct, George Bush was just a little further away from the White House and a little closer to private life.

Tonight, I salute Governor Michael Dukakis. He has run—He has run a well-managed and a dignified campaign. No matter how tired or how tried, he always resisted the temptation to stoop to demagoguery.

I've watched a good mind fast at work, with steel nerves, guiding his campaign out of the crowded field without appeal to the worst in us. I've watched his perspective grow as his environment has expanded. I've seen his toughness and tenacity close up. I know his commitment to public service. Mike Dukakis' parents were a doctor and a teacher; my parents a maid, a beautician, and a janitor. There's a great gap between Brookline, Massachusetts and Haney Street in the Fieldcrest Village housing projects in Greenville, South Carolina.

He studied law; I studied theology. There are differences of religion, region, and race; differences in experiences and perspectives. But the genius of America is that out of the many we become one.

Providence has enabled our paths to intersect. His fore parents came to America on immigrant ships; my fore parents came to America on slave ships. But whatever the original ships, we're in the same boat tonight.

Our ships could pass in the night—if we have a false sense of independence—or they could collide and crash. We would lose our passengers. We can seek a high reality and a greater good. Apart, we can drift on the broken pieces of Reagonomics, satisfy our baser instincts, and exploit the fears of our people. At our highest, we can call upon noble instincts and navigate this vessel to safety. The greater good is the common good.

As Jesus said, "Not My will, but Thine be done." It was his way of saying there's a higher good beyond personal comfort or position.

The good of our Nation is at stake. It's commitment to working men and women, to the poor and the vulnerable, to the many in the world.

With so many guided missiles, and so much misguided leadership, the stakes are exceedingly high. Our choice? Full participation in a democratic government, or more abandonment and neglect. And so this night, we choose not a false sense of independence, not our capacity to survive and endure. Tonight we choose interdependency, and our capacity to act and unite for the greater good.

Common good is finding commitment to new priorities to expansion and inclusion. A commitment to expanded participation in the Democratic Party at every level. A commitment to a shared national campaign strategy and involvement at every level.

A commitment to new priorities that insure that hope will be kept alive. A common ground commitment to a legislative agenda for empowerment, for the John Conyers bill—universal, on-site, same-day registration everywhere. A commitment to D.C. statehood and empowerment—D.C. deserves statehood. A commitment to economic set-asides, commitment to the Dellums bill for comprehensive sanctions against South Africa. A shared commitment to a common direction. Common ground.

Easier said than done. Where do you find common ground? At the point of challenge. This campaign has shown that politics need not be marketed by politicians, packaged by pollsters and pundits. Politics can be a moral arena where people come together to find common ground.

We find common ground at the plant gate that closes on workers without notice. We find common ground at the farm auction, where a good farmer loses his or her land to bad loans or diminishing markets. Common ground at the school yard where teachers cannot get adequate pay, and students cannot get a scholarship, and can't make a loan. Common ground at the hospital admitting room, where somebody tonight is dying because they cannot afford to go upstairs to a bed that's empty waiting for someone with insurance to get sick. We are a better nation than that. We must do better.

Common ground. What is leadership if not present help in a time of crisis? And so I met you at the point of challenge. In Jay, Maine, where paper workers were striking for fair wages; in Greenville, Iowa, where family farmers struggle for a fair price; in Cleveland, Ohio, where working women seek comparable worth; in McFarland, California, where the children of Hispanic farm workers may be dying from poisoned land, dying in clusters with cancer; in an AIDS hospice in Houston, Texas, where the sick support one another, too often rejected by their own parents and friends.

Common ground. America is not a blanket woven from one thread, one color, one cloth. When I was a child growing up in Greenville, South Carolina and grandmamma could not afford a blanket, she didn't complain and we did not freeze. Instead she took pieces of old cloth—patches, wool, silk, gabardine, crockersack—only patches, barely good enough to wipe off your shoes with. But they didn't stay that way very long. With sturdy hands and a strong cord, she sewed them together into a quilt, a thing of beauty and power and culture. Now, Democrats, we must build such a quilt.

Farmers, you seek fair prices and you are right—but you cannot stand alone. Your patch is not big enough.

Workers, you fight for fair wages, you are right—but your patch labor is not big enough.

Women, you seek comparable worth and pay equity, you are right—but your patch is not big enough.

Women, mothers, who seek Head Start, and day care and prenatal care on the front side of life, relevant jail care and welfare on the back side of life, you are right—but your patch is not big enough.

Students, you seek scholarships, you are right—but your patch is not big enough. Blacks and Hispanics, when we fight for civil rights, we are right—but our patch is not big enough.

Gays and lesbians, when you fight against discrimination and a cure for AIDS, you are right—but your patch is not big enough.

Conservatives and progressives, when you fight for what you believe, right wing, left wing, hawk, dove, you are right from your point of view, but your point of view is not enough.

But don't despair. Be as wise as my grandmamma. Pull the patches and the pieces together, bound by a common thread. When we form a great quilt of unity and common ground, we'll have the power to bring about health care and housing and jobs and education and hope to our Nation.

We, the people, can win.

We stand at the end of a long dark night of reaction. We stand tonight united in the commitment to a new direction. For almost eight years we've been led by those who view social good coming from private interest, who view public life as a means to increase private wealth. They have been prepared to sacrifice the common good of the many to satisfy the private interests and the wealth of a few.

We believe in a government that's a tool of our democracy in service to the public, not an instrument of the aristocracy in search of private wealth. We believe in government with the consent of the governed, "of, for and by the people." We must now emerge into a new day with a new direction.

Reaganomics: Based on the belief that the rich had too much money [sic]—too little money and the poor had too much. That's classic Reaganomics. They believe that the poor had too much money and the rich had too little money, so they engaged in reverse Robin Hood—took from the poor, gave to the rich, paid for by the middle class. We cannot stand four more years of Reaganomics in any version, in any disguise.

How do I document that case? Seven years later, the richest 1 percent of our society pays 20 percent less in taxes. The poorest 10 percent pay 20 percent more: Reaganomics.

Reagan gave the rich and the powerful a multibillion-dollar party. Now the party is over. He expects the people to pay for the damage. I take this principal position, convention, let us not raise taxes on the poor and the middle-class, but those who had the party, the rich and the powerful, must pay for the party.

I just want to take common sense to high places. We're spending one hundred and fifty billion dollars a year defending Europe and Japan 43 years after the war is over. We have more troops in Europe tonight than we had seven years ago. Yet the threat of war is ever more remote.

Germany and Japan are now creditor nations; that means they've got a surplus. We are a debtor nation—means we are in debt. Let them share more of the burden of their own defense. Use some of that money to build decent housing. Use some of that money to educate our children. Use some of that money for long-term health care. Use some of that money to wipe out these slums and put America back to work!

I just want to take common sense to high places. If we can bail out Europe and Japan; if we can bail out Continental Bank and Chrysler—and Mr. Iacocca, make [sic] 8,000 dollars an hour—we can bail out the family farmer.

I just want to make common sense. It does not make sense to close down six hundred and fifty thousand family farms in this country while importing food from abroad subsidized by the U.S. Government. Let's make sense.

It does not make sense to be escorting all our tankers up and down the Persian Gulf paying $2.50 for every one dollar worth of oil we bring out, while oil wells are capped in Texas, Oklahoma, and Louisiana. I just want to make sense.

Leadership must meet the moral challenge of its day. What's the moral challenge of our day? We have public accommodations. We have the right to vote. We have open housing. What's the fundamental challenge of our day? It is to end economic violence. Plant closings without notice—economic violence. Even the greedy do not profit long from greed—economic violence.

Most poor people are not lazy. They are not black. They are not brown. They are mostly White and female and young. But whether White, Black or Brown, a hungry baby's belly turned inside out is the same color—color it pain; color it hurt; color it agony.

Most poor people are not on welfare. Some of them are illiterate and can't read the want-ad sections. And when they can, they can't find a job that matches the address. They work hard everyday.

I know. I live amongst them. I'm one of them. I know they work. I'm a witness. They catch the early bus. They work every day.

They raise other people's children. They work everyday.

They clean the streets. They work everyday. They drive dangerous cabs. They work everyday. They change the beds you slept in—in these hotels last night and can't get a union contract. They work everyday.

No, no, they are not lazy! Someone must defend them because it's right, and they cannot speak for themselves. They work in hospitals. I know they do. They wipe the bodies of those who are sick with fever and pain. They empty their bedpans. They clean out their commodes. No job is beneath them, and yet when they get sick they cannot lie in the bed they made up every day. America, that is not right. We are a better Nation than that. We are a better Nation than that. We need a real war on drugs. You can't "just say no." It's deeper than that. You can't just get a palm reader or an astrologer. It's more profound than that.

We are spending a hundred and fifty billion dollars on drugs a year. We've gone from ignoring it to focusing on the children. Children cannot buy a hundred and fifty billion dollars worth of drugs a year; a few high-profile athletes—athletes are not laundering a hundred and fifty billion dollars a year— bankers are.

I met the children in Watts, who, unfortunately, in their despair, their grapes of hope have become raisins of despair, and they're turning on each other and they're self-destructing. But I stayed with them all night long. I wanted to hear their case.

They said, "Jesse Jackson, as you challenge us to say no to drugs, you're right; and to not sell them, you're right; and not use these guns, you're right." (And by the way, the promise of CETA [Comprehensive Employment and Training Act]; they displaced CETA—they did not replace CETA.)

"We have neither jobs nor houses nor services nor training—no way out. Some of us take drugs as anesthesia for our pain. Some take drugs as a way of pleasure, good short-term pleasure and long-term pain. Some sell drugs to make money. It's wrong, we know, but you need to know that we know. We can go and buy the drugs by the boxes at the port. If we can buy the drugs at the port, don't you believe the Federal government can stop it if they want to?"

They say, "We don't have Saturday night specials anymore." They say, "We buy AK47's and Uzi's, the latest make of weapons. We buy them across the along these boulevards."

You cannot fight a war on drugs unless and until you're going to challenge the bankers and the gun sellers and those who grow them. Don't just focus on the children; let's stop drugs at the level of supply and demand. We must end the scourge on the American Culture.

Leadership. What difference will we make? Leadership. Cannot just go along to get along. We must do more than change Presidents. We must change direction.

Leadership must face the moral challenge of our day. The nuclear war build-up is irrational. Strong leadership cannot desire to look tough and let that stand in the way of the pursuit of peace. Leadership must reverse the arms race. At least we should pledge no first use. Why? Because first use begets first retaliation. And that's mutual annihilation. That's not a rational way out.

No use at all. Let's think it out and not fight it out because it's an unwinnable fight. Why hold a card that you can never drop? Let's give peace a chance.

Leadership. We now have this marvelous opportunity to have a breakthrough with the Soviets. Last year 200,000 Americans visited the Soviet Union. There's a chance for joint ventures into space—not Star Wars and war arms escalation but a space defense initiative. Let's build in the space together and demilitarize the heavens. There's a way out.

America, let us expand. When Mr. Reagan and Mr. Gorbachev met there was a big meeting. They represented together one-eighth of the human race. Seven-eighths of the human race was locked out of that room. Most people in the world tonight—half are Asian, one-half of them are Chinese. There are 22 nations in the Middle East. There's Europe; 40 million Latin Americans next door to us; the Caribbean; Africa—a half-billion people.

Most people in the world today are Yellow or Brown or Black, non-Christian, poor, female, young and don't speak English in the real world.

This generation must offer leadership to the real world. We're losing ground in Latin America, Middle East, South Africa because we're not focusing on the real world. That's the real world. We must use basic principles—support international law. We stand the most to gain from it. Support human rights— we believe in that. Support self-determination—we're built on that. Support economic development—you know it's right. Be consistent and gain our moral authority in the world. I challenge you tonight, my friends, let's be bigger and better as a Nation and as a Party.

We have basic challenges—freedom in South Africa. We've already agreed as Democrats to declare South Africa to be a terrorist state. But don't just stop there. Get South Africa out of Angola; free Namibia; support the front line states. We must have a new humane human rights consistent policy in Africa.

I'm often asked, "Jesse, why do you take on these tough issues? They're not very political. We can't win that way."

If an issue is morally right, it will eventually be political. It may be political and never be right. Fannie Lou Hamer didn't have the most votes in Atlantic City, but her principles have outlasted every delegate who voted to lock her out. Rosa Parks did not have the most votes, but she was morally right. Dr. King didn't have the most votes about the Vietnam War, but he was morally right. If we are principled first, our politics will fall in place.

"Jesse, why do you take these big bold initiatives?" A poem by an unknown author went something like this: "We mastered the air, we conquered the sea, annihilated distance and prolonged life, but we're not wise enough to live on this earth without war and without hate."

As for Jesse Jackson: "I'm tired of sailing my little boat, far inside the harbor bar. I want to go out where the big ships float, out on the deep where the great ones are. And should my frail craft prove too slight for waves that sweep those billows o'er, I'd rather go down in the stirring fight than drowse to death at the sheltered shore."

We've got to go out, my friends, where the big boats are.

And then for our children. Young America, hold your head high now. We can win. We must not lose you to drugs and violence, premature pregnancy, suicide, cynicism, pessimism and despair. We can win. Wherever you are tonight, I challenge you to hope and to dream. Don't submerge your dreams.

Exercise above all else, even on drugs, dream of the day you are drug free. Even in the gutter, dream of the day that you will be up on your feet again.

You must never stop dreaming. Face reality, yes, but don't stop with the way things are. Dream of things as they ought to be. Dream. Face pain, but love, hope, faith and dreams will help you rise above the pain. Use hope and imagination as weapons of survival and progress, but you keep on dreaming, young America. Dream of peace. Peace is rational and reasonable. War is irrationable [sic] in this age, and unwinnable.

Dream of teachers who teach for life and not for a living. Dream of doctors who are concerned more about public health than private wealth. Dream of lawyers more concerned about justice than a judgeship. Dream of preachers who are concerned more about prophecy than profiteering. Dream on the high road with sound values.

And then America, as we go forth to September, October, November and then beyond, America must never surrender to a high moral challenge.

Do not surrender to drugs. The best drug policy is a "no first use." Don't surrender with needles and cynicism. Let's have "no first use" on the one hand, or clinics on the other. Never surrender, young America. Go forward.

America must never surrender to malnutrition. We can feed the hungry and clothe the naked. We must never surrender. We must go forward.

We must never surrender to illiteracy. Invest in our children. Never surrender; and go forward. We must never surrender to inequality. Women cannot compromise ERA or comparable worth. Women are making 60 cents on the dollar to what a man makes. Women cannot buy meat cheaper. Women cannot buy bread cheaper. Women cannot buy milk cheaper. Women deserve to get paid for the work that you do. It's right! And it's fair.

Don't surrender, my friends. Those who have AIDS tonight, you deserve our compassion. Even with AIDS you must not surrender.

In your wheelchairs. I see you sitting here tonight in those wheelchairs. I've stayed with you. I've reached out to you across our Nation. And don't you give up. I know it's tough sometimes. People look down on you. It took you a little more effort to get here tonight. And no one should look down on you, but sometimes mean people do. The only justification we have for looking down on someone is that we're going to stop and pick them up.

But even in your wheelchairs, don't you give up. We cannot forget 50 years ago when our backs were against the wall, Roosevelt was in a wheelchair. I would rather have Roosevelt in a wheelchair than Reagan and Bush on a horse. Don't you surrender and don't you give up. Don't surrender and don't give up!

Why I cannot challenge you this way? "Jesse Jackson, you don't understand my situation. You be on television. You don't understand. I see you with the big people. You don't understand my situation."

I understand. You see me on TV, but you don't know the me that makes me, me. They wonder, "Why does Jesse run?" because they see me running for the White House. They don't see the house I'm running from.

I have a story. I wasn't always on television. Writers were not always outside my door. When I was born late one afternoon, October 8th, in Greenville, South Carolina, no writers asked my mother her name. Nobody chose to write down our address. My mama was not supposed to make it, and I was not supposed to make it. You see, I was born of a teen-age mother, who was born of a teen-age mother.

I understand. I know abandonment, and people being mean to you, and saying you're nothing and nobody and can never be anything.

I understand. Jesse Jackson is my third name. I'm adopted. When I had no name, my grandmother gave me her name. My name was Jesse Burns 'til I was 12. So I wouldn't have a blank space, she gave me a name to hold me over. I understand when nobody knows your name. I understand when you have no name.

I understand. I wasn't born in the hospital. Mama didn't have insurance. I was born in the bed at [the] house. I really do understand. Born in a three-room house, bathroom in the backyard, slop jar by the bed, no hot and cold running water. I understand. Wallpaper used for decoration? No. For a windbreaker. I understand. I'm a working person's person. That's why I understand you whether you're Black or White. I understand work. I was not born with a silver spoon in my mouth. I had a shovel programmed for my hand.

My mother, a working woman. So many of the days she went to work early, with runs in her stockings. She knew better, but she wore runs in her stockings so that my brother and I could have matching socks and not be laughed at in school. I understand.

At 3 o'clock on Thanksgiving Day, we couldn't eat turkey because momma was preparing somebody else's turkey at 3 o'clock. We had to play football to entertain ourselves. And then around 6 o'clock she would get off the Alta Vista bus and we would bring up the leftovers and eat our turkey—leftovers, the carcass, the cranberries—around 8 o'clock at night. I really do understand.

Every one of these funny labels they put on you, those of you who are watching this broadcast tonight in the projects, on the corners, I understand. Call you outcast, low down, you can't make it, you're nothing, you're from nobody, subclass, underclass; when you see Jesse Jackson, when my name goes in nomination, your name goes in nomination.

I was born in the slum, but the slum was not born in me. And it wasn't born in you, and you can make it.

Wherever you are tonight, you can make it. Hold your head high; stick your chest out. You can make it. It gets dark sometimes, but the morning comes. Don't you surrender!

Suffering breeds character, character breeds faith. In the end faith will not disappoint. You must not surrender! You may or may not get there but just know that you're qualified! And you hold on, and hold out! We must never surrender!! America will get better and better.

Keep hope alive. Keep hope alive! Keep hope alive! On tomorrow night and beyond, keep hope alive!

I love you very much. I love you very much.

Chapter 24

An Incredible Achievement
"Election Night Victory Speech"

Barack Obama

Editor's Introduction: On November 4, 2008, before a jubilant audience in Grant Park, Chicago, Barack Obama (1961–)delivered his victory speech as President Elect of the United States—the first African American to gain the highest office in the land. He was embraced by African peoples everywhere, and their joy was and continues to be abundant. Further, it was a moment of great pride for millions of Americans who at long last felt that the nation had produced some moral good across racial lines.

Hello Chicago.

If there is anyone out there who still doubts that America is a place where all things are possible, who still wonders if the dream of our founders is alive in our time, who still questions the power of our democracy, tonight is your answer.

It's the answer told by lines that stretched around schools and churches in numbers this nation has never seen, by people who waited three hours and four hours, many for the first time in their lives, because they believed that this time must be different, that their voices could be that difference.

It's the answer spoken by young and old, rich and poor, Democrat and Republican, black, white, Hispanic, Asian, Native American, gay, straight, disabled and not disabled. Americans who sent a message to the world that we have never been just a collection of individuals or a collection of red states and blue states.

We are, and always will be, the United States of America.

It's the answer that led those who've been told for so long by so many to be cynical and fearful and doubtful about what we can achieve to put their hands on the arc of history and bend it once more toward the hope of a better day.

It's been a long time coming, but tonight, because of what we did on this date in this election at this defining moment change has come to America.

A little bit earlier this evening, I received an extraordinarily gracious call from Senator McCain.

Senator McCain fought long and hard in this campaign. And he's fought even longer and harder for the country that he loves. He has endured sacrifices for America that most of us cannot begin to imagine. We are better off for the service rendered by this brave and selfless leader.

I congratulate him; I congratulate Governor Palin for all that they've achieved. And I look forward to working with them to renew this nation's promise in the months ahead.

I want to thank my partner in this journey, a man who campaigned from his heart, and spoke for the men and women he grew up with on the streets of Scranton . . . and rode with on the train home to Delaware, the vice president-elect of the United States, Joe Biden.

And I would not be standing here tonight without the unyielding support of my best friend for the last 16 years . . . the rock of our family, the love of my life, the nation's next first lady . . . Michelle Obama.

Sasha and Malia . . . I love you both more than you can imagine. And you have earned the new puppy that's coming with us . . . to the new White House.

And while she's no longer with us, I know my grandmother's watching, along with the family that made me who I am. I miss them tonight. I know that my debt to them is beyond measure.

To my sister Maya, my sister Alma, all my other brothers and sisters, thank you so much for all the support that you've given me. I am grateful to them.

And to my campaign manager, David Plouffe . . . the unsung hero of this campaign, who built the best—the best political campaign, I think, in the history of the United States of America.

To my chief strategist David Axelrod . . . who's been a partner with me every step of the way.

To the best campaign team ever assembled in the history of politics . . . you made this happen, and I am forever grateful for what you've sacrificed to get it done.

But above all, I will never forget who this victory truly belongs to. It belongs to you. It belongs to you.

I was never the likeliest candidate for this office. We didn't start with much money or many endorsements. Our campaign was not hatched in the halls of Washington. It began in the backyards of Des Moines and the living rooms of Concord and the front porches of Charleston. It was built by working men and women who dug into what little savings they had to give $5 and $10 and $20 to the cause.

It drew strength from the young people who rejected the myth of their generation's apathy . . . who left their homes and their families for jobs that offered little pay and less sleep.

It drew strength from the not-so-young people who braved the bitter cold and scorching heat to knock on doors of perfect strangers, and from the millions of Americans who volunteered and organized and proved that more than two centuries later a government of the people, by the people, and for the people has not perished from the Earth.

This is your victory.

And I know you didn't do this just to win an election. And I know you didn't do it for me.

You did it because you understand the enormity of the task that lies ahead. For even as we celebrate tonight, we know the challenges that tomorrow will bring are the greatest of our lifetime—two wars, a planet in peril, the worst financial crisis in a century.

Even as we stand here tonight, we know there are brave Americans waking up in the deserts of Iraq and the mountains of Afghanistan to risk their lives for us.

There are mothers and fathers who will lie awake after the children fall asleep and wonder how they'll make the mortgage or pay their doctors' bills or save enough for their child's college education.

There's new energy to harness, new jobs to be created, new schools to build, and threats to meet, alliances to repair.

The road ahead will be long. Our climb will be steep. We may not get there in one year or even in one term. But, America, I have never been more hopeful than I am tonight that we will get there.

I promise you, we as a people will get there.

AUDIENCE: Yes we can! Yes we can! Yes we can!

OBAMA: There will be setbacks and false starts. There are many who won't agree with every decision or policy I make as president. And we know the government can't solve every problem.

But I will always be honest with you about the challenges we face. I will listen to you, especially when we disagree. And, above all, I will ask you to join in the work of remaking this nation, the only way it's been done in America for 221 years—block by block, brick by brick, calloused hand by calloused hand.

What began 21 months ago in the depths of winter cannot end on this autumn night.

This victory alone is not the change we seek. It is only the chance for us to make that change. And that cannot happen if we go back to the way things were.

It can't happen without you, without a new spirit of service, a new spirit of sacrifice.

So let us summon a new spirit of patriotism, of responsibility, where each of us resolves to pitch in and work harder and look after not only ourselves but each other.

Let us remember that, if this financial crisis taught us anything, it's that we cannot have a thriving Wall Street while Main Street suffers.

In this country, we rise or fall as one nation, as one people. Let's resist the temptation to fall back on the same partisanship and pettiness and immaturity that has poisoned our politics for so long.

Let's remember that it was a man from this state who first carried the banner of the Republican Party to the White House, a party founded on the values of self-reliance and individual liberty and national unity.

Those are values that we all share. And while the Democratic Party has won a great victory tonight, we do so with a measure of humility and determination to heal the divides that have held back our progress.

As Lincoln said to a nation far more divided than ours, we are not enemies but friends. Though passion may have strained, it must not break our bonds of affection.

And to those Americans whose support I have yet to earn, I may not have won your vote tonight, but I hear your voices. I need your help. And I will be your president, too.

And to all those watching tonight from beyond our shores, from parliaments and palaces, to those who are huddled around radios in the forgotten corners of the world, our stories are singular, but our destiny is shared, and a new dawn of American leadership is at hand.

To those—to those who would tear the world down: We will defeat you. To those who seek peace and security: We support you. And to all those who have wondered if America's beacon still burns as bright: Tonight we proved once more that the true strength of our nation comes not from the might of our arms or the scale of our wealth, but from the enduring power of our ideals: democracy, liberty, opportunity and unyielding hope.

That's the true genius of America: that America can change. Our union can be perfected. What we've already achieved gives us hope for what we can and must achieve tomorrow.

This election had many firsts and many stories that will be told for generations. But one that's on my mind tonight's about a woman who cast her ballot in Atlanta. She's a lot like the millions of others who stood in line to make their voice heard in this election except for one thing: Ann Nixon Cooper is 106 years old.

She was born just a generation past slavery; a time when there were no cars on the road or planes in the sky; when someone like her couldn't vote for two reasons—because she was a woman and because of the color of her skin.

And tonight, I think about all that she's seen throughout her century in America—the heartache and the hope; the struggle and the progress; the times we were told that we can't, and the people who pressed on with that American creed: Yes we can.

At a time when women's voices were silenced and their hopes dismissed, she lived to see them stand up and speak out and reach for the ballot. Yes we can.

When there was despair in the dust bowl and depression across the land, she saw a nation conquer fear itself with a New Deal, new jobs, a new sense of common purpose. Yes we can.

AUDIENCE: Yes we can.

OBAMA: When the bombs fell on our harbor and tyranny threatened the world, she was there to witness a generation rise to greatness and a democracy was saved. Yes we can.

AUDIENCE: Yes we can.

OBAMA: She was there for the buses in Montgomery, the hoses in Birmingham, a bridge in Selma, and a preacher from Atlanta who told a people that We Shall Overcome. Yes we can.

AUDIENCE: Yes we can.

OBAMA: A man touched down on the moon, a wall came down in Berlin, a world was connected by our own science and imagination.

And this year, in this election, she touched her finger to a screen, and cast her vote, because after 106 years in America, through the best of times and the darkest of hours, she knows how America can change.

Yes we can.

AUDIENCE: Yes we can.

OBAMA: America, we have come so far. We have seen so much. But there is so much more to do. So tonight, let us ask ourselves—if our children should live to see the next century; if my daughters should be so lucky to live as long as Ann Nixon Cooper, what change will they see? What progress will we have made?

This is our chance to answer that call. This is our moment.

This is our time, to put our people back to work and open doors of opportunity for our kids; to restore prosperity and promote the cause of peace; to reclaim the American dream and reaffirm that fundamental truth, that, out of many, we are one; that while we breathe, we hope. And where we are met with cynicism and doubts and those who tell us that we can't, we will respond with that timeless creed that sums up the spirit of a people: Yes, we can.

Thank you. God bless you. And may God bless the United States of America.

Chapter 25

Dr. King's Vision of America
"I Have a Dream"

Martin Luther King Jr.

Editor's Introduction: Since many believe that the election of Barack Obama as President of the United States in 2008 constitutes the fulfillment of Martin Luther King Jr.'s dream from 1963, let the readers of this volume compare the two speeches and decide the extent to which they may be right.

I am happy to join with you today in what will go down in history as the greatest demonstration for freedom in the history of our nation. Five score years ago, a great American, in whose symbolic shadow we stand, signed the Emancipation Proclamation. This momentous decree came as a great beacon light of hope to millions of Negro slaves who had been seared in the flames of withering injustice. It came as a joyous daybreak to end the long night of captivity.

But one hundred years later, we must face the tragic fact that the Negro is still not free. One hundred years later, the life of the Negro is still sadly crippled by the manacles of segregation and the chains of discrimination. One hundred years later, the Negro lives on a lonely island of poverty in the midst of a vast ocean of material prosperity. One hundred years later the Negro is still languishing in the comers of American society and finds himself an exile in his own land. So we have come here today to dramatize an appalling condition.

In a sense we have come to our nation's capital to cash a check. When the architects of our republic wrote the magnificent words of the Constitution and the Declaration of Independence, they were signing a promissory note to which every American was to fall heir. This note was a promise that all men would be guaranteed the unalienable rights of life, liberty, and the pursuit of happiness.

It is obvious today that America has defaulted on this promissory note insofar as her citizens of color are concerned. Instead of honoring this sacred obligation, America has given the Negro people a bad check; a check which has come back marked "insufficient funds." But we refuse to believe that the bank of justice is bankrupt. We refuse to believe that there are insufficient funds in the great vaults of opportunity of this nation. So we have come to cash this check a check that will give us upon demand the riches of freedom and the security of justice. We have also come to this hallowed spot to remind America of the fierce urgency of now. This is no time to engage in the luxury of cooling off or to take the tranquilizing drug of gradualism. Now is the time to make real the promises of democracy. Now is the time to rise from the dark and desolate valley of segregation to the sunlit path of racial justice. Now is the time to open the doors of opportunity to all of God's children. Now is the time to lift our nation from the quicksands of racial injustice to the solid rock of brotherhood.

It would be fatal for the nation to overlook the urgency of the moment and to underestimate the determination of the Negro. This sweltering summer of the Negro's legitimate discontent will not pass until there is an invigorating autumn of freedom and equality. Nineteen sixty-three is not an end, but a beginning. Those who hope that the Negro needed to blow off steam and will now be content will have a rude awakening if the nation returns to business as usual. There will be neither rest nor tranquility in America until the Negro is granted his citizenship rights. The whirlwinds of revolt will continue to shake the foundations of our nation until the bright day of justice emerges.

But there is something that I must say to my people who stand on the warm threshold which leads into the palace of justice. In the process of gaining our rightful place, we must not be guilty of wrongful deeds. Let us not seek to satisfy our thirst for freedom by drinking from bitterness and hatred. We must forever conduct our struggle on the high plane of dignity and discipline. We must not allow our creative protest to degenerate into physical violence. Again and again we must rise to the majestic heights of meeting physical force with soul force. The marvelous new militancy which has engulfed the Negro community must not lead us to a distrust of all white people, for many of our white brothers, as evidenced by their presence here today, have come to realize that their destiny is tied up with our destiny and their freedom is inextricably bound to our freedom. We cannot walk alone.

And as we walk, we must make the pledge that we shall march ahead. We cannot turn back. There are those who are asking the devotees of civil rights,

"When will you be satisfied?" We can never be satisfied as long as the Negro is the victim of the unspeakable horrors of police brutality. We can never be satisfied as long as our bodies, heavy with the fatigue of travel, cannot gain lodging in the motels of the highways and the hotels of the cities. We cannot be satisfied as long as the Negro's basic mobility is from a smaller ghetto to a larger one. We can never be satisfied as long as a Negro in Mississippi cannot vote and a Negro in New York believes he has nothing for which to vote. No, no, we are not satisfied, and will not be satisfied until justice rolls down like waters and righteousness like a mighty stream.

I am not unmindful that some of you have come here out of great trials and tribulations. Some of you have come fresh from narrow jail cells. Some of you have come from areas where your quest for freedom left you battered by the storms of persecution and staggered by the winds of police brutality. You have been the veterans of creative suffering. Continue to work with the faith that unearned suffering is redemptive.

Go back to Mississippi, go back to Alabama, go back to South Carolina, go back to Georgia, go back to Louisiana, go back to the slums and ghettos of our modern cities, knowing that somehow this situation can and will be changed. Let us not wallow in the valley of despair.

I say to you today my friends, that in spite of the difficulties and frustrations of the moment I still have a dream. It is a dream deeply rooted in the American dream.

I have a dream that one day this nation will rise up and live out the true meaning of its creed: "We hold these truths to be self-evident; that all men are created equal."

I have a dream that one day on the red hills of Georgia the sons of former slaves and the sons of former slave owners will be able to sit down together at the table of brotherhood.

I have a dream that one day even the state of Mississippi, a desert state sweltering in the heat of injustice and oppression, will be transformed into an oasis of freedom and justice.

I have a dream that my four little children will one day live in a nation where they will not be judged by the color of their skin but by the content of their character.

I have a dream today.

I have a dream that one day the state of Alabama, whose governor's lips are presently dripping with the words of interposition and nullification, will be transformed into a situation where little black boys and black girls will be able to join hands with little white boys and white girls and walk together as sisters and brothers.

I have a dream today.

I have a dream that one day every valley shall be exalted, every hill and mountain shall be made low, the rough places will be made plains, and the crooked places will be made straight, and the glory of the Lord shall be revealed, and all flesh shall see it together.

This is our hope. This is the faith with which I return to the South. With this faith we will be able to hew out of the mountain of despair a stone of hope. With this faith we will be able to transform the jangling discords of our nation into a beautiful symphony of brotherhood. With this faith we will be able to work together, to pray together, to struggle together, to go to jail together, to stand up for freedom together, knowing that we will be free one day.

This will be the day when all of God's children will be able to sing with meaning "My country 'tis of thee, sweet land of liberty, of thee I sing. Land where my fathers died, land of the pilgrim's pride, from every mountainside, let freedom ring."

And if America is to be a great nation this must become true. So let freedom ring from the prodigious hilltops of New Hampshire. Let freedom ring from the mighty mountains of New York. Let freedom ring from the heightening Alleghenies of Pennsylvania!

Let freedom ring from the snowcapped Rockies of Colorado.

Let freedom ring from the curvaceous peaks of California!

But not only that; let freedom ring from Stone Mountain of Georgia!

Let freedom ring from Lookout Mountain of Tennessee!

Let freedom ring from every hill and molehill of Mississippi. From every mountainside, let freedom ring.

When we let freedom ring, when we let it ring from every village and every hamlet, from every state and every city, we will be able to speed up that day when all of God's children, black men and white men, Jews and Gentiles, Protestants and Catholics, will be able to join hands and sing in the words of the old Negro spiritual, "Free at last! Free at last! Thank God Almighty, we are free at last!"

PART 5
AFRICAN AMERICAN
RELIGIOUS CREATIVITY

Chapter 26

The Spirituals
"Understanding Spirituals"

Miles Mark Fisher

.

Editor's Introduction: Miles Mark Fisher (1899–1970), minister,
educator, church historian, published his book *Negro Slave Songs in
the United States* in 1953. The research for the book was undertaken
for his PhD at the University of Chicago. The book won the
American Historical Association's award for the outstanding history
volume of the year. His discussion and analysis of the origins and
functions of the Spirituals has not been surpassed. They constitute
the oldest surviving records of the consciousness of enslaved Africans
and their creative imagination. Most important, the work reveals
the cultural hybridity of their creators, who integrated Western and
African elements of music, lyrics, rhythm, and meter.

The one hundred thirty-six slave songs in the earliest collection, with its
thirty-six variant songs, were products of a particular time and place and were
meaningless outside of that frame of reference. Negro songs collected at a later
date infrequently added fresh spirituals but never altered the story of Negroes in
the Western Hemisphere.

A spiritual may be defined as the utterance of an individual Negro about an experience that had universal application at whatever time that song was popular. . . .

Such a euphonious response included facts with which the singer was acquainted. Derivative or variant spirituals are independent or borrowed reactions to similar environmental circumstances. A combination of several songs which a person might call upon to express his soul upon a particular occasion may form a spiritual medley. The English-speaking people consider as spirituals only Negro songs which incorporate religious terminology, even though differing types of Negro songs often grow from identical experiences.

When the black masses had few thoughts which they could express understandingly about a given situation, their songs were necessarily very brief and often repetitive. As the store of information of an original singer increased, primary themes became the subject of derivative or variant spirituals by the change of just a single word or concept. New stanzas were thus created. Freedmen inherited a meager vocabulary. As they grew in knowledge, they added new themes to their songs, largely by combining existing spirituals with new material into medleys.

The originators of spirituals would hardly have believed their ears had they heard Marian Anderson on Easter, 1939, sing their songs to an estimated 75,000 people at the base of Lincoln's Monument, in Washington, D. C. Spirituals with formal titles are now to be found listed on programs of artists, to be sung either by groups or by soloists, in a cappella fashion or with orchestra, piano, or organ accompaniment. All approximations of the original language of the spirituals simply provide transportation for the thoughts of Negroes. These songs were used by the black masses, and their incorrect grammar is not exaggerated. Only the historical classification of spirituals preserves their primary emphases. Without concern for the music of the masters Negroes employed rhythmical songs to provide creature comforts, to accompany menial labor, to learn facts, to sell commodities, and to share religion. In all life situations Negroes expressed themselves euphoniously. The originators of spirituals would be most surprised to find their musical reactions to their environments catalogued and preserved in libraries purporting to tell this or that about black folk.

Spirituals, though orally transmitted, were actually history . . . The book, *Slave Songs of the United States*, was advertised and widely sold as illumining the history of Negro people in the United States. The collectors of these songs substantiated their assertions with contemporary data. Internal evidence attests that all the songs were developmental. For example, Moses was understood in the eighteenth century to be Bishop Francis Asbury. Later he stood for a Negro and frequently attended camp meetings. All at once he was transported to Africa. There he again assumed religious significance as referred to in sacred literature and Negroes begged him to come back to the United States and miraculously to stretch out his rod in order that slaves might walk to Africa on dry land. One of his main commissions in the United States was to tell Pharaoh to let the slaves go to the Promised Land. In spirituals no distinction was made among the various Biblical Marys. Weeping Mary was ejected from white churches for shouting, was colonized in Africa, and was mysteriously returned to the secret meetings of American slaves. She was at the tomb of Jesus on the resurrection morning. Likewise, heaven was located up north, in Africa, in secret meetings, or up above. Such evolution gave color to spirituals.

Besides giving impressions of real occurrences, spirituals are at the same time contemporary historical documents of these events. Spirituals gave the Negro's side of what happened to him. The original singers did not have enough knowledge to dissemble. No song seemed to have originated without possessing an author, date and place of composition, message, and kindred accompaniments.

At least eight kinds of material went into the making of spirituals. (1) First came the African. Traces of the ancient institution of the secret meetings survived in Negro spirituals. In spirituals African beliefs and customs were preserved. The way in which Africans passed on the traditions of their ancestors from generation to generation through music, instrumental and vocal, and through rhythm or dancing and emotionalism was clearly evident. Professional people, prophets, and "doctors" were the human transmitters of the tradition.

(2) Among those who noticed the influence of *nonhymnal European airs* upon Negro spirituals was Fanny Kemble, who mentioned Scotch and Irish tunes. The former were later noticed by Higginson, the various Fisk collectors, Barton, and Wallaschek. Negroes printed original songs and others for distribution and called them "ballets." This Scotch influence came into Negro singing about 1755 when Presbyterian ministers around Hanover, Virginia, distributed Scotch songbooks among slaves, and Scotch-Irish slaveholders might have continued the process.

(3) About the same time in the eighteenth century *hymns* were introduced among slaves by Samuel Davies. The *Psalms and Hymns* of Isaac Watts and the songs of Charles Wesley, Samuel Davies, John Leland, Lemuel Burkitt, Richard Allen, and others helped to create waves of revivalism. These hymn writers and others through the Civil War period permanently influenced spirituals both in their arrangements, with verses first and then chorus, and in their theology, vocabulary, meter, rhythm, and tunes. Spirituals rendered without part singing show Oriental influence.

(4) *White songs* of the North American nineteenth century possibly influenced spirituals. Many secular songs but no religious ones are cited in *Slave Songs of the United States.*

(5) *Christianity* rarely occurred as an element in antebellum spirituals. The characters mentioned in slave songs were, to be sure, Oriental. The prominence of Moses might be due to Jewish theology. A Haitian has suggested, however, that Moses was a main character of voodooism. When Moses came from the mountain, he found the people worshiping a golden calf, which in that French-speaking country is *veau d'or*, possibly giving a name to voodooism. Negroes

have testified to the presence of supernatural voices and of angels ever since their introduction into the Americas.

(6) Spirituals about Pilgrim, the chief actor of Bunyan's allegorical *Pilgrim's Progress*, were omitted from the earliest collection but not from other songbooks published since Reconstruction days.

(7) *Representative Christians* were not mentioned by spirituals until the nineteenth century, when Richard Fuller and officials of his Beaufort church were definitely named along with the great Lincoln. General Hawley was the only benefactor of Negroes in the Union Army who was mentioned in a slave song. Not one of the numerous missionaries was so honored.

(8) The great spiritual events of *American history* were frequent subjects of spirituals. Slave songs throw light upon camp meetings, African colonization, the oral instruction of Negroes after 1831, work and leisure-time activities of Negro slaves, the Civil War with its soldiers, education, and evangelism, and the Reconstruction. How Negroes accepted Americanization is told with some color. Had every spiritual been preserved, a complete story of every emotion of American Negroes would be available.

The fact that, around New Orleans, spirituals were heard mostly in Baptist churches led one collector to observe that their originators were primarily of that denomination. This conclusion appeared to be rather generally true of freedom spirituals, which coincided in minutiae with the development of that denomination. Pre-Civil War spirituals were not denomination-conscious, being scattered among all the popular Protestant denominations and among Roman Catholic Negroes. To claim that most spirituals were Baptist would be logical as that denomination included the greatest number of the illiterate black masses who had no other means to make known the longings of their hearts.

The nondenominational spirituals express the individuality of their author. As a matter of fact, all except perhaps five slave songs refer to the singer, if no more than to his body, his clothing, his family relations, and his words to an audience. Ordinarily, they are in the first person, using "I," "my," "me," and "we." By this use of the first person in the songs an attempt was made "to find concrete expressions for the origin of a tribe or community" by using personification, as was done in the Old Testament in the case of the Semites.

These individual authors of spirituals described themselves. Some of them were persons who held tenaciously to their African heritage; others of them accepted acculturation; some were slaves; others were freedmen. Perhaps the people of Liberia, either actual or hopeful colonists, emerged as leading makers of spirituals with their themes of "home," "Jacob's ladder," and "roll, Jordan, roll" and with their words "no mo' " rainfall to wet you or "no mo' " peck of corn for me, "I can't stay *behind* [away]," and "swing low, sweet chariot," as well as songs about the ship of Zion. Not one of the originators of spirituals was a preacher in the Christian sense of the word as a person publicly set apart for the ministry. Songsters were lay leaders though "professional" people. They lined or deaconed hymns as was done with the colonial *Bay Psalm Book* of

1640, which used mostly common meter, although some Psalms were in long or hallelujah meter. Among Negroes, who never had sufficient books of praise, this custom proved very convenient. Almost everywhere in the South and in some places in the North, Negro churches lined hymns. Dr. Barton mentioned a "Sister Bumaugh" who was such a song leader; James Weldon Johnson named two more; and the author's Uncle Mark was another. It seems probable that Denmark Vesey, Nat Turner, and Harriet Tubman were authors of specific spirituals.

At first blush, it might appear that these leaders of song were simply furthering the function of American church deacons. They did further their work, but they also continued their African heritage. They originated spirituals to help along their hymns. In song, these leaders would state the theme about which they were singing in a short chorus, the last line of which was the key to what the group should say after each utterance:

> LEADER: There's a union in the heaven where I belong.
> There's a union in the heaven where I belong. There's a union in the heaven where I belong. I belong to the Union band.

By that time the group knew what the leader was saying:

> LEADER: O brother, didn't I tell you so?
> CONGREGATION: I belong to the Union band.

> LEADER: O brothers, didn't I tell you so?
> CONGREGATION: I belong to the Union band.

The chorus sometimes followed two or more utterances of the leader, who made verses about the deacon, sister, preacher, and so forth. This song was originally sung by a Methodist, who used the words, "There's free grace a-plenty where I belong."

There are several objections to the popular Lorenz-White-Johnson-Jackson theory that Negro spirituals were copied from white revival songs of the nineteenth century. The internal and external evidences of slave songs point to conditions under which only Negroes lived and died. The exponents of the white-to-Negro song trend were not familiar with the special historical field to which spirituals belong.

Derivative devotional song material of Negroes, though it might embody musical and folkloristic characteristics and evidence of the behavior of Negroes, is not considered here. The internal evidence of slave songs, shows, first, that they preserve the reactions of Negroes to contemporary situations. As a rule, the Negro occasion for a spiritual antedated the no-occasion of a similar white song. For example, the earliest white song on the "home" concept was printed (probably soon after its origin) nine years after the Negro spiritual on that theme. Sometimes white songs came to life as long as thirty-six years after the occasion for a Negro spiritual. Secondly, only Negroes in the Americas experienced hereditary slavery or the racial emancipation which produced spirituals. Thirdly, Negroes did not sing otherworldly songs like white people, or, if they did, their meaning expressed frustrated this-worldly desires. Finally, simple historical documents are not developed from extended ones, just as the Gospel of Mark did not come from the Gospel of Matthew.

The external evidence of spirituals also disproves the white-to-Negro song trend. Annanias Davisson, the American founder of the so-called "white spirituals," initiated choral church singing by white people because mountain white people protested against slaveholding Presbyterians of Virginia using adult Negro slaves and rearing slave children for choir duty. The whites sang spiritual songs like the Negroes just like the later minstrels invaded the stage. White choral singers frowned upon the "shouting" with which Negroes accompanied their songs, but white people soon incorporated this feature as characteristic of their own efforts. Aristocratic southerners paid no attention to criticisms of their actions and used Negroes for their choirs until the Civil War. It is not known just when untrained white singers were first invited, as were Negroes, to sing to cultivated white audiences.

The earliest and latest spirituals have not been included in this study, which has been limited chiefly to songs of the eighteenth and nineteenth centuries, which outline the history of the residence of Negroes in the United States through the Civil War. Spirituals tell how Negroes attempted to spread brotherhood by the sword, took flight to "better" territory when possible, became pacific in the United States, and laid hold upon another world as a last resort. While constantly keeping in mind their ancient African cult, under the influence of Civil War missionaries Negroes sang old and new songs. Some old songs are in African languages, suggesting that Africans transplanted their native song heritage into the Americas. As a matter of fact, the customs of secret meetings and of elaborate dress for worship arrived with transplanted Africans not later than the sixteenth century. With culture available to the black masses, Negroes seized more literate means of appraising contemporary happenings, keeping records, and promoting religion.

The first areas into which the religious cries of the black masses were introduced were the West Indies and South America, but the same types of Negro song flourished everywhere in the Americas. Spirituals came into North America in Virginia probably with the first Negroes of 1619. As more and more labor came to be supplied by Negroes, spirituals found places in other early settlements along the Atlantic coast. Variant songs followed the population across the Alleghenies, to the Far South, and eventually beyond the Mississippi to the Far West. In the earliest collection of slave songs there seem to be primary historical songs from the West. Spirituals are available particularly from places where something extraordinary in Negro life occurred. These songs outlined the significant developments of the Negro people, which would hardly have been different if every Negro song were found. Knowable facts of life do not vary with environments.

The chief reason for continuing the African institution of the secret meetings upon American soil was to initiate Negro youth into life processes. At first this was done peacefully, until the cult found that it must plan local resistance against those who sought to defeat the religious ideals of Negroes. Virginia legislators were afraid of the insurrectionary possibilities of such meetings as early as 1676. Vocal and instrumental music and bodily rhythm accompanied the ritual and orientation of such meetings. Insurrections practically ceased in the years immediately prior to the American Revolution, for it appeared that all of the slaves would be manumitted. If songs of this epoch in North America were available, some of them would, no doubt, be joyous.

Slave songs reveal the saddened condition of Negro life and the hardships of slave labor after the cotton gin was successfully put into operation. Christian churches did not help the situation when they ejected slaves from their services for demonstrating their religious emotion by shouting. Some Negroes still hoped for a happy solution to their problems in the scheme of the American Colonization Society (1816) to send free Negroes outside the United States, with their consent. Others successfully made their escape from slavery, first with the help of other Negroes and then aided by underground sympathizers along the route to freedom. Still others were militant and plotted local rebellion against white people.

Nat Turner and his associates killed scores of white people in Southampton County, Virginia, in 1831. His revolt left unforgettable memories in the minds of black and white people alike and caused international repercussions. The Negro race was penalized. For the first time conservative leadership gained ascendancy among Negroes and cautioned slaves to do their best to get along with their white overlords in North America. The black masses were not impressed with the kind of life which was expected of them in the South, and thousands ran away annually to escape the terror of retribution after Turner's insurrection. Many of them again hoped for African colonization. This racial and national crisis developed songs of otherworldly yearning. Then it was that abolitionism entered the field. Public opinion debated the merits of the slave system, and the South improved conditions. Not only did Negroes generally receive better treatment, but they were permitted to share somewhat in the administration of the slave system, in which they made a grand success even though the black masses hated their Negro drivers.

The two sections of the United States only drifted farther and farther apart in the dispute over abolition, while the West Indies, South America, and Central America granted Negroes statutory freedom. The Civil War between the North and the South over the slavery issue lasted from 1861 to 1865. In this, the black masses fought heroically both with the North and with the South and in the end gained emancipation. The benefits of education and evangelism both in and out of the army were gratuitously furnished the new freedmen by Yankee soldiers and missionaries, but a reaction against freed Negroes set in all over the South. In an effort to better their conditions, some ex-slaves accepted the Christianity of the missionaries, and some of them went to free territory—most frequently to Canada, the North, and Africa. With their backs to the wall some others resorted to violence, while the black masses of the South suffered and could but rely upon their God. This story was reflected in slave songs.

Derivative devotional songs of the black masses, popularly labeled Negro spirituals, do not illustrate unmistakably that the primary historical purpose of the songs was to recite the story of Negroes in their reactions to incidents in their environment. True spirituals originated shortly after the chief incidents which gave rise to them had passed over, and all the songs derived from them fulfill a threefold secondary purpose: to preserve the outline of the religious development of Negroes, to supply basic songs which could be adapted to other uses, and to describe the conditions under which Negroes had to live.

First, spirituals trace the evolution of the religious institutions of Negroes. This may be illustrated by the following chart:

NEGRO SLAVE SONGS IN THE UNITED STATES

African Secret Meetings

American Valley
or "Wilderness" Convocations

| Praise Houses | Independent Negro Churches | Holiness Movement |

African secret meetings were transplanted to colonies in the Americas. These convocations, sung about in spirituals of the "valley" or the "wilderness," were prohibited by law in North America at Virginia from about 1642. Not only were these secret meetings of "praise" institutionalized in island communities of North America as praise houses, but also these assemblies gave rise to independent Negro churches. David George, pastor of the earliest known Negro church in North America, at Silver Bluff, South Carolina, in about 1773 wrote an account of his first awakening to religion at a secret meeting, saying, "A man of color, named Cyrus, who came from Charleston, South Carolina, to Silver Bluff, told me one day in the woods, that if I lived so (unconverted), I should never see the face of God in glory. . . . I thought then that I must be saved by prayer."[1] Later in the eighteenth century the Bethel African Methodist Episcopal Church and the St. Thomas Protestant Episcopal Church, both of Philadelphia, sprang from the benevolent Free African Society of male members only and dedicated their first houses of worship in 1794.[2] The mother church

1. John Rippon, *The Baptist Annual Register for 1790–1800* (London, [n.d.]), p. 475.
2. Charles H. Wesley, *Richard Allen, Apostle of Freedom* (Washington, ca.1936), pp.61, 78.

of the African Methodist Episcopal Zion denomination was instituted in New York City in 1796 in praise services of ten men.[3] The holiness movement among black people was contained within established churches, as Wesley intended it, until 1889, when the Church of the Living God, Christian Workers for Fellowship, emerged on the Arkansas frontier at Wrightsville with "fraternal points of doctrine known only to members of the organization."[4]

The doctrines of Negro churches were, of course, superficially Christian, but in truth they were the traditional beliefs of the secret meetings. Spirituals stressed the parts of their devotional services which were more important than their denominational tenets, namely, music, reading from a sacred book, preaching, and emotional devotion.

(1) The more emphasis placed upon music, the more attractive have been the praise houses, the independent Negro churches, and the holiness movement. A piano or an organ and musical instruments have come to be substituted for native African instruments. If, at a time of silence in the worship, those modern instruments should strike up a familiar spiritual in rhythm, one would most likely hear feet beating out the time in place of African drums. Syncopated gospel choruses have carried rhythmic singing in Negro churches to the extreme since 1933, while trained choirs have come to supply the music in more conservative areas. The popular hymns of Watts and other hymn writers are retained to this day in the hymnals of independent Negro churches.

(2) Reading from a sacred book has been an element of traditional importance in Negro meetings.

(3) Preaching, or the utterance of a leader of worship, has occupied a unique place. This element obtained from the beginning of spirituals. Preaching to the black masses has in many cases remained a singsong affair with a deep guttural accompaniment like in "a-weeping or a-moaning." It is interesting to note that those independent Negro preachers who can "moan" their gospel, a method now dignified by its resemblance to the intonation and chanting of Roman Catholicism and to the head resonance taught in public speaking, are the pastors of the larger and more influential churches of the black masses, while those who intellectualize the gospel must remain in smaller churches, if at all, or in classrooms denouncing the administrations of independent Negro churches. The pay of a preacher is largely dependent upon his ability to please his audience.

(4) Emotionalism or shouting was once a happy part of devotion to which almost any spiritual was adapted. Summer "revivals" were fixed shouting times for the majority of rural churches. Even urban ones ordinarily included one or two annual revivals in their programs.

3. Christopher Rush, *A Short Account of the Rise and Progress of the African M. E. Church in America* (New York, 1843), p. 10.

4. *United States Census of Religious Bodies: 1936, Bulletin II,* Part I (Washington, 1941), p. 491.

If a preacher who sang was secured to conduct these revivals, the occasion was successful from the start. Shouting might or might not be serious business for Negroes; it certainly was happy recreation for many people.

Secondly, spirituals were developed first, and then so-called secular songs followed. Spirituals gave rise to syncopated rhythm. A Negro dance band in Wheeling, now West Virginia, in the early nineteenth century, consisted of three pieces—"two bangies" and "a lute, through which a chicksaw breathed with much occasional exertion and violent gesticulations."[5] The development of this syncopated rhythm may be traced further in the exploitation of Negro worship on Congo Square in New Orleans for secular purposes. It has been said that jazz sprang from spirituals;[6] swing music also in the nineteenth century has been described as "relatively brief, spontaneous, full of improvisation. . . ." This description coincides precisely with the characteristics which spirituals reveal.

"Blues" originated during the first quarter of the nineteenth century. The black masses used blues "as a vehicle for expressing the individual mood of the moment."[7] This commentator, after the thought of W. C. Handy, wrote that their three lines (instead of two or four) are a structural peculiarity, but spirituals of three lines[8] and with other structural irregularities exist which do not show hymnal influences. It has been admitted that blues are woven from the same stuff as work songs, love songs, and so forth. They are all, in fact, developments from spirituals. A teenager once remarked that jazz made one pat his feet and swing on the outside while a spiritual might create the same emotion on the inside.

Spirituals have furnished the initial tune vocabulary for all kinds of Negro songs.[9] Songs about "de field" and other work songs were developed from spirituals. "Deep River" spirituals about slaves having to work in the burning sun and chilling rains were work songs, as were the spirituals "Rain Fall and Wet Becca Lawton" and "Wait, Poor Daniel." "Poor Rosy, Poor Gal" was a spiritual and also a love song. The "*You'd Better Min'*" song about "rock[a] my soul in a de bosom of Abraham" was a spiritual and a nursery song before there were Negro lullabies. A variant of "Turn, Sinner" was sung while digging a well. In the "I Am Bound for the Promised Land" period, "Jerdan's mills a-grinding" was originated at tasks at the mill. Railroad songs came about after Negroes worked on railroads during the Civil War period.[10] Spirituals have indeed supplied themes for other Negro music.

5. Thomas Ashe, Travels in America, Performed in 1808 (Newburyport, 1808), p. 100.

6. Frederic Ramsey, If. and Charles Edward Smith (ed.), *Jazzmen* (New York, 1939), p. 7; Wilder Hobson, *American Jazz Music* (New York, 1937), p.16.

7. Abbe Niles, "Introduction," in W. C. Handy (ed.), *Blues, an Anthology* (New York, 1921), p. 1.

8. William Francis Allen, Charles Pickard Ware, and Lucy McKim Garrison, *Slave Songs of the United States* (New York, 1929), pp.19,26,59,98,102f.

9. Newman I. White, *American Negro Folk-Songs* (Cambridge, 1928), pp.455; Mellows Kennedy, *Black Cameos* (York, 1925), pp. 20–23, 25, 26ff.

10. Barton, *Old Plantation Hymns*, pp. 33 f.; White, *American Negro Folk-Songs*, pp. 189 ff., 261 ff.

Finally, spirituals have reflected the social conditions under which Negroes were forced to live. Civil War missionaries in North America found two classes of Negroes in the South. In one class were house servants who had been used to the "white" bread of their masters. In the other were field hands, representatives of the black masses, who were half-fed, poorly housed, ignorant, licentious, and sometimes maimed. Because of their lack of opportunity and abject poverty they looked as badly as they were treated. Casual observers could not detect that they were brokenhearted, for they appeared lighthearted. When the thorn pricked them too much, they showed defiance. They found much to laugh at when Americans did not even smile.

The black masses have preserved the spirituals. Acculturated Negroes have generally neglected them unless they were edited. Alexander Payne, during his ministry, about 1845, might be said to have represented the type of educated Negro who opposes the singing of spirituals. Bishop Payne commonly wrote of them as "rings," songs of "fist and heel worshipers," "cornfield ditties," and voodoo dances. He said: "The time is at hand when the ministry of the A.M.E. Church must drive out this heathenish mode of worship or drive out all the intelligence, refinement, and practical Christians . . ."

Uneducated Negroes were so attached to their old songs, their spirituals, that in freedom old spiritual themes were combined with the new songs taught to Negroes by Civil War missionaries. The masses were unprepared, however, to commit to writing the songs which they were singing, and so William Francis Allen, Charles Richard Ware, Lucy McKim, and certain other white people published *Slave Songs of the United States*. In the first sentence of their book the editors wondered "why no systematic effort has hitherto been made to collect and preserve their [Negroes'] melodies." Outside of this collection, the public was content to forget these creative songs. Many Civil War missionaries were unresponsive to them. Later, however, the Fisk University singers met with little success upon concert platforms until they startled their audiences with spirituals. Collectors promptly wrote out the music, rhymed the words, and cheaply sold booklets containing these songs. (The editing done by these collectors fortunately did not completely destroy the spirituals.) Spirituals thereafter were feverishly collected but edited almost out of recognition.

Negroes evidently had something that offset the wretched and unmoral pictures that were usually drawn of their total situations, something that gave them the strength to survive overwhelming hardships. Help from the federal government in preventing starvation and persecution by the Ku Klux Klan in the Reconstruction period and the noble efforts of missionaries, handicapped by lack of workers and means, cannot entirely explain why the turmoil of emancipation did not create a worse reaction in the Negro people. One of the reasons why it did not was the uncommon strength of the Negro spirit, and a major source of this strength was the spirituals. Spirituals were the safety valve of the Negro people through which they permitted pent-up energies to escape, and because of this they saved their souls and did not insist upon unconditional surrender to their ideals even though other Americans did.[11] Many Negroes succumbed to the rigors of American slavery, and all of them might perhaps have become dispirited and have died out, according to expectations, had they not had their songs in the night.

The Negro spirit as displayed through spirituals has permeated and colored the entire United States. Spirituals have introduced certain barbarisms into the American language and they have spread abroad the Negro dialect. The popularity of spirituals in Europe is too well known to need rehearsal here. In both the Eastern and the Western hemispheres have the spirituals captured their listeners. Perhaps never before have the songs of a people woven such charms.

11. Paul Hutchinson, "'Unconditional Surrender'—Again," *Christian Century*, LXV (June 9, 1948), 567–568.

Chapter 27

The Black Church
The Genius of the Negro Church

Benjamin Elijah Mays
and Joseph William Nicholson

Editor's Introduction: Benjamin Elijah Mays (1894–1984), minister, educator, scholar, mentor to Martin Luther King Jr., and president of Morehouse College in Atlanta, Georgia, collaborated with Joseph William Nicholson to write and publish *The Negro's Church* in 1933. The book's title reveals its emphasis on ownership, which, from their point of view, specified the genius of the institution as explicated in the book's final chapter that is printed below. Throughout his life, Mays was interested primarily in two major concerns: namely, the dignity of the individual person and the gap between America's ideals and its practices. The black church's response to both of these interests is contained in the following excerpt as well as being the primary message of Martin Luther King Jr.

THE GENIUS OF THE NEGRO CHURCH

Perhaps the reader feels that the analysis of the Negro church so far presented, though encouraging here and there, gives a rather dark picture; and that it offers nothing exceptionally promising for the future church life of 12,000,000 people.

The analysis reveals that the status of the Negro church is in part the result of the failure of American Christianity in the realm of race-relations; that the church's program, except in rare instances, is static, non-progressive, and fails to challenge the loyalty of many of the most critically-minded Negroes; that the vast majority of its pastors are poorly trained academically, and more poorly trained theologically; that more than half of the sermons analyzed are abstract, other-worldly, and imbued with a magical conception of religion; that in the church school less than one-tenth of the teachers are college graduates; that there are too many Negro churches; that the percentage of Negro churches in debt is high; that for the most part the Negro church is little concerned with juvenile delinquency and other social problems in its environment; that less than half of the reported membership can be relied upon to finance the church regularly and consistently; and that the rural church suffers most because of the instability and poverty of the rural Negroes.

Yet the authors believe that there is in the genius or the "soul" of the Negro church something that gives it life and vitality, that makes it stand out significantly above its buildings, creeds, rituals and doctrines, something that makes it a unique institution. For this reason, the writers, in this chapter, lean more heavily than in previous chapters upon the observations and personal experiences gained during the two year, intensive study of the Negro church; and these are supplemented here and there by the experiences of the race.

THE CHURCH IS THE NEGRO'S VERY OWN

The church was the first community or public organization that the Negro actually owned and completely controlled. And it is possibly true to this day that the Negro church is the most thoroughly owned and controlled public institution of the race. Nothing can compare with this ownership and control except ownership of the home and possibly control of the Negro Lodge. It is to be doubted whether Negro control is as complete in any other area of Negro life, except these two, as it is in the church.

A statement of this character may sound paradoxical in the light of the facts discovered in the chapter on finance, which show that 71.3 per cent of the churches of this study are in debt. But churches are unique institutions, for which reason they enjoy special privileges.

Churches, unlike houses and business enterprises, are not very valuable to their creditors. Residence property, if taken from the buyer, is usually very valuable, and may return a profit. This is not true with churches. A church taken over by creditors is generally of little value to them and usually cannot be used for any other purpose. Ordinarily the financiers want the money and not the church; and they are not concerned with either the ownership or the control of the church. Another reason is the good reputation enjoyed by churches for eventually paying off their debts. Thus, for both of these reasons, indebtedness on churches generally does not involve loss of control to the creditors.

Furthermore, a glance through the chapter on finance shows that the huge total indebtedness of the Negro churches is more striking because of the high percentage of churches in debt than because of the amount of the indebtedness per church.

For example, 45.6 per cent of the 386 churches in debt have an average indebtedness of less than $5,000; and only 15.0 per cent of them have debts ranging between $25,000 and $160,000; with twenty-one owing $50,000 or more, and only three owing more than $100,000.

Even if indebtedness carried control, most of the churches would not be so heavily in debt as to warrant creditor-control. Therefore, whatever the Negro church is in the United States, it is largely the outcome of the Negro's own genius and his ability to organize. Like other institutions it has glaring defects; and improvements in many spheres are greatly needed.

It is equally true, however, that there are hundreds of Negro churches that operate sufficiently well to warrant the commendation of critical minds.

Not only is this institution controlled by Negroes, but nine-tenths of the local churches are self-supporting. A few Negro churches, organically connected with white churches, churches of Negro denominations, and several Baptist churches were helped in an organized way between 1927 and 1931; but during the same period, 88.3 per cent of the churches of this study received no systematic organized support from outside sources. Certainly in the majority of cases the amounts received from outside sources were so negligible that the churches would continue to exist if the outside help were entirely cut off. Even in the cases of the 11.7 per cent of churches that received some organized support due to denominational connections and otherwise, there was sufficient evidence to show that control of the church was primarily in the hands of the Negro congregations.

Through and through, with or without outside help, the Negro churches of this study are principally governed by Negroes. Many Negroes though unable to own homes of their own, take a peculiar pride in their churches. It gives them a sense of ownership that can hardly exist with respect to any other institution in the community. Since thousands do not own their homes, they develop a loyalty and devotion to their churches that command respect and admiration. It is characteristic of the Negro church that the Negro owns it and that it is largely the product of his hand and brain.

OWNERSHIP AND CONTROL PROVIDE OPPORTUNITY FOR THE COMMON MAN

With races and individuals, there must be an opportunity for the development of initiative and self-direction if real character is to be developed, and if hidden potentialities are to be brought to the fore. Certainly the Negro church has been the training school that has given the masses of the race opportunity to develop.

The opportunity found in the Negro church to be recognized, and to be "somebody," has stimulated the pride and preserved the self-respect of many Negroes who would have been entirely beaten by life, and possibly completely submerged. Everyone wants to receive recognition and feel that he is appreciated. The Negro church has supplied this need. A truck driver of average or more than ordinary qualities becomes the chairman of the Deacon Board. A hotel man of some ability is the superintendent of the Sunday church school of a rather important church. A woman who would be hardly noticed, socially or otherwise, becomes a leading woman in the missionary society. A girl of little training and less opportunity for training gets the chance to become the leading soprano in the choir of a great church. These people receive little or no recognition on their daily job. There is nothing to make them feel that they are "somebody." Frequently their souls are crushed and their personalities disregarded. Often they do not feel "at home" in the more sophisticated Negro group. But in the church on X Street, *she* is Mrs. Johnson, the Church Clerk; and *he* is Mr. Jones, the chairman of the Deacon Board.

It can be argued, and justly, that this untrained leadership is partly responsible for the fact that the Negro church has progressed so slowly. But still it is important that recognition and inspiriting opportunity have been given to people who would not have achieved the one or risen to the other elsewhere. Granted also that the same may be said of the churches of other racial groups, nevertheless it can hardly be denied that it is more accentuated among Negroes because they are more highly segregated and restricted in American life.

FREEDOM TO RELAX

The Negro church furnishes the masses, to a less extent now than formerly, an opportunity for self-expression that no other enterprise affords. Not expression in leadership as just described, but release from the restraint, strain and restriction of the daily grind. If in their church services Negroes show more emotion than members of some other racial groups, it can hardly be proved that they are by nature more expressive. The explanation lies in the environmental conditions under which they live. This is true because, as the Negro becomes more intellectual and less restricted in the American life, he becomes less expressive in emotion. A few churches in practically every large-sized American city show the truth of this. But the point urged here is, whatever one may think to the contrary and despite the advance made in the realm of improved race-relations, that as the Negro moves about in most areas of the American Commonwealth he is less free than other Americans. He not only feels, but he knows, that in many places he is not wanted. He knows that in most white churches of the United States he is not desired, even though a sign on the outside of the church may read "Welcome to All." He understands perfectly well that the welcome does not include him. He comprehends clearly that in many of them he would be ushered to the rear or to the gallery, or be refused admission altogether; and in some other instances he would be patronized and tolerated.

A sign on the outside of an important church in a metropolitan southern city reads thus: "We offer riches to the poorest, friendliness to the friendless, comfort to the sorrowing—a welcome to all, step in." But every Negro child in that city is aware of the fact that the invitation is not meant for him . . .

The Negro is conscious of the fact that in many courthouses, city halls, public parks, city auditoriums, institutions supported by the taxes of all the people, he is not a welcomed guest; and that special arrangements must be provided for him. He appreciates the fact that in privately owned stores in many sections, where the money of all groups is sought, places of comfort and relaxation are quite often not provided him; and, if they are, they are provided in such a way as to make him feel humiliated.

The Negro is not unmindful of the fact that as he elbows his way through the crowded thoroughfare, he must be just a little more careful than most people; and that if he were to do what others would be excused for doing, he would be condemned. He works on the job ever aware that to hold his position he must often go the second mile, do more and take more, and work for less money. He must be an epitome of politeness; must smile when ordinarily he would frown; must pretend that it is all right when the respect that is habitually given others is deliberately denied him.

In this tense situation, the Negro lives. In many instances he expresses himself in song, dance and laughter; but for thousands of Negroes this release from restraint, this complete freedom and relaxation for the sake of mere expression, if nothing more than a faint "Amen," a nodding of the head as the minister preaches, a feeling of oneness with the crowd in song and prayer, is to be found only in the Negro church. Here he gathers poise, courage and strength to make it through another week. . . .

It might be urged that this kind of expression is not helpful; that it makes religion an escape from reality; that it serves as an opiate for the people. The possibilities are great that this is true, and that it does happen no one can deny. But whether it is true or not depends in a large measure upon what the minister provides and the kind of instruction he gives the people. If these expressions or outlets help the people to live, they can hardly be set aside as of no value.

NEGRO CHURCH AS COMMUNITY CENTER

Three quotations are illustrative of the use of the Negro church as a social center. George E. Haynes writes:

The Negro as a worker makes contact with the white world when on his job, and receives information, instruction, and stimulus so far as his occupation influences his ways of life. All his leisure-time activities that condition intellectual development and emotional motivation under present conditions of segregated Negro life must find their channel mainly through the principal community agency the Negro has his church.[1]

Forrester Washington states:

From the very beginning the Negro has had to make numerous approximations and substitutions to supply himself with decent recreational opportunities. In both city and country he has made of the Negro church a quasi-community center.[2]

The Mayor's Interracial Committee of Detroit reports in its 1926 Survey:

The Negro has been humiliated in so many public and privately owned institutions and amusement places that he has resorted to the church as a place in which he can be sure of spending his leisure time peacefully. To a large extent it takes the place of the theatre, the dance hall, and similar amusement places, and fills the vacancy created by the failure of public and commercial places of recreation and amusement to give him a cordial welcome. Consequently, the average Negro church in Detroit keeps its doors open constantly for the use of the community. Numerous suppers, lectures, recitals, debates, plays, and the like are given by clubs and individuals from without and within the congregation.

THE CHURCH HAS ENCOURAGED EDUCATION AND NURTURED NEGRO BUSINESS

Through the years, the Negro church through its ministry has encouraged Negroes to educate themselves. The rather naive and blind faith that many Negro parents have had that education is a panacea for all ills came from the Negro pastors. Mostly illiterate, and greatly lacking in formal training himself, he has continually urged the parents of his congregation to sacrifice much in order that their children might enjoy a better day. Many a country boy or girl would never have had the chance to attend college if the pastor of his or her church had not urged it. Even in cases where Negro education was graciously supported by white people who were kindly and justly disposed toward the Negro, the Negro minister was often needed, and relied upon, to give sanction to and boost education. The parents did not always see the light; but the pastor

---

1. Haynes, George E., *The Church and Negro Progress,* The Annals of the American Academy of Political and Social Science, November, 1928.
2. Washington, Forrest B., *Recreational Facilities for the Negro,* The Annals of the American Academy of Political and Social Science, November, 1928.

insisted on it, and somehow the parents believed that the preacher knew. The existence of a large number of weak denominational schools as well as some strong ones is testimony to the fact that the Negro church has greatly encouraged education. Not only has the church urged Negroes to secure an education, but the church has nurtured and still nurtures Negro business. The great medium for the advertisement of Negro business is the church. Not only in sermons but in other ways, the authors were impressed with the way Negro pastors advise their people to help make strong Negro business such as insurance, banking, privately owned Negro enterprises and the like.

DEMOCRATIC FELLOWSHIP

In the main, there are no social classes in the Negro church. In one or two city churches of the 609, there was evidence that some of the members were particular about the people who joined and wanted a "certain brand" for members. In a few cases there was a natural development whereby people of supposedly similar cultural levels assembled. But even in these churches, there are members who represent all grades of culture and varying occupational levels.

In practically all of the 609 churches there exists a thorough democratic spirit. The church is the place where the Negro banker, lawyer, professor, social worker, physician, dentist, and public-school teacher meet the skilled and semi-skilled tradesmen, the maid, the cook, the hotel man, the butler, the chauffeur and the common laborer; and mingle with them. The Negro church still furnishes the best opportunity for Negroes of different social strata and various cultural groups to associate together in a thoroughgoing democratic way.

The Negro race is young in emancipation. It has not had sufficient time to build churches of the wealthy nor of the cultured. As the race gets older in freedom, the number of college-trained business and professional people will inevitably increase. There will be more grouping and mingling among people of similar interest, and the tendency will be in the direction of a more rigid separation between Negroes of different interests and achievements. Up to this time, the Negro church has been one of the most outstanding channels through which this gulf between the "high" and the "low," the "trained" and the "untrained" has been bridged. It will continue to be for years to come; because the vast majority of Negroes who reach the business and professional classes are the sons and daughters of parents whose opportunities for training have been meager and who for the most part have kept this Negro church in operation.

The tendency is, and may continue to be, for the intellectual Negroes to break away from many of our churches because they are not attracted by services that differ so widely from those of the college and university. On the other hand, a good many of these more highly privileged Negroes see great possibilities in Negro churches, and work in them weekly; a goodly number of the Negro students are closely connected with the church. Of 2,594 students, professional and lay people whose attitudes toward the church were ascertained, 67 percent attend church weekly and 56 percent have specific church duties, such as work in the Sunday church school, singing in the choir or some other activity of the church.

As the writers moved about in sixteen communities during the period of the field work of the study, one thing stood out conspicuously—there was a warmth, a spontaneity in worship, and welcome that one could actually feel on entering most Negro churches. In most of them, the atmosphere is congenial and a timid or tense person is set at ease immediately. Perfect relaxation is possible. Frequently it is a hearty handshake by a member of the church, or a cordial greeting by the usher who seems to sense that this man is a stranger, or some word from the pastor in his sermon or at the end of the services. At any rate, the atmosphere is conducive to a feeling of "at-home-ness." To the ultra-sophisticated, it may seem naive and primitive, but there is a virtue in it which the truly wise will not scorn.

TRANSCENDING RACIAL BARRIERS

The democratic fellowship that exists within the race transcends racial barriers in the church. The Negro church generally preaches love and tolerance toward all races and abides by these ideals in its practice. Members of other racial groups are welcomed in Negro churches. Other races experience no rebuffs, no discrimination. Chinese, Japanese, and white people are never deliberately given the back seats in Negro churches. They are never ushered to the gallery for worship. They are never refused admission to Negro churches. If there is any discrimination, it is usually to the advantage of the members of other racial groups. Precaution is taken in Negro churches to see that white visitors are given, not gallery seats, but often the very best seats in the house. The members of churches occupying front seats frequently give their seats to the visitors of other races. They give the stranger and the chance guest of different color, not the worst, but the best.

NEGRO MINISTERS WELCOME WHITE MINISTERS

White ministers are not barred from Negro pulpits.

In the interviews, a few Negro ministers expressed the conviction that they would be perfectly willing to have white ministers preach to their people provided they could preach for the white ministers. But in the vast majority of instances the Negro pastors were willing to have white pastors preach to their people even though they knew that the white ministers would not, or could not, have them preach in their pulpits.

In securing the services of white ministers, most Negro preachers experience no difficulty from their board or congregation. It was the unanimous testimony of the 600 pastors and officials interviewed that their people did not object to visiting white ministers.

Not a single case was observed by the investigators, in interviews and worship, where Negroes did not cordially receive members of other racial groups in their worship. As one minister expressed it: "My church is always glad to have members of any racial group worship with us and I know of no case where our visitors have experienced embarrassments in our church."

Negro ministers who do not invite white pastors because the white ministers cannot invite them, nevertheless insist that in their services no lines shall be drawn against white worshippers.

A POTENTIALLY FREE MINISTRY

It is the firm conviction of the writers that the Negro pastor is one of the freest, as well as most influential, men on the American platform today. This is due to various causes, but chief among them is the factor of the long-time prestige of the Negro minister, the respect for him and for religion; and the poverty and the financial freedom of the Negro church.

It is not the aim of the writers to extol poverty or economic insecurity as a virtue per se. This cannot be done any more than wealth can be set up as a virtue of itself. But there is some virtue in being identified with the under-privileged. It is usually more likely that the man farthest down will advocate complete justice for all than that the man farthest up will. It is hardly possible for the most privileged to be as sensitive to the injustices, the restrictions and the limitations imposed upon the weak as it is for the weak themselves; or for him to feel these wrongs with the same degree of intensity as they are felt by the under-privileged. They who sit in the seat of the mighty, or those who are racially identified with the ruling class, are more likely to feel that they have too much to lose if they begin to champion too ardently the cause of the man farthest down. It is more difficult for them even to see the wrong. The danger is that they view the evil from lofty heights, if at all. They fear economic insecurity and social ostracism, which may come to them if they identify themselves too openly with the oppressed group.

Perhaps the white minister was correct when he said in an interracial seminar that if he were to take an open and vigorous stand in opposing economic and interracial evils the Negroes would have to give him a pastoral charge. Possibly, too, there is much truth in some of the answers given by many white pastors in response to questionnaires on inter-racial church cooperation, that their congregations would not tolerate an exchange of pulpits between Negro and white ministers.

On the other hand, the suffering man feels the sting more keenly and is more likely to complain. Being the under-dog, he has nothing to lose and all to gain when he goes forth in the name of God advocating a square deal for all men. It is not an accident that possibly the most outstanding prophets of religion such as Jesus, Moses, Jeremiah, Isaiah, Micah, Hosea, Amos, and Ezekiel were members of an under-privileged race. It is not argued for a moment that prophets of the ruling class have not and do not exist; but often they must break with the ruling majority and identify themselves with those who suffer. It is simply argued that, all things considered, it is easier for the man who is down to see wrongs and injustices and in many cases easier for him to become an apostle of righteousness.

Thus, one of the main theses of this chapter is that it is a part of the genius of the Negro church that it is owned by a poor race, supported by its members and, further, that this fact alone gives the Negro minister an opportunity and freedom in his church life that ministers of some racial groups might well covet. If the Negro pastor sees fit to condemn from his pulpit practices with respect to low wages, long hours, the working of children in industry, the unfair treatment of women in factories, the denying to the worker the right to organize, and the injustices of an economic system built on competition, self-interest, and profit—he is more likely not to be censured, and less likely to lose his position than his white brother who preaches in the same city. It is more than likely that no committee will wait on him advising him to go slow. No leading financier will walk out of the church threatening never to return. To the contrary, it is highly possible that the Negro minister would receive many congratulations and "Amens" from his congregation if he were to preach such a gospel.

When the Negro pastor feels the urge to preach a thoroughgoing gospel of brotherhood, applying it to the Negroes, whites, Japanese, Chinese, and other races, it is gladly received by Negro audiences. It is taken for granted that Negro ministers will courageously oppose lynching, Jim Crow law, and discrimination in the expenditure of tax money, especially as applied to schools, parks, playgrounds, hospitals, and the like.

This fellowship and freedom inherent in the Negro church should be conducive to spiritual growth of a unique kind. It furnishes the foundation for the Negro church and the Negro ministry to become truly Christian and prophetic in the truest sense. The Negro church has the potentialities to become possibly the greatest spiritual force in the United States. What the Negro church does and will do with these potentialities will depend in a large measure upon the leadership as expressed in the Negro pulpit.

Chapter 28

Black Power
and the Black Churches

Black Theology and Black Power

James H. Cone

Editor's Introduction: On July 31, 1966, a group of black clergy
who were members of the nascent National Conference of Negro
Churchmen (later called National Conference of Black Clergy)
sponsored a full-page ad in the *New York Times* in which they
affirmed the symbol of Black Power. Their action was undertaken at
a time when black churches and civil rights organizations, including
the Southern Christian Leadership Conference, seemed incapable of
responding to what appeared to be an emerging shift among many
toward a more militant race-conscious ideology. It is interesting to
note that most of the signatories to the statement were members
of predominantly white denominations where they had very little
numerical power. Most important, the seven predominantly black
denominations in which the vast majority of black Christians held
membership took no official stance on the issue. Three years later,
following James Forman's widely publicized interruption of the
morning worship service at The Riverside Church in New York
City to read his Black Manifesto demanding reparations, James H.
Cone (1938–) published his *Black Theology and Black Power*, the

185

first of many books that launched and sustained a significantly new movement in theological education. As Professor of Theology at Union Theological Seminary in New York, Cone has attracted and trained at least two generations of African American scholars. The following comprise the respective prefaces to his 1969 and 1989 editions of that first book.

PREFACE TO THE FIRST EDITION

"Black Power" is an emotionally charged term which can evoke either angry rejection or passionate acceptance. Some critics reject Black Power because to them it means blacks hating whites, while others describe it as the doctrine of Booker T. Washington in contemporary form. But the advocates of Black Power hail it as the only viable option for black people. For these persons Black Power means black people taking the dominant role in determining the black-white relationship in American society.

If, as I believe, Black Power is the most important development in American life in this century, there is a need to begin to analyze it from a theological perspective. In this work an effort is made to investigate the concept of Black Power, placing primary emphasis on its relationship to Christianity, the Church, and contemporary American theology.

I know that some religionists would consider Black Power as the work of the Antichrist. Others would suggest that such a concept should be tolerated as an expression of Christian love to the misguided black brother. It is my thesis, however, that Black Power, even in its most radical expression, is not the antithesis of Christianity, nor is it a heretical idea to be tolerated with painful forbearance. It is, rather, Christ's central message to twentieth-century America. And unless the empirical denominational church makes a determined effort to recapture the man Jesus through a total identification with the suffering poor as expressed in Black Power, that church will become exactly what Christ is not.

That most churches see an irreconcilable conflict between Christianity and Black Power is evidenced not only by the de facto segregated structure of their community, but by their typical response to riots: "I deplore the violence but sympathize with the reasons for the violence." Churchmen, laymen and ministers alike, apparently fail to recognize their contribution to the ghetto condition through permissive silence—except for a few resolutions which they usually pass once a year or immediately following a riot and through their co-tenancy of a dehumanizing social structure whose existence depends on the continued enslavement of black people. If the Church is to remain faithful to its Lord, it must make a decisive break with the structure of this society by launching a vehement attack on the evils of racism in all forms. It must become *prophetic,* demanding a radical change in the interlocking structures of this society.

This work, then, is written with a definite attitude, the attitude of an angry black man, disgusted with the oppression of black people in America and with the scholarly demand to be "objective" about it. Too many people have died, and too many are on the edge of death. In fairness to my understanding of the truth, I cannot allow myself to engage in a dispassionate, non-committed debate on the status of the black-white relations in America by assessing the pro and con of Black Power. The scholarly demand for this kind of "objectivity" has come to mean being uninvolved or not taking sides. But as Kenneth B. Clark reminds us, when moral issues are at stake, non-involvement and non-commitment and the exclusion of feeling are neither sophisticated nor objective, but naive and violative of the scientific spirit at its best. When human feelings are part of the evidence, they cannot be ignored. Where anger is the appropriate response, to exclude the recognition and acceptance of anger, and even to avoid the feeling itself as if it were an inevitable contamination, is to set boundaries upon truth itself. If a scholar who studied Nazi concentration camps did not feel revolted by the evidence no one would say he was unobjective but rather fear for his sanity and moral sensitivity. Feeling may twist judgment, but the lack of it may twist it even more.

The prophets certainly spoke in anger, and there is some evidence that Jesus got angry. It may be that the importance of any study in the area of morality or religion is determined in part by the emotion expressed. It seems that one weakness of most theological works is their "coolness" in the investigation of an idea. Is it not time for theologians to get upset?

To say that this book was written in anger and disgust (without denying "a certain dark joy") is to suggest that it is not written chiefly for black people. At least it is no handbook or collection of helpful hints on conducting a revolution. No one can advise another on when or how to die. This is a word to the oppressor, a word to Whitey, not in hope that he will listen (after King's death who can hope?) but in the expectation that my own existence will be clarified. If in this process of speaking for myself, I should happen to touch the souls of black brothers (including black men in white skins), so much the better. I believe that all aspiring black intellectuals share the task that LeRoi Jones has described for the black artist in America: "To aid in the destruction of America as he knows it."

His role is to report and reflect so precisely the nature of the society, that other men will be moved by the exactness of his rendering, and if they are black men, grow strong through this moving, having seen their own strength, and weakness, and if they are white men, tremble, curse, and go mad, because they will be drenched with the filth of their evil.

I am critical of white America, because this is *my* country; and what is mine must not be spared my emotional and intellectual scrutiny. Although my motive for writing was not—did not dare to be—dependent upon the response of white people, I do not rule out the possibility of creative changes, even in the lives of

oppressors. It is illegitimate to sit in judgment on another man, deciding how he
will or must respond. That is another form of oppression.

PREFACE TO THE 1989 EDITION

Black Theology and Black Power was a product of the Civil Rights and Black
Power movements in America during the *1960s*, reflecting both their strengths
and weaknesses. As an example of their strengths, this book was my initial
attempt to identify *liberation* as the heart of the Christian gospel and *blackness* as
the primary mode of God's presence. I wanted to speak on behalf of the voiceless
black masses in the name of Jesus whose gospel I believed had been greatly
distorted by the preaching and theology of white churches.

Although Martin Luther King, Jr., and other civil rights activists did much
to rescue the gospel from the heresy of white churches by demonstrating its life-
giving power in the black freedom movement, they did not liberate Christianity
from its cultural bondage to white, Euro-American values. Unfortunately, even
African-American churches had deviated from their own liberating heritage
through an uncritical imitation of the white denominations from which they
separated. Thus, it was hard to distinguish between the theologies of white and
black churches and the images of God and Jesus they used to express them.
African-Americans, it seemed to me at the time, had assumed that, though
whites did not treat them right, there was nothing wrong with whites' thinking
about God.

It was the challenging and angry voice of Malcolm X that shook me out
of my theological complacency. "Christianity is the white man's religion,"
he proclaimed, again and again, as he urged African-Americans to adopt a
perspective on God that was derived from their own cultural history. He argued:

> Brothers and sisters, the white man has brainwashed us black people to
> fasten our gaze upon a blond-haired, blue-eyed Jesus! We're worshiping a
> Jesus that doesn't even *look* like us! Oh, yes! . . . Now just think of this. The
> blond-haired, blue-eyed white man has taught you and me to worship a
> *white* Jesus, and to shout and sing and pray to this God that's *his* God, the
> white man's God. The white man has taught us to shout and sing and pray
> until we *die*, to wait until *death*, for some dreamy heaven-in-the-hereafter,
> when we're *dead*, while this white man has his milk and honey in the streets
> paved with golden dollars here on *this* earth!

Since I was, like many African-American ministers, a devout follower of
Martin King, I tried initially to ignore Malcolm's cogent *cultural* critique of the
Christianity as it was taught and practiced in black and white churches. I did
not want him to disturb the theological certainties that I had learned in graduate
school. But with the urban unrest in the cities and the rise of Black Power during
the James Meredith March in Mississippi (June 1966), I could no longer ignore

Malcolm's devastating criticisms of Christianity, particularly as they were being expressed in the articulate and passionate voices of Stokely Carmichael, Ron Karenga, the Black Panthers, and other young African-American activists. For me, the burning theological question was, how can I reconcile Christianity and Black Power, Martin Luther King, Jr.'s idea of nonviolence and Malcolm X's 'by any means necessary' philosophy? The writing of *Black Theology and Black Power* was the beginning of my search for a resolution of that dilemma.

Considered within the sociopolitical context of the sixties, I still believe that my answer was correct: "Christianity . . . is Black Power." Since theology is *human* speech and *not* God speaking, I recognize today, as I did then, that *all* attempts to speak about ultimate reality are limited by the social history of the speaker. Thus, I would not use exactly the same language today to speak about God that I used twenty years ago. Times have changed and the current situation demands a language appropriate for the problems we now face. But insofar as racism is still found in the churches and in society, theologians and preachers of the Christian gospel must make it unquestionably clear that the God of Moses and of Jesus makes an unqualified solidarity with the victims, empowering them to fight against injustice.

As in 1969, I unfortunately still see today that most white and black churches alike have lost their way, enslaved to their own bureaucracies with the clergy and staff attending endless meetings and professional theologians reading learned papers to each other, seemingly for the exclusive purpose of advancing their professional careers. In view of the silence of the great majority of white theologians when faced with the realities of slavery and segregation, the white churches' preoccupation with "academic" issues in theology and their avoidance of the issue of justice, especially in the area of race, do not surprise me. What does surprise and sadden me, however, is a similar situation among many African-American churches and their theologians, especially those who claim to speak and act in the name of a black theology of liberation. In view of Sojourner Truth and Fannie Lou Hamer, Martin King and Malcolm X and the tradition of resistance that they and others like them embody, African American ministers and theologians should know better than lose themselves in their own professional advancement, as their people, especially the youth, are being destroyed by drugs, street gangs, and AIDS. More black youth are in jails and prisons than in colleges and universities. Our community is under siege; something must be done before it is too late. If there is to be any genuine future for the black church and black theology, we African-American theologians and preachers must develop the courage to speak the truth about ourselves, saying to each other and to our church leaders what we have often said and still say to whites: *Enough is enough! It is time for this mess to stop!* Hopefully, the re-issuing of *Black Theology and Black Power* will contribute to the development of creative self-criticism in both black and white churches.

An example of the weakness of the 1960s black freedom movement, as defined by *Black Theology and Black Power,* was its complete blindness to the problem of sexism, especially in the black church community. When I read my book today, I am embarrassed by its sexist language and patriarchal perspective. There is not even one reference to a woman in the whole book! With black women playing such a dominant role in the African American liberation struggle, past and present, how could I have been so blind?

The publication of the twentieth-anniversary edition tempted me to rid *Black Theology and Black Power* of its sexist language (as I did in the revised edition of *A Black Theology of Liberation*) [Orbis, 1986] and also insert some references to black women. But I decided to let the language remain unchanged as a reminder of how sexist I once was and also that I might be encouraged never to forget it. It is easy to change the language of oppression without changing the sociopolitical situation of its victims. I know existentially what this means from the vantage point of racism. Whites have learned how to use less offensive language, but they have not changed the power relations between blacks and whites in the society. Because of the process of changing their language, combined with the token presence of middle-class African-Americans in their institutions, it is now even more difficult to define the racist behavior of whites.

The same kind of problem is beginning to emerge in regard to sexism. With the recent development of womanist theology, as expressed in the articulate and challenging voices of Delores Williams, Jackie Grant, Katie Cannon, Renita Weems, Cheryl Gilkes, Kelly Brown, and others, even African-American male ministers and theologians are learning how to talk less offensively about women's liberation. Many seem to have forgotten that they once used exclusive language. Amnesia is an enemy of justice. We must never forget what we once were lest we repeat our evil deeds in new forms. I do not want to forget that I was once silent about the oppression of women in the church and the society. Silence gives support to the powers that be. It is my hope that by speaking out against sexism other male African American preachers and theologians, especially in the historic black churches, will also lift their prophetic voices against this enemy of God in the black church community. So far, too few of us have spoken out in our own denominations.

Black Theology and Black Power is also limited by the Western theological perspective that I was fighting against. After spending six years of studying white theology in graduate school, I knew that the time had come for me to make a decisive break with my theological mentors. But that was easier said than done. I did not know much about my own theological tradition which had given rise to my rebellion. I was struggling to become a *black radical* theologian without much knowledge of the historical development of African-American religion and radicalism. I had studied a little "Negro History" in high school and college, but no text by a black author had been included in my theological curriculum in graduate school. That was one of the things that made me so angry. I had been greatly miseducated in theology, and it showed in the neo-orthodox, Barthian perspective of *Black Theology and Black Power.*

"How can you call what you have written 'black theology,'" African-American theologians pointedly asked me, "when most of the theological sources you use to articulate your position are derived from the white theology you claim to be heretical?" "Your theology," they continued, "is black in name only and not in reality. To be black in the latter sense, you must derive the sources and the norm from the community in whose name you speak." That criticism was totally unexpected, and it shook me as nothing else had. I had expected my black brothers and sisters to support me in my attacks on white theology. But it seemed to me at the time that they were attacking me instead of our enemies. In time, however, I came to see the great value of their criticism. My effort to correct this cultural weakness in my theological perspective has been an on-going process since the publication of *The Spirituals and the Blues* (1972).

As I began to reflect more deeply upon my own cultural history, tracing it back to the African continent, I began to see the great limitations of Karl Barth's influence upon my Christological perspective. Barth's assertion of the Word of God in opposition to natural theology in the context of Germany during the 1930s may have been useful. But the same theological methodology cannot be applied to the cultural history of African Americans in the Americas or to Africans and Asians on their continents. Of course, I knew that when I wrote *Black Theology and Black Power,* but my theological training in neo-orthodoxy hindered my ability to articulate this point.

As in 1969, I still regard Jesus Christ today as the chief focus of my perspective on God but not to the exclusion of other religious perspectives. God's reality is not bound by one manifestation of the divine in Jesus but can be found wherever people are being empowered to fight for freedom. Life-giving power for the poor and the oppressed is the primary criterion that we must use to judge the adequacy of our theology, not abstract concepts. As Malcolm X put it: "I believe in religion that believes in freedom. Any time I have to accept a religion that won't let me fight a battle for my people, I say to hell with that religion."

Another weakness of *Black Theology and Black Power* was my failure to link the African-American struggle for liberation in the United States with similar struggles in the Third World. If I had listened more carefully to Malcolm X and Martin King, I might have avoided that error. Both made it unquestionably clear, especially in their speeches against the U.S. government's involvement in the Congo and Vietnam, that there can be no freedom for African-Americans from racism in this country unless it is tied to the liberation of Third World nations from U.S. imperialism.

"You can't understand what is going on in Mississippi if you don't understand what is going on in the Congo." Malcolm told a Harlem audience. "They're both the same. The same interests are at stake. The same sides are drawn up, the same schemes are at work in the Congo that are at work in Mississippi." During the last year of his life, Malcolm traveled throughout the Middle East and Africa as he sought to place the black freedom struggle in the United States into an international context. When African American leaders questioned the value of his international focus, Malcolm said: "The point that I would like to impress upon every Afro-American leader is that there is no kind of action in this country ever going to bear fruit unless that action is tied in with the overall international struggle."

Martin King shared a similar concern. Against the advice of many friends in the civil rights movement, churches, and government, he refused to separate peace and civil rights issues. His condemnation of his government's involvement in the war in Vietnam, referring to "America as the greatest purveyor of violence in the world today," alienated many supporters in both the white and black communities. Martin King contended that the black freedom struggle and the struggle of the Vietnamese for self-determination were tied together because "injustice anywhere is a threat to justice everywhere."

My failure to link black liberation theology to the global struggles for freedom contributed to my blindness regarding the problem of classism. Class privilege was (and still is) a dominant reality in the white community of the United States as well as in the African-American community. In fact, the problem of oppression in the world today is defined not exclusively in terms of race but also in terms of the great economic gap between rich and poor nations and the haves and havenots within them. Again, if I had listened more attentively to Martin King and Malcolm X, I might have seen what I did not see at the time I wrote *Black Theology and Black Power*. Both turned toward economic issues during their later lives. They saw the great limitations of capitalism and, while rejecting the anti-democratic and atheistic principles of the Soviet Union, Martin and Malcolm began to search for the human, democratic side of socialism. What was clear to both of them, and clear to me now, is that we need to develop a struggle for freedom that moves beyond race to include all oppressed peoples of the world. As Malcolm X told a Columbia University audience a few days before his assassination: "It is incorrect to classify the revolt of the Negro as simply a racial conflict of black against white or as a purely American problem. Rather, we are today seeing a global rebellion of the oppressed against the oppressor, the exploited against the exploiter."

Despite its limitations, I hope that *Black Theology and Black Power* will remind all who read it that good theology is not abstract but concrete, not neutral but committed. Why? Because the poor were created for freedom and not for poverty.

Chapter 29

Womanist Theology

White Women's Christ
and Black Women's Jesus: Feminist
Christology and Womanist Response

Jacquelyn Grant

Editor's Introduction: The struggle for women's equality began
in the 1840s in close association with the abolitionist movement.
The women's suffrage movement was composed of upper class and
middle class white women. Yet they soon enlisted the support of
Sojourner Truth, born a slave by the name of Isabella in Ulster
County, New York (1797–1883). Truth attended the 1851
women's rights meeting in Akron, Ohio, where she made an
extraordinary speech that was destined to constitute her legacy
that would be remembered from that day until the present time.
She had experienced many beatings, including sexual abuse by her
slave masters, and the death of her parents and ten siblings. Though
illiterate she became an itinerant preacher, singer, abolitionist,
women's rights advocate, wife, and mother. She also testified on
several occasions before the United States Congress and visited
President Abraham Lincoln at the White House. Her speech
in Akron is known in history by the title "Ain't I a Woman?"
Embraced by the antislavery and women's rights movements, Truth
made many speeches, the vast majority of which were not reported

by the press because its reporters could not imagine a black woman having anything of importance to say. Thus, Sojourner Truth is a significant ancestor for contemporary theological womanists who emerged at Union Theological Seminary, New York, in the 1980s. At that time a number of African American women pursuing PhD studies in theology and ethics (principally Jacquelyn Grant, Delores Williams, and Katie Cannon) discovered that African American women's experiences were invisible in the writings of both white feminists and black male theologians whom they were studying at the time. That awareness prompted them to seek their own voice for doing theology, and they began mining African American women's traditions in both history and literature. They soon discovered the term "womanist" and its definition in Alice Walker's book *In Search of Our Mothers' Gardens: Womanist Prose*. They found both the word "womanist" and its definition altogether apt for what they were seeking. They quickly adopted it, and consequently a new genre of theology entered the lexicon of the theological academy. Both black theology and womanist theology have had a major influence in expanding the breadth and depth of theological scholarship both at home and abroad by giving visibility and audibility to persons and traditions who traditionally had been excluded from the religious academy.

WOMEN'S EXPERIENCE REVISITED: THE CHALLENGE OF THE DARKER SISTER

Although feminist theology has made an important critique of the sexist limitations of the dominant theologies of Europe and North America, it is not without serious limitations, especially when evaluated in the light of Black women's experience. What are these limitations and how serious are they, especially as they are related to Christology? In this chapter, I will discuss these limitations and, in my concluding remarks, point the way towards a theology that is grounded in Black women's experiences.

A. Limitations of Feminist Theology

1. Feminist theology is inadequate for two reasons: it is White and racist.

Feminist theologians are white in terms of their race and in terms of the *nature of the sources* they use for the development of their theological perspectives. Although there are sharp differences among feminist theologians, as we have seen, they are *all* of the *same* race and the influence of their race has led them to similar sources for the definition of their perspectives on the faith. Of course, chief among the sources is women's experience. However, what is often unmentioned is that feminist theologians' sources for women's experience refer almost exclusively to White women's experience. White women's experience and Black women's experience are not the same. Indeed all experiences are unique to some degree. But in this case the difference is so radical that it may be said that White women and Black women are in completely different realms. Slavery and segregation have created such a gulf between these women, that White feminists' common assumption that all women are in the same situation with respect to sexism is difficult to understand when history so clearly tells us a different story.

a. Black Women's Experience Compared to White Women's Experience During Slavery

The first two and a half centuries of Black presence in the United States was characterized by servitude and slavery.[1] African men, women and children were ruled by their captors, and even owned as property, subject to be sold at the owner's will. Slavery in the United States has been described as one of the most abominable systems in history.[2]

Because Black women were not considered the sisters of White women during slavery, they were not exempt from the tyranny of this system. In fact when we read narratives of slaves and ex-slaves, current "sisterhood" rhetoric appears simply as one of two possibilities: (1) a crude joke, or (2) the conciliatory rhetoric of an advantaged class and race. The life and times of Black women gives evidence of the fact that Black women and White women lived in two very different worlds. The biographies, autobiographies, and narratives reveal many of the stories of how Black women (and men) withstood the physical and

---

1. Herbert Aptheker, ed., *A Documentary History of the Negro People in the United States: From Colonial Times thru the Civil War*, vol. 1 (New York: The Citadel Press, 1971); Herbert Aptheker, ed., *A Documentary History of the Negro People in the United States: From Reconstruction Years* to *the Founding of the NAACP in 1910*, vol. 2 (Secaucus, NJ: The Citadel Press, 1972); Herbert Aptheker, ed., *A Documentary History of the Negro People in the United States: From the Emergence of the NAACP to the Beginning of the New Deal, 1910–1932* (Secaucus, NJ: The Citadel Press, 1973). For a combination of Historical and sociological studies see August Meier and Elliott Rudwick, eds., *The Making of Black America: The Origins of Black Americans*, I (New York: Atheneum, 1969); and Meier and Rudwick, *The Making of Black America: The Black Community in Modern America*.vol. 2 (New York: Atheneum, 1973).

2. For a comparative study of American Slavery and slavery in other places, see Stanley M. Elkins, "Slavery in Capitalist and Capitalist Cultures" in *The Black Family: Essays and Studies* (Belmont, California: Wadsworth Publishing Company, Inc., 1971), pp. 23–16. Elkins says: Neither in Brazil nor in Spanish America did slavery carry with it such precise and irrevocable categories of perpetual servitude, "durante vita" and "for all generations," as in the United States. The presumptions in these countries, should the status of a colored person be in doubt, was that he was free rather than a slave," quoted from William Law Mathieson, *British Slavery and its Abolition* (London: Longmans Green, 1926), pp. 37–38. A slave could be free by a number of ways: (l) He could buy his own freedom. (2) In Cuba and Mexico, the Negro could demand a price declaration which he/she could pay by installments. (3) In Brazil the parents of children might demand his/her freedom. (Johnston, *Negro in the New World*, p. 89) (4) The medieval Spanish code provided for termination of the slave's service if he denounced cases of treason, murder, counterfeiting, or the rape of a virgin or if other meritorious acts are performed (p. 15).

psychological violence of slave existence.[3] They also reveal how Black women experienced White women. White women in slave and ex-slave narratives are always identified as members of the oppressor race. The terms "misus" and "mistress" implied for White women a status which Black women did not have.

Black women, as a part of the servicing class, were not awarded the protection of White patriarchy. Apparently from the point of view of the mistresses, Black women's purpose in life was to serve their domestic needs.[4] No special and very little different treatment was accorded slave women because they were women. The Victorian concept of ladyhood was not applied to slave women. They were treated like slave men as a lower species of animals.

Brutality was administered not only by masters and foremen but also by mistresses, reflecting the fact that White women were just as much participants in this system of slavery as were White men. For every Angelina and Sarah Grimke there were numerous of those like their mother who not only condoned slavery but thought that abolitionists like Angelina and Sarah were agitators, if not in fact heretics.

3. Several biographies of Black women slaves have appeared. Among them are: John Collins, *The Slave-Mother* (Philadelphia: #31 North Fifth Street, 1855). This is a brief account of a runaway slave mother who strategically gave up her infant to gain freedom for them both. Victoria Earle, *Aunt Lindy: A Story Founded on Real Life* (New York: J. J. Little and Co., 1893). This is the story (fictionalized) of an ex-slave Black woman (and Black man) who discovered that a burn victim placed in her care was her ex-master. After a religious meeting she decided to nurse him rather than let him die, consequently in appreciation he helped them to locate their son whom he had sold years earlier. Sarah R. Levering, *Memoirs of Margaret Jane Blake of Baltimore Md.* (Philadelphia: Innes and Son, 1879). Levering gives *her* a brief account of the life of Blake. Blake's mother is said to prefer slavery to freedom for herself and her daughter, Margaret. Levering's paternalistic/maternalistic and racist perspective made it impossible to see that perhaps Margaret's mother was not rejecting freedom, but the unbearable difficulties her weakling and sickly daughter would have to experience as a freed person right after the war. Jim Bearden and Linda Jean Butler, *The Life and Times of Mary Shadd Cary* (Toronto, Ontario: New Canada Publication, a division of NC Press Ltd., 1977). This is a biography of a free Negro woman, who was dedicated to education of Blacks, abolition and women's rights. Also see Conrad Earl, *Harriet Tubman* (Washington, D.C.: The Associated Publishers, Inc., 1943); Sarah Bradford's *Scenes in the life of Harriet Tubman* (1869). *Aunt Sally: A Narrative of the Slave Life and Purchase of the Mother of Rev. Isaac Williams of Detroit, Michigan* (Wheaton, Illinois: Syndale House Publishers, Inc., 1979). First published in 1858 by the American Reform Tract Book Society of Cincinnati, Ohio.

The interplay of racism and sexism is more dramatic in autobiographies and slave narratives. Among the published ones are: Linda Brent, *Incidents in the Life of a Slave Girl* (New York: A Harvest Book, Harcourt, Brace, Jovanovich, Inc.) ed. L. Marie Child (originally published in 1861). New introduction and notes by Walter Teller, 1973. Brent speaks of the physical and mental violence of slavery and other injustices. She appeals to northerners to stop sending fugitive slaves back to the South. Elizabeth Keckley, *Behind the Scenes: Thirty Years a Slave, and Four Years in the White House* (New York: G. W. Carleton and Co., Publishers, 1868). Though attempting to be kind and restrained in her accounts, nonetheless Keckley likewise reveals many of the atrocities of slave existence. Susie King Taylor *Reminiscences of my Life in Camp* (Boston: The Author, 1902). This is an account of Taylor's work among the 33 U.S. Colored Troops.

4. From the point of view of White men, Black women existed not only to serve White women's domestic needs but also to bear the brunt of their sexual exploitation. See discussion in Mary Berry and John Blassingame, *The Black Experience in America* (New York: Oxford University Press, 1982), chapter 4. Also see Calvin Hernton, *Sex and Racism in America* (New York: Grove Press, Inc. 1965).

b. Black Women's Experience Compared to White Women's Experience After Slavery

The abolition of slavery left intact the basic relationship between Black women and White women in particular and Black people and White people in general. For many Black people, emancipation meant slavery without chains.

The end of slavery as a formal, legal institution brought neither change in the image of, nor significant change in the condition of Black people in the United States. The image that Blacks were inferior and that they were intended to service white America remained intact. Consequently, when freed Blacks, sought work they were relegated in the labor market to the same service jobs and menial work which had been forced upon them during slavery. For Black men this meant plantation/farm work, factory work, other menial jobs and often unemployment.[5] For many Black women this meant doing the same work as Black men as well as employment as domestic servants. Black women made up a significant percentage of domestic service workers.[6]

5. See statistics as summarized in the U. S. Department of Commerce, Bureau of the Census, *The Social and Economic Status of the Black Population in the U. S.: American Historical View, 1790–1978* (Current Population Reports Special Studies Series #80). To see the consistent high unemployment rates of Blacks relative to whites (and Black men relative to White men), see reports from the U. S. Department of Labor, Bureau of Labor Statistics.

6. Major studies on Domestic servants are: David Katzman, *Seven Days a Week: Women and Domestic Service in Industrializing America* (New York: Oxford University Press, 1978); Daniel Sutherland, *Americans and Their Servants: Domestic Service in the United States From 1800–1920* (Baton Rouge, LA: Louisiana State University Press, 1981). Faye E. Dudden, *Serving Women: Household Service in Nineteenth-Century America* (Middletown, CT: Wesleyan University Press, 1983). For particular Black emphasis see: Elizabeth Ross Haynes, *Negroes in Domestic Service in the United States* (Washington, D.C.: The Association for the Study of Negro Life and History, Inc., 1923), Reprinted from *The Journal of Negro History*, Vol. VIII, #4 (October 1923). W. E. B. DuBois included in *The Philadelphia Negro* a study of Domestic Servants conducted by Isabel Eaten, "Special Report on Negro Domestic Service in the Seventh Ward" (Millwood, NY: Kraus-Thomas Organization Ltd., 1973). Literary studies include Alice Childress, *Like One of the Family . . . Conversations From a Domestic Life* (Brooklyn, NY: Independence Publishers, 1956) and Trudier Harris, *From Mammies to Militants: Domestics in Black American Literature* (Philadelphia: Temple University Press, 1982).

White females (especially immigrants) used domestic service as a stepping stone to other more decent women's occupations—office clerks, stenographers, typists, bookkeepers, cashiers, accountants, store clerks and saleswomen, and telephone operators. For Black women, domestic service was permanent. In 1890 and 1920 while White female servants declined significantly, Black women in this field increased to 40%. In 1920 they were 73% of all laundresses. In 1910 and 1920 Black women were 0.5% and 1.4% in non-agricultural occupations while (native born) White women were 32.1 and 37.1 in such occupations. By 1920 only 7% native born and 20% immigrant women were servants. Katzman, *Seven Days A Week*, pp. 72–73.

Two reasons can be deduced, from the studies, for the high percentage of Blacks in domestic service. (1) Recognizing that race relations and domestic service were intertwined, Katzman quotes Orra Langhorne's report in 1890 that "among the white people of the South, difficulties about servants are generally spoken of as 'trouble with Negroes;—Negroes and servants being synonymous terms in the average White Southerner's vocabulary.'" (Katzman, *Seven Days A Week*, p. 185). See also Orra Langhorne, "Southern Workman" (October 1890) in Charles E. Wynes (ed.) *Southern Sketches from Virginia 1881–1901* (Charlottesville, VA, 1964), p. 100. (2) Sutherland suggests as another reason for the high percentage of Black domestic servants that negative attitudes towards "new immigration" resulting in their seldom employment as servants. Far worse than the heathen Irish were the culture and tradition differences of Poles, Bohemians, Hungarians, Italians, and Jews

In David Katzman's description, domestic service in the South was a caste system, and domestic labor a part of the larger racial-caste structure which reproduced the social relations of slavery. Blacks were servants and Whites were masters and never were the two to be changed. The domination /subordination relationship within the house hold mirrored the White/Black relationship in general and especially in the South.[7]

In this privatized world of the family the continuation of many of the oppressive practices of slavery can be detected. Though legal slavery was abolished, the relations of Blacks and Whites characteristic of slavery, remained for decades thereafter. Three dimensions of this situation are important for our topic: 1) Physical brutality toward Blacks was continued, and even extended to violence outside of the work context. 2) The immediate relationship between White women and Black women did not change; White women were still oppressors and Black women were still the oppressed. 3) As a part of this continued relationship, Black women were still treated as property. These dynamics between White and Black women represent some of the negative dimensions of Black women's experience.

What is apparent in this historical context is how Black women's experience involves a convergence of racism, sexism, and classism. Within the limited arena of domestic labor, the sexist assumption that women's place is (only) in the home is reconfirmed, as well as the classist practice of paying those who do "menial" jobs little or nothing, and the assumption that such work is more appropriately done by those of the servant class. These patterns are compounded by the racist assumption that White women need protection from actual work and therefore should function in a supervisory capacity.[8] Consequently, as Hooks observes,

---

of all nations. They were seldom employed as servants partially because Americans disliked and distrusted them. [(Sutherland, *Americans, and Their Domestics*, p. 59); see also Mary Grove Smith, "Immigration as a Source of Supply for Domestic Workers," *Bulletin of Inter-Municipal Committee on Household Research*, vol. 2 (May 1906); Rose Cohen, *Out of the Shadows* (New York; Jerome S. Ozer, 1971), 158–59, 171–72; Elizabeth H. Pleck, "A Mother's Wages: Income Earning Among Married Italian and Black women, 1896–1911," in Michael Gordon (ed.), *The American Family in SocialHistorical Perspective* (New York: St. Martins Press, 1978), 495.) (3) A third factor in the high percentage of Blacks as domestics is that while native-White women had non-service occupations opened to them, Blacks were excluded from occupational mobility. Sutherland, Ibid., see also Mary White Ovington, "The Colored Woman in Domestic Service in New York City," *Bulletin of Inter-Municipal Committee on Household Research*, (May 1905), 10–12.

7. Comparing the South with the North and West, Katzman notes that servants were rarely found in lower middle or working class families. However, in the former slave states, Black servants were equally common in households headed by wage earners as in those headed by white collar workers. He further notes that the South has been called a "house-wife's utopia." Katzman, *Seven Days a Week*, 185. Of course this reflected the fact that Black labor was cheap.

8. Because of the strenuousness of housework and the delicateness of White women's physical make-up, White women were taught that they needed protection from the dangers of housework. Katzman recalls: "During the late nineteenth century, medical authorities cautioned women against demanding and enduring physical labor. According to medical guidebooks, adolescent middle-class girls should be excused from such hard physical labor as strenuous domestic chores. More mature women were advised against physical activity during menstruation, and it was widely thought that regular work schedules were injurious to a woman's health." (Katzman, p. 149).

many Black women experienced white women as the white supremacist group who most directly exercised power over them, often in a manner far more brutal and dehumanizing than that of racist White men. (Even) today, despite predominant rule by White supremacist patriarchs, Black women often work in a situation where the immediate supervisor, boss, or authority figure is a White woman.[9]

Thus when theologians speak about women's experience as the source for doing feminist theology, it is necessary to specify which women's experience is being referred to, for the above discussion demonstrates that the experiences of White women and Black women have been far from the same.

2. Feminist Theology as Racist

It would be inaccurate to assert that because feminist theology is White, it is also racist. To be White does not necessarily mean to be racist, though the behavior of Whites makes the distinction difficult. Nevertheless, my claim that feminist theology is racist is best supported by a definition of racism.

Racism, according to Joel Kovel ". . . is the tendency of a society to degrade and do violence to people on the basis of race, and by whatever mediations may exist for this purpose."[10] These mediations are manifested in different forms, and are carried on through various media: the psychology, sociology, history, economics and symbolism of the dominant (White) group. Racism is the domination of a people which is justified by the dominant group on the basis of racial distinctions. It is not only individual acts but a collective, institutionalized activity. As C. Eric Lincoln observed,

> [for racism to flourish with the vigor it enjoys in America, there must be an extensive climate of acceptance and participation by large numbers of people who constitute its power base. It is the consensus of private persons that gives racism its derivative power. . . . The power of racism is the power conceded by those respectable citizens who by their actions or inaction communicate the consensus which directs and empowers the overt bigot to act on their behalf.[11]

Even if some individual feminists are not racists, the movement has been so structured, and therefore takes on a racist character. In a racist society, the oppressor assumes the power of definition and control while the oppressed is objectified and perceived as a thing.[12] As such, White women have defined the movement and presumed to do so not only for themselves but also for non-White women. They have misnamed themselves by calling themselves feminists when in fact they are White feminists, and by appealing to women's experience

9. Hooks, *Feminist Theology*, p. 49.

10. Joel Kovel, *White Racism: A Psychohistory* (New York: Columbia Univ. Press, 1984), p. x.

11. C. Eric Lincoln, *Race Religion and the Continuing American Dilemma* (New York: Hill and Wang, 1984), pp. 11–12.

12. Kovel, *White Racism*, passim.

when in fact they appeal almost exclusively to their own experience. To misname themselves as "feminists" who appeal to "women's experience" is to do what oppressors always do; it is to define the rules and then solicit others to play the game. It is to presume a commonality with oppressed women that oppressed women themselves do not share. If White women's analysis were adequate, they would be more precise in naming their own movement and would not presume to name or define the experiences of others. They have simply accepted and participated in the racism of the larger American society when they have done so. This partially accounts for the negative response which Black women have had with respect to feminism.

Brenda Eichelberger identifies five categories of reasons that lead to Black women's rejection of White feminism.

1) Class differences mean that while Black women are dealing with "survival" issues, White women are dealing with "fulfillment" issues. 2) Negative imagery of Black women derived from physical and cultural stereotypes has resulted in the debased treatment of Black women. 3) The naivete, or basic lack of knowledge of Black women about the women's movement results in their inability to see the relationship between feminist issues and the Black struggle. 4) Black women perceive White feminists to be racists who are interested in them only in order to accomplish the White women's agenda. 5) There is a concern that an alliance of Black women with White women in a feminist agenda may be "detrimental to black men" and therefore divisive of the Black community.[13]

The hostility towards the feminist movement, elaborated by some critics focuses on its implications for family life. Many view feminism as a direct threat to Black family life. Sociologist Iva Carruthers refers to feminism as "one of the most serious assaults on African familyhood.[14] This feminist movement, she maintains, is a "White-family affair" and is therefore totally irrelevant "to the real needs of Black women."[15] Deborah Hines distinguishes between Black women's reality and White women's reality.

> Black women find it extremely difficult to ally themselves with those who say, "We have all suffered the same," when we know it isn't so . . . . We are being told that apples and oranges are the same, when we can see that they are not. You cannot easily substitute one for the other in a recipe. Their odors are different. They appeal to people differently. Even a blind person can tell them apart. Yet, a steady stream of rhetoric is aimed at convincing Black women how much alike their lives, experiences, wishes and decisions are to those of our stepsisters.[16]

13. Brenda Eichelberger, "Voices of Black Feminism," *Quest: A Feminist Quarterly* III (Spring): pp. 16–23.
14. Iva Carruthers, "War in African Familyhood," in *Sturdy Black Bridges: Visions of Black Women in Literature*, eds. Roseann P. Bell, Bettye J. Parker and Beverly Guy-Sheftall (New York: Anchor Books, Doubleday, 1979), p. 9.
15. *Ibid.*, p. 9.
16. Deborah Hines, "Racism Breeds Stereotypes," *The Witness*, 65 (February 1982), p. 7.

To say that many Black women are suspicious of the feminist movement, then, is to speak mildly about their responses to it. Put succinctly, women of the dominant culture are perceived as the enemy. Like their social, sexual and political White male partners, they have as their primary goal the suppression, if not oppression, of the Black race and the advancement of the dominant culture. Because of this perception, many believe that Black feminism is a contradiction in terms.

B. Toward a New Black Women's Consciousness

In spite of the negative responses of Black women to the White women's liberation movement described, there has been a growing feminist consciousness among them, coupled with the increased willingness to do an independent analysis of sexism. This is creating an emerging Black perspective on feminism. Black feminism grows out of Black women's tridimensional reality of race/sex/class. It holds that full human liberation cannot be achieved simply by the elimination of any one form of oppression. Consequently, real liberation must be "broad in the concrete;"[17] it must be based upon a multi-dimensional analysis. Recent writings by secular Black feminists have challenged White feminist analysis and Black race analysis, particularly by introducing data from Black women's experience that has been historically ignored by White feminists and Black male liberationists.

A review of a selected group of literature follows: The first of these publications, *The Black Woman* (1970), an anthology collected by Toni Cade[18] was representative of a variety of disciplines and perspectives. It broke the silence of Black women, declaring that they have a voice that must be heard apart from Black men and White women. Later Ntozake Shange published *For Colored Girls Only Who Have Considered Suicide When the Rainbow is Enuf* (1975),[19] following controversial responses to its production on Broadway. In this choreopoem, Shange exposes the pains and struggles of Black women in Black male/female relationships. Criticized for lacking a social and political context, her poem focused exclusively upon the physical and especially psychological strains of Black women. The work's significance, however, is that it exposed some of the internal problems of the Black community as they relate to sexism.

17. This phrase is used by Anna Cooper in *A Voice From the South by a Black Woman of the South* (Xenia, Ohio, 1892), quoted in Hooks *Ain't I A Woman*, p. 193–194. I use it here to characterize Black women's tri-dimensional experience. To be concerned about Black Woman's issues is to be *concrete*. Yet because of their interconnectedness with Black men (racism), White women (sexism) and the poor (classism), it is also to be, at the same time, concerned with broad issues.
18. Cade (New York: Macmillan Publishing Co., Inc., 1970).
19. Shange (New York: Macmillan Publishing Co., Inc. 1975).

Barbara Smith's essay "Toward a Black Feminist Criticism"[20] (1977), should be noted because it represented the beginnings of an emergent Black feminist theoretical perspective. She articulated an "approach to literature that embodies the realization that the politics of sex as well as the politics of race and class are crucially interlocking factors in the words of Black women writers . . . ."[21]

In 1978, Sharon Harley and Rosalyn Terborg-Penn edited *Afro-American Women*,[22] a book of historical and biographical essays which addressed some issues of race and sex in the labor force, the women's movement, and the White community and Black communities. They also provided some data on the contributions of Black women. In the same year Michelle Wallace, from a perspective similar to Shange's, published a controversial critique of the Black Liberation Movement. In her book, *Black Macho and the Myth of the Superwoman*,[23] she attributed the plight of Black women to Black men's exaggeration of White patriarchally prescribed roles for men, which results in Black male machoism.

By 1981 several other major publications appeared that developed a critique inclusive of the issues of racism, sexism and classism. Angela Davis' *Women, Race and Class*[24] explored the interrelationships between racism, sexism, and labor issues, and is aimed particularly at identifying the class bias that affects the analysis of women's histories. Bell Hooks' *Ain't I A Woman? Black Women and Feminism*[25] simultaneously challenged the White woman's liberation movement for its racism and the Black liberation movement for its sexism. The following year, this tri-dimensional analysis was extended in *All the Women are White, and all the Blacks are Men, But Some of Us are Brave*,[26] a volume edited by Gloria Hull, Patricia Scott and Barbara Smith. These essays seek to advance Black women's studies, by clarifying how analyses of racism, sexism and classism may genuinely illumine Black women's reality. More recently Alice Walker's novel, *The Color Purple*,[27] which received the Pulitzer Prize, portrays the troubles of a Black girl/woman entangled in an oppressive web created by the racism of White America, but in doing so she focused clearly upon the brutal sexism of Black men. In her subsequent collections of prose, *In Search of Our Mother's Garden*, Walker proposes the term womanist, in contradistinction to feminist, to denote feminists of color.[28]

---

20. Smith (Trumanburg, New York: The Crossing Press, 1977), p. 3. Originally published in *Conditions: Two* (October 1977). Brenda Eichelberger's "Voices on Black Feminism" also appeared in 1977, in *Quest* III (Spring, 1977). In this essay she interviews eight Black women on Black women's response to the women's movement and their thoughts on the need for Black feminism.
21. *Ibid.*, Smith, "Towards a Black . . . ," p. 3.
22. Harley and Terborg-Penn (New York: Kennikat Press, 1978).
23. Wallace (New York: Dial Press, 1978).
24. Davis (New York: Vintage Book, 1981).
25. Hooks (Boston: South End Press, 1981).
26. Hull, et al. (Old Westbury, NY: The Feminist Press, 1982).
27. Walker (New York: Harcourt, Brace and Jovanovich, Publishers, 1982).
28. Walker (New York: Harcourt, Brace and Jovanovich, Publishers, 1983).

The publications of Black feminists continue to escalate. In 1984 a significant historical volume on Black women appeared by Paula Giddings, entitled *When and Where I Enter*.[29] This work is an historical account of the impact of Black women on race and sex in America. She chronicles these struggles through the nineteenth and twentieth centuries. Another significant work of literary analysis is Gloria Wade-Gayles' *No Crystal Stair: Visions of Race and Sex in Black Women's Fiction*[30] Wade-Gayles examines the conditions, contradictions and challenges of Black women from 1946 to 1976, through literature. Most recently, Bell Hooks published her second volume, *Feminist Theory: From Margin to Center*,[31] that continues to identify the limitations of bourgeois White feminism and explores the broader implications of a feminism based upon multi-dimensional analysis of oppression.

In few of the above mentioned writings do Black women employ only a gender analysis to treat Black women's reality. Whereas Shange focuses chiefly upon sexism, Wallace, like Walker, presumes that White racism has had an adverse affect upon the Black community in a way that confuses and reinforces the already existing sexism. Harley, Terborg Penn, Giddings and Wade-Gayles all recognize the inclusiveness of the oppressive reality of Black women as they endure racism and sexism and economic oppression. Smith, Hull (et al.), Hooks and Davis particularly explore the implications of this tri-dimensional oppression of Black women. It is clear that through these and other works, Black women have either articulated Black feminist perspectives or develop grounds for doing so. These perspectives, however, have not led to the resolution of tensions between Black women and White women.

On the contrary, the possibly irreparable nature of these tensions is implied in Walker's suggestion that the experience of being a Black woman or a White woman is so different that another word is required to describe the liberative efforts of Black women. Her suggestion that the word "womanist" is more appropriate for Black women is derived from the sense of the word as it is used in Black communities:

> Womanist from womanish. (Opp. of "girlish," i.e., frivolous, irresponsible, not serious.) A Black feminist or feminist of color. From the Black folk expression of mothers to female children, "You acting womanish," i.e., like a woman. Usually referring to outrageous, audacious, courageous or willful behavior. Wanting to know more and in greater depth than is considered

---

29. Giddings (New York: William Morrow and Company, Inc., 1984). Other collections of historical documents include Gerda Lerner, *Black Woman in White America*, and Bert Lowenberg and Ruth Bogin, eds. of *Black Women in Nineteenth-Century American Life: Their Words, Their Thoughts, Their Feelings* (University Park, PA: The Pennsylvania State University Press, 1976). In *We Are Your Sisters: Black Women in the Nineteenth Century*, Dorothy Sterling (ed.) brings together a primary source of Black women letters, interviews, diaries, autobiographies organizational records and newspaper accounts. (New York: W. W. Norton and Company, 1984).

30. Wade-Gayles (New York: Pilgrim Press, 1984).

31. hooks (Boston: South End Press, 1984).

"good" for one. Interest in grown-up doings. Acting grown up. Being
grown up. Interchangeable with another black folk expression: "You trying
to be grown." Responsible. In charge. Serious.[32]

Womanists were Sojourner Truth, Jarena Lee, Amanda Berry Smith, Ida B.
Wells, Mary Church Terrell, Mary McLeod Bethune, Fannie Lou Hamer and
countless others not remembered in any historical study. A womanist then is
a strong Black woman who has sometimes been mislabeled as a domineering
castrating matriarch. A womanist is one who has developed survival strategies
in spite of the oppression of her race and sex in order to save her family and
her people. Walker's womanist notion suggests not "the feminist," but the
active struggle of Black women that makes them who they are. For some Black
women that may involve being feminine as traditionally defined, and for others
it involves being masculine as stereotypically defined. In either case, womanist
just means *being* and *acting* out who you are. It is to the womanist tradition that
Black women must appeal for the doing of theology.

C. Conclusion: The Beginnings of a Womanist
Theology with Special Reference to Christology

Womanist theology begins with the experiences of Black women as its point
of departure. This experience includes not only Black women's activities in the
larger society but also in the churches and reveals that Black women have often
rejected the oppressive structure in the church as well. A brief review of the literature demonstrates this fact.

1. Emerging Black Women's Literature in the Church

Several works have recently appeared which lay the groundwork for the
development of a Black woman's perspective in theology, although at this early
stage, they have appeared primarily in collections of essays in Black and feminist
theological works.

In "Black Women and the Churches: Triple Jeopardy," Theressa Hoover
analyzed the position of Black women in predominantly White denominations,
though she also mentions some of the problems in Black denominations.[33]
She locates the source of Black woman's survival in a faith which has always
strengthened them to struggle against the odds. Pauli Murray, in "Black
Theology and Feminist Theology: A Comparative View," employs the
"inclusionary" principle of White feminist theology to challenge proponents
of Black theology to adopt a spirit of cooperation towards liberation and

---

32. Walker, *In Search* . . . , p. xi.
33. Theressa Hoover, "Black Women and the Churches: Triple Jeopardy" in *Black Theology: A
Documentary History,* eds. Gayraud Wilmore and James Cone (Maryknoll, NY: Orbis Books, 1979),
pp. 377–388. This article was originally published in *Sexist Religion and Women in the Church: No
More Silence!* ed. Alice Hageman (New York: Association Press, 1974).

reconciliation and to take women's role more seriously.[34] In "Black Theology and the Black Woman," I challenge Black theology and the Black church to realize its own proclamation of liberation as the central message of the gospel by extending this principle to Black women.[35] In "Tasks of a Prophetic Church" I define the task of Black feminist liberation theology to be that of exposing the various forms of oppression: racism, classism, sexism and imperialism.[36] I contend that they are all interconnected and none of these forms of oppression can be eliminated by challenging them separately. At the request of a group of Black seminarian women, James Cone has published an essay entitled "New Roles of Women in the Ministry: A Theological Appraisal," which challenges the Black church to divest itself of traditional oppressive attitudes towards women.[37] Later Cone treats the theme of feminism in the Black Church in two of his books in Black theology. In *My Soul Looks Back,* he includes a discussion of "Black Theology, Feminism and Marxism" and in *For My People,* he devotes a chapter to "Black theology, Black Churches and Black Women."[38] He traces Black feminism in the 19th and 20th centuries and elaborates some of the forms of sexism in the Black Church. Cone moves to challenge Black male ministers and theologians to advance Black women's liberation in the church and society. James Evans has written an essay entitled "Black Theology and Black Feminism."[39] Like Cone, he challenged Black theologians to address sexism.

Other articles helped to fill the historical vacuum of Black women's contribution to Black religion particularly in Pentecostal traditions. Pearl Williams-Jones in "Pentecostal Women: A Minority Report," identifies Black women leaders of the 19th and 20th centuries who have held positions and power beyond the spheres usual for women.[40] James S. Tinney in "The Feminist Impulse in Black Pentecostalism"[41] has provided an "historical theological overview of women in Black Pentecostalism." Cheryl Gilkes' "Together and in Harness: Women's Tradition in the Sanctified Church," specifies the activities and strengths of women in Black holiness traditions and identifies how their

---

34. Pauli Murray, "Black Theology and Feminist Theology: A Comparative View," in *Black Theology,* eds. Wilmore and Cone, pp. 398–417.

35. Jacquelyn Grant, "Black Theology and The Black Woman," in *Black Theology,* eds. Wilmore and Cone, pp. 418–433.

36. *Idem,* "Tasks of a Prophetic Church," in *Theology in the Americas,* Cornel West (Maryknoll, NY: Orbis Books, 1982), pp. 136–142.

37. James Cone, "New Roles of Women in the Ministry: A Theological Appraisal," in *Black Theology,* eds. Wilmore and Cone, pp. 380–397.

38. *Idem, My Soul Looks Back* (Nashville, TN: Abingdon Press, 1983), and James Cone, *For My People: Black Theology and the Black Church* (Maryknoll, NY: Orbis Books, 1984).

39. James Evans, "Black Theology and Black Feminism," *Journal of Religious Thought* 38 (Spring/Summer, 1981), pp. 43–53.

40. Pearl Williams Jones, "A Minority Report: Black Pentecostal Women," *Spirit: A Journal of Incident to Black Pentecostalism,* vol. 1 (No. I, 1977), pp. 31–44.

41. An unpublished paper.

contributions are irreplaceable, especially in light of how patriarchy and racism impinge upon their participation.[42]

A number of graduate theses have also appeared to contribute to the development of Black women's theological perspective. Delores Williams' *The Black Woman Portrayed in Selected Black Imaginative Literature and Some Questions for Black Theology*,[43] explores Black women's image (as mother) through the antebellum slave narrative literature and post-bellum literary material such as blues and spirituals. Williams suggests that given the peculiar reality of Black Women, perhaps the dominant Jewish and Christian biblical story of woman which focuses on Sarah, wife of Abraham, is an inadequate model for Black women. She proposes Hagar, the slave woman, as the correlative of Black women's experience. She challenges Black theologians to re-examine the biblical sources of Christian traditions for a Black liberation Theology that could be inclusive of the liberation of Black women.

Acknowledging grounding in both Black and Feminist analyses, LaTaunya Maria Bynum, in *Black Feminist Theology: A New Word About God*,[44] compares the theology of James Cone and Rosemary Ruether and concludes that neither is sufficient to illumine the reality of Black women. Black women must develop a perspective which is both Black and feminist, and which affirms the revolutionary message of Jesus as freedom.

In her dissertation, *Resources for a Constructive Ethic for Black Women with Special Attention to the Life and Work of Zora Neale Hurston*,[45] Katie Cannon explores the possibility of the literary tradition of Black women as the most adequate source for a constructive Black women's ethic. Having engaged some dimensions of Hurston's work with Black theologians Howard Thurman and Martin Luther King, Jr., Cannon concludes that even though Black theologians generally ignore the "victimization of gender discrimination," these two theologians have identified three themes *(imago dei,* love and justice, and community) which Black women need in order to ensure their dignity as persons. These themes, she concludes, were operative in Hurston's work and in the literature of many Black women writers.

Jualynne Dodson has contributed research tracing the history and development of the African Methodist Episcopal Church that gives central attention to the limited data about women's activities in the 19th century. *Women's Collective Power in the African Methodist Episcopal Church*,[46] focuses upon "preaching

42. Cheryl Gilkes, "Togetherness and in Harness: Women's Traditions in the Sanctified Church" (publication forthcoming in *Signs* Quarterly).

43. Delores Williams, *The Black Woman Portrayed in Selected Black Literature and Some Questions for Black Theology* (M.A. Thesis, Columbia University and Union Theological Seminary, 1975).

44. LaTaunya Marie Bynum, *Black Feminist Theology: A New Word About God* (D. Min. Thesis, School of Theology at Claremont, 1980).

45. Katie G. Cannon, *Resources for a Constructive Ethic for Women with Special Attention to the Life and Work of Zora Neale Hurston* (Ph.D. dissertation, Union Theological Seminary, 1983).

46. Jualynne Dodson, *Women's Collective Power in the African Methodist Episcopal Church* (Ph.D. dissertation, University of California at Berkeley, 1983).

women" and "missionary women." She offers a historical synopsis of their contribution to the church, particularly as these initiated structural changes in church life.

In a similar vein, Evelyn Brooks in *The Women's Movements in the Baptist Church, 1880–1920*,[47] traces the development of Black Baptist women's activities, exploring the intersection and interaction of race, class and gender consciousness of those women who created the Women's Convention Auxiliary of the National Baptist Convention, and who thereby provided an arena for the leadership of Black Baptist women.

Though diverse and somewhat more descriptive than normative, these works lay the historical foundation that is needed for the development of a constructive black woman's theological perspective. This perspective in theology which I am calling womanist theology draws upon the life and experiences of some Black women who have created meaningful interpretations of the Christian faith.

2. The Starting Point for Womanist Theology

Because it is important to distinguish Black and White women's experiences, it is also important to note these differences in theological and Christological reflection. To accent the difference between Black and White women's perspective in theology, I maintain that Black women scholars should follow Alice Walker by describing our theological activity as "womanist theology." The term "womanist" refers to Black women's experiences. It accents, as Walker says, our being responsible, in charge, outrageous, courageous and audacious enough to demand the right to think theologically and to do it independently of both White and Black men and White women.

Black women must do theology out of their tridimensional experience of racism/sexism/classism. To ignore any aspect of this experience is to deny the holistic and integrated reality of Black womanhood. When Black women, say that God is on the side of the oppressed, we mean that God is in solidarity with the struggles of those on the underside of humanity.

In a chapter entitled "Black Women: Shaping Feminist Theory," Hooks elaborates the interrelationship of the threefold oppressive reality of Black women and shows some of the weaknesses of White feminist theory. Challenging the racist and classist assumption of White feminism, Hooks writes:

> Racism abounds in the writings of white feminists, reinforcing white supremacy and negating the possibility that women will bond politically across ethnic and racial boundaries. Past feminist refusal to draw attention to and attack racial hierarchy suppressed the link between race and class. Yet class structure in American society has been shaped by the racial politics of white supremacy.[48]

---

47. Evelyn Brooks, *The Women's Movement on the Black Baptist Church, 1880–1920* (Ph.D. dissertation, University of Rochester, 1984).

48. hooks, *Feminist Theology*, p. 3.

This means that Black women, because of oppression determined by race and their subjugation as women, make up a disproportionately high percentage of the poor and working classes. However, the fact that Black women are a subjugated group even within the Black community and the White women's community does not mean that they are alone in their oppression within those communities. In the women's community poor White women are marginalized, and in the Black community, poor Black men are also discriminated against. This suggests that classism, as well as racism and sexism, has a life of its own. Consequently, simply addressing racism and sexism is inadequate to bring about total liberation.[49] Even though there are dimensions of class which are not directly related to race or sex, classism impacts Black women in a peculiar way which results in the fact that they are most often on the bottom of the social and economic ladder. For Black women doing theology, to ignore classism would mean that their theology is no different from any other bourgeois theology. It would be meaningless to the majority of Black women, who are themselves poor. This means that addressing only issues relevant to middle class women or Blacks will simply not do: the daily struggles of poor Black women must serve as the gauge for the verification of the claims of womanist theology.

3. The Use of the Bible in the Womanist Tradition

Theological investigation into the experiences of Christian Black women reveals that Black women considered the Bible to be a major source for religious validation in their lives. Though Black women's relationship with God preceded their introduction to the Bible, this Bible gave some content to their God-consciousness.[50] The source for Black women's understanding of God has been twofold: first, God's revelation directly to them, and secondly, God's revelation as witnessed in the Bible and as read and heard in the context of their experience. The understanding of God as creator, sustainer, comforter, and liberator took on life as they agonized over their pain, and celebrated the hope that as God delivered the Israelites, they would be delivered as well. The God of the Old and New Testament became real in the consciousness of oppressed Black women. Though they were politically impotent, they were able to appropriate certain themes of the Bible which spoke to their reality. For example, Jarena Lee, a nineteenth century Black woman preacher in the African Methodist Episcopal Church constantly emphasized the theme "Life and Liberty" in her sermons which were always biblically based. This interplay of scripture and experience was exercised by many other Black women. An ex-slave woman revealed that when her experience negated certain oppressive interpretations of the Bible

49. This is reflected in the fact that the Black movement (Civil Rights/Black Power) has resulted in advancement of only some Blacks, primarily men, creating an emergent Black middle class. Likewise, the women's movement has meant progress for some women, primarily White, resulting in the increased class stratification in the women's community.

50. Cecil Wayne Cone, *Identity Crisis in Black Theology* (Nashville, TN: African Methodist Episcopal Church, 1975), passim, especially Chapter II.

given by White preachers, she, through engaging the biblical message for herself rejected them. Consequently, she also dismissed White preachers who distorted the message in order to maintain slavery. Her grandson, Howard Thurman, speaks of her use of the Bible in this way:

> "During the days of slavery," she said, "the master's minister would occasionally hold services for the slaves. Always the white minister used as his text something from Paul. 'Slaves be obedient to them that are your masters . . . , as unto Christ.' Then he would go on to show how, if we were good and happy slaves, God would bless us. I promised my Maker that if I ever learned to read and if freedom ever came, I would not read that part of the Bible."[51]

What we see here is perhaps more than a mere rejection of a White preacher's interpretation of the Bible, but an exercise in internal critique of the Bible. The Bible must be read and interpreted in the light of Black women's own experience of oppression and God's revelation within that context. Womanists must, like Sojourner, "compare the teachings of the Bible with the witness" in them.[52]

To do Womanist Theology, then, we must read and hear the Bible and engage it within the context of our own experience. This is the only way that it can make sense to people who are oppressed. Black women of the past did not hesitate in doing this and we must do no less.

4. The Role of Jesus in the Womanist Tradition

In the experiences of Black people, Jesus was "all things."[53] Chief among these however, was the belief in Jesus as the divine co-sufferer, who empowers them in situations of oppression. For Christian Black women in the past, Jesus was their central frame of reference. They identified with Jesus because they believed that Jesus identified with them. As Jesus was persecuted and made to suffer undeservedly, so were they. His suffering culminated in the crucifixion. Their crucifixion included rape, and babies being sold. But Jesus' suffering was not the suffering of a mere human, for Jesus was understood to be God incarnate. As Harold Carter observed of Black prayers in general, there was no difference made between the persons of the trinity, Jesus, God, or the Holy Spirit. "All of these proper names for God were used interchangeably in prayer language. Thus, Jesus was the one who speaks the world into creation. He was the power behind the Church. . . ."[54]

---

51. Howard Thurman, *Jesus and the Disinherited* (Nashville, TN: Abingdon Press, 1949), pp. 30–31.

52. Olive Gilbert, *Sojourner Truth: Narrative and Book of Life*, (1850 and 1875; reprinted, Chicago: Johnson Publishing Co., Inc., 1970), p. 83.

53. Harold A. Carter, *The Prayer Tradition of Black People* (Valley Forge, PA: Judson Press, 1976). Carter, in referring to traditional Black prayer in general, states that Jesus was revealed as one who "was all one needs!" p. 50.

54. *Ibid.*

Black women's affirmation of Jesus as God meant that White people were not God. One old slave woman clearly demonstrated this as she prayed:

> "Dear Massa Jesus, we all uns beg Ooner [you] come make us a call dis yere day. We is nutting but poor Etiopian women and people ain't tink much 'bout we. We ain't trust any of dem great high people for come to we church, but do' you is de one great Massa, great too much dan Massa Linkum, you ain't shame to care for we African people."[55]

This slave woman did not hesitate to identify her struggles and pain with those of Jesus. In fact, the common struggle made her know that Jesus would respond to her beck and call.

> Come to we, dear Massa Jesus. De sun, he hot too much, de road am dat long and boggy (sandy) and we ain't got no buggy for send and fetch Ooner. But Massa, you 'member how you walked dat hard walk up Calvary and ain't weary but tink about we all dat way. We know you ain't weary for to come to we. We pick out de toms, de prickles, de brier, de backslidin' and de quarrel and de sin out of you path so dey shan't hurt Ooner pierce feet no more.[56]

As she is truly among the people at the bottom of humanity, she can make things comfortable for Jesus even though she may have nothing to give him—no water, no food—but she can give tears and love. She continues:

> Come to we, dear Massa Jesus. We all uns ain't got no good cool water for give you when you thirsty. You know, Massa, de drought so long, and the well so low, ain't nutting but mud to drink. But we gwine to take de 'munion cup and fill it wid de tear of repentance, and love clean out of we heart. Oat all we hab to gib you, good Massa.[57]

For Black women, the role of Jesus unraveled as they encountered him in their experience as one who empowers the weak. In this vein, Jesus was such a central part of Sojourner Truth's life that all of her sermons made him the starting point. When asked by a preacher if the source of her preaching was the Bible, she responded "No honey, can't preach from de Bible—can't read a letter."[58] Then she explained; "When I preaches, I has jest one text to preach from, an' I always preaches from this one. My text is, 'When I found Jesus!'"[59] In this sermon Sojourner Truth recounts the events and struggles of her life from the time her parents were brought from Africa and sold "up an' down, an' hither an' yon. . ."[60]

55. *Ibid.*, p. 49.
56. *Ibid.*
57. *Ibid.*
58. Gilbert, *Book of Life*, p. 118.
59. *Ibid.*, p. 119.
60. *Ibid.*

to the time that she met Jesus within the context of her struggles for dignity of Black people and women. Her encounter with Jesus brought such joy that she became overwhelmed with love and praise:

> Praise, praise, praise to the Lord! An' I begun to feel such a love in my soul as I never felt before love to all creatures. An' then, all of a sudden, it stopped, an' I said, Dar's de white folks that have abused you, an' beat you, an' abused your people-think o' them! But then there came another rush of love through my soul, an' I cried out loud-'Lord, I can love *even de white folks!*[61]

This love was not a sentimental, passive love. It was a tough, active love that empowered her to fight more fiercely for the freedom of her people. For the rest of her life she continued speaking at abolition and women's rights gatherings, condemning the horrors of oppression.

5. The Significance of Jesus in the Womanist Tradition

More than anyone, Black theologians have captured the essence of the significance of Jesus in the lives of Black people which to an extent includes Black women. They all hold that the Jesus of history is important for understanding who he was and his significance for us today. By and large they have affirmed that this Jesus is the Christ, that is, God incarnate. They have argued that in the light of our experience, Jesus meant freedom.[62] They have maintained that Jesus means freedom from the sociopsychological, psychocultural, economic and political oppression of Black people. In other words, Jesus is a political messiah.[63] "To free (humans) from bondage was Jesus' own definition of his ministry."[64] This meant that as Jesus identified with the lowly of his day, he now identifies with the lowly of this day, who in the American context are Black people. The identification is so real that Jesus Christ in fact becomes Black. It is important to note that Jesus' blackness is not a result of ideological distortion of a few Black thinkers, but a result of careful Christological investigation. Cone examines the sources of Christology and concludes that Jesus is Black because "Jesus was a Jew." He explains:

> It is on the basis of the soteriological meaning of the particularity of his Jewishness that theology must affirm the Christological significance of Jesus' present blackness. He *is* black because he was a Jew. The affirmation of the Black Christ can be understood when the significance of his past Jewishness is related dialectically to the significance of his present blackness. On the one hand, the Jewishness of Jesus located him in the context

---

61. *Ibid.,* p. 122.

62. J. D. Roberts, *A Black Political Theology* (Philadelphia: The Westminster Press, 1974), p. 138. See especially Chapter 5. See also Noel Erskine, *Decolonizing Theology: A Caribbean Perspective* (New York: Orbis Books, 1980), p. 125.

63. Roberts, *A Black Political Theology,* p. 133.

64. Albert Cleage, *The Black Messiah* (New York: Sheed and Ward, 1968), p. 92.

of the Exodus, thereby connecting his appearance in Palestine with God's liberation of oppressed Israelites from Egypt. Unless Jesus were truly from Jewish ancestry, it would make little theological sense to say that he is the fulfillment of God's covenant with Israel. But on the other hand, the blackness of Jesus brings out the soteriological meaning of his Jewishness for our contemporary situation when Jesus' person is understood in the context of the cross and resurrection are Yahweh's fulfillment of his original intention for Israel . . . .[65]

The condition of Black people today reflects the cross of Jesus. Yet the resurrection brings the hope that liberation from oppression is immanent. The resurrected Black Christ signifies this hope.

Cone further argues that this Christological title, "The Black Christ" is not validated by its universality, but, in fact, by its particularity. Its significance lies in whether or not the Christological title "points to God's universal will to liberate particular oppressed people from inhumanity."[66] These particular oppressed peoples to which Cone refers are characterized in Jesus' parable on the Last Judgment as "the least." "The least in America are literally and symbolically present in Black people."[67] This notion of "the least" is attractive because it descriptively locates the condition of Black women. "The least" are those people who have no water to give, but offer what they have, as the old slave woman cited above says in her prayer. Black women's experience in general is such a reality. Their tri-dimensional reality renders their particular situation a complex one. One could say that not only are they the oppressed of the oppressed, but their situation represents "the particular within the particular."

But is this just another situation that takes us deeper into the abyss of theological relativity? I would argue that it is not, because it is in the context of Black women's experience where the particular connects up with the universal. By this I mean that in each of the three dynamics of oppression, Black women share in the reality of a broader community. They share race suffering with Black men; with White women and other Third World women, they are victims of sexism; and with poor Blacks and Whites, and other Third World peoples, especially women, they are disproportionately poor. To speak of Black women's tridimensional reality, therefore, is not to speak of Black women exclusively, for there is an implied universality which connects them with others.

Likewise, with Jesus Christ, there was an implied universality which made him identify with others—the poor; the woman, the stranger. To affirm Jesus' solidarity with the "least of the people" is not an exercise in romanticized contentment with one's oppressed status in life. For as the Resurrection signified that there is more to life than the cross for Jesus Christ, for Black women it signifies that their tri-dimensional oppressive existence is not the end, but it

---

65. Cone, *God of the Oppressed*, p. 134.
66. *Ibid.*, p. 135.
67. *Ibid.*, p. 136.

merely represents the context in which a particular people struggle to experience hope and liberation. Jesus Christ thus represents a three-fold significance: first he identifies with the "little people," Black women, where they are; secondly, he affirms the basic humanity of these, "the least"; and thirdly, he inspires active hope in the struggle for resurrected, liberated existence.

To locate the Christ in Black people is a radical and necessary step, but an understanding of Black women's reality challenges us to go further. Christ among the least must also mean Christ in the community of Black women. William Eichelberger was able to recognize this as he further particularized the significance of the Blackness of Jesus by locating Christ in Black women's community. He was able to see Christ not only as Black male but also Black female.

> God, in revealing Himself and His attributes from time to time in His creaturely existence, has exercised His freedom to formalize His appearance in a variety of ways. . . . God revealed Himself at a point in the past as Jesus the Christ a Black male. My reasons for affirming the Blackness of Jesus of Nazareth are much different from that of the white apologist. . . God wanted to identify with that segment of mankind which had suffered most, and is still suffering. . . . I am constrained to believe that God in our times has updated His form of revelation to western society. It is my feeling that God is now manifesting Himself, and has been for over 450 years, in the form of the Black American Woman as mother, as wife, as nourisher, sustainer and preserver of life, the Suffering Servant who is despised and rejected by men, a personality of sorrow who is acquainted with grief. The Black Woman has borne our griefs and carried our sorrows. She has been wounded because of American white society's transgressions and bruised by white iniquities. It appears that she may be the instrumentality through whom God will make us whole.[68]

Granted, Eichelberger's categories for God and woman are very traditional. Nevertheless, the significance of his thought is that he was able to conceive of the Divine reality as other than a Black male messianic figure.

6. Challenges for Womanist Christology

Although I have argued that the White feminist analysis of theology and Christology is inadequate for salvific efficacy with respect to Black women, I do contend that it is not totally irrelevant to Black women's needs. I believe that Black women should take seriously the feminist analysis, but they should not allow themselves to be coopted on behalf of the agendas of White women, for as I have argued, they are often racist unintentionally or by intention.

The first challenge therefore, is to Black women. Feminists have identified some problems associated with language and symbolism of the church, theology,

---

68. William Eichelberger, "Reflections on the Person and Personality of the Black Messiah," *The Black Church*, p. 54.

and Christology. They have been able to show that exclusive masculine language and imagery are contributing factors undergirding the oppression of women.

In addressing the present day, womanists must investigate the relationship between the oppression of women and theological symbolism. Even though Black women have been able to transcend some of the oppressive tendencies of White male (and Black male) articulated theologies, careful study reveals that some traditional symbols are inadequate for us today. The Christ understood as the stranger, the outcast, the hungry, the weak, the poor, makes the traditional male Christ (Black and White) less significant. Even our sisters, the womanist of the past though they exemplified no problems with the symbols themselves, they had some suspicions about the effects of a male image of the divine, for they did challenge the oppressive and distorted use of it in the church's theology. In so doing, they were able to move from a traditional oppressive Christology, with respect to women, to an egalitarian Christology. This kind of equalitarian Christology was operative in Jarena Lee's argument for the right of women to preach. She argued ". . . the Saviour died for the woman as well as for the man."[69] The crucifixion was for universal salvation, not just for male salvation or, as we may extend the argument to include, not just for White salvation. Because of this Christ came and died, no less for the woman as for the man, no less for Blacks as for Whites.

> If the man may preach, because the Saviour died for him, why not the woman? Seeing he died for her also. Is he not a whole Saviour, instead of half one? as those who hold it wrong for a woman to preach, would seem to make it appear?[70]

Lee correctly perceives that there is an ontological issue at stake. If Jesus Christ were a Savior of men then it is true the maleness of Christ would be paramount.[71] But if Christ is a Saviour of all, then it is the humanity—the wholeness—of Christ which is significant. Sojourner was aware of the same tendency of some scholars and church leaders to link the maleness of Jesus and the sin of Eve with the status of women and she challenged this notion in her famed speech "Ain't I A Woman?"

> Then that little man in black there, he says women can't have as much rights as men, 'cause Christ wasn't a woman! Where did your Christ come from? Where did your Christ come from? From God and a woman. Man had nothing to do with Him. If the first woman God ever made was strong

---

69. Jarena Lee, *Religious Experiences and Journal of Mrs. Jarena Lee* (Philadelphia, 1849), pp. 15–16.

70. *Ibid.*, p. 16.

71. There is no evidence to suggest that Black women debated the significance of the maleness of Jesus. The fact is that Jesus Christ was a real crucial figure in their lives. Recent feminist scholarship, as reflected in the discussion of Chapters III, IV and V, has been important in showing the relation between the maleness of Christ and the oppression of women.

enough to turn the world upside down all alone, these women together ought to be able to turn it back, and get it right side up again! And now they is asking to do it, the men better let them.[72]

I would argue, as suggested by both Lee and Sojourner, that the significance of Christ is not his maleness, but his humanity. The most significant events of Jesus Christ were the life and ministry, the crucifixion, and the resurrection. The significance of these events, in one sense, is that in them the absolute becomes concrete. God becomes concrete not only in the man Jesus, for he was crucified, but in the lives of those who will accept the challenges of the risen Saviour the Christ.

For Lee, this meant that women could preach; for Sojourner, it meant that women could possibly save the world; for me, it means today, this Christ, found in the experiences of Black women, is a Black woman. The commitment that to struggle not only with symptoms (church structures, structures of society), as Black women have done, but with causes (those beliefs which produce and re-inforce structures) yield deeper theological and Christological questions having to do with images and symbolism. Christ challenges us to ask new questions demanded by the context in which we find ourselves.

The second challenge for Black women is that we must explore more deeply the question of what Christ means in a society in which class distinctions are increasing. If Christ is among "the least" then who are they? Because our foreparents were essentially poor by virtue of their race, there was no real need for them to address classism as a separate reality. Today, in light of the emerging Black middle class we must ask what is the impact of class upon our lives and the lives of other poor Black and Third World women and men.

Another way of addressing the class issue in the church is to recognize the fact that although our race/sex analyses may force us to realize that Blacks and women should share in the leadership of the church, the style of leadership and basic structures of the church virtually insure the continuation of a privileged class.

Contemporary Black women in taking seriously the Christ mandate to be among the least must insist that we address all three aspects of Black women's reality in our analyses. The challenge here for contemporary Black women is to begin to construct a serious analysis which addresses the structural nature of poverty. Black women must recognize that racism, sexism and classism each have lives of their own, and that no one form of oppression is eliminated with the destruction of any other. Though they are interrelated, they must all be addressed.

The third and final challenge for Black women is to do constructive Christology. This Christology must be a liberating one, for both the Black women's community and the larger Black community. A Christology which

---

72. Truth, "Ain't I A Woman," in *Feminism*, ed. Schneir, p. 94.

negates Black male humanity is still destructive to the Black community. We must, therefore, take seriously only the usable aspects of the past.

To be sure, as Black women receive these challenges, their very embodiment represents a challenge to White women. This embodiment (of racism, sexism and classism) says to White women that a wholistic analysis is a minimal requirement for wholistic theology. The task of Black women then, is constructive.

As we organize in this constructive task, we are also challenged to adopt the critical stance of Sojourner with respect to the feminist analysis as reflected in her comment:

> I know that it feel a kind o' hissin' and ticklin' like to see a colored woman get up and tell you about things, and woman's rights. We have all been thrown down so low that nobody thought we' ever get up again, but we have been long enough trodden now; we will come up again, and now I am here. . . . I wanted to tell you a mite about Woman's Rights, and so I came out and said so. I am sittin' among you to watch; and every once in a while I will come out and tell you what time of night it is?[73]

73. *Ibid.*, pp. 96–98.

PART 6
AFRICAN AMERICAN THEMES AND PERSPECTIVES

Chapter 30

A Chronological Overview
The Negro in the United States:
A Brief History

Rayford Logan

Editor's Introduction: Rayford W. Logan (1897–1982) graduated from Williams College and earned his PhD in history from Harvard University. He served a long, distinguished career teaching history at Howard University and was undoubtedly one of America's premier historians of the African American experience. He is known mainly for his work on the post-Reconstruction period, which he described as "the nadir of American race relations." He also served as United States Commissioner for the United Nations Educational, Scientific, and Cultural Organization (UNESCO) and observer at the United Nations for the National Association for the Advancement of Colored People. In 1932 he was appointed by President Franklin Delano Roosevelt to serve on his so-called Negro Cabinet, where he drafted the executive order prohibiting racial discrimination in the military.

SLAVERY AND EMANCIPATION, 1619–1865

Slavery in the Colonies

Negroes participated in some of the earliest explorations by Spaniards in what is now the United States. The best known was Estevanico who accompanied Cabeza de Vaca during his six years of wandering, 1528–1534, Florida into Mexico and who served as guide to the Niza expedition, 1539, from Mexico into Texas and New Mexico. The first Negroes in English America were twenty who were brought to Jamestown, Virginia, by a Dutch man-of-war in 1619. Contemporary Virginia records show that they were probably servants rather than slaves. Slavery there did not receive statutory recognition until 1661. By that time it had become evident that Indians were not satisfactory laborers. Inasmuch as white servants were indentured usually for seven years, they would not fulfill the growing demands for labor.

Thus, economic necessity rather than racial prejudice dictated the beginning of Negro slavery in North America. But by the end of the seventeenth century and thereafter, only Negroes, with few unimportant exceptions, were slaves. The number of Negro slaves in Virginia increased so rapidly after 1661 that by the end of the century their masters began to fear more frequent and more numerous uprisings. The colonial assembly therefore adopted a rigid slave code, restricting the freedom of movement of the slaves, inflicting severe penalties for even minor offenses and denying slaves civil and criminal rights. The number of slaves continued to increase until they constituted more than thirty percent of the population on the eve of the American Revolution.

In all the other colonies, slavery began soon after their founding, increased until the American Revolution, and provoked varying degrees of fears of uprisings and of harshness of slave codes. Since the slaves were relatively most numerous in Delaware, Maryland, South Carolina (where they outnumbered whites two to one) and Georgia, the fears were greater and the slave codes more rigid. In North Carolina, where slaves numbered a little more than one-fourth of the population and where the influence of Quakers, in particular, softened somewhat the rigors of slavery, the tension was less pronounced. The smaller number of slaves in the Northern colonies was due primarily to the fact that these trading and commercial colonies had less need for them than did the planting colonies in the South. On the eve of the American Revolution the percentage of slaves varied from less than one per cent in New Hampshire to about eleven per cent in New York. This latter colony therefore enacted a slave code not unlike the codes in the Southern colonies. But two serious insurrections in New York City, 1712 and 1741, led to a decline in the number of slaves imported and an increase in the number of white workers.

In general, Puritans, the Society for the Propagation of the Gospel in Foreign Parts, and Quakers sought more energetically to Christianize and educate slaves than did religious bodies in the South. John Woolman, a Quaker, was particularly active in New Jersey. In Pennsylvania, Quakers at Germantown issued in 1688 what is generally regarded as the first public denunciation of slavery as a moral wrong. Anthony Benezet, a Philadelphia Huguenot, continued in the eighteenth century to question the right of one man to hold another in bondage. By 1750 Pennsylvania, like New York, was importing few slaves. While slavery was thus a less acute problem in the North than in the South, some Northern traders were particularly active in supplying slaves to both sections.

Opposition to Slavery

From the American Revolution until the invention of the cotton gin in 1793 considerable opposition to slavery and the slave trade developed in the states as far south as South Carolina. This opposition stemmed in part from the realization by some of the Revolutionary leaders of the embarrassing inconsistency between the struggle by white men for freedom from English "tyranny" and the holding by white men of black men in bondage. On October 24, 1774, the Continental Congress resolved not to import or purchase any slave after December 1 of that year. But the advocates of slavery secured the elimination from Thomas Jefferson's initial draft of the Declaration of Independence of the accusation which held the King of England responsible for forcing the slave trade upon the colonies. The final Declaration did, however, declare that "We hold these truths to be self-evident, that all men are created equal, that they are endowed by their Creator with certain unalienable Rights, that among these are Life, Liberty and the Pursuit of Happiness." Jefferson, a slaveholder, may have intended for the natural laws invoked in the Declaration to express opposition to slavery, but few other slaveholders did.

The participation of Negro soldiers in the Revolution did, however, strengthen the opposition to slavery. Crispus Attucks, a runaway slave, was the first to fall in the "Boston Massacre" of 1770. Slaves as well as free Negroes fought in the Battle of Bunker Hill, where Peter Salem killed the British Major Pitcairn. During the Revolution about 5,000 Negroes fought in the land forces and others in the naval, some of them as pilots because of their knowledge of coastal waters. James Madison saw in the emancipation and arming of Negroes the only solution to the vexatious problem in the South, where the British had promised emancipation to every Negro who would desert the Revolutionary army. Alexander Hamilton of New York and Colonel John Laurens of South Carolina urged the employment of Negro soldiers, Hamilton having written to John Jay, President of the Continental Congress on March 14, 1779, "This will secure their fidelity, animate their courage, and, I believe, will have a good influence upon those who remain, by opening the door to their emancipation." Since Negro troops helped to win independence for the United States, continued enslavement probably troubled the consciences of some Americans. Either because of a troubled conscience or because of appreciation for services rendered, masters in many states manumitted hundreds of Negro soldiers and their families after the Revolution.

The first antislavery society had been formed in 1775, and during the next ten years Rhode Island, Connecticut, and Pennsylvania passed laws looking toward the abolition of slavery. In 1783 a decision of the Massachusetts Supreme Court held that slavery violated the state constitution which stated that "all men are born free and equal." Particularly important because of the later crucial controversy over the right of Congress to prohibit slavery in territories was the provision of the Northwest Ordinance of 1787 which stipulated that neither slavery nor involuntary servitude should exist in the territory that became the states of Ohio, Indiana, Illinois, Michigan, and Wisconsin.

The first Congress which met after the ratification of the Constitution on June 25, 1788, re-enacted this Ordinance of the Congress of the Confederation. But the Constitution, which studiously avoided the words slave, slavery, and the slave trade, made three major concessions to slaveholders. Three-fifths of the slaves were to be counted in determining the population of a state for purposes of representation in Congress. Congress could not prohibit prior to 1808 the importation of slaves but might impose a tax not to exceed ten dollars on each slave imported. Slaves escaping into another state had to be surrendered to the slaveholder. On the other hand, when the first Congress met, Georgia was the only state that seemed to retain a pecuniary interest in the importation of slaves. Even South Carolina had passed a law temporarily prohibiting the importation of slaves. The Constitution of Vermont, February 18, 1791, the first new state admitted to the Union, prohibited slavery.

Growth of the Cotton Kingdom

The invention of the cotton gin in 1793 reversed the trend toward the abolition of slavery in the Southern states and state action to end the slave trade. Cotton textiles had been the key industry in the English "Industrial Revolution" which had begun in the middle of the eighteenth century. Since cotton goods were being produced at cheaper prices and in larger quantities for an expanding market, there was need for a larger supply of cotton. The cotton gin, which permitted slaves to devote all their time to planting and hoeing, greatly helped to meet the growing demand. More and more planters in the Southern seaboard states cultivated cotton instead of rice, indigo, and tobacco; planters also opened new cotton fields. The new demand for slaves prevented effective enforcement of the law passed by Congress in 1807 prohibiting the participation by Americans in the slave trade as of January 1, 1808. Even though another law in 1820 made such participation an act of piracy, smuggling continued to the eve of the Civil War. But legislation did not apply to the domestic slave trade which became more profitable after importation became more difficult.

After the first successful power loom was set up in New England in 1814, that section vied with England and European countries for the purchase of cotton. Shortly thereafter the principality of the Southern seaboard states expanded into the cotton kingdom by the opening up of plantations in the new states of Louisiana, Mississippi, and Alabama. Slaves were also extensively used on the sugar cane plantations of Louisiana. By the decade of the thirties these three states were producing ninety per cent more cotton than were the older southeastern states. The South produced nearly twice as much cotton in 1830 as in 1820, twice as much in 1840 as in 1830, and more than three times as much in 1860 as in 1840. Since the highest profits were gained from virgin soil, slaveholders constantly sought new territory, especially Texas. While some planters continued to grow rice, sugar, tobacco, and hemp, many others followed the practice of buying more slaves to grow more cotton. "Cotton was King," but the kingdom was hostage to the slaves it held in bondage. The price of a prime field hand had risen from $200 in 1800 to $1,800 on the eve of the Civil War. At that time there were almost four million slaves with an estimated value of three billion dollars . . . .

Limited Expansion in the Territories

Meanwhile, the contest over slavery in the territories fixed in large measure the limits of the expansion of the Negro population beyond the original thirteen states. The Missouri Compromise of 1820 provided that slavery should not exist above thirty-six degrees, thirty minutes, in that part of the Louisiana Territory that had not been organized into states, but should be permitted south of that line. Since slaveholders were the principal agents in introducing Negroes into new regions, a vast area extending roughly from the Mississippi to the Rockies and from what became the state of Oklahoma to the Canadian border had a very small Negro population. Slavery was forbidden by Congress, 1848, in the Oregon Territory, which included the present state of that name, the states of Washington, Idaho, and part of Montana. The abolition of slavery by Mexico in 1829 virtually destroyed that institution in the land ceded to the United States at the end of the Mexican War, 1848. That cession comprised what became the states of California, Nevada, Utah, Arizona, and portions of New Mexico, Colorado, and Wyoming. With the exception of California, moreover, the terrain did not lend itself to agriculture and enterprises that could use large numbers of slaves. Recognizing this fact, the Compromise of 1850 admitted California as a free state and stipulated that the other territories were to be admitted with or without slavery as their constitutions might provide.

The Kansas-Nebraska Act of 1854 repealed the Missouri Compromise and thereby opened up to slavery the territory in which that Compromise had prohibited it. Since Kansas was contiguous to the slaveholding state of Missouri, slaveholders made strenuous efforts to ensure that Kansas would come into the Union as a slave state. Equally determined opponents of slavery prevailed after years of bitter fighting.

In 1857 the famous Dred Scott decision theoretically opened all territories to slavery. But before any considerable number of slaves could be taken to them, the Civil War began and Congress in 1862 prohibited slavery in the territories. A map of the distribution of slaves in 1860 shows that, with the exception of Kansas, the territories acquired by purchase from France, by cession from Mexico, and by treaty with Great Britain were almost entirely free from slaves. Not until after World War II were some of the states formed from these territories to have sizable Negro populations.

Slave Uprisings

The slave uprisings during the colonial period became more serious in the nineteenth century. In 1800 more than 1,000 Negroes under the leadership of Gabriel Prosser and Jack Bowler planned an attack on Richmond, Virginia. Betrayed by two slaves, the insurrectionists were confronted by some six hundred troops who captured many of them; more than thirty, including Prosser, were executed. During the next twenty years several uprisings and threats of uprisings along the Atlantic seaboard, in Kentucky and Louisiana, spurred the plans to settle free and slave Negroes in foreign lands. Even more serious than the uprising planned by Prosser and Bowler was the abortive plot in Charleston, South Carolina, 1822, led by a free Negro, Denmark Vesey. But foreknowledge again enabled the authorities to crush the incipient insurrection; more than two-score Negroes, including Vesey, were executed.

The insurrection led by a slave, Nat Turner, in Southampton County, Virginia, in 1831, resulted in the killing of some sixty whites. State and federal troops quickly crushed the uprising, killing more than a hundred slaves. Almost a score of other Negroes, including Turner, were hanged. In addition to convincing many whites that Negroes should be deported, the Turner insurrection led to the adoption of more rigid slave codes. The uprisings none the less continued until the Civil War, some of them aided by sympathetic whites. Individual Negroes also killed their masters. Most slaves, however, accepted more or less grudgingly their bondage.

Proposals for the Colonization of Negroes

Some Americans opposed slavery and, for different reasons, advocated various methods for getting rid of it. Two of the least practicable were the forced or voluntary departure of Negroes to places outside the colonies or the United States—to the territories, to Canada, to islands in the Caribbean, to Central and South America, and above all to Africa. While proposals for deportation had been advanced early in the eighteenth century and were renewed after the American Revolution, it was not until early in the nineteenth that the colonization of Negroes abroad began.

In 1815 Paul Cuffe of Massachusetts, the son of an Indian mother and a Negro father who had sailed his own ships to England, Europe, the West Indies, South America, and Africa, took thirty-eight free Negroes to Africa. Organizers of the American Colonization Society, formed in 1816, sought the advice of

Cuffe for guidance in its plans to send larger numbers of Negroes to Africa. But Cuffe, shortly before his death in 1817, came to the conclusion that migration by Negroes from the United States would be interpreted as an admission of their inability to survive there.

The aims of the American Colonization Society were, in fact, mixed. Some leaders were sincerely interested in ridding the United States of slavery; others feared free Negroes as the potential leaders of slave insurrections. Many declared that God had brought Negroes to the United States to be civilized and Christianized so that they could return to Africa and aid in the rehabilitation of their brethren.

Congress appropriated $100,000 in 1819 for the transportation to Africa of Negroes illegally imported to the United States, and in 1821 the Society established the colony of Liberia. But most Negro leaders and many white abolitionists opposed colonization because they suspected the aims of the colonizationists. After the death of Paul Cuffe, James Forten of Philadelphia became the first passionate foe of colonization. A free-born Negro, he fought as a teen-age powder monkey in the American Revolution and became a crusader for temperance, peace, and women's rights. He devoted a large share of his wealth, estimated at about $100,000, to these humanitarian efforts. Forten also was a leader in calling the first convention in 1830 for the discussion of colonization, education, employment, and other problems.

On the other hand, some prominent Negroes concluded by the 1850's that the Negro had little hope for ameliorating his plight in the United States. Among the best known of these advocates of voluntary emigration were Martin R. Delany, Alexander Crummell, and the West-Indian-born Edward W. Blyden. Their numerous writings had little success against their adversaries, who used as their strongest argument the virtual impossibility of transporting large numbers of Negroes to foreign lands. Only about 12,000, most of them free Negroes, migrated to Liberia, and a much smaller number to Haiti. It has been estimated that not more than 25,000 Negroes sought refuge in foreign lands until Marcus Garvey launched a new "Back to Africa" Movement after World War I . . . .

The Abolition Movement

Some abolitionists opposed colonization because they believed that, in due time, Negroes would receive equal treatment in the United States. In 1848 (two years before the passage of the Fugitive Slave Law), Henry Highland Garnet went so far as to hope that, very soon, his country's flag would be hailed by all nations as the emblem of freedom and independence. In the same year, Frederick Douglass advocated equal freedom for Negroes and at the same time urged that they be worthy of it. By 1855, he was convinced that this equal freedom was nearer, because the days of "Black Power," or slave power, were numbered.

Basically, however, abolitionists opposed slavery because it was morally wrong. A few of them, seeing little hope for immediate emancipation, advocated the amelioration of the plight of slaves. Another group, including such staunch crusaders as Theodore Dwight Weld and James G. Birney, favored immediate emancipation followed by gradual stages before the freedmen were given equal status. William Lloyd Garrison presented the doctrine of immediate and unqualified emancipation in the first issue of his magazine, the *Liberator,* January, 1831. Until the adoption of the Thirteenth Amendment in 1865, uncompromising views made him the leading and at the same time the most controversial of the abolitionists. Of the numerous other white abolitionists, Wendell Phillips, Theodore Parker, the Tappan brothers, Elijah P. Lovejoy, Lucretia Mott, Lydia Maria Child, and the Grimke sisters from South Carolina were the most effective. Organized efforts began with the formation in 1831 of a New York Committee and of the New England Anti-slavery Society. Two years later, there was formed the American Antislavery Society.

Negroes participated in the abolition movement in various ways. Their subscriptions helped to keep the *Liberator* alive. They were authors of *slave narratives,* some of them undoubtedly ghost-written. A few, such as those bearing the names of William Wells Brown, Lunsford Lane, J. W. C. Pennington, and J. W. Loguen, were probably the handiwork of the authors. The best known, most authentic, and most influential were those of Frederick Douglass, first published in 1845. He also founded, edited, and published in Rochester, New York, a weekly newspaper, *The North Star,* 1847–1850, which he called after that date until 1865 *Frederick Douglass's Paper.* It was the only long-lived newspaper published by Negroes during this period.

Negro abolitionist orators mounted the platform with their white colleagues and shared with them the same insults and dangers. Most outstanding were Samuel Ringgold Ward, David Ruggles, Charles B. Ray, Charles Lenox Remond and his sister, Sarah, James W. C. Pennington, Alexander Crummell, Henry Highland Garnet, and Sojourner Truth. Preeminent was Frederick Douglass. The abolitionist movement was not only a moral crusade against "man's inhumanity to man"; it was also a part of the nineteenth century "Awakening of the American Mind" that included not only intellectual and cultural activities but also crusades for reform for working men, prisoners, and women, for a wider suffrage for white men, and for public schools, also largely for whites.

The abolitionist movement must also be included in a history of "Freedom to Dissent" and the resultant physical perils. Some Northerners supported abolitionists, even going so far as to use force in attempts to liberate runaway slaves. On the other hand, "doughfaces," the contemptuous but accurate term which identified Northerners who could be molded or kneaded to accept Southern apologies for slavery, used violence to make clear their anti-abolitionist views. Garrison was dragged through the streets of Boston and almost lynched; Elijah P. Lovejoy, editor of a newspaper in Alton, Illinois, was put to death by a mob. Lewd remarks were hurled at white women speakers. Of the numerous Negro abolitionists who refused to submit to abuse and physical attacks, Frederick Douglass has left the most vivid chronicle. Refusing to submit to segregation on the railroad from Boston to Portland, Maine, he used his great muscular strength to prevent several employees from throwing him out of a first-class coach. This early "sit-in" resulted eventually in the abolition of segregated coaches in all of New England, according to Douglass.

The most dramatic episodes of the abolition movement involved escapes of runaway slaves by way of the Underground Railroad and attempts by slaveholders and their sympathizers to recapture them. This "Railroad" consisted of flexibly chosen routes and "stations" or houses of Negroes and sympathetic whites. Courageous whites and Negroes were "conductors." One of the most courageous was Harriet Tubman, the "Moses" of the slaves, who, despite a high price on her head, returned repeatedly to the South. She is said to have led more than 300 slaves out of bondage.

Between the early part of the nineteenth century and 1850, it has been estimated, some 100,000 slaves valued at more than $30,000,000 escaped to the North and Canada. The Southern planters and Northern business interests, which reaped large profits from the sale of manufactured goods to the Southern states, combined to obtain the passage of the Fugitive Slave Law of 1850. Like the Fugitive Slave Law of 1793, it provided that slaveholders or their agents might seize an alleged runaway without legal process or a warrant. New provisions made the 1850 Law more stringent, however. The new Law placed the main burden of enforcement upon United States commissioners and marshals. The commissioners were given concurrent powers with circuit and district judges. The marshals could summon aid of citizens to assist them to make the arrests. Any person obstructing the recovery of a fugitive or assisting him to escape was liable to a fine of $1,000 and a prison sentence of six months. The testimony of the alleged fugitive was not to be admitted as evidence.

On one hand, the 1850 Law reduced the number of runaway slaves. It is estimated that fewer than 10,000 slaves were helped to freedom by the Underground Railroad between 1850 and 1860. On the other hand, the Law led to passive and violent resistance, searching questions of the constitutionality of the Law and increased open defiance and nullification of the Law by several Northern states. In Maine, New Hampshire, Vermont, Massachusetts, New York, Michigan, and Wisconsin, public attorneys were appointed to defend all persons arrested as fugitive slaves. In most of these states, as well as in Rhode Island, Pennsylvania, and Ohio, the use of public buildings, including jails, was denied for the detention of fugitives. Various states adopted anti-kidnapping laws providing for fine and imprisonment, laws stipulating that slaves brought into states were free, and habeas corpus acts. Most important, the Fugitive Slave Law and the Personal Liberty Laws greatly widened the gap between defenders and opponents of slavery; an accommodation between them became increasingly unlikely between 1850 and 1860. The abolition of the slave trade but not of slavery in the District of Columbia by the Compromise of 1850, of which the Fugitive Slave Law was a part, further buttressed the determination to wipe out slavery in the United States and its Territories. The Fugitive Slave

Law probably won more converts to abolition than did any other law except the Kansas-Nebraska Act of 1854.

Southern Opposition to Abolitionism

The activities of the abolitionists, especially their alleged incitement of slave uprisings and the real aid that they gave to runaway slaves, infuriated the South. In 1832, the year after the publication of the first issue of Garrison's *Liberator* and the year after Nat Turner's insurrection, the last significant debate on slavery in a Southern legislature took place in Virginia. In 1835 a mob in Charleston, South Carolina, burned a sack of abolitionist literature. Many Southern postmasters refused to deliver such literature and few persons in the South dared to be found in possession of it. By 1835 most of the Southern states had prohibited or restricted the immigration of free Negroes as well as their right of free assembly. In that same year, North Carolina completed the action of other Southern states in denying Negroes the right to vote. During the 1830's and early 1840's Southern Congressmen succeeded in preventing debates in the House on abolitionist petitions. Ex-President John Quincy Adams, a member of the House, led the fight to have the "Gag Rule" repealed in 1844. John Brown's raid, 1859, on the federal arsenal at Harpers Ferry, West Virginia, with a view to a large-scale operation against slavery in Virginia, infuriated the South more than any other single act because some leading abolitionists were suspected of having helped Brown to plan the raid.

The arguments and activities of the abolitionists led to systematic and increasingly adamant arguments by prominent Southerners in support of slavery. Thomas Roderick Dew, professor and later president at the College of William and Mary, Virginia, John C. Calhoun of South Carolina, and Chancellor William Harper of the Supreme Court of South Carolina insisted that slavery was necessary to permit men of superior intelligence to devote their attention to affairs of government. Calhoun, leader of the nullification movement in South Carolina, 1832, particularly developed the argument that a majority had no right to impose its will upon a minority.

One of the other effective arguments quoted the Bible in support of slavery—for example, although there were slaves when Christ was on earth, He did not preach against it. Many Southerners argued that the Constitution did not prohibit slavery and that it did not give Congress the power to prohibit slavery in the territories. Edmund Ruffin contended that large-scale slavery produced handsome profits, ignoring the facts that only about 100,000 Southerners owned as many as ten slaves, and that, according to Hinton R. Helper's *Impending Crisis,* slavery was responsible for the miserable plight of the non-slaveholding whites. These whites were frequently told that they were superior to the few slaves who fared better than did some poor whites and superior even to free Negroes. The mere fact of being white established their superiority.

Treatment of Slaves

Abolitionists and slaveholders and their respective supporters differed widely in the pictures that they drew of the lot of the slave. In fact, one could prove, then as now, that slavery was horrible or that it was benign and beneficial to the slave. The lot of most slaves was somewhere between the romanticized picture of the literate, well-fed craftsman and of the beloved "mammy" who helped to run the planter's household and to mother his children on the one hand, and of the brutalized slaves in Harriet Beecher Stowe's *Uncle Tom's Cabin* on the other hand. Slaves had poorer food and housing than did workers in the Northern part of the United States, but not much poorer than did workers in the backward parts of Europe. Slaves were treated worse on the large plantations under overseer and absentee management than on the smaller plantations under personal management. Whippings were not uncommon on the large plantations. The breakup of slave families was all too common, as was the practice of slaveholders to have Negro women for their concubines. This common practice, indulged in especially by wealthy slaveholders, created understandable bitterness on the part of their wives. Perhaps the most justifiable indictment of slavery was the fact that the slaves were at the whim of their masters and that they were without legal protection. Probably the most disastrous result of the "peculiar institution" was the fact that the slaveholders had not prepared the slave for freedom since they could not or would not work out a set of human relations between white men and Negro freedmen.

Professors Melville J. Herskovits and E. Franklin Frazier agree that African survivals were less intense in what became the United States than in other parts of the New World. This difference was due primarily to the fact that survivals were largely related to the size of plantations. There were more African slaves concentrated on vast plantations in the West Indies and Brazil, for instance, than in English America. In 1860 in the South as a whole, three-fourths of the farms had fewer than fifty slaves. On these smaller plantations Negroes had more contacts with whites than on the larger. On the islands off the coast of South Carolina and Georgia, where Negroes had few contacts with whites, Professor Lorenzo D. Turner has discovered approximately 4,000 words of African origin in the Gullah vocabulary of Negroes.

Exceptional Negroes Prior to the Civil War

In recent years, painstaking research has discovered a sizable number of college-trained and other well-educated Negroes before 1861. John Chavis, a freeman from North Carolina, perhaps studied at the Princeton Theological Seminary in the latter part of the eighteenth century. He certainly studied at Washington Academy, now Washington and Lee University, Lexington, Virginia. Lemuel Haynes received an honorary degree of Master of Arts from Middlebury College, Vermont, in 1804. Edward Jones graduated from Bowdoin College in

1826 a few weeks before John B. Russwurm, who until now has been called the "first" Negro college graduate. Another colored student finished Ohio University in 1828. George B. Vashon, graduated from Oberlin College in 1844, was one of the three Negroes on the faculty of Central Labor College, McGrawsville, New York, sometimes called "the miniature Oberlin." Five years later, John Mercer Langston, also graduated from Oberlin: in 1852 he received the degree of Master of Arts, and in 1853 he graduated from Oberlin's School of Theology. Jonathan Gibbs received his A. B. degree from Dartmouth College in 1856.

A number of Negroes studied medicine. Records of Bowdoin College and the Medical School of Maine show that James Hall was listed in the class of 1822; Thomas Joiner White and Van Surlay De Grasse both graduated from the Medical School of Maine in 1849. Colored preachers were educated at the Theological Seminary, Gettysburg; the Dartmouth Theological School; Wesleyan Seminary, Wilbraham, Massachusetts; and the Theological Seminary of Charleston, South Carolina.

A few Negroes also studied abroad. Ira Aldridge, one of the most renowned actors of Shakespearean plays in Europe from 1826 until his death in Poland on August 7, 1867, studied briefly at Glasgow University in the 1820's. Alexander Crummell, considered by both his contemporaries and interested modern historians as one of the most learned Negroes of his day, completed his studies for the ministry in Queen's College, Cambridge University, in 1853. A peer of Crummell, Robert Brown Elliott, was graduated from Eton College, University of London, in 1859. James McCune Smith received an A.B. degree at the University of Glasgow in 1834, an A.M. in 1836, and a medical degree in 1837. James W. C. Pennington, considered one of the leading theologians of his day, was given the degree of Doctor of Divinity by the University of Heidelberg before the Civil War. Francis L. Cardozo, who was later nominated for the presidency of Howard University, studied four years at the University of Glasgow and three years at the Presbyterian seminaries in Edinburgh and London before returning to the United States in 1864.

Causes of the Civil War

In the campaign of 1860 the Republican candidate, Abraham Lincoln, was elected president. Seven slave states seceded and organized the Confederate States of America before he took office on March 4, 1861. Confederate troops attacked the federal Fort Sumter, South Carolina, on April 12. The Civil War began and four other slave states joined the Confederacy. Interpretations of the causes of secession and of the Civil War have, like those of other wars, glorified the victors, justified the vanquished, reasserted former positions, and reached a consensus among scholars that has in turn leaned to one side or the other. Thus, slavery was a moral wrong; it was a positive good. Slavery was the main cause of the war; it had nothing to do with it. The Civil War was the Second American Revolution growing out of a conflict of interest between the industrial North and the agricultural South; it was the result of an emotional crisis. The doctrine of state rights was deeply rooted in the slave controversy; the doctrine was primarily a constitutional issue based upon the right of a minority to prevent a majority from imposing its will. The slavocracy—"The Martial South"—was determined to make all free territory slave, to reopen the slave trade and to make all free states slave; it was a conspiracy on the part of the North to impose its way of life on the South. Southerners were incapable of conceiving a plan for the existence of Negro freedmen; if the South had been let alone, it would have abolished slavery. Lincoln's election did not threaten slavery in the states; his election meant that all slave states would become free. The attack on Fort Sumter was an infamous attack; Lincoln maneuvered the South into making the attack. The Civil War was a rebellion on the part of the slave states; it was a war to establish Southern independence. It was an irrepressible conflict; it was a needless war.

Whatever interpretations are accepted—there was no one cause, remote or immediate—the question of slavery and of the Negro was either focal or peripheral.

Emancipation

Regardless of the causes of the war, Northern victory brought the emancipation of the slaves. Negroes played a not inconsiderable part in that victory. Some 186,000 Negro troops took part in 198 battles and skirmishes and suffered 68,000 casualties. The total number of Negroes, including servants, laborers, and spies, amounted to more than 300,000. A much smaller number of Negro soldiers served in the ranks of the Confederate army. Lincoln at first opposed the enlistment of Negro troops and the emancipation of the slaves because he did not wish to lose the support of the border slave-holding states of Delaware, Maryland, Kentucky, and Missouri and because emancipation, after initial Confederate victories, would seem like "the last shriek on the retreat." In the continuing argument about Lincoln's views on emancipation, some historians cite Lincoln's well-known statement that his primary aim was to save the Union; he would do so whether this policy required the emancipation of some, all, or none of the slaves. On this point the evidence is clear that Lincoln, an astute statesman, was wiser than the advocates of a policy which would liberate all and especially those who would free none of the slaves. On July 22, 1862, he told his Cabinet that he was going to issue an Emancipation Proclamation. Following a Union victory at Antietam on September 17, 1862, and to forestall the possibility that England might recognize the Confederacy, he issued a preliminary Emancipation Proclamation on September 22, 1862. On January 1, 1863, acting in his capacity as Commander-in-Chief of the Army and the Navy, he proclaimed the emancipation of all slaves except in those states or parts of states not in rebellion against the United States at that time. *(See Document No. 1A.)* Even before the final Emancipation Proclamation, Negroes had begun to desert the plantations. After the Proclamation, the arrival of Union troops led to even larger-scale flight to the Union forces. On December 18, 1865, the Thirteenth Amendment *(see Document No. 1B)* abolished slavery everywhere in the United States.

Presidential Reconstruction

Revolutionary changes in a way of life generate fresh acts of violence which complicate and prolong the period of adjustment. Such a change was Reconstruction, the twelve years after the Civil War when the federal government attempted to give the freedmen substantially equal rights with those enjoyed by other American citizens. Southerners so strenuously opposed this attempt that the federal government after 1877 left the adjustment almost entirely to the Southern states. In a larger sense, reconstruction of Southern society has continued until today when new federal intervention has provoked again strenuous resistance. The nationalization of the so-called Negro problem by large-scale migration to the North from the South since 1914 has made reconstruction a national problem.

President Lincoln favored a moderate plan, under his own direction, for the restoration of the seceded states. He would have limited Negro suffrage to veterans and "the very intelligent." The states themselves would have determined this question. "With malice toward none, with charity to all," he planned to restore the seceded states to the Union by permitting ten percent of the qualified voters of 1860 in any state, after taking the oath of allegiance, to form a state government. In accordance with this plan, he recognized four state governments in 1864. Congress, however, opposed this "executive usurpation" and denied admission to the representatives and senators chosen by those states. It passed the Wade-Davis Bill which required that a majority of the white citizens of a state take the oath of allegiance. These would elect delegates to a state convention which should pledge the state to abolish slavery and to deny political rights to all high-ranking civil and military officers of the Confederacy. After the constitution had been approved by a majority of the voters and by Congress, the president was to recognize the state government. Lincoln vetoed this Bill. Thus, a basic conflict as to the terms and control of Reconstruction emerged while Lincoln was still president and there were no Southerners in Congress. An open breach was averted when the next session of Congress took no further action on the restoration of the seceded states.

The death of Lincoln on April 15, 1865, a few weeks before the end of the war, greatly augmented the difficulties of healing the nation's wounds. The facts that the "Great Emancipator" had been assassinated by a Southerner and that an attempt had been made at the same time on the life of Secretary of State William H. Seward infuriated public opinion at the North. The fact that Lincoln's successor, Andrew Johnson, on the whole followed Lincoln's plan for restoring the seceded states enraged many members of Congress. Unlike Lincoln, moreover, Johnson did not require that even ten per cent of the white voters would have to take the oath of allegiance before forming a state government. Above all, Johnson refused to call a special session of Congress during the summer and fall of 1865 and presented the Thirty-ninth Congress which convened on December 4, 1865, with a *fait accompli.* All the seceded states except Texas had held constitutional conventions; all others except Mississippi had annulled the acts of secession and ratified the Thirteenth Amendment. They had elected members of state legislatures, representatives to Congress and, with the exception of Florida, senators.

Congressional Reconstruction

Many Congressmen not only opposed Johnson's "executive usurpation" on constitutional grounds but they were also dismayed by its consequences. The Southern states seemed unregenerate. They had elected a large number of ex-Confederates to the state governments and to Congress. Foremost among these was Alexander Stephens, former Vice-President of the Confederacy, who was elected senator from Georgia. None of the states had placed any restrictions on the political rights of former enemies of the Union. The Thirteenth Amendment, proclaimed in effect shortly after Congress convened, would later give the ex-slave states increased representation in Congress—the abolition of slavery meant that all Negroes instead of three-fifths would be counted in the population. None of the slave states, moreover, had made any provisions for Negro suffrage. Congress, paying scant attention to Johnson's temperate justification of his executive plan, quickly voted to establish a Joint Committee of Fifteen to investigate conditions in the former Confederate states and to inquire whether they were entitled to be represented in Congress. Meanwhile, Congress refused to admit the Southern representatives and senators.

The adoption of "Black Codes" *(see Document No. 2)* by the Southern states provided Congressional leaders with further evidence of the obduracy of the Johnson-sponsored governments. In various states these Codes allowed Negroes to testify only in cases in which they were involved. They protected the property rights of Negroes but restricted their right to acquire property, especially real estate. Convinced that the freedmen intended to enjoy their freedom by refusing to work, the framers wrote into the Codes provisions that restricted the freedmen's mobility and that sought to compel them to work—in some instances for their former masters. Although few freedmen could read or write, they had to make written annual contracts for their labor. The South was responding to emancipation by enacting laws that relegated Negroes to a caste not measurably higher than slavery.

For some ten years there ensued a tug-of-war between "Radical Republicans," led by Representative Thaddeus Stevens of Pennsylvania and Senator Charles Sumner of Massachusetts, and Southern "Bourbons" led by "ex-Brigadiers." The more extreme Republicans favored a harsh policy toward the "treasonous" South that had grossly maltreated Northern prisoners of war, especially at Andersonville. Allied with less vindictive Republicans, they insisted upon full political and civil rights for Negroes. (While many Northern states still denied full equality to free Negroes, these states were not seeking to relegate them to a servile status.) More practical politicians sought primarily the establishment of control of the South by the Republican party, based upon Negro suffrage, and the maintenance of Northern industrial supremacy over the agricultural South. Reactionary Southerners, determined to maintain a white man's government free from federal encroachment, fought the Radical Republicans step by step until they won an almost complete victory. The principal sufferers in this tug-of-war were the freedmen.

Early in 1866 the Radical Republicans began to carry out Congressional Reconstruction despite the stubborn opposition of President Johnson. Congress had passed and Lincoln had approved in March, 1865, a bill creating the Bureau of Refugees, Freedmen and Abandoned Lands which was to expire a year after the end of the war. Early in 1866 a bill was introduced to amplify the powers of the Freedmen's Bureau and to make it permanent. Johnson vetoed the bill because of his contention that the Constitution did not authorize Congress, especially one in which the states most concerned were not represented, to support indigent persons or to give permanent aid to one class or color of citizens. In July, 1866, Congress overrode Johnson's veto but limited the powers of the Freedmen's Bureau to two years. The Bureau supplied food, clothing, fuel, and hospital care to a large number of both whites and Negroes. It sought to protect the freedmen from violence and serfdom and to defend their rights to hold property. Its most notable work was in the field of education.

Congress did not enact a Third Freedmen's Bureau Bill, and its activities ceased after 1872. There was thus a clear reluctance on the part of Congress to intervene in economic matters as distinguished from civil and political. The South bitterly criticized the activities of the Freedmen's Bureau because many agents interfered in the relations between masters and servants and encouraged Negroes to vote.

Congress in 1866 adopted two other measures for the protection of the freedmen. A Civil Rights Bill, passed over Johnson's veto, declared that Negroes were citizens of the United States and, as such, were entitled to equal treatment before the law, any "statute to the contrary notwithstanding." One clause stipulated that all such persons would be subject to like punishment, pains, and penalties. Section 2 made it a misdemeanor for any official to violate this provision or to deprive any person of rights secured by the Act. Courts of the United States were granted jurisdiction in case of offenses under the Act. (With some modification, this became Section 2 of the Federal Criminal Code, now generally known as Section 52, Title 18 of the United States Criminal Code. It is this section which was invoked in the 1967 prosecution of Mississippi state officials accused of participating in the murder of two white and one colored civil-rights leaders.)

In an attempt to prevent future contests over the constitutionality of the law and to give Negroes further protection, Congress adopted the Fourteenth

Amendment. *(See Document No. 3A)* The Amendment made Negroes citizens of the states in which they resided as well as of the United States. It forbade a state to make or enforce any law that would abridge the privileges or immunities of citizens of the United States; to deprive any person of life, liberty, or property without due process of law; or to deny to any person within its jurisdiction equal protection of the laws. If a state, for any reason except rebellion or other crime, prohibited adult male citizens from voting, the representation of the state in Congress should be reduced in the proportion that those denied the right to vote bore to the total number of adult male citizens in the state. The Amendment barred from federal and state office many of the most important pre-Civil War Southerners and gave Congress power to enforce the Amendment.

This Amendment constituted, in some ways, a more serious threat to the South than did the Freedmen's Bureau Bill. If adopted, it might mean permanent interference by the federal government. It confronted the states with the dilemma of Negro suffrage or of a loss of representation in the House of Representatives and, consequently, in the Electoral College. Southerners believed that they had a legitimate grievance since the Southern states, although not yet restored to the Union, were asked to ratify the Amendment. All the Southern states, except Tennessee, quickly rejected the Amendment. This rejection led many Northerners to believe that Carl Schurz's severely critical report of conditions in the South, based upon a three-months' tour, was much more accurate than the more favorable report of General Grant, based upon a much shorter investigation. The organization in 1865 of the Ku Klux Klan, followed by that of other private groups, terrorized an increasing number of Negroes, and added to the conviction of many Northerners that even more stringent measures were necessary for the success of congressional Reconstruction. Johnson's intemperate language prior to the Congressional elections of November, 1866, helped the Its Radicals to carry both houses by large majorities.

Congress, overriding Johnson's vetoes, enacted the Reconstruction Acts of March 2 and 23, 1867. They placed all the ex-Confederate states except Tennessee, which had ratified the Fourteenth Amendment, under military governors who were to direct the calling of constitutional conventions elected by colored voters and by those whites who had never been disfranchised for disloyalty. These conventions should draw up new constitutions giving Negroes the right to vote. If the state constitution were adopted by a majority of the Negro and eligible white voters and approved by Congress, if the state legislature elected under this new constitution adopted the Fourteenth Amendment, and if three-fourths of the states ratified it, the state would be restored to the Union and the federal troops withdrawn. Each of the newly elected representatives and senators had to take the "iron clad" oath that he had never given voluntary aid to the Confederacy. The fact that, at about the same time, the Northern states of Minnesota, Kansas, Ohio, and Michigan rejected Negro suffrage by large majorities made many Southerners more determined to resist what they considered federal encroachment upon state rights.

Andrew Johnson, with one exception, consistently opposed bills favorable to the Negro. On the same day, March 2, 1867, that he vetoed the First Reconstruction Act, he signed the bill incorporating Howard University for "the education of youth in the liberal arts and sciences," and other departments, including notably law and medicine. It is not known whether Johnson realized that the Founders of the University interpreted "youth" to mean without discrimination based on race or color (or sex). He vigorously opposed the enforcement of the two Reconstruction Acts of March 2 and 23 as well as subsequent Acts. Since Secretary of War Edwin M. Stanton favored enforcement, Johnson suspended him from office on August 12, 1867. The House of Representatives impeached Johnson, especially for alleged violation of the Tenure of Office Act. But in May, 1868, the Senate acquitted him.

"Black Reconstruction"

In late 1867, Negroes, as provided in the Reconstruction Acts of March 2 and 23, 1867, voted for the first time in large numbers in the former slave states. They and some white voters elected delegates to state constitution conventions which provided for the election of Negroes at whites to state legislatures.

The term "Black Reconstruction" is a misnomer as it generally understood. Only in the South Carolina constitutional convention did Negroes outnumber whites—seventy-six to forty eight. Of the seventy-six, fifty-seven had been slaves. As nearly as can be determined, there were forty-nine colored and forty-nine white delegates to the Louisiana constitutional convention. In all the other constitutional conventions, Negroes were in the minority. Florida had eighteen Negro delegates out of forty-five Virginia, twenty-five out of 108; Georgia, thirty-three out of 170; Alabama, eighteen out of 108; Arkansas, eight out of sixty-six; Mississippi, seventeen out of 100; North Carolina fifteen out of 133; Texas, nine out of ninety. The percentage of Negroes in the state legislatures was about the same.

In most of the states, then, the constitutions and laws were the handiwork of "carpetbaggers" and "scalawags," as well as of Negroes. The first of these were Northerners, mostly white, who have been accused of moving into the South with only a carpetbag (suitcase), empty or partly filled, to batten on the impoverished South and to establish the political and economic control of the "Radicals" in the Republican Party. The "scalawags" have been popularly portrayed as Southern whites, among whom were many poor whites, who basely betrayed the best interests of their states, that is, interests founded upon the reestablishment of white supremacy. Negroes in the constitutional conventions and the state legislatures and in state, county, and municipal offices have been frequently excoriated and ridiculed. Slavery, of course, had not prepared the freedmen for participation in government, and the voteless free Negroes in the South also lacked political experience. In 1867 more than ninety per cent of southern Negroes were illiterate and propertyless; few paid taxes. Many Negroes were intelligent enough, however, to believe that men of their own race and white men who had emancipated them would be more likely to endeavor to promote their interests than would former slaveholders and their sympathizers. If the freedmen did not always distinguish between candidates seeking selfish political power and those earnestly desiring to launch a better way of life, they were little different in from voters in other parts of the country. The devices used by The Union League, many Northern soldiers, and agents of the Freedmen's Bureau, to see to it that Negroes "voted right" were not unlike those used in Northern cities to have foreign-born and the native-born whites "vote right." As the *New York Tribune* had pointed out in 1865, "white men, who are ignorant and vicious, vote."

It was the votes of Negroes, carpetbaggers, and scalawags that provided the majorities in some Southern states for the ratification of the Fourteenth Amendment. *(See Document No. 3A.)* On July 27, 1868, President Johnson announced the ratification and the admission of seven Southern states to Congress. Virginia, Mississippi, and Texas, which still remained under martial law, were required to ratify also the Fifteenth Amendment. *(See Document No. 3B.)* This Amendment stated that the right to vote of citizens of the United States should not be denied or abridged on account of race, color, or previous condition of servitude. Congress was given the power to enforce the Amendment, which was proclaimed in effect on March 30, 1870. Except in Louisiana, where there had been a number of educated, intelligent, and well-to-do free Negroes, many of the Negro delegates, legislators, and officials were illiterate, propertyless, nontaxpaying ex-slaves. There were a few notable exceptions. Jonathan C. Gibbs, Florida secretary of state, 1868–1872 and superintendent of public instruction, 1872–1874, was, according to a white historian, William W. Davis, "the most cultured member of the convention." A graduate of Dartmouth College, New Hampshire, Gibbs was largely responsible for the establishment of the state's system of public schools. Francis L. Cardozo, secretary of state in South Carolina, 1868-1872, and treasurer, 1872–1876, had been educated at the University of Glasgow. Robert Brown Elliott, member of the South Carolina convention and legislature, was educated at Eton College, England. Jonathan Jasper Wright, associate justice of the Supreme Court of South Carolina, 1870–1877, was the first colored man admitted to the bar in Pennsylvania. J. T. Rapier, who had private tutors and who had continued his studies in Canada, was a member of the Alabama convention. James D. Lynch, secretary of state in Mississippi, 1868–1872, was "an able and highly educated Pennsylvanian."

Although the number of Negro college graduates and other unusually well-trained men was exceedingly small, so was that of white members of the Reconstruction governments. Some of the Negroes who had less formal education than those listed above were capable administrators and legislators. Notable among the administrators were three lieutenant-governors of Louisiana: Oscar J. Dunn, 1868–1870; P. B. S. Pinchback, 1871–1872, and governor for forty-three days in 1872; C. C. Antoine, 1872–1876. William G. Brown, superintendent of public instruction in Louisiana, 1872–1876, expanded the public school system started by a Union general in 1864. Antoine Dubudet, state treasurer of Louisiana, 1868–1879, was honest and efficient. James D. Hill "filled quietly and efficiently" the office of secretary of state in Mississippi from 1872 to 1878. Among the more competent members of the conventions and legislatures were T. W. Springer and John R. Lynch in Mississippi, Henry McNeal Turner and Jefferson Long in Georgia.

The collective performance of these carpetbaggers, scalawags, and Negroes can best be evaluated by the constitutions that they drafted, the laws that they enacted, and their management of the states' business.

The constitutions and laws contained many admirable provisions, the most important of which was the inauguration of a mandatory system of state-supported public schools for both whites and Negroes. In various states, other provisions liberalized suffrage and enlarged the rights of women; abolished dueling, imprisonment for debt, the whipping post, the branding iron, and mal stocks; instituted reforms in the organization of the courts, the codes of judicial procedure, and in the system of county Administration; repealed the labor laws of 1865 and 1866. Controversy over the role of Negroes and their allies during reconstruction has generally obscured the fact that the main features of the Black Reconstruction constitutions and laws that did not pertain specifically to Negroes have survived to this day.

The most serious charges leveled at the Black Reconstruction governments have been alleged widespread corruption and enormous increases in the state debts. Corruption was unquestioned; it was participated in by Negroes, carpetbaggers, scalawags, and "loyal" Southern whites. Negroes who shared in the corruption were guilty of pilfering and of accepting petty bribes rather than of plundering; most of the bribing was done by whites. There were honest Negroes like Francis L. Cardozo, treasurer of South Carolina, and dishonest Negroes like his brother, T. W. Cardozo, superintendent of public instruction in Mississippi. Some Negroes accused of defalcations were found not guilty. Others who were probably guilty were not tried.

Few Negroes profited from the increase in the state debts, albeit many of them voted for appropriations that added to the states' financial burdens. The crux of the problem concerns the purposes for which expenditures were made. An inordinate amount was appropriated for stationery, printing, useless clerks, whiskey, and fried-chicken picnics. Most of the increases, however, were for railroads, roads, and other public services in which Northern capital saw an opportunity for profitable investments. There is little correlation between the increase in state indebtedness and the duration or extent of Negro participation in the state governments. In Virginia and Tennessee, for example, where white Southerners were in practically complete control during the brief period of Reconstruction, the indebtedness increased from $52,000,000 in 1860 to $88,000,000 before 1880. In South Carolina, where Negroes exercised the largest share of control for the longest period the indebtedness rose from $6,000,000 in

1860 to $25,000,000 in 1880. Moreover, some of the new agricultural states—Illinois, for example—had a per capita debt comparable to that of the Southern states. During Reconstruction, the Tweed Ring looted New York City out of almost $100,000,000 and the administration of President Grant was one of the most corrupt in the history of the nation. For all these reasons, as Professor Howard K. Beale has urged, the whole question of the great increase in Southern state debts needs to be restudied.

The whole question of Black Reconstruction should also be restudied in terms of the years that Negroes, carpetbaggers, and scalawags participated in government. White rule was restored Tennessee in 1869; in Virginia, North Carolina, and Georgia 1870; in Alabama, Arkansas, and Texas in 1874; and in Mississippi in 1875. Thus, only South Carolina, Louisiana, and Florida remained to be "redeemed" in 1876.

Negroes in Congress

Between 1869 and 1877 two Negroes sat in the Senate of the United States and fourteen different Negroes in the House. Since Hiram R. Revels of Mississippi served only one year, 1870 to 1871, to fill an unexpired term, he accomplished little. Blanche K. Bruce, also Mississippi, was the only Negro to serve a full term in the Senate, 1875–1881. The slave son of a wealthy Virginia planter and of a colored woman, he was educated by a tutor and, after his escape from slavery, for two years at Oberlin College, Ohio. His interests in the Senate covered a wide range. His primary concern was, quite naturally, the Negro: federal aid for Negro emigrants to Liberia; the abolition of separate Negro regiments in the United States army since there was no segregation in the navy; reimbursement of depositors in the bankrupt Freedmen's Savings and Trust Company; the investigation of elections in Mississippi. *(See Document No. 4.)* He also favored an enlightened policy toward Indians and opposed the restriction of Chinese emigration to the United States. He urged federal aid for public education and for internal improvements, and he introduced a bill on the Geneva award for the Alabama Claims.

While few of Bruce's bills, except those for pensions, were enacted into law, he enjoyed the esteem of his colleagues, notably Lamar of Mississippi. Bruce presided briefly over the Senate on two occasions and received eight votes for vice-president at the Republican convention in 1880. He subsequently served two administrations as register of the treasury and one recorder of deeds of the District of Columbia.

Of the fourteen Negro representatives during Reconstruction, one served for all four terms, one for three terms, and two for two terms. One, Robert Brown Elliott of South Carolina, was, as previously noted, a graduate of Eton College. One other had some college training. The other twelve had secondary training or less. It is difficult to evaluate the intellectual level of their speeches, as well as those of their white colleagues, because they underwent considerable revision in the *Congressional Globe* and *Congressional Record.* Most of them fell into obscurity after leaving Congress. A notable exception was John R. Lynch of Mississippi, who was elected temporary chairman of the Republican National Convention in 1884 and who wrote two interesting histories of Reconstruction. Quite understandably, the Negro members of Congress supported bills for the additional protection of Negroes.

Restoration of "Home Rule"

Despite the presence of federal troops and, indeed, with the aid of some Northern soldiers, Southerners used fraud, intimidation, and violence to liquidate Black Reconstruction. Scores of secret organizations committed such numerous outrages, which they justified on the ground of retaliation against similar acts by Negroes, that Congress enacted new legislation in 1870 and 1871.

The Civil Rights Act (First Enforcement Act) of May 31, 1870, was enacted two months after the Fifteenth Amendment was declared in effect. This Act re-enacted and expanded the Civil Rights Act of 1866. It also provided that all citizens otherwise qualified by law to vote in any state or subdivision thereof should be allowed to vote without distinction as to race, color, or previous condition of servitude. By many detailed provisions, the Act implemented this right. This Enforcement Act also made it a felony for two or more persons to conspire together, or to go in disguise to injure, oppress, threaten, or intimidate any citizen, with intent to prevent or hinder his free exercise and enjoyment of any right or privilege granted or secured to him by the Constitution or laws of the United States, or because of his having exercised the same. (With some modifications, it became Section 19 of the Criminal Code, and is generally known now as Section 51, Title 18 of the United States Criminal Code. Under it, persons other than state officials have been prosecuted in the 1960's for participation in acts against civil rights leaders.) The 1870 Act also made more specific than did the 1866 Law acts by officials which would be a misdemeanor.

By the end of 1870, it was clear that the provisions of the First Enforcement Act did not prevent violence and intimidation of large numbers of Negroes seeking to vote. Therefore, on February 28, 1871, the Second Enforcement Act provided for the appointment by federal courts of supervisors of elections and made interference with their duties a federal offense.

Increased lawlessness, especially in South Carolina, led to the Third Enforcement Act of April 20, 1871. Because its primal purpose was to restrict the activities of secret societies such as the Ku Klux Klan, it was commonly referred to as the Ku Klux Klan Act. It repeated the misdemeanor provisions of the 1866 and 1870 Acts and the felony provision of the 1870 Act. In addition, it prohibited conspiracies to overthrow the government of the United States; to prevent the execution of its laws; to use force or threat to prevent any person from holding office or discharging the duties of any office under the United

States; to deter any party or witness from testifying in any United States court; or to influence any juror in any United States court.

The three laws provided inadequate protection to Negroes, and "home rule" or white supremacy was gradually restored in all the states of the Old Confederacy. This restoration was facilitated by other acts of Congress at about the same time that repealed the "iron clad" oath and restored the franchise to all except about 600 ex-Confederate officials.

Last Civil Rights Laws

Congress made three final efforts to legislate in behalf of civil rights for Negroes. Two laws, June 20, 1872, and June 26, 1873, provided that a "respectable well-behaved" person had to be served without regard to race, color, or previous condition of servitude by keepers of hotels and other public places in the District of Columbia. The Civil Rights Act of March 1, 1875, provided that all persons within the jurisdiction of the United States should be entitled to "the full and equal enjoyment of the accommodations, facilities, and privileges of inns, public conveyances on land or water, theatres, and other places of public amusement; subject only to the conditions and limitations established by law, and applicable alike to citizens of every race and color, regardless of any previous condition of servitude." The person aggrieved could recover $500; the offender was guilty of a misdemeanor and federal courts were given exclusive jurisdiction. Although the law applied to the whole nation, it fell with special force upon the South where nine-tenths of all Negroes lived. After considerable debate, a provision requiring the desegregation of public schools was defeated.

Balance Sheet of Reconstruction

While the federal government and the white South were locked in a struggle for power, the baffled and confused pawns were groping to adjust to freedom. Among them were strong men and weaklings; devoted wives, companions and mothers, and loose women; hard workers and scamps; good providers and spendthrifts. Since slavery did not leave a legacy of an overpowering zest for work, many freedmen wandered the countryside and lolled on city streets. Others—whether because of compulsion, temperament or character, precept and example—settled down to the humdrum task of making a hard-won living and a humble home. A fortunate few gained land of their own, in some instances through the benevolence of former masters. But the vast majority were handicapped by the greatest blunder of Reconstruction, the general failure to provide land and tools. Most Southern Negroes, therefore, became a landless proletariat.

A small group went to school. Northern philanthropy, aided for a brief period after the end of the war by the Freedmen's Bureau, established private schools before the Black Reconstruction state governments inaugurated the public school systems. Soon after Union forces gained control of a city or a sizable rural community, freedmen began to learn their three R's. The first school, taught by Mrs. Mary S. Peake, a colored woman, was opened on September 17, 1861, in Hampton, Virginia. By 1869 there were 9,502 teachers in these schools. The American Missionary Association of the Congregational Church, the Baptists, Methodists, Presbyterians, and Episcopalians, especially joined in one of the most moving episodes in the history of American education. Many of the teachers were Northern white women who, as well as men, suffered ostracism, insults, and violence. Some colored teachers were also crusaders, notably Charlotte Forten, a grand-daughter of James Forten, and Francis Cardozo, who was principal of Avery Institute, Charleston, South Carolina.

Most singular, it appeared to scoffers, was the founding of "universities." Edmund A. Ware, a graduate of Yale University, was the first president of Atlanta University, Atlanta, Georgia, that started in a freight car, 1865. Erastus M. Cravath, graduate of Oberlin College, 1857, headed Fisk University, Nashville, Tennessee, which opened in 1866. General Oliver O. Howard, a graduate of Bowdoin College, Maine, who was Commissioner of the Freedmen's Bureau, was the third president of Howard University, Washington, D.C., founded in 1867. While these so-called universities for many years had more elementary, high school, and normal school than college students, they had goals inspired by those of the best Northern institutions of higher learning. Howard and Fisk received in 1953 chapters of Phi Beta Kappa, the national honorary society founded at the College of William and Mary, Virginia, 1776 with the aim: "You are to indulge in matters of speculation, that freedom of inquiry which ever dispels the clouds of falsehood."

These universities, along with thirty other universities and colleges founded in the South during Reconstruction, graduated many teachers and others who constituted a segment of what William Edward Burghardt Du Bois later called "The Talented Tenth." Others attended Northern schools. Three of them, founded before the Civil War—Cheyney Institute and Lincoln University in Pennsylvania and Wilberforce University in Ohio—were for colored students. Some were graduated from white schools: William S. Scarborough, later president of Wilberforce, from Oberlin College, Ohio, in 1875; E. M. Brawley, later president of Selma University, Alabama, from Bucknell College, Pennsylvania, in the same year. By 1877, three Negro physicians, two dentists, and two lawyers had graduated from Harvard University. In 1870 Richard T. Greener, later United States consul to Vladivostok and Bombay, was the first Negro to receive the A.B. degree from Harvard College.

Vocational education, which best suited the needs of most Negroes, was started by General Samuel C. Armstrong, a graduate of Williams College, Williamstown, Massachusetts, at Hampton Institute, Hampton, Virginia, in 1868, with the aims: "To train selected youth who shall go out and reach and lead their people, first by example, by getting land and homes: to give them not a dollar that they can earn for themselves; to teach respect for labor; to replace stupid drudgery with skilled hands; and to these ends to build up an industrial system for the sake of character." It was the forerunner of Tuskegee Institute, Tuskegee, Alabama, founded by Booker T. Washington in 1881, and of other schools that put major emphasis on vocational training.

During this crucial period of adjustment, Negroes suffered cruel blows in addition to the early demise of the Freedmen's Bureau and the failure of the federal government to provide all but a very small number with land and tools. Some freedmen lost their first savings when the Freedmen's Savings and Trust Company went into bankruptcy, 1874. Even more harmful was the policy of segregation adopted by the National Labor Union in 1869. Unaware of, or unimpressed by, the Marxist dogma of the class struggle, this first national federation of workers looked upon black workers as competitors for jobs rather than as allies in the struggle against capitalism. Negroes, led by Isaac Myers, formed in the same year the National Colored Labor Union. To be sure, organized labor did not have at that time the power that it acquired by mid-twentieth century. But within the framework of its limited power it did, as Myers charged, exclude Negroes from the workshops of the nation. Both of these unions disappeared by 1873, the colored one in part because of the attempt of politicians like Frederick Douglass to use it as an arm of the Republican party. This policy of segregation by white workers created a tradition of hostility on the part of black workers against organized labor just as the failure of the Freedmen's Bank generated a distrust of banks in general.

Most devastating were the decisions of The United States Supreme Court which whittled down the protection that the Radical Reconstructionists thought they had written into the Constitution. In the Slaughter House Cases, 1873 (see Document No. 5), the Court ruled that most privileges and immunities inhered in state citizenship and that they, therefore, were not protected by the Fourteenth Amendment. Three years later the Court in United States v. Reese invalidated the provision of the 1870 Act relating to voting rights under the Fifteenth Amendment. The ruling stated that Congress should have limited its legislation to state interference based on race, color, or previous condition of servitude. But the sections invalidated were phrased broadly enough to cover any type of discrimination.

In the same year, 1876, the ruling in United States v. Cruikshank (see Document No. 6) applied the reasoning in the Slaughter House Cases and extended it beyond privileges and immunities to rights. The rights peacefully to assemble, to petition for redress of grievances, and to bear arms were secured to individuals in their capacity as citizens of states, not of the United States. For this reason, the Court struck down the key "conspiracy" provision in the 1870 Act.

The balance sheet of Reconstruction thus showed on the surface a substantial debit. The restoration of white supremacy in the South was well-nigh complete. Pragmatically, the federal government had failed in its experiment to give Southern Negroes the political power to participate effectively in shaping their own destiny. The federal government had quickly abandoned its feeble efforts to intervene in economic matters. The Supreme Court had declared unconstitutional some of the laws passed for the protection of the freedmen. Organized labor had spurned the new contingent of black workers. Black politicians and trade union leaders, understandably, had not been able to cope with the seminal forces aligned against them.

On the other hand, Negroes were learning to survive by grudgingly accommodating themselves to the disappointments of freedom. Their colleges and "universities" would reduce the high rate of illiteracy and train future leaders. Their churches afforded the less fortunate solace to sustain them against their worldly woes. During this post-Civil War period boys and girls were born or already growing up who would demonstrate in some of the nation's best institutions of higher learning their ability to compete on equal terms with white scholars. The "Dream of American Democracy" for Negroes was gaining momentum at the very moment when it seemed to have been stultified.

Chapter 31

Spiritual Strivings

The Souls of Black Folk

W. E. B. DuBois

Editor's Introduction: Clearly one of the classic texts on the African American experience was published in 1903 by one of America's greatest civil rights activists and public intellectuals, W. E. B. DuBois (1868–1963). His long life was devoted fully to the work of scholarship and activism in pursuit of racial justice both at home and abroad. He was the first black to receive his PhD from Harvard University. He was one of the founders of the National Association for the Advancement of Colored People and a chief organizer for the five Pan-African Congresses that met between 1900 and 1945. He wrote more than twenty books and countless articles and essays in numerous literary genres. Some have said that all genres of writings by and about African Americans are indebted to DuBois's perceptive analysis in *The Souls of Black Folk.*

OF OUR SPIRITUAL STRIVINGS

Between me and the other world there is ever an unasked question: unasked by some through feelings of delicacy; by others through the difficulty of rightly framing it. *All,* nevertheless, flutter round it. They approach me in a half-hesitant sort of way, eye me curiously or compassionately, and then, instead of saying directly, How does it feel to be a problem? They say, I know an excellent colored man in my town; or, I fought at Mechanicsville; or, Do not these Southern outrages make your blood boil? At these I smile, or am interested, or reduce the boiling to a simmer, as the occasion may require. To the real question, How does it feel to be a problem? I answer seldom a word.

And yet, being a problem is a strange experience, peculiar even for one who has never been anything else, save perhaps in babyhood and in Europe. It is in the early days of rollicking boyhood that the revelation first bursts upon one, all in a day, as it were. I remember well when the shadow swept across me. I was a little thing, away up in the hills of New England, where the dark Housatonic winds between Hoosac and Taghkanic to the sea. In a wee wooden schoolhouse, something put it into the boys' and girls' heads to buy gorgeous visiting-cards—ten cents a package—and exchange. The exchange was merry, till one girl, a tall newcomer, refused my card,—refused it peremptorily, with a glance. Then it dawned upon me with a certain suddenness that I was different from the others; or like, mayhap, in heart and life and longing, but shut out from their world by a vast veil. I had thereafter no desire to tear down that veil, to creep through; I held all beyond it in common contempt, and lived above it in a region of blue sky and great wandering shadows. That sky was bluest when I could beat my mates at examination-time, or beat them at a foot-race, or even beat their stringy heads. Alas, with the years all this fine contempt began to fade; for the worlds I longed for, and all their dazzling opportunities, were theirs, not mine. But they should not keep these prizes, I said; some, all, I would wrest from them. Just how I would do it I could never decide: by reading law, by healing the sick, by telling the wonderful tales that swam in my head,—some way. With other black boys the strife was not so fiercely sunny: their youth shrunk into tasteless sycophancy, or into silent hatred of the pale world about them and mocking distrust of everything white; or wasted itself in a bitter cry, Why did God make me an outcast and a stranger in mine own house? The shades of the prison-house closed round about us all: walls strait and stubborn to the whitest, but relentlessly narrow, tall, and unscalable to sons of night who must plod darkly on in resignation, or beat unavailing palms against the stone, or steadily, half hopelessly, watch the streak of blue above.

After the Egyptian and Indian, the Greek and Roman, the Teuton and Mongolian, the Negro is a sort of seventh son, born with a veil, and gifted with second-sight in this American world,—a world which yields him no true self-consciousness, but only lets him see himself through the revelation of the other world. It is a peculiar sensation, this double-consciousness, this sense of always looking at one's self through the eyes of others, of measuring one's soul by the tape of a world that looks on in amused contempt and pity. One ever feels his two-nesss,—an American, a Negro; two souls, two thoughts, two unreconciled strivings; two warring ideals in one dark body, whose dogged strength alone keeps it from being torn asunder.

The history of the American Negro is the history of this strife, this longing to attain self-conscious manhood, to merge his double self into a better and truer self. In this merging he wishes neither of the older selves to be lost. He would not Africanize America, for America has too much to teach the world and Africa. He would not bleach his Negro soul in a flood of white Americanism, for he knows that Negro blood has a message for the world. He simply wishes to make it possible for a man to be both a Negro and an American, without being cursed and spit upon by his fellows, without having the doors of Opportunity closed roughly in his face . . . .

This, then, is the end of his striving: to be a co-worker in the kingdom of culture, to escape both death and isolation, to husband and use his best powers and his latent genius. These powers of body and mind have in the past been strangely wasted, dispersed, or forgotten. The shadow of a mighty Negro past flits through the tale of Ethiopia the Shadowy and of Egypt the Sphinx. Throughout history, the powers of single black men flash here and there like falling stars, and die sometimes before the world has rightly gauged their brightness. Here in America, in the few days since Emancipation, the black man's turning hither and thither in hesitant and doubtful striving has often made his very strength to lose effectiveness, to seem like absence of power, like weakness. And yet it is not weakness,—it is the contradiction of double aims. The double-aimed struggle of the black artisan—on the one hand to escape white contempt for a nation of mere hewers of wood and drawers of water, and on the other hand to plough and nail and dig for a poverty stricken horde—could only result in making him a poor craftsman, for he had but half a heart in either cause. By the poverty and ignorance of his people, the Negro minister or doctor was tempted toward quackery and demagogy; and by the criticism of the other world, toward Ideals that made him ashamed of his lowly tasks. The would-be black *savant* was confronted by the paradox that the knowledge his people needed was a twice-told tale to his white neighbors, while the knowledge which would teach the white world was Greek to his own flesh and blood. The innate Jove of harmony and beauty that set the ruder souls of his people a-dancing and a-singing raised but confusion and doubt in the soul of the black artist; for the beauty revealed to him was the soul beauty of a race which his larger audience despised, and he could not articulate the message of another people. This waste of double aims, this seeking to satisfy two unreconciled ideals, has wrought sad havoc with the courage and faith and deeds of ten thousand people,—has sent them often wooing false gods and invoking false means of salvation, and at times has even seemed about to make them ashamed of themselves.

Away back in the days of bondage they thought to see in one divine event the end of all doubt and disappointment; few men ever worshipped

Freedom with half such unquestioning faith as did the American Negro for two centuries. To him, so far as he thought and dreamed, slavery was indeed the sum of all villainies, the cause of all sorrow, the root of all prejudice; Emancipation was the key to a promised land of sweeter beauty than ever stretched before the eyes of wearied Israelites. In song and exhortation swelled one refrain—Liberty; in his tears and curses the God he implored had Freedom in his right hand. At last it came,—suddenly, fearfully, like a dream. With one wild carnival of blood and passion came the message in his own plaintive cadences:—

> "Shout, O children!
> Shout, you're free
> For God has bought your liberty!"

Years have passed away since then—ten, twenty, forty; forty years of national life, forty years of renewal and development, and yet the swarthy spectre sits in its accustomed seat at the Nation's feast. In vain do we cry to this our vastest social problem:—

> "Take any shape but that, and my firm nerves
> Shall never tremble."

The Nation has not yet found peace from its sins; the freedman has not yet found in freedom his promised land. Whatever of good may have come in these years of change, the shadow of a deep disappointment rests upon the Negro people,—a disappointment all the more bitter because the unattained ideal was unbounded save by the simple ignorance of a lowly people.

The first decade was merely a prolongation of the vain search for freedom, the boon that seemed ever barely to elude their grasp,—like a tantalizing will-o'-the-wisp, maddening and misleading the headless host. The holocaust of war, the terrors of the Ku-Klux Klan, the lies of carpet-baggers, the disorganization of industry, and the contradictory advice of friends and foes, left the bewildered serf with no new watch-world beyond the old cry for freedom. As the time flew, however, he began to grasp a new idea. The ideal of liberty demanded for its attainment powerful means, and these the Fifteenth Amendment gave him. The ballot, which before he had looked upon as a visible sign of freedom, he now regarded as the chief means of gaining and perfecting the liberty with which war had partially endowed him. And why not? Had not votes made war and emancipated millions? Had not votes enfranchised the freedmen? Was anything impossible to a power that had done all this? A million black men started with renewed zeal to vote themselves into the kingdom. So the decade flew away, the revolution of 1876 came, and left the half-free serf weary, wondering, but still inspired. Slowly but steadily, in the following years, a new vision began gradually to replace the dream of political power,—a powerful movement, the rise of another ideal to guide the unguided, another pillar of fire by night after a clouded day. It was the ideal of "book-learning"; the curiosity, born of compulsory ignorance, to know and test the power of the cabalistic letters of the white man, the longing to know. Here at last seemed to have been discovered the mountain path to Canaan; longer than the highway of Emancipation and law, steep and rugged, but straight, leading to heights high enough to overlook life.

Up the new path the advance guard toiled, slowly, heavily, doggedly; only those who have watched and guided the faltering feet, the misty minds, the dull understandings, of the dark pupils of these schools know how faithfully, how piteously, this people strove to learn. It was weary work. The cold statistician wrote down the inches of progress here and there, noted also where here and there a foot had slipped or some one had fallen. To the tired climbers, the horizon was ever dark, the mists were often cold, the Canaan was always dim and far away. If, however, the vistas disclosed as yet no goal, no resting-place, little but flattery and criticism, the journey at least gave leisure for reflection and self-examination; it changed the child of Emancipation to the youth with dawning self-consciousness, self-realization, self-respect. In those somber forests of his striving his own soul rose before him, and he saw himself,—darkly as through a veil; and yet he saw in himself some faint revelation of his power, of his mission. He began to have a dim feeling that, to attain his place in the world, he must be himself, and not another. For the first time he sought to analyze the burden he bore upon his back, that dead-weight of social degradation partially masked behind a half-named Negro problem. He felt his poverty; without a cent, without a home, without land, tools, or savings, he had entered into competition with rich, landed, skilled neighbors. To be a poor man is hard, but to be a poor race in a land of dollars is the very bottom of hardships. He felt the weight of his ignorance,—not simply of letters, but of life, of business, of the humanities; the accumulated sloth and shirking and awkwardness of decades and centuries shackled his hands and feet. Nor was his burden all poverty and ignorance. The red stain of bastardy, which two centuries of systematic legal defilement of Negro women had stamped upon his race, meant not only the loss of ancient African chastity, but also the hereditary weight of a mass of corruption from white adulterers, threatening almost the obliteration of the Negro home.

A people thus handicapped ought not to be asked to race with the world, but rather allowed to give all its time and thought to its own social problems. But alas! While sociologists gleefully count his bastards and his prostitutes, the very soul of the toiling, sweating black man is darkened by the shadow of a vast despair. Men call the shadow prejudice, and learnedly explain it as the natural defence of culture against barbarism, learning against ignorance, purity against crime, the "higher" against the "lower" races. To which the Negro cries Amen! and swears that to so much of this strange prejudice as is founded on just homage to civilization, culture, righteousness, and progress, he humbly bows and meekly does obeisance. But before that nameless prejudice that leaps beyond all this he stands helpless, dismayed, and well-nigh speechless; before that personal disrespect and mockery, the ridicule and systematic humiliation, the distortion of fact and wanton license of fancy, the cynical ignoring of the better and the boisterous welcoming of the worse, the all-pervading desire to inculcate disdain for everything black, from Toussaint to the devil,—before this there rises a sickening despair that would disarm and discourage any nation save that black host to whom "discouragement" is an unwritten word.

But the facing of so vast a prejudice could not but bring the inevitable self-questioning, self-disparagement, and lowering of ideas which ever accompany repression and breed in an atmosphere of contempt and hate. Whisperings and portents came borne upon the four winds: Lo! We are diseased and dying, cried the dark hosts; we cannot write, our voting is vain; what need of education, since we must always cook and serve? And the Nation echoed and enforced this self-criticism, saying: Be content to be servants, and nothing more; what need of higher culture for half-men? Away with the black man's ballot, by force or fraud, —and behold the suicide of a race! Nevertheless, out of the evil came something of good,—the more careful adjustment of education to real life, the clearer perception of the Negroes' social responsibilities, and the sobering realization of the meaning of progress.

So dawned the time of *Sturm und Drang:* storm and stress to-day rocks our little boat on the mad waters of the world-sea; there is within and without the sound of conflict, the burning of body and rending of soul; inspiration strives with doubt, and faith with vain questionings. The bright ideals of the past,— physical freedom political power, the training of brains and the training of hands,—all these in turn have waxed and waned, until even the last grows dim and overcast. Are they all wrong,—all false? No, not that, but each alone was over-simple and incomplete,—the dreams of a credulous race-childhood, or the fond imaginings of the other world which does not know and does not want to know our power. To be really true, all these ideals must be melted and welded into one. The training of the schools we need today more than ever,—the training of the schools we need today more than ever,—the training of deft hands, quick eyes and ears, and above all the broader, deeper higher culture of gifted minds and pure hearts. The power of the ballot we need in sheer self-defence,—else what shall save us from a second slavery? Freedom, too, the long-sought, we still seek,—the freedom of life and limb, the freedom to work and think, the freedom to love and aspire. Work, culture, liberty,—all these we need, not singly but together, not successively but together, each growing and aiding each, and all striving toward that vaster ideal that swims before the Negro people, the ideal of human brotherhood, gained through the unifying ideas of Race; the ideal of fostering and developing the traits and talents of the Negro, not in opposition to or contempt for other races, but rather in large conformity to the greater ideals of the American Republic, in order that some day on American soil two world-races may give each to each those chats of the characteristics both so sadly lack. We the darker ones come even now not altogether empty-handed: there are today no truer exponents of the pure human spirit of the Declaration of

Independence than the American Negroes; there is no true American music but the wild sweet melodies of the Negro slave; the American fairly talks and folklore are Indian and African; and, all in all, we black men seem the sole oasis of simply faith and reverence in a dusty desert of dollars and smartness. Will America be poorer if she replace her brutal dyspeptic blundering with light-hearted but determined Negro humility? or her coarse and cruel wit with loving jovial good-humor? or her vulgar music with the soul of the Sorrow Songs?

Merely a concrete test of the underlying principles of the great republic is the Negro Problem, and the spiritual striving of the freedmen's sons is the travail of souls whose burden is almost beyond the measure of their strength, but who bear it in the name of an historic race, in the name of this the land of their fathers' fathers, and in the name of human opportunity.

Chapter 32

Hope

"A Testament of Hope"

Martin Luther King Jr.

Editor's Introduction: No one has described more adequately or analyzed with greater clarity the condition of racial injustice and the struggle to overcome it than Martin Luther King Jr. (1929–1968), the nation's most beloved and most despised son, depending on one's perspective on the issues at hand. No one had a clearer vision of what the nation could be than he, and no one perceived more clearly the impact of the race problem on both black and white Americans than he. Most important, no one embodied more completely the religious, political, and moral dimensions of the problem than he. The following essay on hope was published posthumously.

Whenever I am asked my opinion of the current state of the civil rights movement, I am forced to pause; it is not easy to describe a crisis so profound that it has caused the most powerful nation in the world to stagger in confusion and bewilderment. Today's problems are so acute because the tragic evasions and defaults of several centuries have accumulated to disaster proportions. The luxury of a leisurely approach to urgent solutions—the ease of gradualism—was forfeited by ignoring the issues for too long. The nation waited until the black man was explosive with fury before stirring itself even to partial concern. Confronted now with the interrelated problems of war, inflation, urban decay, white backlash and a climate of violence, it is now *forced* to address itself to race relations and poverty, and it is tragically unprepared. What might once have been a series of separate problems now merge into a social crisis of almost stupefying complexity.

I am not sad that black Americans are rebelling; this was not only inevitable but eminently desirable. Without this magnificent ferment among Negroes, the old evasions and procrastinations would have continued indefinitely. Black men have slammed the door shut on a past of deadening passivity. Except for the Reconstruction years, they have never in their long history on American soil struggled with such creativity and courage for their freedom. These are our bright years of emergence; though they are painful ones, they cannot be avoided.

Yet despite the widening of our stride, history is racing forward so rapidly that the Negro's inherited and imposed disadvantages slow him down to an infuriating crawl. Lack of education, the dislocations of recent urbanization and the hardening of white resistance loom as such tormenting roadblocks that the goal sometimes appears not as a fixed point in the future but as a receding point never to be reached. Still, when doubts emerge, we can remember that only yesterday Negroes were not only grossly exploited but negated as human beings. They were invisible in their misery. But the sullen and silent slave of 10 years ago, an object of scorn at worst or of pity at best, is today's angry man. He is vibrantly on the move; he is forcing change, rather than waiting for it in pathetic futility. In less than two decades, he has roared out of slumber to change so many of his life's conditions that he may yet find the means to accelerate his march forward and overtake the racing locomotive of history.

These words may have an unexpectedly optimistic ring at a time when pessimism is the prevailing mood. People are often surprised to learn that I am an optimist. They know how often I have been jailed, how frequently the days and nights have been filled with frustration and sorrow, how bitter and dangerous are my adversaries. They expect these experiences to harden me into a grim and desperate man. They fail, however, to perceive the sense of affirmation generated by the challenge of embracing struggle and surmounting obstacles. They have no comprehension of the strength that comes from faith in God and man. It is possible for me to falter, but I am profoundly secure in my knowledge that God loves us; he has not worked out a design for our failure. Man has the capacity to do right as well as wrong, and his history is a path upward, not downward. The past is strewn with the ruins of the empires of tyranny, and each is a monument not merely to man's blunders but to his capacity to overcome them. While it is a bitter fact that in America in 1968, I am denied equality solely because I am black, yet I am not a chattel slave. Millions of people have fought thousands of battles to enlarge my freedom; restricted as it still is, progress has been made. This is why I remain an optimist, though I am also a realist, about the barriers before us. Why is the issue of equality still so far from solution in America, a nation that professes itself to be democratic, inventive, hospitable to new ideas, rich, productive and awesomely powerful? The problem is so tenacious because, despite its virtues and attributes, America is deeply racist and its democracy is flawed both economically and socially. All too many Americans believe justice will unfold painlessly or that its absence for black people will be tolerated tranquilly.

Justice for black people will not flow into society merely from court decisions nor from fountains of political oratory. Nor will a few token changes quell all the tempestuous yearnings of millions of disadvantaged black people. White America must recognize that justice for black people cannot be achieved without radical changes in the structure of our society. The comfortable, the entrenched, the privileged cannot continue to tremble at the prospect of change in the status quo.

Stephen Vincent Benet had a message for both white and black Americans in the title of a story, *Freedom Is a Hard Bought Thing*. When millions of people have been cheated for centuries, restitution is a costly process. Inferior education, poor housing, unemployment, inadequate health care—each is a bitter component of the oppression that has been our heritage. Each will require billions of dollars to correct. Justice so long deferred has accumulated interest and its cost for this society will be substantial in financial as well as human terms. This fact has not been fully grasped, because most of the gains of the past decade were obtained at bargain prices. The desegregation of public facilities cost nothing; neither did the election and appointment of a few black public officials.

The price of progress would have been high enough at the best of times, but we are in an agonizing national crisis because a complex of profound problems has intersected in an explosive mixture. The black surge toward freedom has raised justifiable demand for racial justice in our major cities at a time when all the problems of city life have simultaneously erupted. Schools, transportation, water supply, traffic and crime would have been municipal agonies whether or not Negroes lived in our cities. The anarchy of unplanned city growth was destined to confound our confidence. What is unique to this period is our inability to arrange an order of priorities that promises solutions that are decent and just.

Millions of Americans are coming to see that we are fighting an immoral war that costs nearly thirty billion dollars a year, that we are perpetuating racism, that we are tolerating almost forty million poor during an overflowing material abundance. Yet they remain helpless to end the war, to feed the hungry, to make brotherhood a reality; this has to shake our faith in ourselves. If we look honestly at the realities of our national life, it is clear that we are not marching forward; we are groping and stumbling; we are divided and confused. Our moral values and our spiritual confidence sink, even as our material wealth ascends. In these trying circumstances, the black revolution is much more than a struggle for the rights of Negroes. It is forcing America to face all its interrelated flaws—racism, poverty, militarism and materialism. It is exposing evils that are rooted deeply in the whole structure of our society. It reveals systemic rather than superficial flaws and suggests that radical reconstruction of society itself is the real issue to be faced.

It is time that we stopped our blithe lip service to the guarantees of life, liberty and pursuit of happiness. These fine sentiments are embodied in the Declaration of Independence, but that document was always a declaration of intent rather than of reality. There were slaves when it was written; there were still slaves when it was adopted; and to this day, black Americans have not life, liberty nor the privilege of pursuing happiness, and millions of poor white Americans are in economic bondage that is scarcely less oppressive. Americans who genuinely treasure our national ideals, who know they are still elusive dreams for all too many, should welcome the stirring of Negro demands. They are shattering the complacency that allowed a multitude of social evils to accumulate. Negro agitation is requiring America to reexamine its comforting myths and may yet catalyze the drastic reforms that will save us from social catastrophe.

In indicting white America for its ingrained and tenacious racism, I am using the term "white" to describe the majority, not *all* who are white. We have found that there are many white people who clearly perceive the justice of the Negro struggle for human dignity. Many of them joined our struggle and displayed heroism no less inspiring than that of black people. More than a few died by our side; their memories are cherished and are undimmed by time.

Yet the largest portion of white America is still poisoned by racism, which is as native to our soil as pine trees, sagebrush and buffalo grass. Equally native to us is the concept that gross exploitation of the Negro is acceptable, if not commendable. Many whites who concede that Negroes should have equal access to public facilities and the untrammeled right to vote cannot understand that we do not intend to remain the basement of the economic structure; they cannot understand why a porter or a housemaid would dare dream of a day when his work will be more useful, more remunerative and a pathway to rising opportunity. This incomprehension is a heavy burden in our efforts to win white allies for the long struggle.

But the American Negro has in his nature the spiritual and worldly fortitude to eventually win his struggle for justice and freedom. It is a moral fortitude that has been forged by centuries of oppression. In their sorrow and their hardship, Negroes have become almost instinctively cohesive. We band together readily; and against white hostility, we have an intense and wholesome loyalty to one another. But we cannot win our struggle for justice all alone, nor do I think that most Negroes want to exclude well-intentioned whites from participation in the black revolution. I believe there is an important place in our struggle for white liberals and I hope that their present estrangement from our movement is only temporary. But many white people in the past joined our movement with a kind of messianic faith that they were going to save the Negro and solve all of his problems very quickly. They tended, in some instances, to be rather aggressive and insensitive to the opinions and abilities of the black people with whom they were working; this has been especially true of students. In many cases, they simply did not know how to work in a supporting, secondary role. I think this problem became most evident when young men and women from elite northern universities came down to Mississippi to work with the black students at Tougaloo and Rust colleges, who were not quite as articulate, didn't type quite as fast and were not as sophisticated. Inevitably, feeling of white paternalism and black inferiority became exaggerated. The Negroes who rebelled against white liberals were trying to assert their own equality and to cast off the mantle of paternalism.

Fortunately, we haven't had this problem in the Southern Christian Leadership Conference. Most of the white people who were working with us in 1962 and 1963 are still with us. We have always enjoyed a relationship of mutual respect. But I think a great many white liberals outside SCLC also have learned this basic lesson in human relations, thanks largely to Jimmy Baldwin and others who have articulated some of the problems of being black in a multiracial society. And I am happy to report that relationships between whites and Negroes in the human rights movement are now on a much healthier basis.

In society at large, abrasion between the races is far more evident but the hostility was always there. Relations today are different only in the sense that Negroes are expressing the feelings that were so long muted. The constructive achievements of the decade 1955 to 1965 deceived us. Everyone underestimated the amount of violence and rage Negroes were suppressing and the vast amount of bigotry the white majority was disguising. All-black organizations are a reflection of that alienation—but they are only a contemporary way station on the road to freedom. They are a product of this period of identity crisis and directionless confusion. As the human rights movement becomes more confident and aggressive, more nonviolently active, many of these emotional and intellectual problems will be resolved in the heat of battle, and we will not ask what is our neighbor's color but whether he is a brother in the pursuit of racial justice. For much of the fervent idealism of the white liberals has been supplemented recently by a dispassionate recognition of some of the cold realities of the struggle for that justice.

One of the most basic of these realities was pointed out by the President's Riot Commission, which observed that the nature of the American economy in the late nineteenth and early twentieth centuries made is possible for the European immigrants of that time to escape from poverty. It was an economy that had room for—even a great need for—unskilled manual labor. Jobs were available for willing workers, even those with the educational and language liabilities they had brought with them. But the American economy today is radically different. There are fewer and fewer jobs for the culturally and educationally deprived; thus does present day poverty feed upon and perpetuate itself. The Negro today cannot escape from his ghetto in the way that Irish, Italian, Jewish and Polish Immigrants escaped from their ghettos fifty years ago. New methods of escape must be found. And one of these roads to escape will be a more equitable sharing of political power between Negroes and whites. Integration is meaningless without the sharing of power. When I speak of integration, I don't mean a romantic mixing of colors, I mean a real sharing of power and responsibility. We will eventually achieve this, but it is going to be much more difficult for us than for any other minority. After all, no other minority has been so constantly, brutally and deliberately exploited. But because of this very exploitation, Negroes bring a special spiritual and moral contribution to American life—a contribution without which America could not survive.

The implications of true racial integration are more than just national in scope. I don't believe we can have world peace until America has an integrated foreign policy. Our disastrous experiences in Vietnam and the Dominican Republic have been, in one sense, a result of racist decision-making. Men of the white West, whether or not they like it, have grown up in a racist culture, and their thinking is colored by that fact. They have been fed on a false mythology and tradition that blinds them to the aspirations and talents of other men. They don't really respect anyone who is not white. But we simply cannot have peace in the world without mutual respect. I honestly feel that a man without racial blinders—or, even better, a man with personal experience of racial discrimination—would be in a much better position to make policy decisions and to conduct negotiations with the underprivileged and emerging nations of the world (or even with Castro, for that matter) than would an Eisenhower or a Dulles.

The American marines might not even have been needed in Santo Domingo, had the American ambassador there been a man who was sensitive to the color dynamics that pervade the national life of the Dominican Republic. Black men in positions of power in the business world would not be so unconscionable as to trade or traffic with the Union of South Africa, nor would they be so insensitive to the problems and needs of Latin America that they would continue the patterns of American exploitation that now prevail there. When we replace the rabidly segregationist chairman of the Armed Services Committee with a man of good will, when our ambassadors reflect a creative and wholesome interracial background, rather than a cultural heritage that is a conglomeration of Texas and Georgia politics, then we will be able to bring about a qualitative difference in the nature of American foreign policy. This is what we mean when we talk about redeeming the soul of America. Let me make it clear that I don't think white men have a monopoly on sin or greed. But I think there has been a kind of collective experience—a kind of shared misery in the black community—that makes it a little harder for us to exploit other people.

I have come to hope that American Negroes can be a bridge between white civilization and the nonwhite nations of the world, because we have roots in both. Spiritually, Negroes identify understandably with Africa, an identification that is rooted largely in our color; but all of us are a part of the white American world, too. Our education has been Western and our language, our attitudes—though we sometimes tend to deny it—are very much influenced by Western civilization. Even our emotional life has been disciplined and sometimes stifled and inhibited by an essentially European upbringing. So, although in one sense we are neither, in another sense we are both Americans and Africans. Our very bloodlines are a mixture. I hope and feel that out of the universality of our experience, we can help make peace and harmony in this world more possible.

Although American Negroes could, if they were in decision-making positions, give encouragement to the underprivileged and disenfranchised people in other lands, I don't think it can work the other way around. I don't think the nonwhites in other parts of the world can really be of any concrete help to us, given their own problems of development and self-determination. In fact, American Negroes have greater collective buying power than Canada, greater than all four of the Scandinavian countries combined. American Negroes have greater economic potential than most of the nations—perhaps even more than *all* of the nations—of Africa. We don't *need* to look for help from some power outside the boundaries of our country, except in the sense of sympathy and identification. Our challenge, rather, is to organize the power we already have in our midst. The Newark riots, for example, could certainly have been prevented by a more aggressive political involvement on the part of that city's Negroes. There is utterly no reason Addonizio should not be the mayor of Newark, with the Negro majority that exists in that city. Gary, Indiana, is another tinderbox city; but its black mayor, Richard Hatcher, has given Negroes a new faith in the effectiveness of the political process.

One of the most basic weapons in the fight for social justice will be the cumulative political power of the Negro. I can foresee the Negro vote becoming consistently the decisive vote in national elections it is already decisive in states that have large numbers of electoral votes. Even today, the Negroes in New York City strongly influence how New York State will go in national elections, and the Negroes of Chicago have a similar leverage in Illinois. Negroes are even the decisive balance of power in the elections in Georgia, South Carolina and Virginia. So the party and the candidate that get the support of the Negro voter in national elections have a very definite edge, and we intend to use this fact to win advances in the struggle for human rights. I have every confidence that the black vote will ultimately help unseat the diehard opponents of equal rights in Congress who are, incidentally, reactionary on all issues. But the Negro community cannot win this victory alone; indeed, it would be an empty victory even if the Negroes *could* win it alone. Intelligent men of good will everywhere must see this as their task and contribute to its support.

The election of Negro mayors, such as Hatcher in some of the nation's larger cities has also had a tremendous psychological impact upon the Negro. It has shown him that he has the potential to participate in the determination of his own destiny and that of society. We will see more Negro mayors in major cities in the next ten years, but this is not the ultimate answer. Mayors are relatively impotent figures in the scheme of national politics. Even a white mayor such as John Lindsay of New York simply does not have the money and resources to deal with the problems of his city. The necessary money to deal with urban problems must come from the federal government and this money is ultimately controlled by the Congress of the United States. The success of these enlightened mayors is entirely dependent upon the financial support made available by Washington.

The past record of the federal government, however, has not been encouraging. No president has really done very much for the American Negro, though the past two presidents have received much undeserved credit for helping us. This credit has accrued to Lyndon Johnson and John Kennedy only because it was during their administrations that Negroes began doing more for themselves. Kennedy didn't voluntarily submit a civil rights bill, nor did Lyndon Johnson. In fact, both told us at one time that such legislation was impossible. President Johnson did respond realistically to the signs of the times and used his skills as a legislator to get bills through Congress that other men might not have gotten through. I must point out, in all honesty, however, that President Johnson has not been nearly so diligent in *implementing* the bills he has helped shepherd through Congress.

Of the ten titles of the 1964 Civil Rights Act, probably only the one concerning public accommodations—the most bitterly contested section—has been meaningfully enforced and implemented. Most of the other sections have been deliberately ignored. The same is true of the 1965 Voting Rights Act, which provides for federal referees to monitor the registration of voters in counties where Negroes have systematically been denied the right to vote. Yet of the some nine hundred counties that are eligible for federal referees, only fifty-eight counties to date have had them. The 842 other counties remain essentially just as they were before the march on Selma. Look at the pattern of federal referees in Mississippi, for example. They are dispersed in a manner that gives the appearance of change without any real prospect of actually shifting political power or giving Negroes a genuine opportunity to be represented in the government of their state. There is a similar pattern in Alabama, even though that state is currently at odds with the Democratic administration in Washington because of George Wallace. Georgia, until just recently, had no federal referees at all, not even in the hard-core black belt counties. I think it is significant that there are no federal referees at all in the home districts of the most powerful southern senators—particularly Senators Russell, Eastland and Talmadge. The power and moral corruption of these senators remain unchallenged, despite the weapon for change the legislation promised to be. Reform was thwarted when the legislation was inadequately enforced.

But not all is bad in the South, by any means. Though the fruits of our struggle have sometimes been nothing more than bitter despair, I must admit there have been some hopeful signs, some meaningful successes. One of the most hopeful of these changes is the attitude of the southern Negro himself. Benign acceptance of second-class citizenship has been displaced by vigorous demands for full citizenship rights and opportunities. In fact, most of our concrete accomplishments have been limited largely to the South. We have put an end to racial segregation in the South; we have brought about the beginnings of reform in the political system; and, as incongruous as it may seem, a Negro is probably safer in most southern cities than he is in the cities of the North. We have confronted the racist policemen of the South and demanded reforms in the police departments. We have confronted the southern racist power structure and we have elected Negro and liberal white candidates through much of the South in the past ten years. George Wallace is certainly an exception, and Lester Maddox is a sociological fossil. But despite these anachronisms, at the city and county level, there is a new respect for black votes and black citizenship that just did not exist ten years ago. Though school integration has moved at a depressingly slow rate in the South, it *has* moved. Of far more significance is the fact that we have learned that the integration of schools does not necessarily solve the inadequacy of schools. White schools are often just about as bad as black schools, and integrated schools sometimes tend to merge the problems of the two without solving either of them.

There *is* progress in the South, however progress expressed by the presence of Negroes in the Georgia House of Representatives, in the election of a Negro to the Mississippi House of Representatives, in the election of a black sheriff in Tuskegee, Alabama, and, most especially, in the integration of police forces throughout the southern states. There are now even Negro deputy sheriffs in such black belt areas as Dallas County, Alabama. Just three years ago, a Negro could be beaten for going into the county courthouse in Dallas County; now Negroes share in running it. So there *are* some changes. But the changes are basically in the social and political areas; the problems we now face—providing jobs, better housing and better education for the poor throughout the country—will require money for their solution, a fact that makes those solutions all the more difficult.

The need for solutions, meanwhile, becomes more urgent every day, because these problems are far more serious now than they were just a few years ago. Before 1964, things were getting better economically for the Negro; but after that year, things began to take a turn for the worse. In particular, automation began to cut into our jobs very badly, and this snuffed out the few sparks of hope the black people had begun to nurture. As long as there was some measurable and steady economic progress, Negroes were willing and able to press harder and work harder and hope for something better. But when the door began to close on the few avenues of progress, then hopeless despair began to set in.

The fact that most white people do not comprehend this situation—which prevails in the North as well as in the South—is due largely to the press, which molds the opinions of the white community. Many whites hasten to congratulate themselves on what little progress we Negroes have made. I'm sure that most whites felt that with the passage of the 1964 Civil Rights Act, all race problems were automatically solved. Because most white people are so far removed from the life of the average Negro, there has been little to challenge this assumption. Yet Negroes continue to live with racism every day. It doesn't matter where we are individually in the scheme of things, how near we may be either to the top or to the bottom of society; the cold facts of racism slap each of us in the face. A friend of mine is a lawyer, one of the most brilliant young men I know. Were he a white lawyer, I have no doubt that he would be in a hundred-thousand-dollar job with a major corporation or heading his own independent firm. As it is, he makes a mere twenty thousand dollars a year. This may seem like a lot of money and, to most of us, it is; but the point is that this young man's background and abilities would, if his skin color were different, entitle him to an income many times that amount.

I don't think there is a single major insurance company that hires Negro lawyers. Even within the agencies of the federal government, most Negro employees are in the lower echelons; only a handful of Negroes in federal employment are in upper-income brackets. This is a situation that cuts across this country's economic spectrum. The Chicago Urban League recently conducted a research project in the Kenwood community on the South Side. They discovered that the average educational grade level of Negroes in that community was 10.6 years and the median income was about forty-two hundred dollars a year. In nearby Gage Park, the medial educational grade level of the whites was 8.6 years, but the median income was ninety-six hundred dollars per year. In fact, the average white high school dropout makes as much as, if not more than, the average Negro college graduate.

Solutions for these problems, urgent as they are, must be constructive and rational. Rioting and violence provide no solutions for economic problems. Much of the justification for rioting has come from the thesis—originally set forth by Franz Fanon—that violence has a certain cleansing effect. Perhaps, in a special psychological sense, he may have had a point. But we have seen a better and more constructive cleansing process in our nonviolent demonstrations. Another theory to justify violent revolution is that rioting enables Negroes to overcome their fear of the white man. But they are just as afraid of the power structure after the riot as before. I remember that was true when our staff went to Rochester, New York, after the riot of 1964. When we discussed the possibility of going down to talk with the police, the people who had been most aggressive in the violence were afraid to talk. They still had a sense of inferiority; and not until they were bolstered by the presence of our staff and given reassurance of their political power and the rightness of their cause and the justness of their grievances were they able and willing to sit down and talk to the police chief and the city manager about the conditions that had produced the riot.

As a matter of fact, I think the aura of paramilitarism among the black militant groups speaks much more of fear than it does of confidence. I know, in my own experience, that I was much more afraid in Montgomery when I had a gun in my house. When I decided that, as a teacher of the philosophy of nonviolence, I couldn't keep a gun, I came face to face with the question of death and I dealt with it. And from that point on, I no longer needed a gun nor have I been afraid. Ultimately, one's sense of manhood must come from within him.

The riots in Negro ghettos have been, in one sense merely another expression of the growing climate of violence in America. When a culture begins to feel threatened by its own inadequacies, the majority of men tend to prop themselves up by artificial means, rather than dig down deep into their spiritual and cultural wellsprings. America seems to have reached this point. Americans as a whole feel threatened by communism on one hand and, on the other, by the rising tide of aspirations among the undeveloped nations. I think most Americans know in their hearts that their country has been terribly wrong in its dealings with other peoples around the world. When Rome began to disintegrate from within, it turned to a strengthening of the military establishment, rather than to a correction of the corruption within the society. We are doing the same thing in this country and the result will probably be the same unless, and here I admit to a bit of chauvinism, the black man in America can provide a new soul force for all Americans, a new expression of the American dream that need not be realized at the expense of other men around the world, but a dream of opportunity and life that can be shared with the rest of the world.

It seems glaringly obvious to me that the development of a humanitarian means of dealing with some of the social problems of the world—and the correlative revolution in American values that this will entail—is a much better way of protecting ourselves against the threat of violence than the military means we have chosen. On these grounds, I must indict the Johnson administration. It has seemed amazingly devoid of statesmanship; and when creative statesmanship wanes, irrational militarism increases. In this sense, President Kennedy was far more of a statesman than President Johnson. He was a man who was big enough to admit when he was wrong—as he did after the Bay of Pigs incident. But Lyndon Johnson seems to be unable to make this kind of statesmanlike gesture in connection with Vietnam. And I think that this has led as Senator Fulbright has said, to such a strengthening of the military industrial complex of this country that the president now finds himself almost totally trapped by it. Even at this point, when he can readily summon popular support to end the bombing in Vietnam, he persists. Yet bombs in Vietnam also explode at home; they destroy the hopes and possibilities for a decent America

In our efforts to dispel this atmosphere of violence in this country, we cannot afford to overlook the root cause of the riots. The President's Riot Commission concluded that most violence-prone Negroes are teenagers or young adults who, almost invariably, are underemployed ("underemployed" means working every day but earning an income below the poverty level) or who are employed in menial jobs. And according to a recent Department of Labor statistical report, 24.8 percent of Negro youth are currently unemployed, a statistic that does not include the drifters who avoid the census takers. Actually, it's my guess that the statistics are very, very conservative in this area. The Bureau of the Census has admitted a ten-percent error in this age group, and the unemployment statistics are based on those who are actually applying for jobs. But it isn't just a lack of work; it's also a lack of *meaningful* work. In Cleveland, fifty-eight percent of the young men between the ages of sixteen and twenty-five were estimated to be either unemployed or underemployed. This appalling situation is probably ninety percent of the root cause of the Negro riots. A Negro who has finished high school often watches his white classmates go out into the job market and earn one hundred dollars a week, while he, because he is black, is expected to work for forty dollars a week. Hence, there is a tremendous hostility and resentment that only a difference in race keeps him out of an adequate job. This situation is social dynamite. When you add the lack of recreational facilities and adequate job counseling, and the continuation of an aggressively hostile police environment, you have a truly explosive situation. Any night on any street corner in any Negro ghetto of the country, a nervous policeman can start a riot simply by being impolite or by expressing racial prejudice. And white people are sadly unaware how routinely and frequently this occurs.

It hardly needs to be said that solutions to these critical problems are overwhelmingly urgent. The President's Riot Commission recommended that funds for summer programs aimed at young Negroes should be increased. New York is already spending more on its special summer programs than on its year-round poverty efforts, but these are only tentative and emergency steps toward a truly meaningful and permanent solution. And the negative thinking in this area voiced by many whites does not help the situation. Unfortunately, many white people think that we merely "reward" a rioter by taking positive action to better his situation. What these white people do not realize is that the Negroes who riot have given up on America. When nothing is done to alleviate their plight, this merely confirms the Negroes' conviction that America is a hopelessly decadent society. When something positive is done, however, when constructive action follows a riot, a rioter's despair is allayed and he is forced to reevaluate America and to consider whether some good might eventually come from our society after all.

But, I repeat, the recent curative steps that have been taken are, at best, inadequate. The summer poverty programs, like most other government projects, function well in some places and are totally ineffective in others. The difference, in large measure, is one of citizen participation; that is the key to success or failure. In cases such as the Farmers' Marketing Cooperative Association in the black belt of Alabama and the Child Development Group in Mississippi, where the people were really involved in the planning and action of the program, it was one of the best experiences in self-help and grass roots initiative. But in places like Chicago, where poverty programs are used strictly as a tool of the political machinery and for dispensing party patronage, the very concept of helping the poor is defiled and the poverty program becomes just another form of enslavement. I still wouldn't want to do away with it, though, even in Chicago. We must simply fight at both the local and the national levels to gain as much community control as possible over the poverty program.

But there is no single answer to the plight of the American Negro. Conditions and needs vary greatly in different sections of the country. I think that the place to start, however, is in the area of human relations, and especially in the area of community-police relations. This is a sensitive and touchy problem that has rarely been adequately emphasized. Virtually every riot has begun from some police action. If you try to tell the people in most Negro communities that the police are their friends, they just laugh at you. Obviously, something desperately needs to be done to correct this. I have been particularly impressed by the fact that even in the state of Mississippi, where the FBI did a significant training job with the Mississippi police, the police are much more courteous to Negroes than they are in Chicago or New York. Our police forces simply must develop an attitude of courtesy and respect for the ordinary citizen. If we can just stop policemen from using profanity in their encounters with black people, we will have accomplished a lot. In the larger sense, police must cease being occupation troops in the ghetto and start protecting its residents. Yet very few cities have really faced up to this problem and tried to do something about it. It is the most abrasive element in Negro-white relations, but it is the last to be scientifically and objectively appraised. . . .

Chapter 33

Black America's Major Threat

Nihilism in Black America

Cornel West

Editor's Introduction: Professor Cornel West (1953–) is one of the nation's most widely known public intellectuals, who for a generation has been thinking, speaking, and writing as a cultural critic with deep philosophical, theological, and ethical roots in Western philosophy, Christian prophetic thought, and African American cultural history. Throughout his career he seems to be driven by an enduring concern for the steady rise of meaninglessness and hopelessness that he discerns in the heart of urban America where countless numbers of people are threatened daily by the forces of racism, sexism, homophobism, violence, and poverty, to mention only a few. West has named this problem nihilism.

The Proper starting point for the crucial debate about the prospects for black America is an examination of the nihilism that increasingly pervades black communities. *Nihilism is to be understood here not as a philosophic doctrine that there are no rational grounds for legitimate standards or authority; it is, far more, the lived experience of coping with a life of horrifying meaninglessness; hopelessness, and (most important) lovelessness.* The frightening result is a numbing detachment from others and a self-destructive disposition toward the world. Life without meaning, hope, and love breeds a coldhearted, mean-spirited outlook that destroys both the individual and others.

Nihilism is not new in black America. The first African encounter with the New World was an encounter with a distinctive form of the Absurd. The initial black struggle against degradation and devaluation in the enslaved circumstances of the New World was, in part, a struggle against nihilism. In fact, the major enemy of black survival in America has been and is neither oppression nor exploitation but rather the nihilistic threat that is, loss of hope and absence of meaning. For as long as hope remains and meaning is preserved, the possibility of overcoming oppression stays alive. The self-fulfilling prophecy of the nihilistic threat is that without hope there can be no future, that without meaning there can be no struggle.

The genius of our black foremothers and forefathers was to create powerful buffers to ward off the nihilistic threat, to equip black folk with cultural armor to beat back the demons of hopelessness, meaninglessness, and lovelessness. These buffers consisted of cultural structures of meaning and feeling that created and sustained communities; this armor constituted ways of life and struggle that embodied values of service and sacrifice, love and care, discipline and excellence. In other words, traditions for black surviving and thriving under usually adverse New World conditions were major barriers against the nihilistic threat. These traditions consist primarily of black religious and civic institutions that sustained familial and communal networks of support. If cultures are, in part, what human beings create (out of antecedent fragments of other cultures) in order to convince themselves not to commit suicide, then black foremothers and forefathers are to be applauded. In fact, until the early seventies black Americans had the lowest suicide rate in the United States. But now young black people lead the nation in the rate of increase in suicides.

What has changed? What went wrong? The bitter irony of integration? The cumulative effects of a genocidal conspiracy? The virtual collapse of rising expectations after the optimistic sixties? None of us fully understands why the cultural structures that once sustained black life in America are no longer able to fend off the nihilistic threat. I believe that two significant reasons why the threat is more powerful now than ever before are the saturation of market forces and market moralities in black life and the present crisis in black leadership. The recent market-driven shattering of black civil society—black families, neighborhoods, schools, churches, mosques leaves more and more black people vulnerable to daily lives endured with little sense of self and fragile existential moorings.

Black people have always been in America's wilderness in search of a promised land. Yet many black folk now reside in a jungle ruled by a cutthroat market morality devoid of any faith in deliverance or hope for freedom. Contrary to the superficial claims of conservative behaviorists, these jungles are not primarily the result of pathological behavior. Rather, this behavior is the tragic response of a people bereft of resources in confronting the workings of U.S. capitalist society. Saying this is not the same as asserting that individual black people are not responsible for their actions—black murderers and rapists should go to jail. But it must be recognized that the nihilistic threat contributes to criminal behavior. It is a threat that feeds on poverty and shattered cultural institutions and grows more powerful as the armors to ward against it are weakened.

BUT WHY IS THIS SHATTERING of black civil society occurring? What has led to the weakening of black cultural institutions in asphalt jungles? Corporate market institutions have contributed greatly to their collapse. By corporate market institutions I mean that complex set of interlocking enterprises that have a disproportionate amount of capital, power, and exercise a disproportionate influence on how our society is run and how our culture is shaped. Needless to say, the primary motivation of these institutions is to make profits, and their basic strategy is to convince the public to consume. These institutions have helped create a seductive way of life, a culture of consumption that capitalizes on every opportunity to make money. Market calculations and cost-benefit analyses hold sway in almost every sphere of U.S. society.

The common denominator of these calculations and analyses is usually the provision, expansion, and intensification of *pleasure*. Pleasure is a multivalent term; it means different things to many people. In the American way of life pleasure involves comfort, convenience, and sexual stimulation. Pleasure, so defined, has little to do with the past and views the future as no more than a repetition of a hedonistically driven present. This market morality stigmatizes others as objects for personal pleasure or bodily stimulation. Conservative behaviorists have alleged that traditional morality has been undermined by radical feminists and the cultural radicals of the sixties. But it is clear that corporate market institutions have greatly contributed to undermining traditional morality in order to stay in business and make a profit. The reduction of individuals to objects of pleasure is especially evident in the culture industries—television, radio, video, music—in which gestures of sexual foreplay and orgiastic pleasure flood the marketplace.

Like all Americans, African-Americans are influenced greatly by the images of comfort, convenience, machismo, femininity, violence, and sexual stimulation that bombard consumers. These seductive images contribute to the predominance of the market-inspired way of life over all others and thereby edge out nonmarket values—love, care, service to others—handed down by preceding generations. The predominance of this way of life among those living in poverty-ridden conditions, with a limited capacity to ward off self-contempt and self-hatred, results in the possible triumph of the nihilistic threat in black America.

A MAJOR CONTEMPORARY STRATEGY for holding the nihilistic threat at bay is a direct attack on the sense of worthlessness and self-loathing in black America. This *angst* resembles a kind of collective clinical depression in significant pockets of black America. The eclipse of hope and collapse of meaning in much of black America is linked to the structural dynamics of corporate market institutions that affect all Americans. Under these circumstances black existential *angst* derives from the lived reveals the devastating effect of pervasive European ideals of beauty on the self-image of young black women. Morrison's exposure of the harmful extent to which these white ideals affect the black self-image is a first step toward rejecting these ideals and overcoming the nihilistic self-loathing they engender in blacks.

The accumulated effect of the black wounds and scars suffered in a white-dominated society is a deep-seated anger, a boiling sense of rage, and a passionate pessimism regarding America's will to justice. Under conditions of slavery and Jim Crow segregation, this anger, rage, and pessimism remained relatively muted because of a well-justified fear of brutal white retaliation. The major breakthroughs of the sixties—more physically than politically—swept this fear away. Sadly, the combination of the market way of life, poverty-ridden conditions, black existential *angst,* and the lessening of fear of white authorities has directed most of the anger, rage, and despair toward fellow black citizens, especially toward black women, who are the most vulnerable in our society and in black communities. Only recently has this nihilistic threat—and its ugly inhumane outlook and actions—surfaced in the larger American society. And its appearance surely reveals one of the many instances of cultural decay in a declining empire.

WHAT IS TO BE DONE about this nihilistic threat? Is there really any hope, given our shattered civil society, market-driven corporate enterprises, and white supremacism? If one begins with the threat of concrete nihilism, then one must talk about some kind of *politics of conversion.* New models of collective black leadership must promote a version of this politics. Like alcoholism and drug addiction, nihilism is a disease of the soul. It can never be completely cured, and there is always the possibility of relapse. But there is always a chance for conversion—a chance for people to believe that there is hope for the future and a meaning to struggle. This chance rests neither on an agreement about what justice consists of nor on an analysis of how racism, sexism, or class subordination operate. Such arguments and analyses are indispensable. But a politics of conversion requires more. Nihilism is not overcome by arguments or analyses; it is tamed by love and care. Any disease of the soul must be conquered by a turning of one's soul. This turning is done through one's own affirmation of one's worth—an affirmation fueled by the concern of others. A love ethic must be at the center of a politics of conversion.

A love ethic has nothing to do with sentimental feelings or tribal connections. Rather it is a last attempt at generating a sense of agency among a downtrodden people. The best exemplar of this love ethic is depicted on a number of levels in Toni Morrison's great novel *Beloved.* Self-love and love of others are both modes toward increasing self-valuation and encouraging political resistance in one's community. These modes of valuation and resistance are rooted in a subversive memory—the best of one's past without romantic nostalgia—guided by a universal love ethic. For my purposes here, *Beloved* can be construed as bringing together the loving yet critical affirmation of black humanity found in the best of black nationalist movements, the perennial hope against hope for trans-racial coalition in progressive movements, and the painful struggle for self-affirming sanity in a history in which the nihilistic threat seems insurmountable.

The politics of conversion proceeds principally on the local level—in those institutions in civil society still vital enough to promote self-worth and self-affirmation. It surfaces on the state and national levels only when grassroots democratic organizations put forward a collective leadership that has earned the love and respect of and, most important, has proved itself accountable to these organizations. This collective leadership must exemplify moral integrity, character, and democratic statesmanship within itself and within its organizations.

Like liberal structuralists, the advocates of a politics of conversion never lose sight of the structural conditions that shape the sufferings and lives of people. Yet, unlike liberal structuralism, the politics of conversion meets the nihilistic threat head-on. Like conservative behaviorism, the politics of conversion meets the nihilistic threat head-on. Like conservative behaviorism, the politics of conversion openly confronts the self-destructive and inhumane actions of black people. Unlike conservative behaviorists, the politics of conversion situates these actions within inhumane circumstances (but does not thereby exonerate them). The politics of conversion shuns the limelight—a limelight that solicits status seekers and ingratiates egomaniacs. Instead, it stays on the ground among the toiling everyday people, ushering forth humble freedom fighters both followers and leaders—who have the audacity to take the nihilistic threat by the neck and turn back its deadly assaults.

Chapter 34

The Problem of Theodicy

Is God a White Racist?

William R. Jones

Editor's Introduction: Shortly after the emergence of James Cone's black theology, his project was challenged by an African American colleague who was teaching philosophical theology at Yale Divinity School. William R. Jones (1933—2012) viewed himself as a humanist who was not able to accept the many assumptions underlying Christian theology in general and black theology in particular. His provocative book, *Is God a White Racist? A Preamble to Black Theology* surprised most African American religious scholars who had not questioned black theology's assumptions. Consequently, Jones's book has endured as the most critical challenge to that theological enterprise by bringing to the center of attention the classical problem of theodicy contextualized for African Americans. How can theology claim to be liberative if there is no empirical evidence of liberation? These questions continue to stimulate the interest of a growing number of young contemporary African American scholars.

Each of the current black theologians—Albert Cleage, James Cone, Major Jones, J. Deotis Roberts, and Joseph Washington—has answered in his own way

Du Bois' perplexing question, What meaneth black suffering? However, their answers, individually and collectively, compound the confusion of an already inscrutable mystery. They have painstakingly drawn a theological road map to guide the black faithful from distorted conceptions to prophetic enlightenment. But the road is full of logical potholes, theological washouts, and elaborate but unsound detours. Consequently the theological terrain they have scouted must be surveyed again.

It has often been said that asking the right question is as important as supplying the correct answer. Whether correct or incorrect, this generalization describes the purpose in the following pages. To paraphrase Kant's admonition, my objective is to force the black theologians and their readers to pause a moment and, neglecting all that they have said and done, to reconsider their conclusions in the light of another question: Is God a white racist? My concern throughout is to illuminate the issues this pregnant question introduces into the arena of black theology and religion. The black theologian, I contend, cannot avoid this issue of divine racism, because it is implicit in his theological method, purpose, and content.

No doubt the combination of terms "divine" and "racism" is novel—some will say blasphemous. But the ideas and categories the concept expresses are time-honored and familiar themes in philosophy and theology. To raise the question of divine racism is actually to revive a perennial issue in black religion: what is the meaning, the cause, and the "why" of black suffering? It is to resurrect for this day and time the same question Du Bois probed a half century ago.

In a more general vein the issue of divine racism is simply another way of addressing the traditional problem of evil and human suffering. "The Problem of Suffering Revisited" is an apt description of a central emphasis of this book. In more technical terms the question "Is God a white racist?" pushes the issue of theodicy[1] to the forefront of theological discussion.

Because the concept of divine racism is novel, it is perhaps best to begin the analysis autobiographically, tracing, as it were, the evolution of the concept in my own mind.

A number of experiences and influences converged to give form and flesh to the concept of divine racism as I have entertained it. First among these is my status as a member of an oppressed minority. To be oppressed, in the final analysis, is to suffer, and to suffer in a way that differs radically from the suffering of those who have not known oppression. Indeed it would be surprising if the oppressed did not reflect upon the nature, the cause, and the justice of their suffering, since suffering prescribes the permanent predicament of the oppressed.

---

1. Theodicy, from the Greek *theos*, God, and *dikē*, justice, is the common term for the field of inquiry that deals with the issue of evil and human suffering. Most often it signifies the attempts to account for human suffering and evil in the framework of one's affirmations about the nature and activity of God. I shall use the term, however, in a different sense. My stipulative definition is given on pp. xviii–xx of this [Jones's] book. Source: William R. Jones. *Is God a White Racist?: A Preamble to Black Theology* (Boston: Beacon Press, 1973), xix–xxviii.

Allied to this general influence is my background in the black church—though I admit that the reader may be hard pressed to detect its traces on these pages. The sermons of my grandfather, Sunday-school lessons on the Exodus, the Cross, the suffering servant, etc., provided my earliest answers to the enigma of black suffering. It will become evident that I have rejected these solutions forged in my childhood, but one must not conclude that to reject what is learned in one's youth is necessarily to be free of its formative influences.

These influences account in large part for my enduring interest in the problem of evil and human suffering. A quick survey of my undergraduate and graduate term papers and of the courses I have taught reveals the problem of evil to be the single and most prominent thread running through the whole skein of my personal and scholarly interests.

There is also a group of thinkers I label "black humanists." I have in mind those few but fearless spokesmen who rejected the biblical and Christian models for explaining black suffering, who were unafraid to doubt God's intrinsic goodness relative to blacks, who questioned God's existence and relevance in the struggle for black freedom.[2] It is characteristic of most writers on black religion to relegate black humanism to a theological limbo. James Cone and Benjamin Mays, for instance, classify it as "secular," "non-religious" and "antireligious,"[3] thus denying its value and status as an authentic expression of the black religious experience. This interpretation of black humanism must be challenged. Black humanism is antithetical to traditional Western theism, black or white, but we can label it non-religious only if we equate religion and theism. An indirect concern of this study is to compel a rehearing for this aspect of black religious thought. It is also my concern to make this humanistic wing of black religion the norm for contemporary black theology, thereby providing a more realistic interpretation of the meaning of the black experience.

Add to these black humanists the humanism of Albert Camus and Jean-Paul Sartre, the French existentialists. I have benefited from the influence of both, although my own philosophical position is much closer to my understanding of Sartre's humanistic existentialism. My own thinking and my reading of the black humanists, of Camus and Sartre, and of certain others[4] suggest the following concepts, which undergird the central argument of this [Jones's] book: theodicy as the central theological category, the possibility of a demonic God, and the intimate connection between theodicy and oppression. These propositions, coupled with some salient critiques of the principal theodicies in the Christian tradition, inform my critical understanding of the central issues in black theology and black religion.

---

2. For a discussion of black humanists see pp. 29–44 of this book.
3. James H. Cone, *The Spirituals and The Blues* (New York: Seabury Press, 1972), p. 109.
4. Bertrand Russell's essay "A Free Man's Worship" helped, for instance, to clarify the concept of a demonic diety, See p. 66 of this [Jones's] book.

An obvious place to look for parallels to the black experience in religion is the theological treatment of Jewish oppression, the suffering of another ethnic minority. One work stands out here, Rabbi Richard Rubenstein's *After Auschwitz*.[5] His analysis of Jewish suffering forced me to pose a troublesome question that he does not explicitly consider: Is God an anti-Semite? The implications of his study for my own explorations in black theology were direct and immediate. In the light of black suffering, a suffering that may exceed that of the Jews,[6] the unsettling question becomes: Is God a white racist?

Moreover, Rubenstein, like the black humanists and like Camus and Sartre, pressed certain points of critical import for theological method. The oppression and slaughter of the Jews in World War II convinced him that only one standard should be used to evaluate Jewish theology: its ability to assimilate the horror of Auschwitz, the mass murder of six million Jews. Thus Rubenstein's argument makes the analysis of Jewish suffering the necessary point of departure for the Jewish theologian, and the viability of its theodicy becomes the touchstone for an authentic Jewish theology.

At this juncture of the investigation the inevitable conclusion seemed that the correlative concepts of black suffering and theodicy were the imperative foci for a black theology worthy of acceptance, and my reading of the inner logic of the extant black theologians reaffirmed this conclusion. Subsequent investigations added nothing substantially new to the general position already supported methodologically by Frederick Sontag's analyses in *God, Why Did You Do That?*[7] and *The God of Evil*.[8] Hence the major contours of the concept and its methodological implications were already firmly established.

A further conclusion—and here begins the outline of the three divisions of this [Jones's] book—is that the issue of divine racism emerges only in particular theological contexts; not every theological framework forces this issue. The first purpose of Part I is to identify the combination of theological categories and frameworks that makes it necessary to ask, Is God a white racist? The issue of divine racism surfaces whenever a specific type of suffering, which I identify as *ethnic suffering*, is joined with particular interpretations of God's sovereignty over human history and His activity within human history or both. Hence the initial exploration of the concept of human suffering from several perspectives, with the intent of establishing divine racism as not only a legitimate but an irreducible theological category.

5. Richard Rubenstein, *After Auschwitz* (New York: Bobbs-Merrill Company, 1966).

6. The point is not essential for my argument, but I would regard black suffering as more severe than Jewish suffering. Basil Davidson, for instance, estimates that slavery before and after embarkation cost fifty million black souls. *Black Mother* (Boston: Little, Brown & Company, 1961), p. 80. Yet numbers alone do not tell the total story, I do not detect decimation of Jewish culture and tradition, but decimation of black culture and tradition characteristics life in America.

7. Frederick Sontag, *God, Why Did You Do That?* (Philadelphia: Westminster Press, 1970).

8. Frederick Sontag, *The God of Evil* (New York: Harper & Row, 1970).

The description and analysis of the category of divine racism serve as the background for the second purpose of Part I, which is to establish the centrality of theodicy for black theology. Johannes Metz has argued that the demands of Christian faith require "the development of theology as eschatology." He further concludes that eschatology "must not be reduced to a *part* of Christian theology but must be understood radically: as the determining factor in all theological statements."[9] I maintain that black theology demands a different arrangement of the theological furniture. For it, theodicy must assume the first rank, which Metz assigns to eschatology.

A former colleague responded to my claim about the centrality of theodicy with this criticism: My concern to make theodicy the essential nucleus of black theology is illegitimate, for it means that I am forcing the formal question of theodicy. That is to say, I am comprehending black theology in the tradition of Western religious philosophy and its conventional problems. In sum, he concluded, I do not sufficiently honor the black perspective.

This is an eminently fair challenge, and the bulk of this book is an implicit reply to it. I would argue that I am not elevating theodicy to a rank it does not already enjoy in black theology and theology in general. Theodicy, I will show, is already at the heart of theology; I simply call attention to this fact.

I conclude that each person has a functional theodicy; there is an aspect of his over-all world view that treats the issue of suffering and relates it to his prevailing beliefs about the nature of ultimate reality and man. It is not difficult, for instance, to demonstrate that each individual makes a fundamental judgment about the character of specific sufferings, whether each is good (positive), bad (negative), or neutral; whether he must endure the suffering he encounters or should annihilate it; whether suffering can be eliminated or whether it is an inevitable part of the human condition. Each person also acts on the basis of some conclusion about the source or cause of suffering. Indeed it would be surprising if mankind as a whole did not ordinarily reflect upon suffering, since it appears to be an inescapable aspect of the human condition.[10]

The universal concern with the issue of suffering and theodicy is often overlooked, and the reason is not hard to isolate. Theodicy, we must first consider, is defined too narrowly. The common understanding of theodicy places too much emphasis upon its etymology; for too many, *theos*, God, and *dike*, justice, comprise the total meaning. But an etymological analysis illuminates only one aspect of the enterprise of theodicy, namely the apologetic. Theodicy is more than the attempt to exonerate and justify God's purpose and works in the face of contrary

9. Cited in *New Theology No. 5*, ed. by Martin E. Marty and Dean G. Peerman (New York: The Macmillan Co., 1968), p. 135.

10. It is well to recall here the perceptive observation of John Bowker. "If the different religions have a common factor in their treatment of suffering, it is that they start with the facts of suffering as they are, not with suffering as conceived as a theoretical problem. Suffering becomes a problem when it is related to other facts or other propositions which seem to be contradicted by it." *Problems of Suffering in Religions of the World* (London: Cambridge University Press, 1970), p. 5.

evidence. There is another dimension; for instance, a concern to determine the cause of suffering. In fact every apologetic approach to human suffering is at the same time an implicit conclusion about the cause or origin of suffering.

Theodicy is also defined too narrowly if it is perceived as an abstract and theoretical enterprise executed only by professional philosophers and theologians. What is the suffering servant theme in Isaiah but a theodicy in miniature? Is not Du Bois engaged in the enterprise of theodicy when he asks, "What meaneth this?"

Indeed it does not do violence to the total salvation history second coming of Jesus—to interpret it as a pattern of theodicy as well as salvation. In fact I would argue that theodicy is the necessary ground for salvation. That is to say, theodicy is logically prior to the affirmation of the salvation of man. To talk about the *saving* work of God is to presuppose a conclusion about the *benevolence* of God; it is to assert the essential goodness of God in spite of the prior "evil" that makes his "saving" work necessary. In sum, salvation is meaningless without the prior affirmation of God's benevolence toward man. The priority of theodicy is further underscored when we consider—and one of the major arguments of this book is to demonstrate the point—that every alleged act of God's benevolence can easily be interpreted as an instance of His malevolence.

Several arguments will establish that theodicy is the controlling category for black theology, and this will be accomplished in a manner that does not involve the use of concepts alien to a black perspective. One argument will show that theodicy is central because black theology defines itself as a theology of liberation. Accordingly, the special requirements of a theology of liberation necessitate consideration of the theodicy issue. This becomes clear if some of the essentials of a theology of liberation are identified by considering some general observations about oppression and suffering.

Oppression, I contend, is reducible to a form of suffering. If one dichotomizes between negative and positive suffering, oppression is a variety of negative suffering. It involves a suffering that is either detrimental or irrelevant to one's highest good. It is also noteworthy that if a positive quality is assigned to suffering, as for instance in masochism, suffering is welcomed and willingly endured. However, to define suffering as negative motivates one to crush it. The theologian of liberation, by definition, is committed to annihilate oppression, which is to say, to eliminate the suffering that is the heart of oppression. Thus he must provide an explanation that perceives the suffering as negative. He must show that the suffering that is oppression is not God's will or sanctioned by nature. He must, in sum, desanctify the suffering in question, or else the oppressed will not regard their suffering as oppressive and will not be motivated to attack it. The theologian or philosopher of liberation, in short, *must* engage in the enterprise of theodicy if he is to accomplish his task.

A second argument for the centrality of theodicy concludes that the unique character of black suffering forces the question of divine racism, and to pose this question is to initiate the theodicy debate. The black theologian is obliged to reconcile the inordinate amount of black suffering, which is implied in his claim that the black situation is oppressive, with his affirmations about the nature of God and God's sovereignty over human history.

Jürgen Moltmann has correctly perceived that today the theodicy question has assumed a new form and also a new importance in theology:

> Since we experience reality as history and no longer as cosmos, the fundamental theodicy question is still with us and is more pressing than before. For us it has no longer only its old naturalistic form, as in the earthquake of Lisbon in 1775. It appears today in a political form, as in the question of Auschwitz. . . . We ask the question: *An Deus sit?* ("Whether God is") on grounds of history and its crimes. . . .[11]

I suggest that, at least for America, it is black suffering, not Auschwitz, that introduces the theodicy question. Accordingly, a viable theodicy, one that refutes the charge of divine racism, must be the point of departure and the necessary foundation for the construction of a black theology. This is not to demand that a theodicy must be a kind of preface to any black theology. Rather, my contention is that the theodicy question must control the entire theological enterprise and be its ultimate foundation. What the black theologian wishes to assert about the person and work of Jesus (Christology) or the ultimate consummation of human destiny (eschatology) must be viewed in terms of its connection to the problem of black suffering. In short the essential conclusion of Part I is that black theology must be an extended theodicy.

Part II of this [Jones's] study critically analyzes the respective positions of the most popular black theologians—Albert Cleage, James Cone, Major Jones, J. Deotis Roberts, and Joseph Washington—on the issue of black suffering. Part I provides the critical apparatus for that analysis. It is possible to read and appreciate Part I without a knowledge of the field of black theology and its literature. Part II, however, one cannot. In a real sense it is a "family squabble" internal to black theology. The present situation in black theology and the peculiar themes of this study mean that throughout, but particularly in Part II, I am engaged, hopefully, in an instructive debate with the best-known black theologians.

Part II aims at several demonstrations: I purport to show that the issue of divine racism is in fact forced by the black theologians' own conclusions and presuppositions. Having adopted specific theological frameworks and concepts, e.g. the politics of God, the question "Is God a white racist?" inexorably surfaces. Moreover, I contend that the scaffolding of their respective systems collapses if they do not refute the charge of divine racism.

Having shown the necessity of a viable theodicy that invalidates the claim of divine racism, I then proceed to analyze critically the respective answers the

---

11. Jürgen Moltmann, *Religion, Revolution, and the Future* (New York: Charles Scribner's Sons, 1969), p. 205.

black theologians give to the mystery of black suffering. The critical test I utilize is whether the black theologian consistently disproves the charge of divine racism and whether his account of black suffering provides a coherent and sturdy foundation for the theology of liberation advanced as its explicit purpose. When this test is applied, I reach the unobscure conclusion that each of the black theologies examined is defective. All leave the issue of divine racism unresolved. In some cases the issue is not even raised for consideration, even though its refutation is presupposed by the essential position taken by the black theologian. The resolution thus begs the question: it takes for granted what must be proved. In other instances the argument is not tenable because of the questionable logical and theological positions it requires for its support.

The conclusions of Parts I and II force an issue that is the focus of Part III. Given the necessity of a viable theodicy (the conclusion of Part I) and given that none of the black theologians provides that indispensable theodicy (the conclusion of Part II), it is necessary to determine what other theodicies can meet the needs of an authentic black theodicy. This is the purpose of Part III.

Though an extensive discussion of classical solutions to the theodicy question falls outside the scope of my present analysis, I feel compelled to state that my research in this area indicates that they are not adequate to account for ethnic suffering. Nor do I find that the solution of John Hick[12] and the theologians of hope fares better than those of the black theologians. Hence my conclusion that a new model for treating black suffering must be sought. I suggest that what I term *humanocentric theism* and *"secular" humanism* are the best candidates. The essential feature of both is the advocacy of the *functional ultimacy of man*. Man must act *as if* he were the ultimate valuator or the ultimate agent in human history or both. Thus God's responsibility for the crimes and errors of human history is reduced if not effectively eliminated.

Of special interest in this respect is the identification of those features of the black theologians that must be modified if humanocentric theism or secular humanism is accepted as normative. The belief, for instance, that blacks are God's chosen people must be abandoned. This section also serves as a brief introduction to my own statement of a theology or philosophy of liberation that is still in its formative stage.

---

12. John Hick, *Evil and the God of Love* (London: Macmillan & Co. 1966).

Chapter 35

An Alternative View of Religion

"Perspectives for a Study of Afro-American Religion in the United States"

Charles H. Long

Editor's Introduction: Charles H. Long, (1926–) was born and raised in the segregated city of Little Rock, Arkansas, received his PhD in the History of Religions at the University of Chicago, where he remained as a teacher rising through the ranks to full professor. Subsequently, he taught on the faculties of University of Southern California at Santa Barbara and the University of North Carolina at Chapel Hill. He has taught and mentored numerous scholars in the field who view him as a model of academic excellence. Throughout his career he has striven to find a methodology that would enable him to grasp the meaning of religion for oppressed peoples. His findings in that quest have led to a profound criticism of Western religion that oppresses others in contrast to the religion of the oppressed that liberates.

Americans of African descent have for some time been the subject of countless studies and research projects—projects extending from the physical through the social sciences. The religion of this culture has not been overlooked.[1]

Most of the studies of religion have employed the methodology of the social sciences; hardly any of the studies have come to terms with the specifically religious elements in the religion of black Americans: We have not yet seen anything on the order of Pierre Verger's[2] study of African religion in South America or of Alfred Metraux's[3] study of the same phenomenon in the Atlantic islands.

On the contemporary scene, a group of black scholars have been about the task of writing a distinctively "black theology." I refer here to the works of Joseph Washington (*Black Religion* [Boston, 1961]) and James Cone (*Black Theology and Black Power* [New York, 1969]), and to Albert Cleage's sermons (*The Black Messiah* [New York, 1968]). In this enterprise these men place themselves in the religious tradition of David Walker, Henry Garnet, Martin Delany, and W E. B. DuBois. They are essentially apologetic theologians working implicitly and explicitly from the Christian theological tradition.

What we have, in fact, are two kinds of studies: those arising from the social sciences, and an explicitly theological apologetic tradition. This limitation of methodological perspectives has led to a narrowness of understanding and the failure to perceive certain creative possibilities in the black community in America.

One of the most telling examples of this limitation of perspectives in the study of black religion is to be found in Joseph Washington's work cited above. Washington has correctly seen that black religion is not to be understood as a black imitation of the religion of the majority population. His religious norm is Christianity, and the internal norm for Christianity is faith expressing itself in theology. From his analysis he concludes that black religion is not Christian, thus does not embody faith, and therefore has produced no theology. Black

---

1. W. E. B. DuBois, ed., *The Negro Church* (Atlanta: Atlanta University Press, 1903); Carter G. Woodson, *The History of the Negro Church* (Washington, D.C.: Associated Publishers, 1921); Benjamin E. Mays and Joseph W Nicholson, *The Negro's Church* (New York: Russell & Russell, 1969); Arthur Fauset, *Black Gods in the Metropolis* (Philadelphia: University of Pennsylvania Press, 1944; London: Oxford University Press, 1944); E. Franklin Frazier, *The Negro Church in America* (New York: Schocken Books, 1962); Howard Bratz, *The Black Jews of Harlem* (New York: Schocken Books, 1970); C. Eric Lincoln, *The Black Muslims in America* (New York: Beacon Press, 1961); and E. U. Essien-Udom, *Black Nationalism: The Search for an Identity in America* (Chicago and London: University of Chicago Press, 1962).

2. Pierre Verger, *Notes sur le culte des Orisa at Vodun à Bahia la Baie de tous les saints au Bresil et à l'ancienne Cote des esclaves en Afrique* (Dakar, 1957).

3. Alfred Metraux, *Le Vaudou haitien* (Paris, 1958).

religion has, in his view, been more concerned with civil rights and protest, and hardly, if ever, concerned with genuine Christian faith.

I do not wish to take issue with Washington regarding his understanding of Christian faith and theology, for this lies outside the scope of the concerns in this essay. However, a word or two must be said in passing. Washington seems to conceive of Christianity and theology in static terms unrelated to historical experience. He seems to be unaware of the historical situations that were correlative to European and American theology, and he seems equally unaware that Americans have produced few theologians of the variety that would meet his norm. In short, his critique of black religion from the stance of Christian theology is blunted by the lack of his historical understanding of theology.

But now, to the point that is most relevant for this discussion: the distinctive nature of black religion. Washington's insights here are very accurate, for he shows in his work how folkloric materials, social protest, and Negro fraternalism, along with biblical imagery, are all aspects of black religion. He experiences a difficulty here, for he is unable to deal with religion outside the normative framework of Christian theology. But even if one is to have a theology, it must arise from religion, something that is prior to theology.

For some time I have felt the need to present a systematic study of black religion—a kind of initial ordering of the religious experiences and expressions of the black communities in America. Such a study should not be equated with Christianity, or any other religion for that matter. It is, rather, an attempt to see what kinds of images and meanings lie behind the religious experiences of the black communities in America. While recognizing the uniqueness of this community, I am also working as a historian of religions. These perspectives constitute symbolic images as well as methodological principles. They are:

1. Africa as historical reality and religious image
2. The involuntary presence of the black community in America
3. The experience and symbol of God in the religious experience of blacks.

AFRICA AS HISTORICAL REALITY AND RELIGIOUS IMAGE

It is a historical fact that the existence of the black communities in America is due to the slave trade of numerous European countries from the seventeenth to the nineteenth century (slaves were still being illegally smuggled into the United States as late as the 1880s). The issue of the persistence of African elements in the black community is a hotly debated issue. On the one hand, we have the positions of E. Franklin Frazier and W. E. B. DuBois,[4] emphasizing the lack of

---

4. See W. E. B. DuBois, *The Souls of Black Folk* (Basic Afro-American Reprint Library, Johnson reprint; originally published in Chicago: A. C. McClurg, 1903).

any significant persisting elements of Africanism in America. Melville Herskovits held this same position but reversed his position in the *Myth of the Negro Past* (Boston, 1958), where he places a greater emphasis on the persistence of African elements among the descendants of the slaves in North America. One of the issues in this discussion had to do with the comparative level of the studies. Invariably, the norm for comparison was the black communities in the Atlantic islands and in South America. In the latter, the African elements are very distinctive, and, in the case of Brazil, Africans have gone back and forth between Africa and Brazil.[5] African languages are still spoken by blacks in Brazil. Indeed, Pierre Verger first became interested in Yoruba religion when he saw it being practiced in South America!

It is obvious that nothing of this sort has existed in the United States. The slave system of the United States systematically broke down the linguistic and cultural patterns of the slaves, but even a protagonist for the loss of all Africanisms, such as E. Franklin Frazier, acknowledges the persistence of "shout songs," African rhythm, and dance in American culture. Frazier, and in this matter DuBois, while acknowledging such elements, did not see these elements of ultimate significance, for they could not see these forms playing an important role in the social cohesion of the black community. Without resolving this discussion, we need to raise another issue. The persistence of elements of what some anthropologists have called "soft culture" means that, given even the systematic breakdowns of cultural forms in the history of North American slavery, the slaves did not confront America with a religious *tabula rasa*. If not the content of culture, a characteristic mode of orienting and perceiving reality has probably persisted. We know, for example, that a great majority of the slaves came from West Africa, and we also know from the studies of Daryll Forde that West Africa is a cultural as well as a geographical unit.[6] Underlying the empirical diversity of languages, religions and social forms, there is, according to Forde, a structural unity discernible in language and religious forms.[7] With the breakdown of the empirical forms of language and religion as determinants for the social group, this persisting structural mode and the common situation as slaves in America may be the basis for the persistence of an African style among the descendants of the Africans.

In addition to this, in the accounts of the slaves and their owners we read of "meetings" which took place secretly in the woods. It is obvious that these "meetings" were not devoted to the practice of the masters' religion. They were

5. See Verger, *Notes sur le cults des Orisa.*
6. Daryll Forde, "The Cultural Map of West Africa: Successive Adaptations to Tropical Forests and Grassland," in *Cultures and Societies of Africa,* ed. Simon Ottenberg and Phoebe Ottenberg (New York: Random House, 1960).
7. Joseph Greenberg makes a similar argument for the structural similarity of West African languages in his *Studies in African Linguistic Classification* (New Haven: Yale University Press, 1955).

related to what the slaves themselves called "conjuring," and the connotation reminds one of voodoo rites in Haiti.

Added to this is the precise manner in which slaves, by being slaves, black persons, were isolated from any self-determined legitimacy in the society of which they were a part and were recognized by their physiological characteristics. This constituted a complexity of experience revolving around the relationship between their physical being and their origins. So even if they had no conscious memory of Africa, the image of Africa played an enormous part in the religion of the blacks. The image of Africa, an image related to historical beginnings, has been one of the primordial religious images of great significance. It constitutes the religious revalorization of the land, a place where the natural and ordinary gestures of the blacks were and could be authenticated. In this connection, one can trace almost every nationalistic movement among the blacks and find Africa to be the dominating and guiding image. Even among religious groups not strongly nationalistic, the image of Africa or Ethiopia still has relevance.[8] This is present in such diverse figures as Richard Allen, who organized the African Methodist Episcopal Church in the late eighteenth century, through Martin Delany in the late nineteenth century, and then again in Marcus Garvey's,[9] "back to Africa movement" of the immediate post-World War I period, and finally in the taking up of this issue again among black leaders of the present time.

The image of Africa as it appears in black religion is unique for the black community in America is a landless people. Unlike the American Indian, the land was not taken from them, and unlike the black Africans in South Africa or Zimbabwe (Rhodesia), the land is not occupied by groups whom they consider aliens. Their image of the land points to the religious meaning of land even in the absence of these forms of authentication. It thus emerges as an image that is always invested with historical and religious possibilities.

THE INVOLUNTARY PRESENCE OF THE BLACK COMMUNITY IN AMERICA

Implied in the discussion concerning the land and the physiological characteristics of the blacks is the significance attributed to this meaning in America. The stance has, on the one hand, been necessitated by historical conditions and, on the other hand, been grasped as creative possibility. From the very beginning, the presence of slaves in the country has been involuntary; they were brought to

---

8. See especially Edward W. Blyden, *Christianity, Islam and the Negro Race* (London, 1887). Blyden, though born in the Virgin Islands and ordained as a Presbyterian minister, was one of the early leaders in pan-Africanism. It is interesting to note that he set the problem within a religious context. The publication of his work is directly related to the problems created in the 1840s by the passage of the Fugitive Slave Law and the Dred Score decision of the United States Supreme Court.

9. See E. David Cronon, *Black Moses* (Madison: University of Wisconsin Press, 1962).

America in chains, and this country has attempted to keep them in this condition in one way or another. Their very presence as *human beings* in the United States has always constituted a threat to the majority population. From the point of view of the majority population, they have been simply and purely legal entities, first as slaves defined in terms of property, and then, after the abolition of chattel property, as citizens who had to seek legal redress before they could use the common facilities of the country—water fountains, public accommodations, restaurants, schools, and so on. There is no need to repeat this history; it is too well known, and the point I wish to make is more subtle than these specific issues, important as they may be.

In addition to the image and historical reality of Africa, one must add, as another persisting datum, the involuntary presence and orientation as a religious meaning. I have stated elsewhere the importance of the involuntary structure of the religious consciousness in the terms of oppugnancy.[10] In the case of the slaves, America presented a bizarre reality, not simply because of the novelty of a radical change of status and culture but equally because their presence as slaves pointed to a radical contradiction within the dominant culture itself. The impact of America was a discovery, but one had little ability to move from the bizarre reality of discovery to the level of general social rules of conduct, which happens in the case of other communities presented with an ultimate discovery. In addition to this, to normalize the condition of slavery would be to deny the existence of the slaves as human beings.

The slaves had to come to terms with the opaqueness of their condition and at the same time oppose it. They had to experience the truth of their negativity and at the same time transform and create *an-other* reality. Given the limitations imposed upon them, they created on the level of the religious consciousness. Not only did this transformation produce new cultural forms but its significance must be understood from the point of view of the creativity of the transforming process itself.

Three short illustrations of this phenomenon must suffice at this point. Listen to the words of this spiritual:

> He's so high, you can't get over him,
> He's so low, you can't get under him,
> So round, you can't get around him,
> You got to go right through the door.

The musical phenomenon called the blues is another expression of the same consciousness. What is portrayed here is a religious consciousness that has experienced the "hardness" of life, whether the form of that reality is the slave system, God, or simply life itself. It is from such a consciousness that the power

---

10. See Charles H. Long, "Prolegomenon to a Religious Hermeneutic," *History of Religion* 6, no. 3 (February 1967): 254–64; chap. 2 in this [Long's] volume.

to resist and yet maintain one's humanity has emerged. Though the worship and religious life of blacks have often been referred to as forms of escapism, one must always remember that there has always been an integral relationship between the "hardness" of life and the ecstasy of religious worship. It is, in my opinion, an example of what Gaston Bachelard described in Hegelian language as the lithic imagination. Bachelard had reference to the imaginary structure of consciousness that arises in relationship to the natural form of the stone and the manner in which the volitional character of human consciousness is related to this imaginary form.[11] The black community in America has confronted the reality of the historical situation as immutable, impenetrable, but this experience has not produced passivity; it has, rather, found expression as forms of the involuntary and transformative nature of the religious consciousness. In connection with this point, I shall illustrate by returning to the meaning of the image and historical reality of Africa.

Over and over again this image has ebbed and flowed in the religious consciousness. It has found expression in music, dance, and political theorizing. There has been an equally persistent war against the image in the religion of black folk. This war against the image of Africa and blackness can be seen in the political and social movements connected with the stratagems of segregation and integration. Even more telling is the history of the names by which the community has chosen to call itself. From African to colored, to Negro, Afro-American, and, presently, black. The history of these designations can be seen as a religious history through which this community was coming to terms with a primary symbol of opacity.

Recall the words of Gerardus van der Leeuw. He said, "Religious experience, in other terms, is concerned with a 'Somewhat.' But this assertion often means no more than this 'Somewhat' is merely a vague 'something,' and in order that man may be able to make more significant statements about this 'Somewhat,' it must force itself upon him, oppose it to him as being Something Other. Thus the first statement we can make about religion is that it is a highly exceptional and extremely impressive 'Other.'"[12] From the point of view of religious history, one could say that this community in its own self-interpretation has moved from a vague "Somewhat" to the religious experience of a highly exceptional and *extremely impressive* "Other." The contemporary expressions of black power attest to this fact, and the universalizing of this notion in terms of pan-Africanism, negritude, or neo-Marxian and Christian conceptions must equally be noted.

The meaning of the involuntary structure or the opacity of the religious symbol has within this community held together eschatological hopes and the archaic religious consciousness. In both secular and religious groups, new expressions such as Moorish Temple, Black Jews, and Black Muslims retain an

11. See Gaston Bachelard, *La terre et les rêveries de la volonté* (Paris, 1948).
12. Gerardus van der Leeuw, *Religion in Essence and Manifestation*, trans. J. E. Turner (London: George Allen & Unwin, 1938), 23.

archaic structure in their religious consciousness, and this structure is never quite settled, for it is there as a datum to be deciphered in the context of their present experience.

THE EXPERIENCE AND SYMBOL OF GOD

The sources for my interpretation of the experience of the holy in this community are from the folkloric tradition. By this, I mean an oral tradition that exists in its integrity as an oral tradition, the writing down of which is a concession to scholarship.

These sources are slave narratives, sermons, the words and music of spirituals and the blues, the cycles of Brer Rabbit and High John, the Conqueror, stories. These materials reveal a range of religious meanings extending from trickster-transformer hero to High God.

To be sure, the imagery of the Bible plays a large role in the symbolic presentations, but to move from this fact to any simplistic notion of blacks as slaves or former slaves converted to Christianity would, I think, miss several important religious meanings.

The biblical imagery was used because it was at hand; it was adapted to and invested with the experience of the slave. Strangely enough, it was the slave who gave a religious meaning to the notions of freedom and land. The deliverance of the Children of Israel from the Egyptians became an archetype which enabled the slave to live with promise.

God for this community appears as an all-powerful and moral deity, though one hardly ever knows why he has willed this or that. God is never, or hardly ever, blamed for the situation of humanity, for somehow in an inscrutable manner there is a reason for all of this. By and large, a fundamental distinction is made between God and Jesus Christ. To the extent that the language of Christianity is used, black Americans have held to the Trinitarian distinction, but adherence to this distinction has been for experiential rather than dogmatic reasons. Historians of religions have known for a long time that the Supreme Being appears in differing forms. To be sure, God, the first person of the Trinity, is a powerful creator deity.

It is not so much the dogma of the Trinity as it is the modalities of experience of the Trinity which is most important. The experience of God is thus placed within the context of the other images and experiences of black religion. God, as first person of the Trinity, is, of course, a powerful Creator and Supreme deity. Though biblical language is used to speak of his historical presence and intervention in history, we have neither a clear Hebraic nor what has become a Christian interpretation of history. I am not implying that the deity is a *deus otiosus,* for there is an acceptance of historical reality, but in neither its Hebraic nor its traditional Christian mode. We must remember that the historicity of these two traditions was related to the possession of a land, and this has not been the case for blacks in America. In one sense, it is possible to say that their history in America has always presented to them a situation of crisis. The intervention of the deity into their community has not been synonymous with the confirmation of the reality of their being within the structures of America. God has been more often a transformer of their consciousness, the basis for a resource that enabled them to maintain the human image without completely acquiescing to the norms of the majority population. He provided a norm of self-criticism that was not derivative from those who enslaved them. I cite two examples as illustrations:

> When I was very small my people thought I was going to die. Mama used to tell my sister that I was puny and that she didn't think that she would be able to raise me. I used to dream nearly all the time and see all kinds of wild-looking animals. I would nearly always get scared and nervous.
>
> Some time later I got heavy one day and began to die. For days I couldn't eat, I couldn't sleep; even the water I drank seemed to swell in my mouth. A voice said to me one day, "Nora you haven't done what you promised." And again it said, "You saw the sun rise, but you shall die before it goes down." I began to pray. I was making up my bed. A light seemed to come down from heaven, and it looked like it just split me open from my head to my feet. A voice said to me, "Ye are freed and free indeed. My son set you free. Behold, I give you everlasting life."
>
> During all this time I was just dumb. I couldn't speak or move. I heard a moaning sound, and a voice said, "Follow me, my little one, and I will show you the marvelous works of God." I got up it seems, and started to traveling.
>
> I was not my natural self but a little angel. We went and came to a sea of glass, and it was mingled with fire. I opened my mouth and began to pray, "Lord, I will perish in there." Then I saw a path that led through the fire, I journeyed in this path and came to a green pasture where there were a lot of sheep. They were all of the same size and bleated in a mournful tone. A voice spoke to me, and it sounded like a roar of thunder: "Ye are my workmanship and the creation of my hand. I will drive all fears away. Go, and I go with you. You have a deed to your name, and you shall never perish."[13]

> Everybody seemed to be getting along well but poor me. I told him so. I said, "Lord, it looks like you come to everybody's house but mine. I never bother my neighbors or cause any disturbance. I have lived as it is becoming a poor widow woman to live and yes, Lord, it looks like I have a harder time than anybody." When I said this, something told me to turn around and look. I put my bundle down and looked towards the east part of the world. A voice spoke to me as plain as day, but it was inward and said, " I am an on time-God working after the counsel of my own will. In due time I will bring all things to you. Remember and cause your heart to sing."
>
> When God struck me dead with his power I was living on Fourteenth Avenue. It was the year of the Centennial. I was in my house alone, and I

13. Clifton H. Johnson, ed., *God Struck Me Dead*, Religious Conversion Experiences and Auto-biographies of Ex-Slaves (Boston: Pilgrim Press, 1969), 62–63.

declare to you, when his power struck me I died. I fell out on the floor flat on my back. I could neither speak nor move, for my tongue stuck to the roof of my mouth; my jaws were locked and my limbs were stiff.[14]

These two narratives are illustrative of the inner dynamics of the conversion experience. The narratives combine and interweave the ordinary events with the transformation of the religious consciousness. It is not merely a case of God acting in history, for the historical events are not the locus of the activity but then neither do we have a complete lack of concern for historical events in favor of a mystification of consciousness. It is the combination of these two structures that is distinctive in these narratives; clues such as these might help us to understand the specific nature of the black religious consciousness.

But this structure of the deity is present in non-Christian movements among the blacks; the transforming power of the deity may be seen among the Black Muslims and the Black Jews. This quality of the presence of the deity has enabled blacks to affirm the historical mode by seeing it more in terms of an initiatory structure than in terms of a progressive or evolutionary understanding of temporality.

Continuing with the Christian language of the Trinity, Jesus has been experienced more in the form of a demi-deity[15] than as conquering hero. One could make the case that this understanding of Jesus Christ has always been present in the history of the Western church, but it is clear that this image of the Christ has not been experienced as a symbol of Western culture as a whole since the seventeenth century. Christ as fellow sufferer, as the little child, as the companion, as the man who understands—these symbols of Christ have been dominant. Consider, for example, the spirituals:

I told Jesus it would be all right if he changed my name,
Jesus told me that the world would hate me if he changed my name.
Poor little Jesus boy, made him to be born in a manger. World treated him so
  mean,
Treats me mean too . . . .

But there is more than biblical imagery as a datum. In the folklore we see what appears as the trickster-transformer hero. More than often he appears in the Brer Rabbit cycle of stories, which seem related to similar West African stories of Ananse, the Spider.

14. Ibid., 58–59.
15. Adolf E. Jensen defined this religious structure as a result of his researches in Ceram. See his *Hainuwele* (Frankfurt, 1939) and *Myth and Cult Among Primitive Peoples* (Chicago and London: University of Chicago Press, 1963). I do not wish to say that Jesus Christ is understood in any complete sense as a dema-deity in black religion; I am saying that it is from this religious structure that one should begin the deciphering of the meaning of Jesus. Essential to this structure is the notion of the deity as companion and creator, a deity related more to the human condition than deities of the sky, and the subjection of this deity in the hands of human beings.

This is one of the cycles of the Brer Rabbit stories.[16] Brer Rabbit, Brer Fox, and Brer Wolf were experiencing a season of drought. They met to decide the proper action to take. It was decided that they should dig a well so that they would have a plenteous supply of water. Brer Rabbit said that he thought this was a very good plan, although he did not wish to participate in the digging of the well, because, he said, he arose early in the morning and drank the dew from the grass and thus did not wish to participate in the arduous task of digging. Brer Fox and Brer Wolf proceeded with their task and completed the digging of the deep well. After the well was dug, Brer Rabbit arose early each morning and went to the well and drank his fill, pretending all the time that he was drinking the morning dew. After a while, Brer Fox and Brer Wolf became suspicious of Brer Rabbit and set about to spy upon him. Sure enough, they caught him one morning drinking from their well. They subjected him to some punishment, which we need not go into, for the point of the story has been made.

Brer Rabbit is not simply lazy and clever; it is clear that he feels that he has something else to do—that life cannot be dealt with in purely conventional terms and committee meetings. In many respects the preacher in the black community exhibits many of the traits of Brer Rabbit, and it was often the preacher who kept alive the possibility of another life, or who protested and affirmed by doing nothing.

One other instance should be mentioned: High John, the Conqueror. It is stated explicitly in the Folklore that High John came dancing over the waves from Africa, or that he was in the hold of the slave ship. High John is a flamboyant character. He possesses great physical strength and conquers more by an audacious display of his power than through any subtlety or cunning. He is the Folkloric side of a conquering Christ, though with less definite goals.

The essential element in the expression and experience of God is his transforming ability. This is true in the case of God as absolute moral ruler as well as in Brer Rabbit or High John, the Conqueror. Insofar as society at large was not an agent of transformation, the inner resources of consciousness and the internal structures of the blacks' own history and community became not simply the locus for new symbols but the basis for a new consciousness for the blacks.

It is therefore the religious consciousness of the blacks in America which is the repository of who they are, where they have been, and where they are going. A purely existential analysis cannot do justice to this religious experience. A new interpretation of American religion would come about if careful attention were given to the religious history of this strange American.

---

16. See T. F. Crane, "Plantation Folklore," in *The Negro and His Folklore*, ed. Bruce Jackson (Austin: University of Texas Press, 1967), 157–67.

Chapter 36

A Poem on Memory and Hope
"Lift Every Voice"

James Weldon Johnson

Editor's Introduction: James Weldon Johnson (1871–1938), then principal of the segregated Stanton school in Florida, wrote the lyrics of "Lift Every Voice and Sing" for his students to read at a celebration of the birthday of Abraham Lincoln on February 12, 1900. The poem and its reading also served as a welcoming gesture for the event's distinguished speaker, Booker T. Washington. In 1905 the lyrics were set to music by Johnson's brother Rosamond. In 1919 the National Association for the Advancement of Colored People declared the song to be the Negro National Anthem, and soon thereafter it was widely distributed and sung in black churches that often pasted its words into their hymnals. The poem aptly expresses the themes of memory and hope that constitute the title of this chapter. Most important, it has been an effective means of keeping the story of memory and hope alive and passing it on from one generation to another. On January 20, 2008, the Reverend Joseph Lowery, former president of the Southern Christian Leadership Conference, cited the words of the third stanza at the beginning

of his benediction at the inauguration of President Barack Hussein
Obama as the first African American president of the United States.

"Lift Every Voice"

Lift every voice and sing,
'Til earth and heaven ring,
Ring with the harmonies of Liberty;
Let our rejoicing rise
High as the listening skies,
Let it resound loud as the rolling sea.
Sing a song full of the faith that the dark past has taught us,
Sing a song full of the hope that the present has brought us;
Facing the rising sun of our new day begun,
Let us march on 'til victory is won.

Stony the road we trod,
Bitter the chast'ning rod,
Felt in the days when hope unborn had died;
Yet with a steady beat,
Have not our weary feet
Come to the place for which our fathers sighed?
We have come over a way that with tears has been watered,
We have come, treading our path through the blood of the slaughtered,
Out from the gloomy past,
'Til now we stand at last
Where the white gleam of our bright star is cast.

God of our weary years,
God of our silent tears,
Thou who has brought us thus far on the way;
Thou who has by Thy might
Led us into the light,
Keep us forever in the path, we pray.
Lest our feet stray from the places, our God, where we met Thee,
Lest, our hearts drunk with the wine of the world, we forget Thee;
Shadowed beneath Thy hand,
May we forever stand,
True to our God,
True to our native land.

Chapter 37

The Theologies of Black Folk in North America

Presidential Address to the American Theological Society, March 30, 2012

Peter J. Paris

Editor's Introduction: Peter J. Paris (1933–) is the only author in this anthology who enjoys dual citizenship in the United States and Canada. Born and raised in Nova Scotia, he has lived in the United States since 1965, when he began his pursuit of the PhD degree in Ethics and Society at the University of Chicago Divinity School. Two of his books have been basic texts in black church studies for several decades, namely, *Black Religious Leaders: Conflict in Unity* and *The Social Teaching of the Black Churches.* The following address demonstrates how various forms of resistance to racial injustice have evolved and been embraced by blacks in their enduring quest for racial justice. Consequently, five types of theology have emerged with corresponding implications for social ethics.

The purpose of this address is to explain how the various theologies of black folk are virtually variations on the theme of freedom, where each theology is correlated with the ethics of freedom. Most importantly, the theologies of black folk invariably explicate the substance of black religion as located respectively in what Benjamin Mays called more than eight decades ago, The Negro's God[1] and The Negro's Church.[2] Those various theologies originated in the context of chattel slavery, where enslaved Africans gradually constructed an alternative understanding of Jesus from that which they had received from their cruel owners. Though illiterate for the most part, they relied on their oral traditions to create and preserve a radically new tradition within the confines of slavery, one which eventually was institutionalized in their independent black churches.

I begin this lecture with a broad brush depicting white America's discovery of the black churches during the 1955 Montgomery Bus Boycott. I then provide an outline of the birth, growth, and modifications of the black churches from the eighteenth century up to the present era. At every stage of their development the theologies of the black churches have been closely related with the spiritual, social, economic, political, and moral needs of their people whether or not they were members of the churches. That is to say, no sphere of the people's lives was outside the purview of their theologies, which may be one of the most telling marks of their deep African roots where all life is directly related to the sacred.

With variations within each of them, the theologies of black folk are five-fold: (1) the invisible theology of enslaved Africans; (2) the public theology of free Negroes in their independent churches; (3) the public theology of Martin Luther King, Jr.; (d) black theology in the theological academy; and (5) womanist theology in the theological academy.

THE INVISIBLE THEOLOGY OF ENSLAVED AFRICANS

Now, the black churches had been invisible to white America for almost a century following emancipation. Born in the cauldron of slavery their founders considered it necessary to conceal their religious practices from their oppressors as they had done in an earlier period with the religious beliefs and practices they had brought with them from Africa and were forbidden to practice. At this time, they had an even greater need to conceal their practice because they were developing in those secret spaces an understanding of God and of humanity that radically differed from that of their owners. In other words, they had begun to construct an alternative understanding of their slave owners' Christianity. Needless to say, perhaps, this activity was an altogether radical and dangerous undertaking.

In the early days of the trans-Atlantic slave trade most of the traders and the owners believed that Africans were subhumans and had no souls. Thus, there was no need to try to convert them to Christianity. Long after that anthropology

---

1. Benjamin E. Mays, *The Negro's God as Reflected in His Literature* (New York: Atheneum, 1938).
2. Benjamin Elijah Mays and Joseph William Nicholson, *The Negro's Church* (Institute of Social and Religious Research, 1933).

was modified, however, most slave owners continued to deny white evangelists permission to preach to their slaves less they think that a common baptism implied equality of civil status or be motivated to demand such. Thus, it was not until those fears had been minimized by legal enactments that some owners permitted their slaves to hear the Gospel proclaimed either by their hired preachers or sometimes by a trusted slave who would preach in the presence of the owner or his appointed representative.

Since the enslaved Africans were never able to muster any reasonable amount of respect for the Christianity promulgated by their slave owners' preachers, it took them a very long while to develop any desire for Christian conversion. Since Africans probably caught their first glimpse of the name "Jesus" in 1562 when they saw the words "The Good Ship Jesus" emblazoned on the hull of a British slave ship bringing its first cargo of enslaved Africans from Sierra Leone to the Dominican Republic, that fact alone should make it obvious why they would have no interest in converting to Christianity.

While undergoing the brutal experiences of chattel slavery the only source of hope that the Africans had lay in their familial and tribal ancestors whom they believed interceded with their God to effect freedom and the restoration of personal dignity and communal belonging. Those who had the privilege to attend their slave owners' churches sometimes caught a glimpse of such a vision in the teaching and personality of Jesus of Nazareth as they heard their owners' preachers proclaim him the savior of the world. Since the only savior for them would be one who could set them free from their bondage, they saw no such salvation in the preaching of anyone who viewed God's will as synonymous with that of their slave owners. Unwilling, therefore, to accept any word from their slave owners' preachers as truth, some began rethinking the stories about Jesus in their own secret meeting places.

In due course, these enslaved Africans discovered an immense difference between the religion of their slave owners and many of the biblical stories about God and God's son Jesus. After discerning that the God who brought Jesus into the world was the same God who had called Moses to challenge the pharaoh in Egypt to set his people free from slavery, the basis for a new hope began to take root in their minds and souls. Gradually, they discovered many other things about Jesus with which they could easily identify, including the following: that Jesus had been born into a working-class family and while he was still an infant his parents were forced to seek refuge in a minority immigrant community in Egypt; that Jesus began his ministry by accepting for himself the vocation of the prophet Isaiah to preach good news to the poor, to proclaim release to the captives, recovery of sight to the blind, and to set at liberty those who were oppressed (Isa 60:1; Luke 4:18); and that he was betrayed by his own people, captured, accused of sedition, tortured, and sentenced to death by the colonial ruler by crucifixion, the most tortuous method of the day.

Thus, they soon identified with Jesus completely, empathized with his suffering, rejoiced over his rising from the dead, and viewed him as their divine friend who would always protect them. As they began viewing the Bible through these lenses they gradually embraced Jesus as their savior and placed their hope in the heavenly vision he proclaimed: the vision of an alternative world where God's love would be all pervasive and everybody would be delivered from their sufferings and treated with dignity, respect, and fairness. While their slave owners viewed heaven as a reward to be earned after death, enslaved Africans soon added to that understanding a view of heaven as a symbol of social criticism on the immoral practices of slavery.

Like the Israelites, many blacks soon came to view themselves as God's chosen people called to be God's special representatives of love and justice to God's wayward people, including their oppressors.

Thus the contrast between the Christianity of their slave owners and that of the enslaved Africans is seen vividly in their respective understandings of God. On the one hand, these suffering Africans viewed Jesus as one who proclaimed a message concerning the God of truth, freedom, love, hope, and justice who had commissioned him to usher in what he called "the Kingdom of God" wherein all things would be restored to their original state of wholeness. On the other hand, the slave owners' preachers proclaimed a God who had created whites as a superior race destined to own and control the inferior race of African peoples by treating them with impunity. We can readily see why the enslaved Africans would prefer the message of Jesus to that of their slave owners' preachers. The former contained the good news of freedom: the substance of their hopes and dreams. The latter provided divine sanction for their oppression.

Now, it is important to emphasize that the enslaved Africans did not merely become Christians by embracing their owners' religion. Rather, led by the Spirit of the Jesus whom they encountered in the Bible they refashioned an alternative to slave-owning Christianity by finding within the Bible salvific resources with which to address their needs. Accordingly, little by little they discovered many biblical principles, stories, events, icons, prayers, meditations, and symbols that enabled them to construct an understanding of Jesus Christ as their spiritual ancestor which, as implied above, is the highest honor that Africans can bestow on humans in gratitude and reverence for the goodness they had bequeathed to their people during their lifetime. Thus a covenant occurred. The people resolved to keep the memory of their ancestors alive with regular devotions in return for their intercessions with God on their behalf. This covenant with Jesus Christ as ancestor took precedence over all their other ancestral covenants and it was renewed each time the people ended their prayers with the words, "in the name of Jesus Christ, we pray. Amen."

In short, this band of illiterate enslaved African Christians, meeting secretly in the hush harbors, gave birth to the "invisible enslaved African church" which remained a hidden reality for a very long while. It was in those meetings where they comforted one another by praying, testifying, preaching, and composing and singing their songs of faith that we now call the "spirituals." Through the oral tradition they wrote this revised Christian Gospel on their hearts and passed it on through song to succeeding generations. They created their songs by adapting the various rhythmic patterns of African music to lyrics that expressed biblical messages of hope, trust, freedom, mercy, love, and fairness as contained in the Gospel of Jesus Christ which they viewed as deeply embedded in the deliverance of the Israelites from their bondage. This revised Gospel coincided with their hopes for freedom, which were reinforced whenever they sang about their God who they believed would do for them what God had done for the Israelites. Thus, they composed what has become one of the most beloved songs of the ages:

> Go down Moses, way down in Egypt's land,
> Tell'old Pharaoh, to let my people go.
>
> When israel was in Egypt's land, let my people go,
> Oppressed so hard, they could not stand, let my people go.

Similarly, their faith in a God who would comfort them in their suffering was expressed in another song inspired by Jeremiah's spiritually depressed cry, "Is there no balm in Gilead?" According to the theologian Howard Thurman, "The slave caught the mood of this spiritual dilemma, and with it did an amazing thing. He straightened the question mark in Jeremiah's sentence into an exclamation point: 'There Is a balm in Gilead!' Here is a note of creative triumph."[3]

> There is a balm in Gilead to make the wounded whole.
> There is a balm in Gilead to heal the sin-sick soul.

Clearly their songs of faith did not focus exclusively on the triumphal event of the afterlife but also on the relation between that finale and their present strivings for freedom. In other words, they also sang about the ethics implied by their theology. Since it was often necessary to conceal the ethics, some of the songs had double meanings: one for the ears of the slaves and the other for the ears of their owners. Thus, in somber tones they sang,

> Steal away; steal away,
> Steal away to Jesus.
> Steal away, steal away home,
> I ain't got long to stay here.

Some might have thought that the slaves were singing only about their mortality. But, they may have been singing also about a plan to escape. Such double entendre helped to keep alive their spirit of resistance. In other words, the slaves discerned no disjunction between their religious strivings and their daily needs.

---

3. Howard Thurman, *Deep River and The Negro Spiritual Speaks of Life and Death* (Richmond, IN: Friends United, 1975), 56.

Similarly, the song, "Wade in the water, wade in the water children, / Wade in the water, God's gonna' trouble the waters." Once again the slave owners might have thought they were singing about baptism, a song that is still sung at many Baptist baptism ceremonies. But they may also have been singing about crossing the Ohio River or even crossing over into Canada via the underground railroad.

And as a not so subtle criticism of their slave owners' beliefs that heaven was racially segregated, they sang,

> I've got shoes, you got shoes,
> All God's chil'un got shoes,
> When i get to heaven gonna put on my shoes,
> And walk all ober God's heaven.

And with a gentle nod to the slave owners they sang the refrain,

> Heaben, heaben,
> Everybody talkin' about heaben ain't a gonna there,
> Heaben, heaben,
> Gonna walk all ober God's heaben.

And the stanzas that speak about having a robe and a crown when we get to heaven, clearly signify their human dignity as recognized by their creator God if not by their oppressors.

Since the depth and breadth of their suffering was so traumatic and expansive Jesus was their only source of comfort and trust. And so they sang,

> I want Jesus to walk with me;
> I want Jesus to walk with me;
> All along my pilgrim journey,
> I want Jesus to walk with me;
>
> In my trials lord, walk with me.
> In my trials lord, walk with me.
> All along my pilgrim journey,
> I want Jesus to walk with me.

Analyses of over 600 spirituals reveal an astounding diversity in content and form; rhythm and mood. There are songs of immense pathos like "Sometimes I feel like a motherless child" or "Nobody knows the trouble I see, / nobody knows my sorrow. / Nobody knows the trouble I see, / Glory Hallelujah." Songs of joy like "Walk together Children" or "Git on Board Little chillen, There's room for plenty a mo'." Songs of excitement like "Joshua Fit the Battle of Jericho, Jericho, Jericho, And the Walls Came Tumblin' down." Songs with a soft lull like, "Swing low Sweet Chariot, Coming for to carry me home." Songs of sadness like, "My Lord What a Morning, My Lord What a morning, When the sun refused to shine." Songs of spiritual confidence like, "I'm satisfied; I'm satisfied; King Jesus standin' by my side, Lord I'm satisfied."

Some of the most beloved of these spirituals spoke about Christ's suffering and death, which were also very common experiences for enslaved Africans. The following has become a great Easter hymn that is sung today around the world:

Were you there when they crucified my Lord?
Were you there when they crucified my lord? . . .

Were you there when they hanged him on the tree?
Were you there when they hanged him on the tree? . . .

Were you there when the sun refused to shine?
Were you there when the sun refused to shine? . . .

Were you there when they laid him in the grave?
Were you there when they laid him in the grave? . . .

Were you there when he rose up from the grave?
Were you there when he rose up from the grave? . . .

And after each verse, the singers repeat the moving refrain of personal empathy:

Oh, sometimes it causes me to tremble, tremble, tremble,
Were you there when they crucified my lord.

In their secret gatherings they also composed that great call to the Lord's supper which is the central ritual of remembering Christ's suffering, death, and resurrection.

Let us break bread together, on our knees,
Let us break bread together, on our knees.
When i fall on my knees,
With my eyes to the risin' sun,
O lord, have mercy on me.

Let us drink wine together on our knees,
Let us drink wine together on our knees,
When i fall on my knees,
With my eyes to the risin' sun,
O lord, have mercy on me.

Let us praise god together on our knees,
Let us praise god together on our knees,
When i fall on my knees,
With my eyes to the risin' sun,
O lord, have mercy on me

While the story of the Christ's suffering, death, and resurrection occur often in the spirituals, very few deal with his birth for reasons that are unknown. Nonetheless, among the few are these:

> Mary had a baby, yes Lord,
> Mary had a baby, yes Lord,
> What did she name him, my Lord?
> What did she name him, my Lord?
> She named him king Jesus, my Lord.
> She named him king, Jesus, my Lord.

We can only imagine how empowering that song must have been for young women who also must have dreamed about giving birth one day to a savior whom they would name themselves as Mary had done with no patriarchal involvement whatsoever.

Another such song was this one:

> Go tell it on the mountain,
> Over the hills and every where,
> Go tell it on the mountain,
> That Jesus Christ is born.

There were also songs declaring the need for prayer:

> It's me, it's me, it's me, O Lord,
> Standing in the need of prayer;
> It's me, it's me O Lord,
> Standing in the need of prayer;
>
> Tain't my mother or my father, but it's me O Lord,
> Standing in the need of prayer;
> Tain't the preacher or the deacon, but it's me O Lord,
> Standing in the need of prayer . . .

No spiritual represents the call to evangelism more than this one:

> Somebody's knockin' at your door,
> Somebody's knockin' at your door,
> Oh sinner, why don't you answer,
> Somebody's knockin' at your door.

The spirituals also speak about God as deliverer:

> Didn't my Lord deliver Daniel, Daniel, Daniel,
> Didn't my Lord deliver Daniel,
> Then why not everyman.

Undoubtedly, the spirituals are community songs in their origin, content, and performance. As such they reveal the centrality of community in the African experience before, during, and after slavery. Thus, in that regard also, the black churches manifest continuity with traditional familial and communal life in Africa.

In their churches (invisible to their slave owners though deliberately concealed by the slaves themselves) enslaved Africans radically revised the Christianity of their slave owners by embracing the ethic of inclusion and never practicing racism. In fact, black churches have been the only institutions in America with a non-racist history and that constitutes their uniqueness on the American landscape.

Though blacks suffered greatly for two-and-a-half centuries of slavery followed by another century of second-class citizenship, they were always more than mere victims. As a matter of fact, they overcame their suffering by striving to be like Jesus. Thus, they developed a legacy of love and goodwill not for what America was but for what it could become. Accordingly, they composed the song,

Lord I want to be a Christian, in'a my soul, in'a my soul.
Lord I want to be a Christian, in'a my soul.

Lord, I want to be more loving, in'a my soul; in'a my soul.
Lord, I want to be more loving, in'a my soul.

Lord, I want to be like Jesus, in'a my soul; in'a my soul.
Lord, I want to be like Jesus, in'a my soul.

Clearly, these descendants of enslaved Africans have bequeathed to the world not only a portion of its most beloved music and songs but a reconciling spirit towards the heirs of their former oppressors. Their continuous strivings to heal the nation of all traces of racism by expanding democracy for all citizens evidence their love for the so-called American dream from which they had been excluded for such a long time.

Under the conditions of chattel slavery, the theology of this so-called invisible church may be rightly called "the invisible theology of enslaved Africans." It was a survivalist theology set in motion by the strivings of enslaved Africans for freedom from physical pain, psychological suffering, material deprivation, endless terror, brutal oppression, and diminished humanity: a theology deeply rooted in the understanding of a God who was both personal and communal; one who they hoped would deliver them from slavery as with the Israelites of long ago.

This invisible theology of enslaved Africans provided the spiritual foundation for relieving the burdens of their people through many different forms of actions that ranged from the extreme passivity of submission to the extreme aggressive forms of violent uprisings. The great diversity of responses included the following: helping runaway escapees whenever possible; inspiring rebellions, especially those led by preachers; pretending to be content with slavery by keeping their true feelings concealed; devising various devious means of resistance; supporting the nationalist aim to form a colony of free blacks in Africa which culminated in their settlement in Liberia in 1822; and giving assistance to the enemy during the War of Independence in return for free passage along the Atlantic seaboard, either to Nova Scotia with Reverend David George in 1782 or to Jamaica with Reverend George Liele in 1783 where they became the pioneers in establishing enduring Baptist churches in both countries. Let me hasten to say that less than a decade later, because of the racial hostilities they suffered in Nova Scotia, David George led a sizable group of blacks from Nova Scotia in 1791 to found Freetown in Sierra Leone, the first British colony in West Africa. It was there that he planted another Baptist church.[4]

THE PUBLIC THEOLOGY OF FREE NEGROES
IN THEIR INDEPENDENT CHURCHES

This theology of enslaved Africans ended its tradition of invisibility in 1787 by morphing into the independent church movement of Richard Allen. While the Constitution of the United States was being ratified in Philadelphia in that year, a mere six blocks away on Lombard Street, Richard Allen was leading a group of blacks out of St. George's Methodist Church. He had been forced off his knees during prayers because he chose to sit in the white section of the church. He and those who left with him later formed the Bethel African Methodist Episcopal Church, the mother congregation of the denomination by the same name that was established in 1816 with the motto, "God our Father; Christ our Redeemer; Man our Brother." Suffice it to say that Allen's action initiated a movement among so-called free Negroes who established various independent churches that continue to be moral centers in the black community from that day up to the present. Further, the act of "kneel-ins" in white churches during the Civil Rights Movement had its historical roots in Allen's deliberate "kneel-in" in 1787.

For the most part, the various independent churches formed thereafter combined the polity they had inherited from their respective white denominations with the invisible theology of enslaved Africans to form what I call "the public theology of free Negroes in their independent churches." Upon close analysis, one discovers that the invisible theology of enslaved Africans not only became visible in independent black churches but it played a major role in developing a moral social order among free blacks from the time of the revolutionary War

---

4. For further study, see Grant Gordon, *From Slavery to Freedom: The Life of David George, Pioneer Black Baptist Minister* (Hantsport, NS: Lancelot, 1992).

of Independence through the Civil War and up to the middle of the twentieth century.

This second phase of theological development endured for approximately 175 years. Many different types of black churches were supported by its thought, which included predominantly black denominations and black congregations in predominantly white protestant denominations such as Methodists, Presbyterians, Baptists, Anglicans, Lutherans, Congregationalists, and others.

It should be noted, however, that the theology of free Negroes in their independent churches also supported the rise of a tradition of Christianity that had no antecedent in the mainstream white Protestant churches, namely the Pentecostal tradition that began with the 1906 revival meetings at the Azusa Street Mission,[5] a predominantly black congregation in Los Angeles led by William J. Seymour. That revival attracted many whites and other ethnic groups. In fact, many whites joined the mission and remained there for several decades, helping to preserve and expand the principle teachings of baptism by the Holy Spirit and glossolalia (speaking in tongues). Eventually, however, they broke away and joined the larger white community in preferring to form and maintain their own racially separate churches and denominations.

Thus, for several decades the sociology of black Pentecostals differed from the so-called main stream white churches by promoting and preserving inter-racial congregations with a racial balance not only in the pew but also in its bishopric. Since their members were predominantly poor with very limited education, their churches easily attracted large numbers of the southern migrants as they moved into northern and western cities throughout the first half of the twentieth century. Understandably, these churches undertook a necessary pastoral ministry by focusing primarily on matters pertaining to personal morality (abstinence from smoking, drinking, dancing, cursing, and gambling) and spiritual holiness (i.e., faithfulness to family and church).[6] Yet, a growing number of contemporary black Pentecostal scholars[7] are striving to persuade black Pentecostal churches to return to the prophetic ministry implied by their founders' countercultural orientation. Such a ministry would also be a counter-force to the many contemporary charismatic televangelists busily proclaiming what many view as an idolatrous prosperity Gospel.[8]

Clearly, the most enduring contribution of African American Pentecostalism to the black church tradition has been that of varying the sound of the spirituals

---

5. See Cecil M. Robeck, Jr., "The Azusa Street Mission and Historic Black Churches: Two Worlds in Conflict in Los Angeles' African American Community," in *Afro-Pentecostalism: Black Pentecostal and Charismatic Christianity in History and Culture*, ed. Amos Yong and Estrelda Y. Alexander (New York: New York University, 2011), 29ff.

6. See David D. Daniels III, "Navigating the Territory: Early Afro-Pentecostalism as a Movement within Black Civil Society," in ibid., 44.

7. See Cheryl J. Sanders, "Pentecostal Ethics and Prosperity Gospel: Is There a Prophet in the House?," in ibid., 142–44.

8. Ibid., 148–51.

into a "sanctified sound" which became the forerunner to gospel music destined to gain ascendancy in the mid- to late-twentieth century through its indelible imprint on the music of most contemporary independent black churches.[9]

For 175 years the public theology of free Negroes in their independent churches employed the method of moral suasion whenever they sought the help of whites for improving the plight of their people. This was done through reasoned arguments in letters, speeches, and face-to-face contact with white authorities. During slavery their theology supported that method but also such additional strategies as the following: the work of the New York Anti-Slavery Society in which the first black graduate of Princeton Theological Seminary, Theodore S. Wright (1828) was a founding member; the courageous ministry of the black Presbyterian abolitionist, Henry Highland Garnet; the mission of black newspapers like The North Star, founded and edited by the renowned Frederick Douglass, an escaped slave and foremost black abolitionist, orator, and writer; the Pan-African endeavors of Alexander Crummell and Martin Delany in calling for the colonization of free blacks to Africa; the work of two preachers, Nat Turner and Gabriel Prosser, who led rebellions against slavery in 1820 and 1830 respectively; the underground railroad where black churches joined others in aiding escapees from slavery and by facilitating their movement from place to place en route to Canada; and the founding of mutual aid societies, schools, hospitals, and businesses. Black churches viewed all of these diverse activities as essential parts of their respective ministries.

From the time of Reconstruction onwards black churches have lent their support to candidates for electoral office whose work they believed would assist them in their activities of uplifting the race. Also, from the beginning of their founding in the early twentieth century, the black churches have given their full support to traditional civil rights organizations such as the National Association for the Advancement of Colored People (NAACP) and the National Urban League, founded in the early decades of the twentieth century.

It is also important to note that the public theology of free Negroes in independent black churches was thoroughly ecumenical. It permeated every denomination (Episcopalian, Presbyterian, Methodist, Baptist, and others) and shaped its ethos. Following Vatican II it found a larger space in the predominantly black congregations of the Roman Catholic Church as well.

As stated above, from the beginning of their history black churches made the Christian Gospel their own by Africanizing their practices through music, dance, song, preaching, testimonies, prayers, body movements, spirit possession, communal belonging, and hospitality to all peoples. Much more could be said at this point about the content and style of this renewal process as well as its continuity with their African past, but suffice it to say that their constructive

---

9. Ibid., 49.

revision of white Christianity clearly evidenced that they were the sole agents in that process and not mere benefactors of their oppressors' benevolence.[10]

THE PUBLIC THEOLOGY OF MARTIN LUTHER KING, JR.

Clearly the black churches in America gained national visibility during the mid-twentieth-century Civil Rights Movement under the leadership of Martin Luther King, Jr. Prior to that event white America knew very little about the black churches and theological education or paid no attention to them whatsoever. Long concealed from the eyes and ears of white America, the black church's sudden public appearance greatly surprised the nation. While there was nothing unexpected about the main features of the boycott itself, namely the emptiness of the Montgomery buses and hundreds of black women walking to their domestic jobs, there was something else that was altogether new to white journalists and their readers. Close observation of the event revealed that the boycotters gathered in black churches each evening for what they called mass rallies. There they joyfully participated in programs that highlighted many of the traditional religious practices of the black churches: joyful hymns, spirituals, gospel music, prayers, testimonies, and dynamic preaching, all of which provided the necessary inspiration and encouragement that the people needed for continuing the boycott. Most importantly, their official spokesperson, Dr. Martin Luther King, Jr., speaking with an eloquence rarely heard since Abraham Lincoln, gave theological meaning to the resistance they were orchestrating against racial segregation and discrimination. Further, he repeatedly justified the boycott by appeals to the Bible, the Declaration of Independence, and the Constitution of the United States, which he often blended together as if they were parts of a single document.

Although not every black person in Montgomery attended the mass rallies, it soon became clear that those who participated in the boycott enjoyed an overwhelming consensus of black support for the action itself. Gradually, the nation was able to recognize the symbiotic relationship that had long existed between the black churches and the larger black community.

At the Montgomery Bus Boycott in 1955 the public theology of free Negroes in their independent churches underwent a striking transformation, not so much in substance as in its public style. For the first time in their history, black churches directly confronted the political and economic authorities of southern cities in protesting racial injustice, first by waging a year-long bus boycott and

---

10. Significant historical sources on slave religion and the independent black churches are the following: Albert J. Raboteau, *Slave Religion: The Invisible Institution in the Antebellum South*, rev. ed. (New York: Oxford, 2004); Gayraud S. Wilmore, *Black Religion and Black Radicalism: An Interpretation of the Religious History of African Americans*, 3rd ed. (New York: Orbis, 1999). A major sociological resource is C. Eric Lincoln and Lawrence H. Mamiya, *The Black Church in the African American Experience* (Durham, NC: Duke, 1990).

later by numerous mass demonstrations. Most importantly, they courageously introduced the nation to the practice of nonviolent resistance as they willingly presented their bodies to absorb the violence of the police and the terror of the Ku Klux Klan.

Propelled by the instrumentality of the public media, the speeches and sermons of Dr. Martin Luther King, Jr., saturated the nation's airwaves for the greater part of a decade. King's advanced learning enabled him to augment his inherited public theology of free Negroes in their independent churches with insights gained from his exposure to the liberal wing of the white male theological academy, which included the Social Gospel movement, philosophical and theological personalism, and the theologies of Reinhold Niebuhr and Paul Tillich. Clearly those academic resources merely supplemented his inherited public theology of free Negroes in their independent churches, which he modified in such a way that its ethics appealed not only to his own people but to liberal white Protestants, Jews, and many Roman Catholics as well. Since its impact on both whites and blacks was so great, and since his movement undertook the first nonviolent direct confrontation with the white power structure by blacks, C. Eric Lincoln marked that period as a watershed event when the so-called "negro church" actually became the "black church."[11] Thus, we can rightly claim that in contrast with any notion of submissiveness or passivity, the public theology of free Negroes in their independent churches became more self-determinative, assertive, and confident in the Southern Christian Leadership Conference which Dr. King founded and led. Following the debates of the 1960s about "black power," the former so-called Negro churches began renaming themselves the "black churches," wherein the theology of Martin Luther King, Jr., continues to dominate its prophetic orientation.

During that period King revealed to the nation and world the traditional black belief in the God of Freedom who he believed ordained Jesus Christ to announce the coming of the "beloved community" where the diverse peoples of the world would live in harmony and peace. That same theology laid the foundation for the ensuing conflict that occurred between him and the advocates of black power. In his last book, *Where Do We Go from Here? Chaos or Community?*, King engaged in a rigorous discussion about the concept of "black power." In doing so, he sought to affirm the notion of power per se while rejecting the adjective "black" because he believed it implied both racial chauvinism and the use of violence.

No one should assume that that debate was new. On the contrary, the black churches had had a long history of conflict among various camps within its domain advocating passive accommodation, legitimate protest, and nationalist separation. In fact, local black churches and some denominations became identified with one or other of those orientations. Yet, during the post-civil rights

---

11. See C. Eric Lincoln, *The Black Church since Frazier* (New York: Schocken, 1974), 114–15.

era, the achievements of Dr. King's nonviolent protest movement facilitated the ascendancy of the strident black power movement that was soon embraced by the nascent black theology movement.

BLACK THEOLOGY IN THE THEOLOGICAL ACADEMY

During the year after Dr. King's assassination, Professor James H. Cone of Union Theological Seminary in New York published his first book entitled Black Theology and Black Power, which provided a theological rationale for the controversial concept of black power by arguing that God was on the side of oppressed peoples using power for the sake of their liberation. Key biblical passages drawn upon were those pertaining to the Exodus and Luke 4:18–20. Cone's book launched a novel event in the American theological academy that was kept alive by the demands of black students, whose numbers, after King's death, had rapidly increased in predominantly white seminaries, divinity schools, and religious studies departments.

Most importantly, Cone's black theology marked the entrance of the black Christian tradition in the theological academy. Soon thereafter Professor Preston N. Williams of Harvard Divinity School organized the first Group Session in the American Academy of Religion entitled, "African American Religious History," which was later chaired for several years by Cone's colleague at Union Theological Seminary, the late James M. Washington.

In 1971 an appreciative though critical response to James Cone's first book was published by Professor J. Deotis Roberts in his book, *Liberation and Reconciliation: A Black Theology*. For several years thereafter a debate between these two black theologians became dominant. Other constructive criticisms of the black theology project gradually emerged from such scholars as Cecil W. Cone, Major Jones, William R. Jones, Charles H. Long, and Gayraud Wilmore. A few white theologians also contributed their criticisms including John C. Bennett, Helmut Gollwitzer, Paul Lehmann, Paul Holmer, and G. Clarke Chapman.

The most radical form of black theology, however, was represented by Albert B. Cleage, Jr., whose first book entitled *The Black Messiah* claimed that Jesus and all of his disciples were black. He had also founded the Shrine of the Black Madonna in Detroit, which eventually expanded to other cities. His second book was entitled *Black Christian Nationalism*, which lay the groundwork for his increasing ecclesiastical separation from the black church tradition in this country by directly connecting with the Orthodox Church tradition in Africa. Thereafter his church took the name Pan-African Orthodox Christian Church, and he changed his name to Jaramogi Abebe Agyeman, Swahili names for Liberator, Holy man, and Savior of the nation.

In 1970 the few blacks who were teaching in theological education at that time came together and formed the Society for the Study of Black Religion (SSBR) as a forum where black scholars could freely discuss and critique one another's research projects as well as challenge one another to discern how to relate Cone's black theology to their respective disciplines. The purpose of the SSBR was never to replace the American Academy of Religion but to encourage black scholars to participate more effectively by offering papers at its annual meetings.

In its early days and for a long while afterwards the relationship between academic black theology and the black churches was strained because the black churches had never had a close relationship with the academic scholarship of predominantly white seminaries and divinity schools. Nonetheless, many of the black church leaders were familiar with all of the main tenets of black theology because they had encountered it in some of its notable nineteenth-century leaders who had emphasized them from time to time; leaders like Bishop Henry McNeil Turner, Alexander Crummell, David Walker, and Henry Highland Garnet, as well as such contemporaries as Herbert Edwards, Vincent Harding, Henry Mitchell, Ella Mitchell, Cornish Rogers, Hycel Taylor, Gayraud Wilmore, and Henry Young, to mention a few.

Clearly black theology has been largely an academic enterprise situated in and motivated by the demands of the academy. In fact, it originated with the questions and concerns of an ecumenical group of black leaders, many of whom were members of predominantly white denominations. On July 31, 1966 they took out a full-page ad in the *New York Times* in support of black power. Later in the following year they formed the National Conference of Negro Churchmen, which they later called the National Conference of Black Clergy.

Cone's writings enabled them to discern deeper theological grounds for their embrace of black power. Yet both then and now the concerns of blacks in the theological academy were far removed from those in the black churches. The awareness of that gap and various attempts to address it have been a work-in-progress for more than four decades. Nonetheless, the presence of black theology on the various seminary curricula has given visibility and relevance to the concerns of blacks and others as they pursue degrees in ministry and/or advanced theological studies.

As the decades have unfolded and more blacks have been admitted to the various degree programs in theological education and religious studies programs, the face of the academy has changed radically. Four decades ago one could count on one's fingers the number of blacks in attendance at the American Academy of Religion. Today, several hundred attend, not only from the United States but from round the world. Also, each year the various book exhibitions reveal increasing numbers of books authored by black religious scholars in all the various disciplines of theological study. Further, a virtual cultural revolution has occurred along the lines of gender in that same arena. Most importantly, African American women theologians known as "womanist scholars" have gained high visibility in all areas of the theological academy.

Today, most African Americans in any field of theological education readily expect the opportunity to explore the content of black theology and womanist theology in order to discern the extent to which they will be helpful to them in their work as pastors, teachers, and scholars. Most black religious scholars use one or other genres as hermeneutic guides in their work. Yet, it is important to note that since most black theological scholars do not teach in institutions that offer Ph.D. programs, their continuing impact on the theological academy is uncertain. Nonetheless, some brilliant texts on the relation between black theology and the black churches have been published in recent years, the most impressive of which is James H. Evans, Jr.'s *We Have Been Believers*.[12]

WOMANIST THEOLOGY
IN THE THEOLOGICAL ACADEMY

In the early 1980s, African American women pursuing advanced degrees in theology at Union Theological Seminary in New York discovered that since black theology was a male-centered discourse it had rendered woman's voices silent. This disturbed them because the experience of black women differed in many ways from that of black men, as did their theology. As soon as that critique reached Cone's ears he did not hesitate to confess guilt and apologized for the oversight, which he considered a serious one. He then encouraged the women to address the issue themselves, which they did. Soon, Jacquelyn Grant published her book, the title of which is both provocative and perceptive, *White Women's Christ and Black Women's Jesus: Feminist Christology and Womanist Response*.[13]

Among other things, Grant's book demonstrated a strong willingness to dialogue with white feminists, in large part because they shared patriarchy as a common enemy. But, unlike white feminists who struggled with sexism and classism, black women's experience was shaped by the additional factor of racism. Since black male theologians had no similar kinship with white male theologians, interracial theological dialogue for them has been much more difficult to begin.

Womanist theologian Delores S. Williams's book, *Sisters in the Wilderness: The Challenge of Womanist God-Talk*, comprises a radical critique of the traditional doctrines of the atonement because they fail to address the experiences of black women. The book claims that the biblical figure of Hagar, who was cast away by her master and mistress, is a prototype of black women's experience as slave, abused, castaway, surrogate mother, whose survival depended only on her trust in God.

Like black male theology, womanist theology was also born in the theological academy and, hence, continues to have difficulty in being embraced fully by the

---

12. James H. Evans, Jr., *We Have Been Believers* (Minneapolis: Fortress, 1992).
13. The term womanist was borrowed from Alice Walker's adoption of it in her book, *In Search of Our Mothers' Gardens* (New York: Harcourt Brace Jovanovich, 1983), xi–xii.

black churches. Ironically, black men and black women steeped in black theology and womanist theology often find it necessary to de-center the impact of those theologies on their thought when seeking a call to pastor a congregation.

A few black male theologian pastors have been effective, however, in persuading their churches to Africanize their aesthetic tastes in their personal dress, choir, and pastor's robes, as well as various images of ecclesial ancestors, including Jesus and his disciples. This so-called Afri-centric orientation has been enhanced further by the recent publication of the African American Bible (a King James Version supplemented with various commentaries and essays by black scholars). The New International Version of the Bible, subtitled Aspire: The New Women of Color Study Bible, has a similar purpose.

CONCLUSION

Until more African Americans are teaching in theological institutions that offer PhD degrees, one is not likely to see much scholarly conversation about the theologies of black folk between black and white scholars. Thus, the ongoing academic discussion about the theologies of black folk is likely to occur largely among African Americans themselves and a very small number of whites, as the various sessions at the American Academy of Religion and other academic associations presently indicate.

Let me hasten to point out, however, a major problem that attends the theologies of black folk both in the churches and the academy, namely their lack of critical attention to a broad range of moral problems confronting the nation in general and African Americans in particular. Although those theologies have a long tradition of critiquing the ways that race and racism diminish the lives of African Americans and the moral character of the nation, both black churches and their theologies maintain strong patriotic loyalties to the nation itself. Their uncritical acceptance of many of the nation's conservative moral traditions makes them more likely to be pro-life than pro-choice on the concerns of women, homophobia, fatalism vis-à-vis the disproportionate amount of poverty among blacks and its concomitant effects on education, employment, crime, incarceration, environmental conditions, domestic abuse, teenage pregnancies, unstable families, to mention only a few. In short, the theologies of black folk and the religion of the black churches must expand their prophetic purview in order to address the broad range of moral concerns and social justice advocacy that are related to but not consumed by the traditional focus on race and racism alone.

Index

CPSIA information can be obtained
at www.ICGtesting.com
Printed in the USA
FFOW01n1530090116
20284FF